DATE DUE			

Developing Effective
Communications Strategy

RONALD SERIES ON MARKETING MANAGEMENT

Series Editor: **FREDERICK E. WEBSTER, Jr.**
*The Amos Tuck School
of Business Administration
Dartmouth College*

FRANK H. MOSSMAN, W. J. E. CRISSY, and PAUL M. FISHER, *Financial Dimensions in Marketing Management*

JACOB JACOBY and ROBERT W. CHESTNUT, *Brand Loyalty: Measurement and Management*

WILLIAM E. COX, Jr., *Industrial Marketing Research*

CLARK LAMBERT, *Field Sales Performance Appraisal*

JEAN-MARIE CHOFFRAY and GARY LILIEN, *Market Planning for New Industrial Products*

EUGENE J. CAFARELLI, *Developing New Products and Repositioning Mature Brands: A Risk-Reduction System that Produces Investment Alternatives*

GARY M. GRIKSCHEIT, HAROLD C. CASH, and W. J. E. CRISSY, *Handbook of Selling: Psychological, Managerial, and Marketing Basis*

MELVIN PRINCE, *Consumer Research for Management Decisions*

WILLIAM H. DAVIDSON, *Global Strategic Management*

FREDERICK E. WEBSTER, Jr., *Field Sales Management*

DAN AILLONI-CHARAS, *Promotion: A Guide to Effective Promotional Planning, Strategies, and Executions*

DAVID A. AAKER, *Developing Business Strategies*

FREDERICK E. WEBSTER, Jr., *Industrial Marketing Strategy,* Second Edition

JOHN M. KEIL, *The Creative Mystique: How to Manage It, Nurture It, and Make It Pay*

RUSSELL I. HALEY, *Developing Effective Communications Strategy: A Benefit Segmentation Approach*

WILLIAM F. COPACINO, DONALD B. ROSENFIELD, AND JOHN F. MAGEE, *Modern Logistics Management: Integrating Marketing, Manufacturing, and Physical Distribution*

Developing Effective Communications Strategy

A Benefit Segmentation Approach

RUSSELL I. HALEY
Whittemore School of Business and Economics
University of New Hampshire

A RONALD PRESS PUBLICATION

JOHN WILEY & SONS

New York · Chichester · Brisbane · Toronto · Singapore

Library of Congress Cataloging in Publication Data
Haley, Russell I.
    Developing effective communications strategy.

    (Ronald series on marketing management, ISSN 0275-
875X)
    "A Ronald Press publication."
    Includes bibliographical references and index.
    1. Communications in marketing.   2. Market segmentation.
I. Title.   II. Series.

HF5415.123.H35   1985   658.8′02   84-26983
ISBN 0-471-81262-5

Preface

Knowledge transfer and use is an emerging discipline, which is based on the premise that learning can occur either from experimentation—the scientific approach—or from life experience.[1] The latter type of learning is often unstructured and qualitative in nature, and, there is increasing recognition that it is no less valid. Consequently a great deal of effort is currently being devoted to developing methods for transferring knowledge gained from life experience to other people. This book is philosophically compatible with that goal. It is an attempt by a practitioner, more recently a professor, to summarize a little more than 20 years of experience with an approach that has become known as Benefit Segmentation.

The book represents a personal point of view based partly on experimental evidence but, more important, on the experience of having been deeply involved in over 120 Benefit Segmentation studies. Although significant references are cited where it is thought that they will be helpful to readers wishing to pursue areas that are merely touched upon, no attempt has been made to develop a comprehensive bibliography on market segmentation. Such bibliographies are available elsewhere.[2]

The book addresses one central issue—one involving questions that are easy to ask but difficult to answer. How can a company, or any organization, discover an effective communications strategy, and, once it has been discovered, how can it be sure that it has been properly executed and that it is having the desired effect upon the market?

It is customary at this point to thank those who have been helpful in the development of the book. I would particularly like to thank my son, Douglas Haley, who is also a market research professional, for his helpful

[1] Knowledge Use Training Program, University of Pittsburgh, October 18 and 19, 1982.
[2] Ronald D. Michman, Myron Gable and Walter Gross (Eds.), Market Segmentation: A Selected and Annotated Bibliography, Bibliography Series #28, New York, American Marketing Association, 1977.

suggestions; my secretary, Shirley Bastianelli, for what must have seemed like endless typing; and my wife, Neale, for her patience while I scribbled away, ignoring everything else.

RUSSELL I. HALEY

Durham, New Hampshire
January 1985

Series Editor's Foreword

As business encounters challenges of the 1980s, top management is increasingly looking to marketing for sharpened competitive effectiveness. The emphasis on strategy formulation and financial performance at the corporate level that characterized the previous decade is now evolving toward a broader concern for total strategic management. This sharpens the focus on marketing as the prime vehicle for implementing corporate and business strategies.

Marketing management is the most dynamic of the business functions. Marketing must respond to the everchanging marketplace and the constant evolution of customer preference and buying habits, technology, and competition. Marketing management continually grows in sophistication and complexity as developments in management science are applied to the work of the marketing manager.

The books in The Ronald Series on Marketing Management have been written for managers. They combine a concern for management application with an appreciation for the relevance of developments in such areas as behavioral science, financial analysis, and mathematical modeling, as well as the insights gained from analyzing successful experience in the marketplace. The Ronald Series on Marketing Management is thus intended to communicate the state-of-the-art in marketing to managers.

Both marketing practitioners and academic teacher/scholars have contributed to the works in this series which now includes coverage of advertising management, sales promotion, public relations, consumer research, industrial marketing, brand loyalty, financial analysis for marketing decisions, the impact of government regulation, selling and field sales management, new product development, and market planning for new industrial products. As new insights based on research and managerial practice in

vii

marketing management are brought forward, this series will continue to offer new entries that convey the state-of-the-art in a manner that permits practicing managers to extend their own experience by using new analytical frameworks, and which acquaint students of marketing with the work of the professional marketing manager.

FREDERICK E. WEBSTER, JR.

Hanover, New Hampshire
September, 1982

Contents

1. **Premises of Market Segmentation**   1

   Psychographics, 6
   Benefit Segmentation, 14

2. **Models of the Communication Process**   19

   How Advertising Works, 20
   The Richardson-Haley Model, 23
   Selective Processes, 29
   Persuasion, 47

3. **Measuring Attitudes and Images**   53

   Methods of Attitude Measurement, 53
   Attitude Scaling Alternatives, 58
   Scale Choice Decisions, 63
   Evaluative Attitude Scales, 65
   Descriptive Attitude Scales, 78

4. **Constructing an Image Measurement Tool**   81

   Selecting the Stimuli—Exploratory Work, 81
   Conducting Consumer Interviews to Identify Key Attitude
      Factors, 83
   Scale Scoring, 85
   Factor Analysis, 86
   Assignment of Importance Weights, 87
   Validation Evidence, 90

5. Developing Effective Communications Strategies   93

Market Definition, 94
Choosing an Effective Buying Incentive, 109
Choice Criteria, 112
Selecting a Market Target, 118
Criteria for Segment Selection, 125

6. Conducting Attitude Segmentation Research   131

Organizing for a Segmentation Study, 132
Defining Objectives, 136
What a Segmentation Study Can and Can't Do, 139

7. Benefit Segmentation Premises   143

How Advertising Works, 143
An Experiment on the Relationship Between Benefits and
    Attention, 144
Selecting the Messages and Designing the Advertisements, 145
Developing the Questionnaire, 148
Exposing Respondents to Messages and Measuring Reactions, 149
Measuring Communications Effects, 151
When Persuasion Is Effective, 159
General Conclusions About the Communications Process, 164
Rules of Thumb for Communications, 166

8. Benefit Segmentation Methodology   171

Types of Information Gathered, 171
Overall Study Design, 174
Analysis of Phase III Results, 202
Methodological Tricks and Traps, 208
Conjoint Measurement and Tradeoff Analysis, 209
Determining the Best Method for Segmenting a Market, 215
Deriving the Segments, 219

9. Interpreting Segmentation Study Results   225

Benefit Segmentation Principles, 231
Communications and Other Marketing Implications, 239

Examples Illustrating the Versatility of the Benefit Segmentation
   Method, 249
Generalizations, 250
Generalized Benefit Segments, 251

10. **Presenting Results and Beginning Follow-Through Activities**   263

Presentation Formats, 264
Communicating with the Project Task Force, 267
Communicating with Creative People, 271
Types of Follow-Through Required, 277

11. **Copy Research Follow-Through**   279

State-of-the-Art of Copy Testing, 279
The General Measurement Approach, 291
Measurements to Be Taken, 292
Diagnostic Measures, 299
Measuring Nonverbal Factors, 302
Analysis of the Results, 306
Stage 1 Conclusions and Stage 2 Plans, 311
The Form of the Advertising, 325
Sampling, 337
Syndicated Services, 340
Copy Testing in a Segmented Market, 346

12. **Media Planning and Other Forms of Follow-Through**   355

Media Planning in a Segmented Market, 355
Packaging, Sales Promotion, Pricing, and Product Planning, 359
Follow-up Tracking Systems, 362

13. **Successful Benefit Segmentation Case Histories**   373

14. **An Overview of Attitude Segmentation Research**   383

**Appendix A. Copy Executions from Experiment on Predicting
            Attention**   395

Appendix B. Benefit Segmentation Exercise   413

Appendix C.   Flow Chart for Prototypical
              Benefit Segmentation Study   441

Appendix D.   Benefit Segmentation Study   445

Author Index   501

Subject Index   505

Developing Effective Communications Strategy

ONE

Premises of
Market Segmentation

Market segmentation is a topic of continuing interest among marketing people. It is probably of more interest today than it was in the 1960s. Several parallel trends are fueling its increased emphasis.

First, there is the growth in population. In 1960, 179 million people lived in this country. Today the population is 234 million. In the year 2000 it will be 268 million. The more people there are the more likelihood that segments large enough to be profitable can be found among the populace.

Second, there is the growth in individualism. People are steadily becoming more interested in differentiating themselves from the general population. Note the growth of the "I-am-me" segment in the VALS-lifestyle service[1] (characterized as exhibitionistic, narcissistic, young, impulsive, dramatic, experimental, active, and inventive), and a trend toward strong focus on self-fulfillment and self-realization (as opposed to more traditional concerns about family, community, and nation) evident in the Yankelovich Monitor.[2] A number of people have commented on this trend. For example, Bruce Crawford said "we are in the Age of Me, with its hunger for personal success, money, and personalization."[3]

Third, there is increased competition and the accompanying brand proliferation. The average supermarket now has 12,000 to 14,000 items on its shelves. Companies no longer attempt to dominate a market with a single product. History suggests that that is a high risk strategy. Consequently,

---

[1] VALS (Values and Lifestyles Program), SRI International, Menlo Park, CA.
[2] Yankelovich Monitor, Yankelovich, Skelly & White, New York. A subscription service.
[3] Bruce Crawford, " 'Age of Me' Poses New Problems for Marketers," *Marketing News*, June 30, 1978, p. 3.

1

most companies, especially in package goods markets, have introduced a series of so-called *flanker brands* to protect the flanks of their major entry, often called the *flagship brand.* Thus General Foods has introduced Brim to accompany Sanka, Chesebrough-Ponds offers Vaseline Intensive Care Lotion not only in its original form but with an herbal line extension and one for problem hands, and Tide is now available in liquid form. The examples are endless. The more products available in a market, however, the more necessary it is for individual brands (if they wish to survive) to locate market segments within which they can become a dominant product.

Finally there are the "new media"—cable, video-discs, video tape recorders, and satellite transmissions. These make it increasingly possible to reach smaller and smaller segments of the market with special interests or special needs. The term *narrowcasting,* as opposed to broadcasting, has been coined to describe the kinds of segmentation potential offered by these media. Speaking at the Twenty-ninth ARF Conference in New York in March 1983, Stephen P. Arbeit, Senior Vice President, Marketing Director, Ogilvy & Mather, Inc. said: "When he turns on his television set he doesn't just have three networks and perhaps an independent as his options, but he has 60, 80, 110 channels of programming choices, therefore . . . all advertisers will be forced to design products that fit with the multiplicity of channels, with a multiplicity of discrete consumer target audiences." Media proliferation seems destined inevitably to follow product proliferation, and these converging forces guarantee that market segmentation will remain in the forefront of marketing planning activities.

Market segmentation is by no means a new phenomenon in marketing. It was reviewed in depth as far back as 1956 by Wendell Smith in a seminal article entitled "Product Differentiation and Market Segmentation as Alternative Product Strategies."[4] Historically, at least three kinds of segmentation gained widespread use.

Probably the first form was geographic segmentation. Small manufacturers who wished to limit their investments, or whose distribution channels were not extensive enough to cover the entire country, segmented the U.S. market, in effect, by selling their products only in certain geographic areas.[5] This form of segmentation continues to be popular among small manufacturers, retailers, banks, and service organizations.

As more and more brands became national and as the national media

---

[4] Wendell R. Smith, *Journal of Marketing,* Vol. XXI, July 1956, pp. 3–8.

[5] J. Garreau, "The Nine Nations of North America," *Marketing News,* Vol. 17, No. 2, January 21, 1983, p. 1, suggests that geographic segmentation still is important. Also the so-called geo-demographic services of PRIZM, Acorn, and Cluster-Plus are very popular, especially among media people.

needed to reach geographically dispersed markets, however, the second major form of segmentation—demographic segmentation—became popular. Under this philosophy targets were defined as all men 18 years of age or over, people earning $25,000 or over, working women, and so on. This form of segmentation is still popular, primarily because of the ready availability of detailed demographic data from governmental and media sources. A number of studies have shown that demographic variables such as age, sex, income, occupation, and race are, in general, poor predictors of behavior and consequently are less than ideal bases for segmentation strategies.[6]

This is not to say that demographic segmentation is useless. It can be very helpful, in defining targets for the generic expansion of markets with low incidence of use. For example, the demographic characteristics of bus travelers (younger age groups, older age groups, and lower income groups) are sharply different from those of non-bus travelers. Accordingly it would probably be a mistake to mount an advertising campaign targeted on upper income people, at least without significant changes in the product.

Similarly the demographic characteristics of users of new products such as home security systems, often provide guidance concerning the types of people most likely to be good prospects in the near term.

For more broadly based products, and especially for product categories where brands are not strongly differentiated from each other in a physical sense, however, the demographic characteristics of the users of one brand are likely to be similar to those of the users of competitive brands. Consequently it is necessary to go beyond demographics.

A third form of segmentation, behavioral segmentation, divides consumers into groups based upon their behavior in the marketplace. The earliest form, volumetric segmentation, attempts to go straight to the heart of the sales maximization problem. In the mid-1960s, Dik Twedt, then with the Oscar Mayer Company, developed the "heavy-half" theory, demonstrating that in most product categories it is normal for one-half of the consumers to account for about 80 percent of total consumption.[7] If this is true, according to the logic, it makes sense for any knowledgeable marketer to concentrate his or her efforts on these high-volume consumers. Certainly they are the most *valuable* consumers.

This view is endorsed by a large number of brand managers in major

[6] R. E. Frank, "Is Brand Loyalty a Useful Basis for Market Segmentation?," *Journal of Advertising Research*, Vol. 7, June 1967, pp. 27–33. Also, A. S. Boote, "Market Segmentation by Personal Values and Salient Product Attributes," *Journal of Advertising Research*, Vol. 21, February 1981, pp. 29–35.

[7] Dik W. Twedt, "Some Practical Applications of 'Heavy Half' Theory," Proceedings of the 10th Annual Conference of the ARF, October 1964; "How Important to Marketing Strategy Is the Heavy User?" *Journal of Marketing*, Vol. 28, January 1964, pp. 71–72.

package goods companies and by leading advertising agencies such as BBDO. They routinely seek out and analyze the characteristics of the heavy users, and usually define them as their market target.

There are two problems with this line of reasoning. First it assumes that heavy users are generally available to the brand in question—that they are all seeking a similar benefit or benefit set and that the brand will be able to deliver the desired benefit or benefits. This is frequently not true. In most categories there are two types of heavy users—quality-oriented heavy users and price-oriented heavy users. For example, in the coffee market the quality-oriented people feel that the small additional amount of money required to buy such brands as Yuban, Martinson's, and Savarin is more than justified by their fuller taste. They perceive significant differences among brands and believe that premium brands are worth their prices. The price-oriented buyer, on the other hand, sees brand differences as minor and is likely to buy store brands or generics.

Both of these groups are heavy users. Yet one feels that, because they drink so much coffee, it makes sense to treat themselves to a superior product. The other feels that, because they drink so much coffee and because the differences among brands are not significant, it is sensible to buy a relatively inexpensive brand. These two groups of people, although they are both members of the "heavy-half" segment, are not equally good prospects for any one brand, nor can they be expected to respond to the same advertising claims.

Parenthetically it is apparent that these two segments exist in most, if not all, markets. Today it is common to observe that premium-priced quality brands are prospering and that low-priced brands are prospering, but that brands caught between these two positions often experience difficulties. That is frequently because they do not have positions that are compatible with the needs of well-defined market segments. This issue will be treated in detail in later chapters.

A second form of behavioral segmentation groups people by their patterns of brand loyalty. This has been done in a variety of ways. One long-standing method characterizes people as current users, nonusers (sometimes called "never-users"), and past users (also called "trier/rejectors"). Each of these groups is then analyzed in depth and tactics are devised for increasing future sales to one or more of these groups.

An alternative, and somewhat newer approach, is to use a constant sum scale[8] to measure the extent to which each brand has been bought the last 10 times a purchase was made, or to measure future purchase intentions by brand. Persons assigning 10 points to a single brand are labeled "loyal" or

---

[8] W. S. Torgerson, *Theory and Methods of Scaling,* New York: Wiley, 1958.

"regular" buyers; persons assigning six to nine points to the brand are labeled "frequent purchasers"; those assigning one to five points are called "occasional purchasers"; and people who give the brand no points at all are called "nonpurchasers." As in the previous approach these groups are analyzed and means of increasing sales to them are developed.

The most recent, and one of the most sophisticated, of these approaches is that used by William T. Moran of Moran & Tucker, Inc. He develops what he calls a "Substitutability Index"[9] by asking people how they are likely to react if the brand they intend to buy is out of stock. A forced choice is made among the following alternatives:

Switch to another brand.

Wait until it comes back into stock.

Go to another store.

Buy any brand available.

This is an outgrowth of work done by Mr. Moran with the Hendry Corporation,[10] while at Lever Brothers, and Young & Rubicam, Inc. They found a common pattern of U-shaped loyalty distributions with the proportion of uncommitted people (people in the trough of the "U") being a significant indicator of how responsive a brand is likely to be to advertising or promotional efforts. For a full discussion of this approach see Kalwani and Morrison.[11] Some companies have defined communications targets on the basis of these distributions.[12]

Behavioral segmentation also suffers from one important limitation. It assumes that similar behaviors are the result of similar causes. Unfortunately this is often not the case. For example, loyal customers may be loyal for quite different reasons.[13] Someone who buys the same brand 10 times in a row may believe it to be a superior product or may simply be repeating a familiar action. People who feel brands are basically interchangeable may "satisfize"—find a brand that meets their minimum requirements and then buy that brand over and over—sometimes only recognizing the package, and being unable to supply the brand name without help.

Similarly a person who is willing to wait for a brand to reappear in his or

[9] "Tracking Advertising Profitability," ANA Advertising Research Workshop, New York, December 9, 1981.

[10] "Hendry System Gives Marketers Handle on Buyers Prior to New Brand Introduction," *Marketing News*, September 8, 1978, p. 5.

[11] M. U. Kalwani and D. G. Morrison, "A Parsimonious Description of the Hendry System," *Management Science*, Vol. 23, No. 5, January 1977, p. 467.

[12] Norton Simon—J. McMennamin, 1981. Unpublished paper.

[13] J. Jacoby and D. B. Kyner, "Brand Loyalty versus Repeat Purchasing Behavior," *Journal of Marketing Research*, Vol. 10, February 1973, p. 2.

her store may be no more loyal than someone who will switch to another brand. The latter person may simply be a heavier user and unable to wait without running out of stock. Unless people have similar mental and perceptual attitudes toward the brand it is difficult to persuade them effectively and efficiently.

Still another method of behavioral segmentation is to group people by occasions of use or consumption situations. This has been an effective strategy for brands such as Nyquil (the "nighttime cold remedy"), for airlines and motel chains that successfully focus on business or vacation travelers, for fast-food outlets who have increased sales by adding the breakfast menus, and even for universities who have expanded summer, evening, and off-campus study occasions. Conversely, some products have found themselves too tighty locked into a single occasion and have tried to broaden their markets by extending beyond their traditional occasion (e.g., Orange juice: "It's not just for breakfast any more").

Occasion segmentation can be an effective strategy. However, it is based on the assumption that people consuming the product for a given occasion are seeking similar benefits. To the extent that this is true an occasion segmentation strategy makes sense.

PSYCHOGRAPHICS

There is some confusion about the origin of the term *Psychographics*, and its origin has been described erroneously in several publications.[14] The facts are these. In the summer of 1965 several Grey research and creative executives were reviewing the results of the most recent "attitude segmentation"[15] study. The creative people were showing considerable enthusiasm for the alternative targeting possibilities revealed by the attitudinal segments "discovered" in the process of the research. One of the creative people asserted that this was the first research he had ever seen that was truly helpful in providing creative guidance. Looking at the full-blown segment descriptions, which included behavioral information, demographic data, benefits sought, and personality and lifestyle characteristics, he observed, "Boy, this stuff goes way beyond standard demographics. Why, you've gone into people's psychologies! These are Psychographics." The word was im-

---

[14] E. Demby, "Psychographics and from Whence It Came," in W. D. Wells (Ed.), *Life Style and Psychographics*, Chicago: American Marketing Association, 1974.
[15] A term used originally to describe the method which was introduced in 1961 and which later evolved into the approach known as Benefit Segmentation.

mediately recognized as an appropriate label, and when the question of a good subject for the next issue of *Grey Matter*[16] arose, it was suggested that the creative department write one on Psychographics. That newsletter was issued in November 1965, and it was the first time the word *Psychographics* had appeared in print. (See Figure 1.1.)

The newsletter at that time had a substantial circulation, including a number of mass media subscribers, so the word spread rapidly. Almost as important as the newsletter was the diffusion of Grey Advertising researchers throughout the research community. Still another influence was a computer expert who was doing data processing work for Grey and for other advertising agencies and market research firms. He described the process to them and its potential was quickly recognized. The term *Psychographics* was not used in the 1964 *HBR* article by Daniel Yankelovich[17] because it had not yet been coined. A little later a senior member of the Grey Research Department joined Emanuel Demby at Motivational Programmers, Inc.; they also began to make heavy use of the term.[18] In no time at all *Psychographics* had been made a permanent part of marketing research jargon.

Originally the word was intended as an umbrella term to cover all measures of the mind, as distinguished from behavioral and demographic measures, and that is how it will be used in this book. Consequently it includes such universes of content as benefits, problems, lifestyles, personality measures, beliefs, and perceptions. Psychographic segmentation therefore can be accomplished through use of any one or more of these universes of content.

Probably the most frequently used universe of content is lifestyle measures. Operationally it is very difficult to separate personality measures from lifestyle measures. It has been said that personality measures largely have their roots in clinical psychology, whereas lifestyle measures have primarily come out of social psychology. In any event the extent of overlap between these two types of measures is substantial. Thus, personality and lifestyle measures will be considered a single universe of content.

One of the first researchers to investigate the potential of these measures for marketing and communications problems was Arthur Kaponen[19] of the

[16] A monthly newsletter issued by Grey Advertising, Inc., 777 Third Ave., NY, 10017 (Volume 36, No. 11).
[17] Daniel Yankelovich, "New Criteria for Market Segmentation," *Harvard Business Review*, Vol. 42, March/April, 1964, pp. 83–90.
[18] Demby, "Psychographics."
[19] Arthur Kaponen, "Personality Characteristics of Purchasers," *Journal of Advertising Research*, Vol. 1, September 1960, pp. 6–12.

volume 36

november 1965

number 11

Thoughts and Ideas on Advertising and Marketing

Grey Advertising, Inc.

SPOTLIGHT ON PSYCHOGRAPHIC MARKET SEGMENTATION

Pages of business literature, whirlwinds of words from convention rostrums, extol the value of market segmentation as <u>preferred</u> strategy in today's marketing planning.

And for many businesses this is <u>sound advice.</u> Unfortunately, as so often happens, the tendency of people is to be swept along by currents, thus <u>overlooking</u> rich opportunities.

To most marketers "market segmentation" means cutting markets into <u>slices</u> -- demographically, geographically, according to economic status, race, national origin, education, sex and other established criteria.

But the idea of relating marketing strategy to <u>psychological</u> differences among consumers has been slow to germinate. We call it "Psychographic Market Segmentation."

The strategy of isolating a market by selecting people who react <u>en masse</u> to a particular <u>emotional appeal</u> or who share common <u>behavioral patterns</u> has been overshadowed by the concentration on <u>easily discernible</u> market divisions such as youth, sex, financial status, education, location and others.

BREAK TRADITIONAL BOUNDARIES

Psychographic segmentation breaks across the boundaries of these traditional market sectors and discovers a <u>homogeneity</u> or linkage among people who have been considered as belonging to <u>diverse</u> markets.

For example, the assistant principal of a school and a truckman may be earning identical salaries and perhaps living not very far apart. They may also be in the same age group and of the same ethnic origin. But <u>emotionally</u> and <u>psychologically</u> they may be at opposite poles.

Psychographic segmentation places them into the marketing segments in which they belong <u>psychologically.</u>

Want extra copies of this issue of Grey Matter? We're happy to take care of your needs. Up to 10 copies —free. Over 10 copies — 25¢ per copy. We are equally happy to extend reprint privileges on request.

Figure 1.1. The first mention in print of the word *Psychographics*

Conversely, a family in the middle forties in age and middle income status may have the same outlook and youthful attitude as a young newly-formed family unit. Psychologically, they belong in the youth market segment for many products.

The profit potential in psychographic segmentation of markets is greater than is generally realized and those advertisers who see these opportunities clearly, and exploit them skillfully, are scoring and will score triumphs, while those who continue to dissipate competitive energy only on established notions of market segmentation may find themselves on a "me too" merry-go-round.

FABLES AND FOIBLES

Every departure from herd thinking seems to create a mystique which acts as a barrier to the less venturesome. This is true of psychographic segmentation, too.

For instance, the prevailing notion in marketing circles is that an appeal to a limited group is of necessity limited in its impact.

Holders of this view fail to realize that there are no rigid boundaries circumscribing people's attitudes. On the contrary, these are fluid, and an idea tossed into what seems to be a tiny pool more often than not ripples out in widening circles until what appeared to be a small market becomes a huge market.

Let's take the case of Maclean's tooth paste. These marketers reasoned that since 70% of the population is concerned with tooth decay, it would be sound strategy to aim at that part of the remaining market (30%) composed of people who are psychologically or emotionally more concerned with "whiteness," the cosmetic effect of brushing their teeth, than with cavities. The success of this manouvor in gaining a share of the tooth paste market beyong their expectations is well known to the marketing world.

A SHIFT ON A GIANT SCALE

The foible still lingers that it's tactically unsound for a company to aim products and promotion at specific markets while its overall strategy is to court the mass market. The weakness of this stance is best illustrated by the automobile industry.

Let's go back five years or so.

A significant under-the-surface trend in mass consumer marketing almost went unnoticed by automobile manufacturers. For many years planners in this giant industry focused on bigness, flashiness and standard designs until "the peas-in-a-pod" appearance of automobiles became a subject of universal comment.

Meanwhile the small foreign car began making inroads and seemed to be the answer to mass marketing of automobiles.

But, in reality, the consumer mass market was breaking into psychological segments. Differing groups of people were demanding greater differences in automobiles than the industry had heretofore realized.

In 1962 the marketing world sensed a new trend in the action of Chevrolet. (Actually the trend was not new. It had been going on unnoticed by most advertisers.) But the automobile industry made it new in magnitude, if not

Grey Matter—Grey Advertising, Inc.

Figure 1.1.   Continued

9

in conception. It made the shift on a giant scale...a shift away from look-alike products to a strategy of fitting products and advertising to "psychographically" segmented markets as a means of obtaining a larger share of the total mass market.

This marketing philosophy was explained by Semon E. Knudsen, Chevrolet's manager, in these words:

> "Four distinct lines of products, appealing to four different segments of the buying public, give a choice of product to fit most needs, either emotional or practical." (The emphasis is ours.)

This was recognition of market segmentation based on psychological as well as practical needs of people. The success of this philosophy for Chevrolet is history. Its significance is in the thrust it gave to psychographic market segmentation in the automotive industry which will be felt throughout the marketing world.

The impact of Chevrolet's action is especially evident in the advertising of all the competitors in the so-called "mass brands" of the industry: Chevrolet, Ford, Plymouth and Rambler.

Take Plymouth. Under the umbrella "There's something for everyone in Plymouth '66," each brand aims at a specific psychological target while not neglecting its economy status.

> The new "elegant" VIP is a "limousine in looks, power and ride. But it's a Plymouth in price."

> The "Bold Fury...a great big beauty."

> Barracuda is a new version of the "fast back...if you go in for bucket seats."

> The Valiant "really lets you live within your budget."

At this point we'd like to make it clear that we are not passing judgment on the advertisements per se. We're merely commenting on the psychographic market segmentation they represent.

Interestingly, Russell Baker, famed columnist of the New York Times, undoubtedly with a twinkle in his eye, comments on the psychographic segmentation of automobile marketing in this manner:

> "It is becoming harder and harder to buy a new car without psychiatric help. As the ads for the new models show all too clearly, what Detroit is now selling is not so much a car as a personality."

ENTER THE DISSENTERS

But there are those who pooh-pooh the whole idea of market segmentation.

Professor William H. Reynolds, of the University of Southern California, writing in the September-October 1965 Harvard Business Review, says that psychological market segmentation is nothing more than variety marketing with a different name. He brushes aside the evidence of success of this approach with the statement: "Granting the existence of subcultures, there is an amazing uniformity to the American culture from border to border."

We're not so naive as to ignore the influence of the norm on the buying behavior of the individual. Nor do we overlook mass motivation as a

Grey Matter—Grey Advertising, Inc.

Figure 1.1. Continued

10

generator of sales of mass products. Our point is that to overlook Psycho-graphic Market Segmentation as a marketing strategy for many mass products means missing rich profit opportunities.

A myopic attitude about the homogeneity of the American consumer can lead to losses, for the desire of the individual for change and for self expression has become ingrained in the American character.

Even in suburbia (the alleged symbol of uniformity of living) there is a restless urge to be different while conforming to the community pattern. There are social, intellectual and economic islands in apparently homogeneous suburban towns. The urge to differ is often much more powerful than the desire to conform.

The noted sociologist, David Reisman, of the University of Chicago, put his finger on the problem when he said: "Differentiation is as strong as homogenization in the market, and the very effort to get everybody will alienate many bodies."

SUMMING IT ALL UP

For companies with limited budgets it may be a matter of survival to discover and concentrate on a segment of the market which presents the richest potentials. But for large volume advertisers, too, it is often sound strategy to aim at groups instead of shooting the works at the mass.

In the dynamic expansion which our economy is undergoing, the mass consumer will become more complex, more puzzling and less mass. The tremendous increase in population will result in larger heterogeneous groups of consumers who will have to be taken into account in marketing strategy.

However, there will be less need for trying to find the mass consumer. For specific segments of the market can be large enough in themselves to be cultivated profitably by mass marketers. Fact is that even today astute advertisers are finding it profitable to pick segments of the market and to develop them deeply and intensively.

Aiming advertising at the mass consumer may be the only effective strategy for many products, but it often results in a sameness of products and advertising which dilutes advertising effectiveness.

Certainly research will have to apply itself more and more to finding and identifying psychographic segments of the market, each large enough to return a handsome profit to the marketer.

Grey Advertising Inc.

777 Third Avenue, New York, New York 10017
Beverly Hills, Montreal, Toronto

International Partners: Australia: *Brown, Bruce and Grey Pty. Ltd., Melbourne and Sydney* • Belgium: *Dorland & Grey, S.A., Brussels* •
England: *Charles Hobson & Grey, Ltd., London* • France: *Dorland & Grey, S.A., Paris* • Germany: *Gramm & Grey International Partners, GmbH, Dusseldorf* •
Italy: *Milano e Grey S.p.A., Milan* • Japan: *Grey-Daiko Advertising, Inc., Tokyo* • Spain: *Rasgo-Grey, S.A., Madrid* • Venezuela: *Kittay-Grey Advertising, C.A., Caracas*

Figure 1.1. Continued

J. Walter Thompson Company. He attempted to relate the 15 factors of the Edwards Personal Preference Schedule[20] to sales of products in over a dozen fields, from consumer durables to groceries.

Other pioneers of lifestyle measures in marketing and advertising research include Clark Wilson of BBDO and Mike Pessemier of Purdue University, both of whom presented seminal papers on lifestyles at the 1965 conference of the American Marketing Association.[21]

Work with lifestyles has been reported by Tigert,[22] Wells,[23] and Plummer.[24] The pursuit of lifestyle information has generated enough interest to support at least two continuous tracking systems[25] that attempt to measure and project trends in major consumer lifestyles and lifestyle segments. Similarly, they are included in at least two major media databank services as standard practice. Numerous uses of this information have been reported in marketing literature and at marketing conferences.[26]

Despite the popularity of lifestyle information, users of lifestyle segmentation approaches have found that they suffer from a number of shortcomings.[27] Perhaps the most important one is the large gap between lifestyles and product or brand-specific behavior. For example, introversion and extroversion, however they are measured and labeled, may be related to magazine preferences. But they bear a much less predictable relationship to preference for brands of laundry detergents. Certainly not all lifestyles are relevant for all product categories. Unless a great deal of care is taken in selecting specific lifestyle measures, lifestyle segmentation runs a sizable risk of producing segments that have little or no marketing significance for the product or brand of interest. Lifestyles are, in effect, expressions of life goals. It seems highly unlikely that the choice of a spray deodorant is strongly related to a life goal.

Another limitation is the mistaken assumption that lifestyles are stable

---

[20] A. L. Edwards, *Edwards Personal Preference Schedule*, New York: The Psychological Corporation, 1959.

[21] Proceedings, 48th National Conference of the American Marketing Association, "New Directions in Marketing," New York, NY, June 14–16, 1965, F. E. Webster(ed).

[22] W. D. Wells and D. Tigert, "Activities, Interests, and Opinions," *Journal of Advertising Research*, Vol. 11, 1971, pp. 27–35.

[23] William D. Wells, "Psychographics: A Critical Review," *Journal of Marketing Research*, Vol. 11, May 1975, pp. 196–213.

[24] J. T. Plummer, "Lifestyle Patterns and Commercial Bank Credit Card Usage," *Journal of Marketing*, Vol. 35, No. 2, April 1971, pp. 35–41.

[25] For example Yankelovich Monitor and S.R.I. VALS.

[26] J. T. Plummer, "The Concept and Application of Lifestyle Segmentation," *Journal of Marketing*, Vol. 38, No. 1, January 1974, pp. 33–37.

[27] Anthony J. Adams, "Why Lifestyles Research Rarely Works," 13th Annual Attitude Research Conference: American Marketing Association, Scottsdale, AZ, February 8, 1982.

across product categories—that a price-conscious buyer in one product category is also a price-conscious buyer in another. Among other considerations it depends upon the magnitude of perceived differences between choice alternatives within the category. If differences are perceived to be small, the consumer may be very sensitive to price difference. If significant differences are seen, however, those differences and the benefits they suggest are likely to play a larger role in choice than is price.

For some product categories, however, people do express who they are by the brands they choose. This is particularly true for products or brands that are consumed conspicuously, such as brands of liquor, brands of cigarettes, and styles of clothing. In categories such as these lifestyle segmentation can be extremely useful. In general, however, lifestyles explain only about 10% of the variance in micro-behavior. Although this is a substantial improvement over the amount that can be explained by demographic characteristics (usually about 5%)[28] it still leaves a substantial amount of room for improvement.

Another approach to psychographic segmentation is through perceptions. The most frequent variation is to attempt to use multidimensional scaling techniques or discriminant function analysis to position people in N-dimensional space. They can then be grouped by "explicit" or "inferred" ideal points. Or, as Johnson points out,[29] respondents need not be grouped at all. This type of segmentation has been covered thoroughly in Frank, Massy, and Wind.[30] Although it is popular with academics and academic consultants it has not been as broadly accepted among marketing research practitioners as other forms of segmentation. Perhaps this is because it usually employs newer and, consequently, less familiar statistical methods. An excellent review of the various ideas in segmentation research is provided by Wilkie and Cohen.[31]

Geographic, demographic, and behavioral segmentation methods have been used because they provide helpful guidance in certain marketing decision areas. For example, geographic segmentation, because it describes the market in a discrete way, provides definite direction in media purchas-

[28] C. L. Wilson, "Homemaker Living Patterns and Marketplace Behavior," in J. S. Wright and J. L. Goldstocker (Eds.), *New Ideas for Successful Marketing*, American Marketing Association, Proceedings of the 1966 World Congress.

[29] Richard M. Johnson, "Market Segmentation: A Strategic Management Tool," *Journal of Marketing Research*, Vol. 8, February 1971, pp. 13–18.

[30] R. E. Frank, W. F. Massy and Y. Wind, *Market Segmentation*, Englewood Cliffs, NJ: Prentice-Hall, 1972.

[31] William L. Wilkie and Joel B. Cohen, "An Overview of Market Segmentation: Behavioral Concepts and Research Approaches," *Marketing Science Institute Working Paper*, June 1977.

ing. Spot TV, radio, newspapers, and local editions of magazines can be bought for the geographical segment selected for concentrated effort. Similarly, demographic segmentation allows media to be bought more efficiently because demographic data on readers, viewers, and listeners are readily available for most media vehicles. Demographic variables are extremely helpful in differentiating users from nonusers, especially in new product categories. For example, when instant potatoes were first introduced, it soon became evident that working women were an especially attractive target.

The heavy-half philosophy is especially effective in directing dollars toward the most important parts of the market. And lifestyle segmentation is extremely helpful in communicating to creative people in advertising agencies a feeling for the types of persons they are attempting to persuade.

However, demographic and behavioral systems of segmentation are handicapped by an underlying disadvantage inherent in their nature. They are based on an ex post facto decision about the kinds of people who comprise various segments of a market. People have been categorized into segments by the analyst, often arbitrarily. Thus these systems of segmentation rely on *descriptive* factors rather than on *causal* factors, which is why the segments are often irrelevant to the future marketing actions of the respondents. They are relatively poor predictors of how people are likely to respond to new advertising themes, new products, price changes, promotions, or other marketing tactics.

BENEFIT SEGMENTATION

In 1968 the first article on Benefit Segmentation was published.[32] Actually, the development of the approach began a number of years earlier, the first study having been done in 1961 for that most respected of American marketers, Procter & Gamble.[33]

Much has been written in professional journals about "secret research techniques" that are discovered by a company or an advertising agency and then held confidential. Although it is unfortunate that progress in understanding consumer behavior has been slowed by the suppression of these studies, to a large extent this is an inaccurate supposition. Most of the so-called secret studies have not been published because they cannot with-

---

[32] Russell I. Haley, "Benefit Segmentation: A Decision Oriented Tool," *Journal of Marketing*, Vol. 32, July 1968, pp. 30–35.
[33] R. I. Haley, *Experimental Research on Attitudes Toward Shampoos*, unpublished paper, New York, Grey Advertising, 1961.

stand the criticism of the research community. Because of the substantial number of people who become involved in the development and use of any successful technique, it is impossible to prevent the spread of information about them. If the developer does not publish, others will do so. At the most the widespread disseminations of information on the method can be delayed for a few years.

By the time three or four attitude segmentation studies had been completed at the agency where the technique originated, its potential in improving the effectiveness of communications was appreciated. The agency then had to choose between the value of attempting to keep the method confidential and the value of obtaining favorable publicity for having developed the approach. The following letter is evidence of that struggle:

Grey Advertising, Inc.   December 1, 1966
   House Correspondence   Copy to:
To:
From:
Subject: Our Attitude Segmentation Approach

We've got to get a segmentation article into print someplace as soon as we can.

As you know, _____ beat us into print with the *concept* having picked up the idea from _____ who was doing tab work for them. Now _____ of _____ is making a speech on the *techniques* of segmentation, having picked them up from work he has done for us and for _____. As you know, I've talked to our lawyers about stopping him from disclosing anything we consider proprietary, but we can hardly stop him from suggesting that Q analysis, an old technique in the area of personality measurement, can be fruitfully applied to attitude segmentation problems in marketing research. If we don't hurry, there won't be anything left for us.

Because outside organizations were involved in the multivariate processing of questionnaire data they, and the consultants they used, became familiar with the procedures developed at Grey. They began to suggest them to their other clients and their consultants began to write about various aspects of the methodology. The agency had opted for confidentiality and so it attempted to restrict these practices, as evidenced by this letter.

Dear _____:
Just a note to follow up on our conversation yesterday. You will remember that you raised the question of how we would feel about having our procedures written up anywhere. Just to be sure that what I told you was correct I have double checked our positions with _____.

We would indeed take a *very* dim view of any write-up of our procedures without our express and written consent. We have spent a great deal of time and money in developing them thus far and we do indeed consider our approaches proprietary. I have always assumed, and I am sure correctly, that we were dealing with you on a confidential basis—that the methods we employ are strictly between you and ourselves and will not be shared with any of your other clients. If this is not the case please let me know immediately.

I am sorry that we have to take this firm position but I am sure that you will understand. The agency business is highly competitive and we have to take all steps necessary to protect the interests of our clients.

I'd appreciate your informing _____ of our feelings also.

Sincerely yours,

Despite some success in delaying would-be publicizers, however, it eventually became apparent that it would be impossible to keep the method confidential. By the mid-1960s a great many people had begun to work with the approach.[34] Some of these had been involved in the developmental work at Grey Advertising. Many more had learned of the methods indirectly, through Grey suppliers, through friends who were employees, through ex-employees, or through Grey clients for whom early studies had been done. A few had discovered similar approaches independently, stimulated by the increasing availability of large computers and multivariate software.

Most of these early experimenters were either currently employed by advertising agencies, had recently worked for agencies, or were connected with them as consultants or clients. Unlike recent work in information processing and statistical methods, where R&D efforts have largely been centered in universities, the earliest R&D efforts in psychographic segmentation were centered in advertising agencies. This is because, although the area has applications in new product and other marketing decisions, the primary payoffs for psychographic segmentation have always been in communications. Agencies were quick to appreciate this. However, with few exceptions they were generally reluctant to publish the results of segmentation studies in marketing or research journals. This was partly because companies rightfully felt that the studies gave them a competitive edge, and they could see no advantage in publishing their findings while

---

[34] A. Achenbaum, L. Alpert, K. Athaide, J. Baumwoll, M. Chotin, K. Clancy, E. Demby, T. Dunn, E. Fishman, R. Frank, R. Gatty, A. Goldberg, M. Greenberg, H. Heller, R. Johnson, E. Lambek, S. Melvin, R. Nelson, D. Neswald, C. Overholser, L. Ott, F. Posner, R. Reiser, J. Robbin, M. Schoenwold, S. Shiller, J. Swartz, B. Solov, M. Watts, D. Yankelovich, S. Young, S. Yuspeh, R. Ziff and others.

they were current. According to one executive who refused a request from his agency to show some data from his research in a professional conference, such actions were equivalent to "giving away the store." Even later, when the studies were out of date and had lost their competitive meaning, the people involved in them too often had moved on to new studies and had lost interest in publishing the earlier studies.

Another reason for the relative absence of publications documenting early segmentation work is the disinclination of practitioners to publish. Those few who tried found that it was troublesome and time-consuming to attempt to meet the standards of the editorial review boards, of professional journals which were composed almost entirely of professors. Their views of what was worth publishing were often at variance with those of practitioners. This conflict has been commented upon elsewhere.[35]

Meanwhile the professional journals were being deluged by articles prepared by academics and carefully designed to meet the standards of other academics. The number of journals was limited, the number of marketing professors was expanding rapidly, and publication in professional journals had become one of the key criteria for promotion and tenure decisions. The net result was that the overwhelming preponderance of articles in the professional journals were written by academics, and that situation remains largely unchanged today.[36]

By the late 1960s and early 1970s segmentation studies had become a fad. Almost every consumer products company was doing or had done a segmentation study.[37] However, many companies found that they were not sure how to handle the results once they had obtained them. Their inclination was then to blame the method for their troubles. While saying that "segmentation research does work and can be immensely valuable," Tauber points out that the method is still being blamed today.[38] Consequently although segmentation studies continue to be done with reasonably high frequency, they are probably less popular today than they were in their prime. This seems an appropriate time to reassess the methods being employed and to encourage their proper positioning in our kit of useful marketing research tools.

---

[35] A. J. Kover, "Careers and Noncommunication: The Case of Academic and Applied Marketing Research," *Journal of Marketing Research*, Vol. 13, November 1976, pp. 339–344.
[36] Editorial by Wind on stepping down as editor of *The Journal of Marketing* (*Journal of Marketing*, Fall 1981).
[37] Any research involving the gathering of scaled ratings, factor analyzing these, clustering respondents into groups, and analyzing the resultant groups was called a segmentation study.
[38] E. M. Tauber, "Stamp Out the Generic Segmentation Study," *Journal of Advertising Research*, Vol. 23, No. 2, April–May 1983, p. 7.

TWO

Models of the Communication Process

It has often been charged that segmentation studies lack a theoretical foundation, and it is true that it has not been made explicit in the literature. Again this is largely attributable to the comparative lack of publishing from practitioners. However, efforts have been made by a few researchers to spell out the explicit or implicit assumptions involved. Given the communications orientation of segmentation studies, these necessarily relate to how the advertising process operates.

In 1970 Alice E. Courtney, under the sponsorship of the Marketing Science Institute, published the results of personal interviews with the research directors of leading advertising agencies about their assumptions as to how advertising works.[1] Although there were many similarities among agencies, it was also apparent that a great many different assumptions were being made about the means by which advertising achieves its effects. There is no reason to believe that situation has changed today.

The acid test of the validity of any model of communications is its ability to predict the responses after exposure to a communications stimulus. In the context of this book the stimulus will be an advertising message. However, it could be any element that communicates information about the product—the package, promotional material, the price, or the reputation of the stores in which the product is sold.

The focus here is on advertising—first, because a straightforward and generally accepted criterion of effectiveness is available, namely sales. And,

[1] Alice E. Courtney, *Practitioners' Conceptions of the Advertising Process,* Cambridge, MA: Marketing Science Institute, 1970.

19

second, because the original applications of attitude segmentation mainly concerned advertising. Finally advertising is the author's primary area of expertise. However, the conceptual model involved is thought to have broad applicability in areas such as social marketing, politics, and education.

Advertising is viewed in the broadest sense of the term. It concludes not only conventional media but publicity, promotion, packaging, personal contact, and even nonverbal communications elements. Pricing, distribution outlets, the appearance and manner of salespeople, and the design and physical characteristics of the product itself all deliver messages. The term *message* is also used in the broad sense, to encompass any single message, set of messages, or message program that the advertiser wishes to communicate to his or her customers and potential customers or to significant other publics such as employees, tradespeople, stockholders, legislators, regulators, or townspeople in the areas surrounding the plants and offices of the advertiser.

HOW ADVERTISING WORKS

Although the problem is one of long standing there is still no general agreement about how advertising works. The literature on consumer information processing, advertising, and persuasion is replete with models diagramming the process that is assumed to be operating.[2] Each new textbook on advertising seems to have a model that differs slightly or significantly from those presented in other texts.

Early models tended to be simplistic, and perhaps for that reason have survived both in the literature and in practice. Most of the early models assumed that advertising operates in a straightforward "one-way" manner. The advertiser decides upon a message, encodes it in the form of an advertisement, and delivers it through mass media to a basically passive or receptive audience. The audience attends, partially attends, or does not attend to the message and remembers all, part, or none of it. Although initial exposures may not result in behavioral changes, the cumulative weight of a good campaign is considered to be persuasive and can cause increased numbers of people to buy the product or service.

[2] G. D. Hughes and M. L. Ray (Eds.), *Buyer/Consumer Information Processing*, Chapel Hill: University of North Carolina Press, 1974. See also R. E. Smith and W. R. Swinyard, "Information Response Models: An Integrated Approach," *Journal of the American Marketing Association*, Winter 1982, pp. 81–93.

In one popular model, people were assumed to be going through a process that has been labeled AIDA:

Attention
Interest
Desire
Action

In other words, the job of the advertising was assumed to be first to call attention to the fact that the product or service was available. Once that had been accomplished the advertising was supposed to build interest in the product, to encourage potential customers to seek out information about it from whatever sources they customarily use to gather such information.

That having been accomplished the advertising was then supposed to create an active desire to try the product—to persuade people that it was a desirable purchase. Then, finally, the advertising was supposed to cause sales.

An expanded version of this model was published by Grey Advertising in 1962 under the title of *Sense and Nonsense in Creative Research*. It developed what was then called the "Staircase of Influence" leading from Attention to Sales. It hypothesized six steps[3]—attention, interest, comprehension, impact, attitude, and sale. In academic circles this type of model has come to be known as the *Hierarchy of Effects* model.[4]

A number of experiments[5] have shown that there are many situations in which this sort of straightforward one-way model does not apply. Quantitative evidence suggests[6] that steps are frequently skipped or reversed or both. Consequently, a wide variety of more complex models has been proposed to account for discrepancies between theories of consumer behavior and data from consumer behavior experiments. In general these models have been expanded to represent not only advertising but all of the factors presumed to play a role in the consumer purchase decision process. One of

[3] N. Kominik (Ed.), *Sense and Nonsense in Creative Research*, Grey Advertising, Inc., June 1962.
[4] Kristian S. Palda, "The Hypothesis of a Hierarchy of Effects: A Partial Evaluation," *Journal of Marketing Research*, Vol. 3, February 1966, pp. 13–24.
[5] D. A. Aaker and G. S. Day, "A Dynamic Model of Relationships Among Advertising, Consumer Awareness, Attitudes and Behavior," *Journal of Applied Psychology*, Vol. 59, 1974, pp. 281–286.
[6] M. L. Ray, "Marketing Communications and the Hierarchy-of-Effects" in Peter Clarke (Ed.), *New Models for Mass Communication Research*, Vol. 11, Sage Annual Reviews of Communication Research, Beverly Hills: Sage Publications, 1973.

the most complete (although it may be considered somewhat cumbersome by practitioners) is the Howard/Sheth model.[7]

Most of the consumer information processing models presuppose that most information gathering activities and most cognitive activities take place *before* a purchase decision has been reached. Several experimenters[8, 9] have expressed reservations about the applicability of these models to the types of decisions in which risks are low; risk being defined in either financial, physical, or psychological terms. In such "low involvement" situations they maintain that a trial-and-error model is more appropriate than an information seeking model.

As an example of this school of thought consider the ATR model of Ehrenberg. He hypothesizes that awareness leads directly to trial and that attitudes come into play only afterward, when trial-generated attitudes are reinforced by advertising.

One investigator[10] has tested the applicability of the AIDA model and the ATR model to purchase decisions concerning consumer durables and to those involving consumer packaged goods. His intuitively pleasing conclusions are that the AIDA model does a better job of describing durables decisions, whereas the ATR model does a better job of explaining packaged goods choices.

With increasing frequency researchers are now beginning to classify products into high involvement and low involvement categories. For example, Foote-Cone and Belding determines the appropriateness of different types of advertising appeals by relating the natures of the appeals to levels of involvement and assumed sequences of thinking, feeling, and acting.[11] Ray offers a similar matrix in his advertising text.[12]

Although this matter of conceptualizing underlying processes appears to hold promise, it might be pressed even further. Rather than categorizing products into high and low involvement types, *consumers* within a given category could productively be classified by their individual levels of cate-

[7] John L. Howard and Jagdish N. Sheth, *The Theory of Buyer Behavior,* New York: Wiley, 1969.

[8] H. E. Krugman, "The Impact of Television Advertising: Learning Without Involvement," *Public Opinion Quarterly,* Vol. 29, Fall 1965, pp. 349–356.

[9] M. L. Ray, "Psychological Theories and Interpretations of Learning," in S. Ward and T. S. Robertson (Eds.), *Consumer Behavior: Theoretical Sources,* Englewood Cliffs, NJ: Prentice-Hall, 1973.

[10] N. K. Dhalla, *Causal Influences in Attitude Research,* American Marketing Association Conference on Attitude Research, Las Vegas, 1977.

[11] *Advertising Age,* October 26, 1981, pp. S-36 to S-39.

[12] M. L. Ray, *Advertising and Communication Management,* Englewood Cliffs, NJ: Prentice-Hall, 1982.

gory and brand involvement.[13] Although automobiles are clearly a high involvement category, there are people who feel all similarly priced models are virtually interchangeable and who simply buy from a conveniently located dealer with very little information seeking. Conversely although laundry detergents are usually considered a low involvement category, some individuals check them carefully in *Consumer Reports* and ask friends, neighbors, and retailers about them. For them the choice of the best possible detergent can be involved and important. Consequently, it may be productive to look at high and low involvement groups of consumers within a product category, whether that category is generally a high or a low involvement product category. This will be discussed in greater detail in the chapters on segmentation.

THE RICHARDSON-HALEY MODEL

Because all advertising researchers make underlying assumptions about the way in which advertising works, and because they frequently codify them into a model, Chapter 3 will review the author's assumptions and will present them in the form of a model. The model to be discussed was developed jointly by Jack Richardson, Director of Research of the Warner-Lambert Company, and the author (in the summer of 1980) as the basis for a corporate system of copy testing. It was believed that any corporate system of copy testing should begin with explicit underlying assumptions about how exposure to advertising copy relates to product purchase. The Richardson-Haley model represents the formalization of these assumptions.

This model has its roots in the two-way communications process suggested by Bauer[14] in 1964. He held that the consumer was not an inert, passive target for messages—one that can be manipulated by advertising. Instead he believed that the recipients of messages were active participants in the communications process. They screen them, distorting, adding, subtracting, counterarguing,[15] and mentally rehearsing portions of the messages. They largely receive what they want to receive and believe what they want to believe.

---

[13] See also, Melody Douglas-Tate, *Facing Up to the Underlying Models and Assumptions Used in the Evaluation and Selection of Copy,* 8th Annual Mid-year Conference of the Advertising Research Foundation, September 15–17, 1982, Chicago.

[14] Raymond A. Bauer, "The Obstinate Audience," *American Psychologist,* 1964, pp. 319–328.

[15] Counterarguing refers to the mental arguments people make to themselves in opposition to the theme of the advertising; mental rehearsal refers to the process of repeating to oneself positive aspects of the message.

This suggests that a productive way to study communications is to analyze them from the standpoint of the functions that they perform for the recipient. People are not receptive to messages unless they receive some benefit from doing so. Essentially the benefits of advertising can be grouped into three types:

1. *Information.* News, facts, or impressions that can be helpful, usually in purchase decisions. Sometimes, however, useful information is given on a topic of interest to the message recipient in the hope that he or she will favor the products or services of the advertiser in gratitude for the information.

2. *Entertainment.* Something that is pleasant or amusing to watch, listen to, or read. Again it is hoped that gratitude to the advertiser or affiliative feelings toward the brand advertised will favorably influence brand choice.

3. *Emotional Reinforcement.* A major function of advertising is to reassure purchasers that they have made a correct choice, to encourage favorable word of mouth about the product or services purchased, and to develop loyal repeat purchase behavior. One of the most attentive audiences for the advertising of a product is those who have just bought that product. This is particularly true for products where risk is high. For example, it will normally be found that readers of Rolls-Royce advertisements contain many times the proportion of Rolls purchasers found in the general population. It is sometimes erroneously concluded, on the basis of the sharply higher proportions of purchases occurring among people recalling advertising in such situations, that the advertising has *caused* the purchases. More frequently, however, purchasers are simply immersing themselves in the ads because of the strong emotional reinforcement that they provide.

The Richardson-Haley model strongly endorses the two-way model of the advertising process. The consumer being exposed to an advertising message is by no means a blank slate. He brings to the exposure situation his previous experience, his values and interests, his personality and lifestyle, his moods and his habits. Moreover, he brings with him a well-developed perceptual screening process—the process he has developed for identifying those stimuli in the environment that warrant his attention. Each of these factors has a bearing on how this consumer reacts to the advertising.

Reactions are largely idiosyncratic, unique to the individual. To understand them it is necessary to understand the recipient's attitudes before being exposed to the advertising.[16] In the words of one analyst "What messages do to people isn't nearly as important as what people do to messages." People instinctively process messages using the selective techniques that they have developed over the course of their lives. They protect themselves from unwanted messages and are perceptually vigilant to the occurrence of things that interest them. This selective processing of messages is done automatically, largely without conscious thought.

Selective processing has important implications for advertisers. It suggests that every message, whether or not the advertiser wishes it, selects its own audience. It does this by the way in which it is constructed and through the message elements it contains. If a message shows a golfer, it is likely to contain in its audience[17] a disproportionately large proportion of golfers. This is fine if those in the market target are particularly interested in golf. If they are not, then the effectiveness of the advertising becomes much more a matter of luck.

This points up the importance of market research to the development of effective communications. It is important to know the target people in depth—in enough depth to be able to anticipate how they are likely to react to different types of messages.

This is no easy task. As mentioned earlier, reactions to advertising messages are largely idiosyncratic. How then can an advertiser anticipate the reactions of large groups of people to messages? Two research tools can be very helpful—segmentation research and analysis of message content. The first of these areas is well developed and is one of the primary topics of this book. The second is not as familiar to advertisers, but is of equal importance.

The objective of market segmentation is to group people by criteria which will allow the message sender to predict responses to advertising messages. That is the justification for Benefit Segmentation. Knowledge of the benefits that are important to an individual can be helpful in predicting responses to advertising incorporating those benefits. Evidence in support of this point is presented in Chapter 7.

---

[16] The copy testing process involves the simultaneous evaluation of several copy executions which are exposed to independent samples of consumers in the market target for the brand in question. To be sure that differences in commercial performance are a function of the commercials themselves rather than of differences in the types of people exposed, the samples exposed to each execution are precisely matched. In developing the matching process it was found that the single factor most strongly related to changes in overall attitudes of advertised brands was the types and intensities of beliefs held before exposure.

[17] Audience, used in this sense, refers to people who have been *mentally* exposed to the advertising not just the *physically* exposed audience.

Although responses to advertising messages are highly individual they are not unique. People can be grouped by the similarities of their responses to individual message elements. The question is which message elements form the most reasonable basis for such grouping.

Messages are complex stimuli consisting of a great number of perceptual, cognitive, and emotional elements. Some are verbal, but most are nonverbal. The basic message of the advertising is usually carried by the verbal elements and reinforced by nonverbal factors such as color, music, graphics, pace, setting, and casting.

Advertising messages usually communicate a limited number of benefits. These may be categorized into several classes:

Cognitive benefits.   Logical and rational benefits such as durability, low price, and product performance.

Sensory benefits.   How attractive the taste, feel, smell, appearance, and/or sound of the product are.

Emotional benefits.   How you feel when you buy, use, or simply own the product. Reinforcement of self-image through user images is the key in this class.

Affiliative benefits.   Intangibles such as the reputation of the company offering the product or service, liking their style, admiring their advertising.

Any of these benefits, individually or in sets, can form the basis for a communications strategy.

A schematic of the Richardson-Haley model is presented on page 27. (See Figure 2.1). This model suggests that the planning process should start with a thorough review of the product, brand, or service to be advertised and what it means to people. Areas to be covered include characteristics inherent in the product itself (e.g., its function, its quality level, its size, its price, distinguishing characteristics, its general level of complexity, etc.— what the product is), physical benefits it delivers (what it does), sensory benefits, emotional or symbolic benefits, affiliative benefits, brand image, the types of people who are perceived to use it, the types who actually do use it, the conditions or occasions of use, and the conditions or occasions of purchase.

The second step is the development of a communications strategy. This involves a definition of the product category within which the brand is competing and whether incremental volume is expected to come from primary competitors, other products, new occasions of use or larger quantities of consumption per use occasion, the choice of a single-minded buying incentive, demonstration or support for that incentive, and the identification

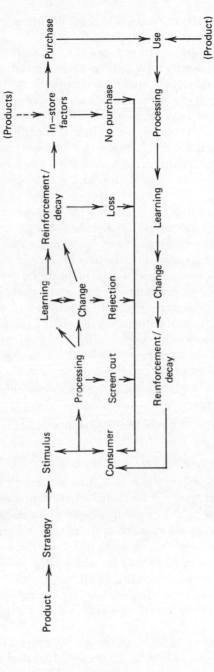

Figure 2.1. Richardson-Haley model of the communication process

27

of a specific market target. Frequently these decisions are crystallized in a copy platform or copy strategy statement.

Next the advertising stimulus is developed. This involves decisions as to the core idea, the message type (intellectual or emotional), support type (sensory cues, demonstrations, spokespersons or characters, and nonverbal forms of support, such as music, casting, and voices), format (e.g., slice-of-life, problem/solution, testimonial, direct sell, mood, etc.), media considerations (type, program/editorial environment, specific vehicles, and locations), frequency/prominence/scheduling (commercial or ad exposure considerations, brand identification), and the complexity of the message (the amount of information to be delivered, the type, and its intellectual difficulty).

At this point the stimulus is exposed to the consumer. However, the consumer brings to the exposure situation a number of things that can have a strong effect upon her reactions at the moment of exposure. These include her perceived and latent needs and the benefits being sought, brand salience and perceptions, her interest and involvement in the product category, the amount of risk (physical, economic, or social) she perceives to be involved in brand choice, her general receptivity to advertising and the purposes it serves for her (information, entertainment, and/or reinforcement), and her beliefs about the product category.

The term *beliefs* deserves some clarification. In this model it refers to general perceptions about the product category and is measured by the extent to which people agree or disagree with statements such as:

"All brands are the same."

"The higher the price the better the quality."

"Gum is bad for the teeth."

"Laxatives are as much a preventative as a cure."

Also affecting responses are the information processing styles and purchasing and use styles of the individual. Information processing styles include the ways in which people use information to make decisions, the extent to which they are seeking information and the types of information they are seeking, and the purchase influences to which they are subject. Purchasing styles include the types of outlets in which they normally buy, the frequency of their purchases, quantities purchased, the timing of purchases, and whether they plan their purchases or buy on impulse. Use includes the purpose or purposes for which the product is used, frequency, quantity, and timing of use.

The final set of personal factors having a bearing on response are the so-called classification data—who the person is. Included here are his or her personality and the style characteristics as well as the person's demographic characteristics.

In any event some form of message processing takes place, and it can be extremely brief. A person can say, subconsciously, "I am not interested" and screen out the message. On the other hand, it can register in short-term or long-term memory. However, it usually does not register in complete and perfect form. There are additions, deletions, distortions and misinterpretations, connections with the personal life and values of the individual, source derogation, discrediting of spokespersons, counter- and/or supporting arguments, and mental rehearsals.

Processing results in changes in people's attitudes about and predispositions toward the advertised product. Learning is also involved. The net effect can be positive or negative; it can result in rejection or positive reinforcement.

Consumers are also likely to be exposed to multiple messages from the advertised brand and to messages from competing products. If they receive no further messages, the effects of the initial exposure can be expected to diminish or "decay." Multiple messages are normally aimed at reinforcement.

Before buying, other influences—notably in-store influences—come into play. These include distribution, display, price, packaging, promotion, word-of-mouth, influence of store personnel, activity of other shoppers, and the ambience of the store itself.

If a purchase is not made, the cycle begins all over again. If the advertised brand is bought, the product then becomes the primary stimulus. Experience with it in use situations causes further processing which in turn leads to learning and change, and is subject to reinforcement and decay.

SELECTIVE PROCESSES

One key element, probably *the* key element, in explaining how advertising works is the selective processes that underlie the way in which advertising messages reach consumers. They operate at several levels:

Message avoidance and pursuit
Selective attention
Selective perception
Selective retention

Message Avoidance and Pursuit

This process involves the scheduling of people's activities so that they are not likely to be exposed to messages of low interest and, conversely, so that they are likely to receive supportive, interesting, and pleasant messages.

Thus people who are not interested in religion normally do not go to church; people who are staunch liberal democrats do not listen to the speeches of conservative republicans; and people who are not interested in sports do not buy *Sports Illustrated.* Conversely, people who are very interested in current events probably subscribe to *Time, Newsweek,* or *U.S. News and World Report* and are likely to watch television news programs. Leaving the room during television commercials, changing channels, talking to other people in the room, or engaging in other activities such as reading or sewing are some ways of avoiding commercial messages.

Advertisers are well aware of this and try to place their advertisements in media vehicles whose audiences have interests that relate to the product or service to be advertised and in locations where they will be difficult to avoid. Thus manufacturers of sports car equipment often advertise in *Road and Track, Car and Driver,* and *Motor Trends.* Similarly, manufacturers of golf clubs are likely to advertise in *Golf Digest* or *Golf Magazine,* depending on costs per thousand[18] and other considerations.

Selective Attention

Selective attention involves whether or not the message is received once it is physically presented to the intended recipient. In the golf club situation, for example, an experiment conducted by a marketer of women's golf clubs illustrated the importance of an appropriate media environment. Women in the market target for this product were exposed to golf club ads in *Baby Talk,* a magazine whose primary focus (as the title suggests) is on babies, and through identical ads in *Sports Illustrated.* It had been reasoned that the "shock value" of seeing an incongruous advertisement for golf clubs in the midst of ads for baby food and baby clothes, plus the fact that the ad was the *only* ad for golf clubs in *Baby Talk,* would generate high levels of attention. In fact, however, the ads in *Baby Talk* generated extremely low recall scores. The same ad in *Sports Illustrated* produced high scores.

The explanation for these results is obvious. Women have expectations as to the kinds of ads they can expect to find in differing media environments. They screen *in* ads that are consistent with those expectations and screen *out* those that are not. Thus the ads in *Baby Talk* were not seen, whereas women in the market for golf clubs may well seek out magazines such as *Sports Illustrated* to see what sorts of merchandise are potentially available to them.

The subject of attention has itself received a great deal of attention both in psychology and in advertising, and its selective nature is well docu-

---

[18] A standard measure of media efficiency. The cost associated with delivering the advertising message to 1000 prospects.

mented. Attention has been defined by William James as "the taking possession by the mind, in clear and vivid form of one out of what seem several simultaneously possible objects or trains of thought. It implies withdrawal from some things in order to deal effectively with others . . ."[19] Selective attention depends upon five major factors:

1. *Message Characteristics.* The aesthetic physical and psychological characteristics—the way in which the message is constructed.

2. *Characteristics of the Message Recipient.* Information processing styles and previous experience or learning as it affects the expectations of the person being physically exposed to the message.

3. *Source Influences.* The expertise, trustworthiness, attractiveness, and familiarity of the perceived source of the message.

4. *Situational or Environmental Factors.* When the message is received, where, and the motives in play at the time of exposure—the needs, wants, wishes, and interests of the person physically exposed.

5. *Channel Influences.* The role played by the medium as it interacts with the message. The available evidence suggests that print messages operate quite differently than broadcast messages. Also, as pointed out earlier, people have expectations about the kinds of messages that are likely to appear in individual media vehicles and are more likely to receive messages that appear in the expected context.

Although a great deal of research has been done on attention, relatively few principles have found their way into advertising practice. Advertising has remained largely an art form. In part this is because much of the experimental work has been seriously flawed.[20] In most instances one or more of the five receptivity factors has been either measured poorly or ignored entirely. Perhaps for this reason the conclusions reached have too often been contradictory. And because academics have been unable to agree, applied researchers have relied largely upon experiential learning and conventional wisdom.

From an applied standpoint, what do we know about the five key receptivity factors? Unfortunately we know very little about channel characteristics. Although it is appreciated that print and broadcast media operate differently, most experiments by applied researchers have treated these dif-

---

[19] William James, *The Principles of Psychology*, Vol. 1, New York: Dover Publications, 1950. (Originally published in 1890!)

[20] M. L. Ray and A. A. Mitchell, "When Does Information Processing Research Have Anything to Do with Consumer Information Processing?," pp. 372–375, Also, J. C. Olsen, "Cognitive Effects of Advertising Repetition," pp. 213–220, both articles in W. D. Perrault, Jr. (Ed.) *Advances in Consumer Research*, Vol. 4, Atlanta, 1977.

ferences in a "black box" manner, simply assigning varying weights to different media types and measuring effects on chosen criterion measures. Different effects on information processing activities have rarely been studied.[21] The same applies to situational and environmental influences, although in recent years there has been an upsurge in interest in this area in academic circles.[22]

We are in somewhat better shape with respect to source influences. For example, a considerable amount of attention has been given to the choice of presenters of television commercials and to the roles of spokespersons,[23-25] and primary dimensions of evaluation such as trustworthiness, attractiveness, expertise, and familiarity have been identified. However, much remains to be done in integrating the effects of this receptivity factor with those of the others.

The two areas considered to be the most important, judging from the amount of attention they have received, are the message and the way it is constructed and the audience and how it interacts with the message. The largest body of work interrelating these two factors is, of course, copy testing. Situational, source, and channel influences are usually either assumed to be negligible, are held constant through the experimental methods employed, or are made as typical as possible under the conditions of the test.

A number of studies have been done on message elements that are related to message recall, a popular measure of attention and retention.[26-28] The following factors are among those having a bearing on attention.

Novelty, Incongruity, or Surprise

People continuously monitor their environments and screen *out* stimuli that are normal or ordinary. Things that are not in line with their expectations

---

[21] Exceptions include H. R. Krugman's "Brain Wave Measure of Media Involvement," *Journal of Advertising Research*, Vol. 11, 1971, pp. 3–10.

[22] J. C. Olson (Ed.) *Advances in Consumer Research*, Vol. 7, 1979, Research on Situational Factors, five papers, pp. 639–663.

[23] C. Atkin and M. Block, "Effectiveness of Celebrity Endorsers," *Journal of Advertising Research*, February/March 1983, Vol. 23, No. 1, pp. 57–61.

[24] H. Friedman, S. Termini, and R. Washington, "The Effectiveness of Advertisements Using Four Types of Endorsers," *Journal of Advertising*, Vol. 6, 1977, pp. 22–24.

[25] J. C. Mowen, "On Product Endorser Effectiveness: A Balance Model Approach," *Current Issues and Research in Advertising*, 1980, pp. 41–58, Graduate School of Business Administration, University of Michigan.

[26] K. J. Clancy and D. M. Kweskin, "TV Commercial Recall Correlates," *Journal of Advertising Research*, Vol. 11, April 1971, p. 18ff.

[27] R. Valiente, "Mechanical Correlates of Ad Recognition," *Journal of Advertising Research*, Vol. 13, No. 3, June 1973, pp. 13–18.

[28] G. Fennell, "Attention Engagement," *Current Issues and Research in Advertising*, 1979, pp. 17–33, Graduate School of Business Administration, University of Michigan.

and experience are screened *in* for further processing. Physical advertising elements that affect screening for incongruity include loudness, brightness, color, changes of pace, and visual distortion. The more intense these stimuli the more attention they are likely to attract. Extreme intensity is likely to be unpleasant as well, however, and thus may detract from the effectiveness of the commercial.

Uncertainty, defined as simultaneously aroused expectations, and conflict, defined as simultaneously aroused responses, also fall under this general heading, as does message complexity. In the latter area it appears that the best strategy is to use few dimensions but relevant ones. Eye camera work by Krugman[29] and replicated by Haley[30] suggests that there is a *negative* correlation between time spent with print advertising and its memorability.

Valued or Pleasant Stimuli; Emotional Arousal

People are inclined to screen in stimuli that are pleasurable and to screen out those that are not. For example, valued words are recalled more readily than neutral words.[31] Valued positions evoke similar responses. In one classic experiment[32] people known to be pro and anti-Communist were exposed to a series of statements favoring and opposing Communism. They tended to remember the statements that were compatible with their own positions. Humor also tends to be screened in, at least on first exposure. Connecting it to specific products in such a way as to cause them to be viewed favorably, however, poses a real challenge to creative departments.

There is ample evidence that strong fear appeals can cause messages to be screened out. Insurance advertisements regularly receive Starch "noting" scores[33] that are among the lowest of any category monitored. And nonsmokers are much more likely to attend antismoking messages than are smokers.[34]

---

[29] H. E. Krugman, "Processes Underlying Exposure to Advertising," *American Psychologist,* Vol. 23, No. 4, April 1968, pp. 245–253.

[30] R. I. Haley, *Effective Communications: With Application to Marketing and Social Marketing,* Unpublished dissertation, Union Graduate School, October 1974.

[31] L. Postman, J. S. Brunner, E. McGinness, "Personal Values as Selective Factors in Perception" in J. P. Chaplin and T. S. Kraw (Eds.), *Systems and Theories of Psychology,* New York: Holt, Rinehart and Winston, 1962.

[32] J. M. Levine and G. Murphy, "The Learning and Forgetting of Controversial Material," *Journal of Abnormal and Social Psychology,* Vol. 38, 1943, pp. 507–517.

[33] W. J. Wilson, "Women's Purchasing Influence: How Much Has It Changed in 30 Years?," Marketing to Women Conference, New York Chapter, American Marketing Association, March 30, 1978.

[34] Sixty-seven percent of nonsmokers compared to 44 percent of smokers, according to one study.

Familiar stimuli, such as commercials involving products or services being used, are likely to be screened in because they offer positive and reinforcing information. Familiar stimuli are easily understood and are processed with no emotional dissonance.

Repetition serves two functions. For those who are familiar with the advertised products it is reinforcing and encourages repeat behavior when purchase needs arise. In one study, it was found that significantly more people who had just bought a new car noticed ads for that car than noticed ads for cars they had not bought, or than noticed ads for cars they had considered but not bought.[35] Similarly, the primary impact of election debates is to reinforce partisan predispositions.[36] For people not familiar with products advertised, repetition encourages "tuning in" to scan a message which they may recognize they have seen before but have not processed. Advertisers have capitalized upon this tendency by tactics such as buying every car card in a bus (a bus "spectacular") and by running the same commercial twice with a minimal amount of time, often only a few seconds, between airings. In this situation people may effectively screen out the first exposure. When exposed a second time, however, a natural reaction is "Didn't I just see that commercial?," and to determine whether this is true they carefully watch the commercial. At that point they *really* have been exposed.

Information—News, Problem-solving Methods, or Information Relevant to Present or Probable Future Activities, Interests, or Opinions

People also maintain perceptual vigilance for any information that is potentially interesting or useful to them and screen it in. Although the screening is done subconsciously, the processing is largely a cognitive activity.

Context

The scheduling of the message also has a bearing on the amount of attention that is paid to it. Program influence can be substantial. One carefully designed study[37] indicated that commercial recall varied substantially not only from program to program but also from episode to episode of the same program. When commercials are grouped together in a "pod," the position of the commercial in the pod can affect its recall level. The well-known pri-

[35] Ian Hare, "Cognitive Dissonance and the New Car Buyer: A British Study," *Quarterly Review of Marketing,* Spring 1977, pp. 1–3.
[36] A. H. Miller and M. Mackuen, "Learning About the Candidates: The 1976 Presidential Debates," *Public Opinion Quarterly,* Fall 1979, pp. 326–358.
[37] *Program Environment Copy Test,* J. Walter Thompson Co., New York, July 1977.

macy/recency[38] effect is usually present, together with lead-in, lead-out effects. The latter occur when commercials for products of general interest are placed back-to-back with products with comparatively narrow audiences (e.g., denture adhesives). If the commercial for the product with limited interest is placed ahead of that for the general interest product, it can sharply lower its recall score. When people are exposed to the commercial for the special interest product, all but those who are interested in it tune out. And they often do not bother to tune back in for the subsequent commercial. If the general interest product is scheduled first, it is likely to have much less influence on the commercial that follows.

Turning now to what is known about the influence of audience factors on attention levels, the first thing of note is that because of the strong interaction of audiences and messages it is very difficult to separate the influences of message characteristics and audience characteristics. Physical characteristics such as loudness, brightness, and color are usually considered to be inherent in the message. However, individual differences in information processing methods can cause sharply different responses to a common stimulus. What seems unusually loud to one person, and for that reason is noted, may seem ordinary to another person and thus may be ignored. And what may seem a brilliant color to one person may be gray to someone who is color blind. Similarly, what is familiar to one person may not be familiar to another, and interest in problems may vary depending upon the frequency and seriousness of the problem to the message recipient. Thus because of the individual nature of response, the audience deserves at least as much study as the message.

Presumably, if we can determine the causal factors behind the responses of an individual, we can aggregate individuals into response segments. One central factor in predicting response is involvement in the product category. Those planning to buy products involving risk consciously attend advertising messages for those products.[39] People's involvement in the decision progess is directly related to their involvement in the product category. This is clearly demonstrated by the strong correlations found between relative male/female purchase influences as reflected by the Haley-Overholser Purchase Influence study[40] and the relative Starch noting scores (measures of attention to print advertising) of males and females in 91 product categories.[41] People who are interested in a given product category are more likely to attend messages relating to that category and to make finer distinctions among brands in it. Similarly, they are interested in a wider

---

[38] The tendency to have higher recall for the first and last items in a string of items.
[39] Burleigh B. Gardner, "A Battle to Persuade," *Advertising Age*, June 22, 1981, p. 52.
[40] *Purchase Influence: Measures of Husband/Wife Influence on Buying Decisions*, New Canaan, Conn.: Haley, Overholser Associates, Inc., January 1975.
[41] William J. Wilson, Marketing to Women Conference, March 30, 1978, New York.

range of benefits. This has sometimes been confused with "yeasaying," a tendency to respond positively on rating scales.[42] However, independent validation[43] shows that those indicating interest in a wider range of benefits are also heavier consumers of the product category.

Message content—the benefits communicated by the message—also affect attention,[44] and the specific benefits that are considered important or desirable by the message recipient have a definite effect on recall levels of differing message types.[45] Other factors that bear a strong relationship to the attention levels of individual audience members include:

Interests.   Hobbies, activities, people, countries, and subjects.

Lifestyles.   Admired lifestyles and ones with which that the respondent can empathize.

Values.   Those held to be important by the individual.

Beliefs and Perceptions.   Commercials that are compatible with these are more likely to be attended.

Complexity of Cognitive Structure.   Some people use relatively few dimensions of evaluation; others use a great many. The number used is related to involvement but it also is determined by the person's basic information processing style. This will be discussed in more detail when we deal with perception. Tuchman[46] has isolated four cognitive systems, but there are probably more.

Personalization of the Message.   The feeling that "they are talking directly to me." This is a gestalt reaction that cuts across all message factors. It involves using words of the right types, familiar sentences and pace, and showing people and scenes to which the message recipient can easily relate.

Selective Perception

Perception is defined as "the way things look to us, or the way they sound, feel, taste or smell . . . perception also involves, to some degree, an under-

---

[42] B. Gold and W. Salkind, "What Do Top Scores Measure?," *Journal of Advertising Research*, Vol. 14, March 1974, pp. 19–23.

[43] *Bank of America Segmentation Study*, San Francisco, May 1976.

[44] M. B. Holbrook and D. R. Lehmann, "Form Versus Content in Predicting Starch Scores," *Journal of Advertising Research*, Vol. 20, No. 4, August 1980, pp. 53–64.

[45] R. I. Haley, "Beyond Benefit Segmentation," *Journal of Advertising Research*, Vol. 11, August 1971, pp. 3–8.

[46] B. W. Tuchman, "Integrative Complexity: Its Measurement and Relation to Creativity," *Educational and Psychological Measurement*, Vol. 26, No. 4, Winter 1966, pp. 369–382.

standing awareness, a 'meaning' or a 'recognition' of these objects." In short, perception is how we organize what is attended.[47]

Perception is selective. Because it is so highly interrelated with attention, it is difficult to separate the two. Perceptual mechanisms have a lot to do with what is attended. When people are exposed to a picture, they tend to look at only about 10 percent of it (the most easily recognized part).[48] Pictorial information is processed slowly; unwanted details are not noticed. In reading a paper, people scan, looking for peripheral cues as to things that might be of interest. They are almost grateful for cues which indicate that they can safely ignore material. Ads placed near fast-moving articles are compatible with the scanning process. Consequently, they are remembered better than ads near slow-paced articles.[49]

People are active participants in the perception process. They do not simply record portions of the advertising stimulus presented; mostly they see what they want to see. Messages that conflict with existing predispositions are likely to be screened out.[50] They select from a message the meanings that are most consistent with their previous experience and beliefs. In experiments in binocular rivalry, where people look through field-glass type eyepieces and simultaneously see two pictures—one with each eye—this conclusion is well documented. When Latin Americans and North Americans are exposed to simultaneous pictures of a bullfighter and a baseball player, the Latin Americans are more likely to see the bullfighter, whereas North Americans are more likely to see baseball players.

In a parallel experiment, respondents were exposed to simultaneous pictures of a nude woman and a clothed woman. Very few saw the clothed woman. And in still another experiment subjects were shown simultaneous pictures of two *very* unattractive women. When asked to describe what they had seen, some people described an attractive woman, one that had not appeared in either of the two pictures.

People reshape messages so that they better fit their preconceptions. They may add material that has not been presented, especially things from past advertising, or they may place major emphasis on seemingly minor parts of the advertising. This process is called sharpening.[51] People more frequently delete all or parts of messages they receive, subtracting meanings and ignoring meanings that are not acceptable to them; this process is called leveling. Selective processes are potent. In fact, Hyman and Sheatsley, in reviewing reasons that public service campaigns fail, conclude that

---

[47] Fred Webster, Jr., *Marketing Communication*, New York: Ronald Press, 1971.

[48] Leo Bogart, *Strategy in Advertising*, New York: Harcourt Brace & World, Inc., 1967.

[49] D. B. Lucas and S. H. Britt, *Advertising Psychology and Research*, New York: McGraw-Hill, 1963.

[50] J. T. Klapper, *The Effects of Mass Communication*, New York: Free Press, 1963.

[51] Webster, *Marketing Communication*.

mass communications of information rarely have important persuasive impact because of selective exposure.[52]

Other defense mechanisms that prevent people from dealing with unwanted messages include:

Source Derogation. Recognizing the purpose of the message. "Aw, they're just trying to sell me."

Discrediting the Spokesperson. If a person who saves at Citibank sees a commercial in which Joe DiMaggio is extolling the virtues of the Bowery Bank, and if that person greatly admires DiMaggio, the commercial may cause a certain amount of dissonance. One way by which the person can reduce this dissonance is to discredit the spokesperson. "Gee, I hadn't realized how old Joe is getting."

Distortion. In one commercial for a floor cleaner two mops were shown simultaneously cleaning the floor. One had been saturated with the advertised brand and the other with the leading brand in the category. The demonstration showed the advertised brand to be doing a better job. However, users of the leading brand perceived the person using the advertised brand to be exerting more pressure on her mop than the other person. Neutral observers saw no difference in the amounts of pressure being exerted.

Similarly, one comparative ad for Fresca and Pepsi-Cola, written in support of Fresca, claimed that, in "blind" tests[53] 40 percent of Pepsi drinkers actually preferred Fresca to Pepsi. The playback among Fresca drinkers was to the effect that Pepsi drinkers prefer Fresca to Pepsi.

One simple but prevalent form of distortion is to misidentify the sponsor of the commercial. A leading copy testing firm reports that "In a typical example of six established competitive food brands, we found that on the average only 52 percent of the viewers could correctly identify the brand. The range ran from a low of 37 percent to a high of 70 percent. The average misidentification was 17 percent, but the no identification group ranged from 16 to 45 percent."[54]

Misidentification often operates in favor of the category leader, although some of the incorrect brand association may be an artifact of direct questioning and the guessing that this often stimulates. People also tend to attribute advertising they like to brands that they like, even though it may be

---

[52] "Some Reasons Why Information Campaigns Fail," *POQ*, Vol. II, 1947, pp. 413–423.
[53] Blind tests are tests in which the respondent is not aware of the identity of the product being tested.
[54] H. Spielman, AMA New York Chapter Television Testing Conference, April 7, 1970.

for another product. In one humorous and somewhat embarrassing situation, a group of judges, attempting to select the most effective commercials of the year, misidentified the sponsorship of the commercial they selected as the winner.[55]

Counterargumentation. To avoid conflicts in commercials favoring the brands they represent people often have contrary thoughts. "Yes, but it costs twice as much to use that product" or "It sure doesn't work that way in my house." By indicating to themselves that the commercial is misleading, it is more easily dismissed. This process is called counterargumentation.[56]

Mental Rehearsal. This is the opposite of counterargumentation. It involves repeating all or parts of supportive elements in the message. It is often practiced by users of products while being exposed to commercials for those products. It is reinforcing and reassuring to have this kind of support for decisions you have made or are about to make.

A thorough review of the extensive literature on perception and selective processes is beyond the scope of this chapter. The interested reader is referred to Wasson,[57] Abelson,[58] and McGuire.[59]

Selective Retention

The final element in the main chain of selective processes is selective retention. If people do, despite their perceptual defenses, receive messages that they would rather not have received, they can fall back on their ultimate defense. They can forget the message as quickly as possible. In an experiment involving public service messages (see Chapter 7), these messages were found not only to have lower recall levels than messages for commercial products (due, no doubt, to perceptual screening of unwanted requests for money, time, or other forms of help), but they have faster rates of decay. People who receive public service messages forget them more rapidly than do recipients of commercial messages.

[55] *Advertising Age,* October 18, 1976, p. 74.
[56] P. L. Wright, "The Cognitive Processes Mediating Acceptance of Advertising," *Journal of Marketing Research,* Vol. 10, February 1973, pp. 53–62.
[57] C. R. Wasson, *Consumer Behavior: A Managerial Viewpoint,* Austin, TX: Austin Press, 1975, Chapter 6.
[58] R. P. Abelson et al. (Eds.), *Theories of Cognitive Consistency: A Sourcebook,* Chicago: Rand McNally, 1968.
[59] W. J. McGuire, *The Guiding Theories Behind Attitude Change Research,* 3rd Annual Attitude Research Conference, American Marketing Association, March 1970.

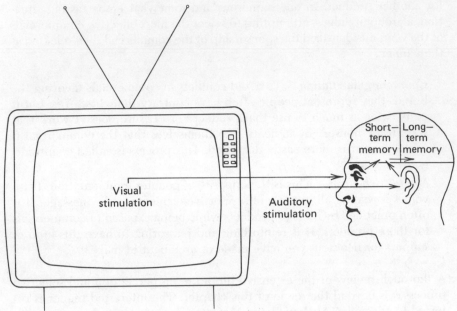

Figure 2.2. An information processing model

A number of information-processing models have been proposed for the recall function. One is presented in Figure 2.2. It involves three factors:

Visual stimulation

Auditory stimulation

The interaction of the two in short-term memory, feeding into long-term memory and/or response

Visual stimuli are processed rapidly, coded visually, and briefly stored into what is called *iconic* storage. At the same time auditory stimuli are coded auditorially and stored briefly in what is called *echoic* storage. These two forms of storage are immediately combined in short-term memory. Haber and Hershenson[60] claim ". . . in any perceptual task, the perceiver has little more than ¼ of a second in which to process the content of this initial visual representation so that the information can be transformed to a somewhat more stable or permanent storage."

[60] R. N. Haber and M. Hershenson, *The Psychology of Visual Perception*, New York: Holt, Rinehart and Winston, 1973, p. 163.

Once iconic and echoic storage have taken place a visual and auditory image is developed. This is the conscious awareness of the stimuli the point at which the act of perceiving and storage in short-term memory occurs. It is also the point at which mental rehearsal can occur. The mind can be "turned on" to review the stimuli if, subconsciously, they appear to be worthy of review. If not there is no mental rehearsal and part or all of the stimuli will be lost.

The normal amount of processing time in short-term memory is several seconds, longer if rehearsal occurs. Surviving information passes into long-term memory. It then affects not only future stimuli and future actions, but also past stimuli, replacing some and modifying others. Long-term and short-term storage interact, each affecting the other.

Recall is one of the oldest criteria of effective copy as measured by copy research, and it remains popular today. Recall is defined as the ability to play back elements of the advertising message after exposure. It is normally obtained without reexposing people to the advertising.

A related measure is recognition. In recognition tests people are shown all or part of the original ad and asked if they remember having seen it. As might be expected, levels of claimed exposure are higher with recognition tests than with recall tests. However, part of the higher level is probably attributable to confusion and to guessing. On the other hand, part of the reason for the low recall scores probably is related to the inability to retrieve the message from the memory code under which it is stored.

The message factors relating to recognition and recall of advertising messages have been studied frequently. For example, one study by Marplan,[61] a division of Interpublic, identified five factors that were significantly related to Starch noting scores. These were:

1. Layout (illustrations at the top of the page, ones with a single focal point, and ones that have simple layout generate the highest scores).
2. Illustration (large illustration area, use of a structured illustration as opposed to a silhouette, photographic realism, proximity dominance, and vividness are best).
3. Headline (shorter headlines score better, one line or at the most two).
4. Text (smaller areas are related to higher scores).
5. Signature or product identification symbol (small amounts of space perform better than larger amounts of space).

[61] D. W. Hendon, "How Mechanical Factors Affect Ad Perception," *Journal of Advertising Research*, Vol. 13, No. 4, August 1973, pp. 39–45.

In another study conducted at Leo Burnett, similar conclusions were reached.[62] The size of the illustration was found to be positively related to Starch noting scores, whereas tle size of the headline and the number of elements in the illustration, a measure of complexity, was found to be negatively related to Starch scores.

Most recently Ogilvy and Raphaelson[63] have provided several rules of thumb for television commercials. This in turn comes largely from data supplied by Mapes and Ross, a leading copy testing firm. In terms of ability to change brand preference the following techniques are reported to score above average:

1. Problem/solution
2. Humor pertinent to the buying incentive
3. Characters developed by the advertising and associated with the brand
4. Slice-of-life scenes in which a doubter is converted
5. Genuine news
6. Candid camera testimonials
7. Demonstrations

It is carefully pointed out, however, that these are no more than averages and, as has been noted in the instance of segmented markets, averages are often misleading. Certainly "built" commercials that do no more than conform to the averages are not likely to be exciting or highly motivating.

Effects of Selective Processes on the Power of Advertising

There is ample evidence that people screen out most of the advertising to which they are exposed. The average copy testing recall score for television commercials is about 20. This means that when people are contacted approximately 24 hours after being exposed to a television commercial, only 20% can remember enough about it to prove that they have seen it. In other words, nearly 80% of all of the people who have been exposed have largely screened it out. Statistics such as this have a strong bearing on the popularity of intrusive media such as television and radio and upon the high frequency levels in most media schedules.

Evidence of the limiting effects of selective processes comes also from a joint study made by the American Association of Advertising Agencies

---

[62] Hendon, "Mechanical Factors."
[63] D. Ogilvy and J. Raphaelson, "Research on Advertising Techniques That Work—and Don't Work," *Harvard Business Review*, Vol. 60, No. 4, July–August 1982, pp. 14–18.

(AAAA) and Harvard University.[64] In this study a large national sample of respondents was equipped with hand counters and asked to register every advertisement that they saw. Respondents were enlisted for half a day each.

Estimates of the number of ads to which the average American is exposed in a half day are necessarily approximate. In one study conducted by BBD&O,[65] however, it was estimated that the average American male is exposed to 285 advertisements a day in television, radio, magazines, and outdoor, and the average female to 305. So, in round numbers, the average number of messages for a half-day period can be estimated at about 150.

Returning to the AAAA research, it could be argued that the respondents might be expected to miss a number of the ads to which they were actually exposed. On the other hand, it might be expected that people who were aware that they were taking part in an experiment, and who were continually reminded of that fact by the presence of the hand counters, would be sensitized to the presence of any and all advertising. In the latter case they could be expected to pick up a large portion—perhaps most—of the 150 exposures that we estimate would occur.

However this might be reasoned, the actual "modal" category (the one registered most frequently by the people doing the counting) of exposures was 11–20. This suggests that people's screening processes are well imbedded—not easily changed even when they are participating in experimental activities such as the AAAA study.

The British Market Research Bureau also gathered some relevant data based on a technique developed at the Institute for Economic Psychology in Mannheim, West Germany.[66] In this design subjects are invited to participate in a focus group, a form of group discussion. When they arrive at the location for the meeting, they are ushered into a waiting room and asked to make themselves comfortable until the discussion is ready to begin. In the waiting room is a table on which a magazine lies, and the only chair in the room is placed by the table. Finding himself alone, the subject almost invariably begins to read the magazine. A cleverly concealed camera keeps track of the pages to which he directs his attention and the amount of time he spends looking at them. Later a "reading and noting" interview of the sort conducted by Starch is given. Thus actual physical exposure can be compared with remembered exposure. One such comparison is presented in Table 2.1.

[64] R. A. Bauer and S. A. Greyser, *Advertising in America: The Consumer View*, Cambridge, MA: Harvard University Press, 1968.
[65] "A Mere 305 Ads Hit Mom Every Day Not 1500, BBDO Reports," *Advertising Age*, October 19, 1970, p. 1.
[66] Based on a technique developed at the Institute for Economic Psychology in Mannheim, West Germany (1970).

TABLE 2.1   Relationship Between Time Spent with Ads and Recall

Time Spent Looking at Ad	Less than 2.5 Seconds	2.5 to 5.0 Seconds	5.0 Seconds or More	Mean Level
Physically exposed but not recalled	85%	74%	64%	81%
Recalled the ad	15	26	36	19
Total	100%	100%	100%	100%
Base	(874)	(211)	(141)	(1226)

It is apparent that, in general, the longer people looked at ads the more likely they were to remember them. Even at the 5-second or more exposure length, however, only about a third of the respondents were able to remember the advertisements. Interestingly, the overall average level of recall is around the 20 percent level normally associated with day-after recall levels for television commercials.

Laboratory work revealing the effects of selective processes has also been done with newspapers.[67] Bogart had a small group of women look through a newspaper under laboratory conditions. Exposure to the advertisements in the newspaper was measured with a special camera which recorded the spot on the page to which women were directing their attention. A half-hour after exposure he asked about noting and reading both for editorial items and for advertisements. There were 510 ads in the newspaper, and 29 pages of the newspaper were used for test purposes.

All respondents opened all of the test pages. Of the ads for women's products 87% were looked at. For other products only 56% were looked at—some 31 percentage points fewer. This is clear evidence of selective perception. Women were able to find cues indicating whether the products were designed with them in mind and paid more attention to those that were. Recall figures showed a similar pattern. Of the ads for women's products which they had looked at, they were able to recall 70%. They could recall only 52% of the ads for other products, however, evidence of selective retention at work.

Advertising agencies also have impressive evidence of the power of selective processes. For example, one major agency—Grey Advertising—has conducted a huge number of copy tests over the past 20 years using a method they call TV-matic. This involves the use of rear screen projectors

[67] L. Bogart, *Strategy in Advertising*, New York: Harcourt Brace & Jovanovich, 1967. "Looking with Learning versus Looking without Learning: An Exploratory Study of Eye Movement Patterns when Viewing Advertisements," American Newspaper Publishers Association, Inc., 1967.

in which a pilot film for a television program that has not yet been aired is stored. Typically three commercials are spliced into this film. One of these is the commercial of primary interest, the one which is to be evaluated by the test. A second is one that is included largely for purposes of distracting people from the purposes of the test. And the third is a long-running commercial such as "Smokey the Bear," included for purposes of control in every test. A large bank of "norms" is available with respect to the latter commercial. This allows the researchers to spot respondent groups that have atypical reactions.

Respondents are randomly recruited in the guise of being asked to evaluate the pilot film. Those who accept are visited in their homes and are shown the pilot film, together with the three commercials imbedded in it. No indication is given to respondents at the time of exposure that they are involved in a commercial test. Instead they are asked questions about the casting, the plot, and how interested they would be in viewing the next episode of the program.

The next day, however, they are recontacted and asked if they remember having seen any commercials in the program they had viewed. It should be observed that exposure was in a quasi-laboratory situation, even though respondents were exposed in their own homes. They undoubtedly paid more attention to the program than they would have under normal conditions. Also the presence of the interviewer probably restricted activities such as talking to other family members, reading during commercial breaks, going to the bathroom during breaks in the program, and so on. Nevertheless, despite the more involving conditions under which people are exposed and the fact that they are exposed to three commercials, over one-third of the respondents typically cannot recall having been exposed to *any* commercials.

It could perhaps be argued that because people were so interested in evaluating the program, commercial screening activities were operating at higher levels than they normally would. However, the evidence on effects of program context points in the opposite direction. Yuspeh, in a very large test, found that higher levels of involvement in the program generally led to higher recall scores.[68] Similarly, Clancy and Kweskin found in 25 tests that the more likely respondents were to consider a program as "one of my favorites" the more likely they were to recall commercials that appeared in those programs.[69]

[68] S. Yuspeh, "The Medium Versus the Message (The Effects of Program Environment on the Performance of Commercials)," 10th Attitude Research Conference, American Marketing Association, Hilton Head, SC, February 17, 1979.
[69] K. J. Clancy and D. M. Kweskin, "TV Commercial Recall Correlates," *Journal of Advertising Research*, Vol. 11, No. 2, April 1971, p. 18–20.

Not only do people screen out vast quantities of the advertising to which they are exposed, they appear to get their perceptual screens working very early in a campaign. Krugman has hypothesized that about three exposures are sufficient to allow a commercial to have any potential impact.[70] He calls the first exposure the "What is it?" exposure. When the commercial is first seen, most time is spent in seeing what is happening and hearing what is being said. The second exposure he calls the "What of it?" exposure. The second time people see a commercial they determine its relevance to their personal situation, delving into its meaning a little more deeply. The third exposure allows integration of impressions received during the first exposure with those received during the second.

Other investigators have reached similar conclusions. The early work by Grass at Dupont with the CONPAAD machine is a case in point.[71, 72] This machine includes a television screen and two foot pedals. Respondents can only see and hear the programs (and commercials) on the screen by pumping the foot pedals at a fairly vigorous rate. One of the pedals controls the brightness of the screen and the other the loudness of the sound. Attention levels are measured by a criterion measure sometimes facetiously called "pumps per minute." When respondents are exposed to the same commercial several times, the measure shows an early peak followed by steady declines thereafter.

MacDonald,[73] in a highy creative and careful analysis of the effects of advertising on a panel of respondents, also concluded that two or three exposures were sufficient, as have Axelrod,[74] Naples,[75] Tortoloni,[76] and McCollum-Spielman.[77]

Not only are selective processes a powerful brake on the effects of advertising there are indications that people's abilities to screen out commercials have been improving over the years. In one major agency, for example, television recall "norms" were dropped by more than a third in one 10-year

[70] H. Krugman, "Why Three Exposures May Be Enough," *Journal of Advertising Research*, Vol. 12, No. 6, December 1972, pp. 11–14.

[71] R. C. Grass, "Satiation Effects of Advertising," 14th Annual Conference of the Advertising Research Foundation, New York, 1968.

[72] R. C. Grass and W. H. Wallace, "Satiation Effects of TV Commercials," *Journal of Advertising Research*, September 1969, pp. 3–9.

[73] C. MacDonald, "What Is the Short Term Effect of Advertising?," Marketing Science Institute, Special Report No. 71–142, February 1971.

[74] J. Axelrod, "Choosing the Best Advertising Alternative," Association of National Advertisers, New York, December 1971.

[75] J. Naples, "Effective Frequency: The Relationship Between Frequency and Advertising Effectiveness," Association of National Advertisers, New York, 1979.

[76] R. Tortoloni, "Testing Your TV Spot? Once Is Not Enough," *Advertising Age*, November 15, 1976.

[77] McCollum-Spielman, "The Need for Multiple Exposure," *Topline*, Vol. 1, No. 1, October 1978.

period in the 1960s and 1970s. Starch print norms have also edged downward during the last 20 years.

A number of hypotheses have been advanced to account for the declines,[78] among them:

Increasing clutter (between 1967 and 1981 the number of network commercials rose from 1856 to 4079 a week and 15 second commercials are rapidly becoming popular.)[79]

Boredom with television

Erosion of product protection policies that require minimum time intervals between commercials for directly competing products

Increased amounts of commercial time

Copy restrictions requiring concrete support for claims and, in the eyes of some critics of governmental regulation of advertising, resulting in innocuous copy

More advertising messages per capita resulting from more stations, shorter commercials, etc.

More advertisers and more products advertised

Less precise but equally relevant was the comment of Mary Wells Lawrence to the effect that "People are tired. They see lots of ads. They have seen lots of ads."

PERSUASION

Most advertising professionals do not believe that advertising has done its job if it simply delivers its message to the intended respondent. They want it to go further—to cause the recipient to see the product in a more favorable light and thereby to increase the probability that it will be purchased. It is not necessary that this effect be achieved in a single exposure or even in two or three. It is hoped and expected, however, that it will be obtained at some point during the campaign. This effect is normally called "attitude change" or "attitude shift," and it has become a popular effectiveness criterion both in copy tests and in tracking studies.[80]

---

[78] E. Meyer, "Is the Golden Goose Beginning to Lay Leaden Eggs?," ANA Seminar on TV Advertising Management, New York, April 1970.

[79] L. Bogart and C. Lehman, "The Case of the 30-second Commercial," *Journal of Advertising Research*, Vol. 23, No. 1, February/March 1982, pp. 11–19.

[80] A continuous monitoring of advertising effects via consumer interviews. See, Russell I. Haley and R. Gatty, "Monitor Your Market Continuously," *Harvard Business Review*, Vol. 46, No. 3, May–June 1968, pp. 65–69.

Although it is true that advertising can and does operate in this manner there is increasing evidence that advertising can achieve its ultimate goal—favorably influencing sales—in a number of ways. Among those most evident are the following:

By its very presence

Through increasing brand salience

Through "mobilizing" information

Through agenda setting

Through image change—either the images of the kinds of people perceived to be users of the brand or of the kinds of benefits to be expected from its use (cognitive, sensory, emotional, or affiliative)

Through changing overall attitudes toward the brand directly

The effects of advertising on sales have been a more or less continuous topic of study, not only by advertisers and advertising researchers, but by economists.[81, 82] One economist has hypothesized that advertising has an effect on sales *simply through its presence*.[83] He believes that consumers relate the presence of advertising to "good value" and goes on to offer data in support of that proposition. He reasons that advertisers do not continuously back poor products with an advertising investment, because it is not in their best interests to do so. Consequently, heavily advertised brands are ones in which the companies offering them have confidence. Consumers have intuitively recognized this and take it into consideration in making their choices. Moreover, their confidence in advertised brands is not misplaced. Nelson shows that profit margins for advertised products (after advertising costs have been deducted) are smaller than those for unadvertised products. He attributes this to the lower unit costs associated with the higher volume that advertising presumably stimulates.

The *brand salience* hypothesis comes from the "low involvement" school of thought. The assumption here is that, for low involvement products, many consumers simply purchase the first acceptable brand that comes to mind. They "satisfize" rather than optimize. In supermarkets, where the average consumer makes a large number of decisions in a relatively short time, this makes intuitive good sense.

Thus, the reasoning goes, the job of advertising is simply to get the brand

---

[81] B. Klein and K. B. Leffier, "The Role of Market Forces in Assuring Contractual Performance," *Journal of Political Economy*, Vol. 89, No. 4, 1981, pp. 615–641.

[82] G. A. Akerlof and W. T. Dickens, "The Economic Consequences of Cognitive Dissonance," *American Economic Review*, June 1982, pp. 307–319.

[83] P. J. Nelson, *Business Week*, December 22, 1975, pp. 49–54.

into the consumers evoked set.[84] It has been shown[85] that there is a considerable amount of apparently random behavior in making choices within the evoked set. So if advertising causes an increase in salience, it can reasonably be expected that purchases will increase as well.

It should be noted that increasing brand awareness is one of the oldest goals in advertising. The so-called creative boutique agencies usually feel that the problem can be solved simply through the creativity of their copywriters, artists, and production staff. Undoubtedly there have been cases of highly successful campaigns based on advertising intuition. However, these successes are like those of the "producers view" marketers who guess what products consumers would like, make them, and then discover that they were right. The success is impressive, but the situation is one in which risks are high.

Some agencies have tried to solve the brand awareness problem by employing some rather extreme attention-getting devices—raging bulls smashing furniture, professional fighters threatening to punch viewers who take away their favorite brand of beer, and so on. Marion Harper once complained in a speech that creators of advertising, through the use of exotic locales, bizarre plots, and overstated characterizations were "using technical fireworks as a substitute for message—to a degree that is reducing the airwaves to an absolute babble."

From the standpoint of public attitudes toward the advertising industry there are some real dangers in resorting to this sort of approach. As the AAAA study showed, one of the major consumer complaints about advertising is receiving messages that they do not want. They resent the intrusiveness of media and being told about products which, on one hand are dull and boring and, on the other, embarrassing or of an intimate, personal nature.

Even when it is not objectionable the "fireworks" approach is wasteful. It is a shotgun approach; many of the people whose attention is attracted are not legitimate prospects for the products advertised and consequently are unlikely to change their purchasing patterns as a result of having been exposed to the advertising. Finally, it places a heavy burden on creative people. Overstressing the value of attention can work against building a favorable brand image, and thus long-term sales gains may be sacrificed for short-term increases.

The hypothesis involving "mobilizing" information comes from studies

---

[84] Evoked set refers to the group of brands that a consumer can recall without aid and that he finds acceptable purchase alternatives.
[85] F. M. Bass, "Unexplained Variance in Studies of Consumer Behavior," Paper No. 339, November 1971, Herman C. Krannert Graduate School of Industrial Administration, Purdue University, Lafayette, Indiana.

by sociologists of how the mass media affects the public opinion process. The traditional view was that public opinion is changed by changing the attitudes of individuals. The aggregate of individual effects was taken to represent the general change in public opinion. More recently sociologists have come to believe that mass media when they have any effect at all, affect the public opinion process in ways other than by changing individual attitudes. One author[86] talks of "mobilizing information," the kind of information that helps people act on attitudes that they already have. An example of this approach in the field of product advertising might be the highly successful "Soup Is Good Food" campaign run by Backer & Spielvogel on behalf of Campbell soup. Pointing to the nutritional values of soup, the advertising claims that "Everything you always knew about the goodness of soup has just been proved true." Consumers did not feel they had learned anything new from this campaign. Yet it significantly increased both purchase and use of soup.

Agenda setting is an approach which appears to have been successful on occasion in political persuasion.[87] In a marketing context it would mean ignoring the possibility of changing the brand image, something that appears to be very difficult to do. To digress, there have been occasions, cases of successful *image change*. Marlboro cigarettes at one time were longer than other cigarettes, were cork tipped when special tips were less prevalent, and were considered to be feminine. Similarly Miller High Life had as its slogan "The Champagne of Bottled Beers" and definitely had limited appeal to blue-collar workers. However, both of these cases involved huge advertising expenditures and extended periods of time. At best any substantial image change is a major undertaking. Even when an all-out campaign is launched, success is by no means assured. The roots of the difficulty again lie in selective processes. Once people feel they are familiar with a product or a service they endow it with a brand image and this rapidly becomes stereotyped. Once it has, advertising that is not compatible with the accepted image is likely to be screened out.

Agenda setting does not attempt image change. Instead it tries to increase people's perceptions of the importance of benefits on which the advertised brand is acknowledged to be strong. Mazola cooking Oil, for example, tries to emphasize the perceived importance of its corn oil ingredient.

[86] James B. Lemert, *Does Mass Communication Change Public Opinion After All? A New Approach to Effects Analysis,* Chicago: Nelson-Hall, 1981.
[87] Fay Lomax Cook et al., "Media and Agenda Setting: Effects on the Public, Interest Group Leaders, Policy Makers, and Policy," *Public Opinion Quarterly,* Spring 1983, pp. 16–35, and M. Sutherland and J. Galloway, "Role of Advertising: Persuasion or Agenda Setting," *Journal of Advertising Research,* October 1981.

Attitude Change

Other theories of how advertising affects sales have been advanced.[88-90] None, however, has yet captured the full attention of the advertising research community. Most advertisers concentrate primarily on building more favorable overall attitudes toward the brands advertised. One popular way of trying to understand attitudes is to view them as having three major components: (1) the affective or evaluative component, (2) the cognitive or descriptive component, and (3) the conative or "behavioral tendency" component.

In a marketing sense, the affective component deals with whether people like a brand. It can be measured by attitude scales such as "like/dislike" or "excellent to poor." These are sometimes called hedonic scales. More simply they might be called *"good/bad" scales* (see Figure 2.3).

The cognitive component deals with how people see things, and it is descriptive rather than evaluative in nature. This is the component that contains brand images. Individual elements in the brand image are often measured with scales such as masculine/feminine, expensive/inexpensive, and modern/old fashioned. Measurements such as these fall within the cognitive component. In a simple sense these can be called *"yes/no" scales.* Unfortunately, the cognitive component is not completely independent of the affective component. Thus whenever it is measured it is subject to the well-known "halo effect." When people like a brand, they tend to rate it high on everything. Conversely, when they don't like it, they tend to rate it low across the board.

The third component, the conative component, goes one step beyond predisposition. It concerns the tendency to act in the direction of the predisposition. Operationally, in market research, it is measured by scales such as *purchase intent scales* or by examining past behavior. As will be shown later in this chapter, scales measuring the affective component are highly correlated with those measuring the conative component. There are at least two circumstances where they are less well correlated, however. These are first, where price is a barrier to purchase (e.g., a Cadillac may be rated above a Chevrolet on an "excellent to poor" scale but below it on a Purchase Intent scale) and, second, where the respondent is purchasing with the tastes of other family members in mind as well as his or her own (e.g., a

[88] J. N. Sheth, "Measurement of Advertising Effectiveness: Some Theoretical Considerations," *Journal of Advertising,* Vol. 3, No. 1, 1974, pp. 6–11.
[89] J. C. Maloney, "Is Advertising Believability Really Important?," *Journal of Marketing,* Vol. 27, October 1963, pp. 1–80.
[90] J. B. Haskins, *How to Evaluate Mass Communications: The Controlled Field Experiment,* New York: Advertising Research Foundation, 1973.

A. *A Hedonic Scale*
Excellent ☐
Very good ☐
Good ☐
Fair ☐
Not so good ☐
Poor ☐

B. *A Cognitive Scale*
Agree completely ☐
Mostly agree ☐
Agree a little more than disagree ☐
Disagree a little more than agree ☐
Mostly disagree ☐
Disagree completely ☐

C. *A Purchase Intent Scale*
Definitely will buy ☐
Probably will buy ☐
Might or might not buy ☐
Probably will not buy ☐
Definitely will not buy ☐

Figure 2.3. Examples of alternative types of attitude scales.

homemaker may rate a food product as "excellent" but not be inclined to buy it because other members of the family will reject it). (See Figure 2.3.)

Attitudinal information is generally considered to be of greater value than any other type of market research information in developing communications strategies, particularly in the key decision areas of selecting a market target and a buying incentive. This is true because attitudinal information—information on the kinds of satisfactions a consumer seeks when buying a product and on his or her images of various brands—is causative rather than merely descriptive. Numerous studies support the premise that the way a person feels and thinks, his or her psychographic profile, has an important role in determining how the person will behave in the marketplace. Demographic and behavioral data are primarily descriptive, whereas attitudinal data are predictive.

THREE

Measuring Attitudes and Images

METHODS OF ATTITUDE MEASUREMENT

The central issue of this chapter is how information on consumer attitudes can be obtained in valid, reliable, and practical ways. To do so we must solve the standard communications problem of how best to establish effective two-way communications with the consumer. There are a number of obstacles to this, some of which relate to the respondent and others that relate to the researcher. Those relating to the respondent include:

Lack of willingness to participate in interviews
   Desire for privacy
   Suspicion of strangers
   Low interest levels
   Fatigue
   Unwillingness to sacrifice the time required
Inability to analyze himself on the spot, tendency to respond in stereotypes
   Inability to express feelings accurately

Those tracing to the researcher include:

Inability to ask the right questions
   To provide a uniform stimulus
   To cover all relevant attitudes thoroughly

To cover all relevant attitudes efficiently

To avoid redundancy in the questionnaire

Inability to record answers accurately

Interviewer shortcomings

Coder shortcomings

Not only must the consumer be willing and able to answer the questions asked, but researchers must ask questions that are relevant to the experience of the consumer and to record his or her responses quickly and accurately.

Traditional question-and-answer approaches have not met these objectives very well. Often respondents are not interested in participating in a survey. With the spread of research much of the novelty of being a respondent has disappeared. The lack of interest is reflected in rising refusal rates,[1,2] but it also permeates our data in more subtle ways. Many people do not wish to appear unpleasant. Consequently, they will go along with the interview but in a halfhearted way. This results in a high proportion of short, incomplete, stereotypical, and just plain inaccurate answers. Furthermore, not only the respondent but the interviewer would like to complete the interview as quickly as possible. As a result, a heavy burden is placed on the conscientiousness of the interviewer, who must probe for full answers and must encourage respondents to be properly reflective even though he or she would like the interview to proceed smoothly and rapidly. Fortunately, there is a happy correlation between volume of product consumption and interest levels. Respondents who are relatively heavy consumers of the product category with which the questionnaire is concerned are likely to be those who are most interested in it and thus to give fuller answers to interview questions.

However, even the most interested and cooperative respondent is likely to tire of questions at some point during the interview, and probably sooner than we anticipate. Moreover, fatigue can badly distort our data. For example, one experiment was conducted with two probability samples, each with a base in excess of 1000 respondents. In the first sample, incidence of usage was obtained in the first question. In the second it was obtained after 10 minutes of a traditional question-and-answer interview. Reported incidence in the second sample was 22.7% lower than the level reported in the

[1] K. Marquis, "Survey Response Rates: Some Trends, Causes, and Correlates," in L. Reeder (Ed.), *Health Survey Research Methods: Second Biennial Conference*, Williamsburg, VA, Washington, DC: U.S. Government Printing Office.

[2] L. M. Sharp and J. Frankel, "Respondent Burden: A Test of Some Common Assumptions," *Public Opinion Quarterly*, Vol. 47, No. 1, Spring 1983, pp. 36–53.

first sample. Outside data showed quite clearly that the figure obtained in the first study was the more reliable figure.

What this means is that in consumer interviews the researcher has a limited amount of time in which to obtain the required information. In effect, researchers are working inside a time box of almost fixed size. If they conduct a long and tiring interview and then treat the data obtained as though it were completely accurate, they are almost certainly overly optimistic. Respondents will answer most of questions, but the validity of their answers is open to serious question.

In addition to ignoring, or at best dealing partially with, the problem of the *willingness* of respondents to answer questions conscientiously, it is often tacitly assumed that respondents have the *ability* to answer the kinds of questions we would like to ask. Yet to provide the kind of information needed the consumer must possess the ability to analyze himself on the spot and report accurately on his attitudes and motivations. This is asking a lot. In all probability it is unrealistic to assume that it can be done with any degree of consistency. It assumes that humans are purely cognitive and that they not only can tell us what they think but that they understand the role that their emotions play in their brand choices and that they can accurately report on those also.

It is likely that when an interviewer appears at the door or telephones and asks the respondent a series of questions about the product of interest, the respondent is giving that product considered thought for the first time in his or her life. And although this product may be of great interest to the marketer, particularly subtle differences in brand images, it is likely that the consumer has given it little more than an occasional passing thought. Consequently, when the respondent answers questions, even if he makes an honest effort to do so, he is not likely to supply a full and accurate explanation for his behavior.

Added to this is the problem of differing levels of articulation among respondents. With some respondents it is difficult to extract more than a few meaninglessly stereotyped answers. With others the problem is how to record and include in tabulations the huge volume of information they supply.

As noted earlier, the researcher is also a potential barrier to understanding consumer attitudes. Perhaps the researcher's most important function is to ask the right questions, questions that are relevant to the experience of the consumer and that fit into his or her mental set. This is no easy job. Different researchers are likely to choose different question areas. This, of course, moves survey research away from being a scientific discipline and in the direction of being an art form, with results largely dependent on the analyst conducting the research.

In addition to choosing the right questions, the analyst must, of course, make sure that the questions are clear and are understood by all respondents. In other words, they must represent a uniform stimulus. Similarly, they must cover every important aspect of consumer attitudes—thoroughly, efficiently, and without unnecessary redundancy.

The analyst's problem of understanding the attitudes of respondents is further complicated by the recording agents—the people who stand between him or her and the consumer—the interviewer and the coder. Before the researcher can analyze the data, he or she must be willing to assume that the interviewer has been able to establish rapport with the consumer, has asked questions in a consistent manner, and has recorded the respondent's answers accurately and in great detail. Similarly the researcher must assume that the coder has been perceptive enough to analyze the material supplied by the interviewer and that he or she has been able to classify responses objectively into appropriate categories.

These assumptions taken as a set represent a sizable problem in measurement, one that few researchers have been willing to face squarely. Because the situation is bothersome, it is tempting to sweep it under a handy rug (like the rug under which the problems of controlling the quality of fieldwork are frequently swept) and move forward to the more interesting problem of how best to analyze the responses obtained. However, our ability to advance the "state of the art" is materially slowed by that kind of process. The facts are that today's respondents generally are *not* enthusiastic about participating in interviews, respondents are *not* able to analyze their motivations, respondents *are* likely to express themselves in stereotypes (partially through lack of articulation but mostly to complete the interview as quickly as possible), and not all market researchers ask the same questions. Similarly, interviewers do *not* ask questions in a uniform way (one firm[3] once taped all their interviews, and found those tapes as appalling as the Watergate tapes). Interviewers do not record respondents' answers reliably and completely, and even trained coders differ substantially in their classification of open-ended responses.

Recognizing these problems, some market analysts have sought the aid of clinical psychologists to help measure consumer attitudes. Experiments have been carried out with projective techniques such as picture drawing, sentence completion, balloon tests, and thematic apperception tests. But these have proven to be expensive, cumbersome, wasteful of valuable interview time, and highly dependent upon both the interviewer and the person interpreting the results. Accordingly, in recent years such methods have been largely confined to small-scale exploratory studies and pretests.

[3] Grudin-Appel-Haley, Inc., New York

Another method that has been and continues to be popular is the use of physiological approaches. These have a great deal of appeal because of their apparent objectivity and the pseudoscientific aura that surrounds their use. Included in this category in the past have been the lie detector (psychogalvanometer), basal skin response, the eye camera, the twitch test (amount of movement in seats), eye blink rate, and CONPAAD (equipment that measures the amount of work a person will do to view and hear a commercial). Work is still being done on an active basis with the eye camera, pupil dilation, voice analysis, and brain wave measures. Because of a number of shortcomings, however, devices such as these have never achieved broad-scale acceptance among the research community. Reliability has often proved questionable and the responses obtained can often be attributed to more than a single cause (e.g., to confusion as well as to interest, or to interest in executional elements as well as to liking the product). Moreover, such devices are usually cumbersome and thus expensive to use—particularly so because it appears that the information obtained is no more useful than that which can be obtained by less-expensive alternatives.

Consequently, researchers have tended toward greater use of rating scales. They have been found to have a number of significant advantages over alternative approaches to attitude measurement. From the standpoint of both the willingness and the ability of respondents to supply information on their attitudes:

They encourage respondent participation by involving them in an interesting, quasi game-playing situation.

Because the individual stimuli are generally succinct they permit coverage of a broad range of attitudes in a relatively short period of time.

In relation to the amount of ground covered, respondent fatigue is held to a minimum.

Differences in articulateness among respondents are evened out. Each respondent makes a similar number of judgments and thus has an approximately equivalent weight in the results.

Moreover, they aid researchers in interpreting survey results.

All respondents are presented with a uniform stimulus, a fact that is translated into relatively reliable results.

Differences in questioning from interviewer to interviewer are reduced because the interviewer has little discretion in the administration of the interview.

Results can be coded and tabulated quickly, easily, and objectively.

There is little chance for personal viewpoints to be imposed on the data. Reliance on the judgment of coders to classify responses properly is eliminated because responses are all precoded. Similarly differences among coders are eliminated.

Because of these advantages the research community appears to have converged on the conclusion that, all things considered, attitude rating scales are the best way to measure consumer attitudes. However, this leaves open a large number of scaling alternatives. Some of the key ones will be reviewed in the following section.

ATTITUDE SCALING ALTERNATIVES

Attitude scaling had its earliest beginnings in psychophysics. Phenomena such as brightness, loudness, and weight were scaled in an effort to develop firm quantitative assessments for subjective responses. This technique was adapted by L. L. Thurstone in the 1920s to survey measures of attitudes.[4] His work in turn was extended in a classic work on attitude measurement by Guilford.[5]

Before reviewing specific scaling alternatives it may be well to summarize some of the more important criteria by which the value of alternative attitude measures can be assessed.

The first criterion usually cited is validity[6]—the scale should measure what it purports to measure. It should allow a respondent to express him or herself accurately.

Second, it should be *reliable*. Repeating the measurement should produce the same results provided there is no significant intervening stimulus. Ideally this should hold true for individual respondents as well as for groups of respondents.

A third criterion is *discrimination*. If a set of objects is to be tested (whether the objects are copy executions, packages, or product names), the method should differentiate them from each other.

Next the scale should be *sensitive*. It should reflect subtle changes in feelings resulting from exposure to stimuli. It should also be *additive*. All respondents should understand it and should use it in an essentially similar manner.

[4] L. L. Thurstone and E. J. Chave, *The Measurement of Attitude*, Chicago: University of Chicago Press, 1929.
[5] J. P. Guilford, *Psychometric Methods*, New York: McGraw-Hill, 1954.
[6] M. L. Ray, "Special Section: Measurement and Marketing Research," *Journal of Marketing Research*, Vol. 16, February 1979, pp. 1–5.

And, finally, it should be *practical* in the sense that it is easy for interviewers to use, easy for analysts to interpret, easy to tabulate, adaptable to a wide range of products, and not limited by an inordinate cost.

Unfortunately, these criteria often lead to conflicts. The longer the scale the more likely it is to discriminate. A scale with 1000 points can be expected to discriminate better than a scale with only two or three points. The longer the scale, however, the more likely it is to be treated differently by different respondents.

The ability of respondents to translate their feelings into the values represented by the scale is a key consideration. A good rule of thumb is that the simpler and easier to understand the scale, the more likely it is to perform well on the preceding criteria. Many people are not numerically oriented; consequently, scales that are anchored by words generally are more easily understood than those that are anchored by numbers. Similarly, lower income groups tend to have trouble with scales requiring the perception of spatial relationships.

A great variety of scales has been proposed in the past. Among the major types have been:

Thurstone scales[7]

- A large number of statements of varying intensity are assembled.
- Results are evaluated for each statement and a final set of statements is chosen to represent the various positions on the scale. Small variance is also a major criterion affecting statement choice. In other words, all judges will see a good statement as having about the same level of intensity.

Likert scales[8]

These involve asking respondents both whether they agree or disagree with a given statement and how much they agree or disagree.

Guttman scales[9]

Derived by following a rigorous set of rules—so rigorous, in fact, that, throughout World War II, a team of psychologists studying servicemen's attitudes toward the armed services was able to develop less than 20 such scales. In general, these rules are derived in such a way that a person's response to any one statement in the scale accurately predicts his or her

---

[7] Ibid.

[8] R. Likert, "A Technique for the Measurement of Attitudes," *Archives of Psychology* No. 140, 1932.

[9] L. Guttman, "The Problem of Attitude and Opinion Measurement," in S. A. Stouffer et al. (Eds.), *Measurement and Prediction*, Princeton, NJ: Princeton University Press, 1950.

response to all other statements included in it. One such scale concerned divorce, when attitudes toward adultery were more disapproving than they are today. The scale went as follows:

- Divorce is never permissible.
- Divorce is permissible with adultery.
- Divorce is permissible with cruelty.
- Divorce is permissible when there are no children.

A person agreeing with any of these four statements will automatically agree with all statements above it. Similarly if a person disagrees with one of the statements, he or she will disagree with all statements below it. A term called the *coefficient of reproducibility* measures how well any scale conforms to the rigorous conditions set forth by Guttman.

Paired comparison[10]

A scaling procedure whereby each of the objects to be scaled is compared with all other objects to be scaled, taking the objects two at a time. Sometimes 10 points are divided between each pair. Sometimes a simple count is taken of the number of times an item is preferred. At other times each pair is compared on a scale such as shown in Figure 3.1, comparing product A with product B.

Semantic differential[11]

Seven point scale with words that are polar opposites anchoring the ends of the scales. The five points in the middle of the scale are not anchored (see Figure 3.2).

Numerical scales[12]

These are simply scales in which numbers are used to indicate levels of intensity. One simple variant is a scale scored sequentially from 1 to 10. As noted earlier, however, lower-income groups are likely to have some degree of difficulty with scales of this type. Concentrations of ratings are likely to appear at 10, 8, 5, and 1. Conversely 9 and 2 are likely to be underutilized.

Another popular numerical scale is the Stapel scale. This is simply a series of 11 numbers ranging from plus five through zero to minus five.

[10] Allen L. Edwards, *Techniques of Attitude Scale Construction,* New York: Appleton, 1957, pp. 19–50.
[11] C. Osgood, G. Suci, and P. Tannenbaum, *The Measurement of Meaning,* Urbana: University of Illinois Press, 1957.
[12] J. Stapel, "Predictive Attitudes," in L. Adler and I. Crespi (Eds.), *Attitude Research on the Rocks,* Chicago: American Marketing Association, 1968, pp. 96–115.

| Strongly | Moderately | Slightly | No Preference | Slightly | Moderately | Strongly |

Prefer A [table of cells] Prefer F

Figure 3.1 A paired comparison scale

Masculine [table of cells] Feminine

Figure 3.2 A semantic differential scale

When used in conjunction with ratings of consumer products, however, the negative points on the scale are usually underutilized. Consequently few applied researchers favor this scale.

Verbal scales[13]

Scales such as "Excellent, Very Good, Good, Fair, Poor" are easy for consumers to understand and have been widely used. If they have a fault it is that their levels of discrimination have not always been as high as one might wish. Nevertheless, it is true that the well-known Buying Intent scale (definitely will buy, probably will buy, might or might not buy, probably will not buy, and definitely will not buy) is a valid and reasonably accurate predictor of trial rates for new products.

Constant sum scales[14]

Constant sum scales require the respondent to allocate a number of points across a fixed set of alternatives to show their relative appeal to the respondent. Often in market research or in copy testing the number of points is 10 and the alternatives are brands in the product category of interest. This scale is particularly useful in predicting behavior when respondents are likely to have positive feelings toward several brands. It is also used in before/after tests to show which brands are most likely to be affected by changes in the marketing activities of one of the brands.

Nonverbal scales[15]

To avoid problems of selecting good scale anchors some analysts have opted for nonverbal scales. One version of such a scale is the Line scale. In this approach respondents are simply given a horizontal line on a piece of paper and told to place an x on it to reflect their attitude toward

[13] W. D. Wells and G. Smith," Four Semantic Rating Scales Compared," *Journal of Applied Psychology*, Vol. 44, No. 6 December 1960, pp. 393–397.
[14] G. D. Hughes, *Attitude Measurement for Marketing Strategies*, Glenview, Ill.: Scott, Foresman, 1971.
[15] F. Cutler, "To Meet Criticisms of TV Ads Researchers Find New Ways to Measure Children's Attitudes," *Marketing News*, January 27, 1978, p. 16.

the product being evaluated. The farther to the left the x is placed the more favorable their opinion and the farther to the right the more unfavorable their opinion. This has the advantage of permitting analysts to choose any interval they wish for purposes of scoring. If they wish to convert results to a three-point scale, they will simply place a transparent grid with three cells over the line. If they wish to convert them to a seven-point scale, they will use a transparent grid with seven boxes.

Another example of this type scale is the "Smile scale" used by General Foods. This was designed for use with children who may not have the ability to reflect their feelings accurately with a verbal scale or a numerical scale. It shows a series of faces that begin with one showing a broad smile and end with one showing a deep frown. The child is asked to choose the face that most closely reflects his or her feelings. Unfortunately experience with the scale has shown that children are prone to choose the faces at the ends of the scale. Of course children's feelings may fluctuate more widely than those of adults and they may have stronger feelings, both positively and negatively.

Combination scales[16]

Some analysts have resolved the question of whether to use verbal or numerical scales by using both. Examples of this are the P&G Thermometer scale and the well-known Census Buying Intentions scale. Evidence on responses to these will be presented later in this chapter. The central problem with them appears to be that some respondents use the numbers, some the words, and some both, which reduces the additivity of the responses. In other words, because respondents use the scale differently, adding their scale scores together may make results somewhat ambiguous.

Still another example is the scale which uses both words and the sizes of the words to communicate intensity. An example of this is the scale shown in Figure 3.3.

Miscellaneous additional scales

The foregoing list of scale types by no means exhausts the possibilities for attitude scales variations. There are also ratio or magnitude estimation scales,[17] adjective checklists (which in reality are two-point scales), and scales using pennies, marbles, or poker chips instead of printed material. Even Response Latency[18] can be considered a form of attitude scaling.

[16] F. T. Juster, "Consumer Buying Intentions and Purchase Probability: An Experiment in Survey Design," NBER Occasional Paper 99, New York: Columbia University Press, 1966.
[17] H. R. Moskowitz and B. Jacobs, "Ratio Scaling of Perception Versus Image: Its Use in Evaluating Advertising Promise Versus Product Delivery," *Current Issues and Research in Advertising,* 1980, pp. 59–95.
[18] J. MacLachlan, *"Response Latency," New Measure of Advertising,* New York: Advertising Research Foundation, 1977.

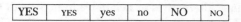

Figure 3.3.   A scale using word size to communicate intensity

SCALE CHOICE DECISIONS

Even if an analyst decides to use a relatively straightforward verbal or numerical scale he or she must still make a number of decisions. Among the more important questions to be answered are the following:

1.   How long should the scale be?

The work done in developing the semantic differential scaling approach concluded that scale lengths of from five to eight points best met the requirements of an ideal scale.[19]

2.   Should the scale be anchored or unanchored? If it is to be anchored, which specific anchors should be used?

Verbal anchors are generally preferable to numerical anchors. Adjective intensity studies are helpful in choosing the specific anchors. These have as their objective a smooth progression of intensity from point to point on the scale.

3.   Should the scale be balanced or unbalanced? In other words, should an equal number of positive and negative points be included or should, for example, more positive than negative points be included?

The answer to this question depends upon the stimuli to be rated. If they are likely to engender primarily positive responses, then the scale should have more positive than negative points. If positive and negative responses are likely to be equally balanced, then the scale used should be a balanced scale.

4.   Should an odd or an even number of points be used?

This does not appear to be a crucial issue. However, a rectangular distribution of responses shows full utilization of all scale points. If one scale form (odd or even) results in a more even distribution, then it is preferable.

5.   Should "no answer" responses be allowed or should respondents be forced to provide ratings for every scale used?

There are two schools of thought on this issue. Those who believe that respondents should be forced to guess on all scales believe that the inclusion of a "no answer" square provides a refuge for the lazy respondent and that he will use that square to avoid having to think about the item being rated. Those on the other side believe that some respondents genuinely do not know how to rate some of the items on which they are asked to make judg-

[19] Osgood, Suci, and Tannenbaum, *Measurement of Meaning.*

TABLE 3.1   Scaling Alternatives in Relationship to Stimuli to Be Rated

Stimulus to Be Rated	Perceptual Scales (yes/no)	Evaluative Scales (good/bad)	Action Probability
Overall reactions to products or concepts	Agree/Disagree	Excellent/Poor	Buying Intent Constant Sum
Image characteristics	Agree/Disagree	Excellent/Poor	Does not apply
Benefits, needs, values	Does not apply	Important/Not important Desirable/Undesirable	Does not apply
Personality and lifestyle characteristics	Like me/not like me As others see me	Important/Not important Desirable/Undesirable As I would like to be	Does not apply

ments. When they are forced to do so, they become frustrated and the quality of their responses deteriorates. Those who use this system usually base scale scores only on those who respond. This means a shifting base from item to item and tacitly assumes that nonresponders would have behaved much like responders had they been forced to respond.

The Arrowhead #9 study[20] investigated this assumption. It found that when nonresponders are forced to respond, they do *not* behave as responders; instead they supply distinctly lower ratings. Presumably they did not respond because they felt they lacked enough information to do so. When forced to respond, they assumed that the lack of information meant that the product was probably not very good.

A compromise position on this issue is to show respondents a scale without a "no answer" box, but to provide interviewers with a space on their questionnaires for recording "no answers" if respondents insist that that is the only response they can legitimately make. This minimizes nonresponses without completely frustrating strong-minded respondents who feel they cannot legitimately guess.

   6. In dealing with evaluative scales is it better to get a single overall

---

[20] R. I. Haley and P. B. Case, "Testing 13 Attitude Scales for Agreement and Brand Discrimination," *Journal of Marketing*, Vol. 43, October 1979, pp. 20–32.

response or to get a number of evaluative responses and average them?

Experimental work done at Grey Advertising in the 1960s suggests that the averaging procedure increases the test/retest reliability of scores for individual respondents but slightly decreases overall predictive validity. Thus if samples are small and reliability of individual respondents is a likely problem, the averaging approach is preferable. For larger samples, say samples of 300 or more, the single overall response may be preferable.

An overview of scaling alternatives can be provided by returning to the basic components of an attitude (mentioned earlier in this chapter) and summarizing ways in which they can be measured when dealing with the kinds of stimuli for which market researchers regularly use attitude scales (see Table 3.1). Note that only two basic types of scales are suggested for the area of Action Probability. As was observed earlier this type of scale normally correlates highly with evaluative scale types. For this reason it is convenient to consider the scales used by market researchers as belonging primarily to one of two types—evaluative or descriptive (perceptual). So let us review each of these major categories in some depth.

EVALUATIVE ATTITUDE SCALES

To date, one of the most thorough examinations of the kinds of evaluative scales used by market researchers has been the Arrowhead #9 project.[21] Its objectives were to provide the answers to two questions: First, to what extent are all rating scales measuring the same thing? Second, which scales discriminate best between brands?

With the second question in mind, it was decided to restrict efforts to package goods with relatively high frequency of purchase. Six product categories were chosen—analgesics, toothpaste, colas, regular coffee, detergents, and toilet soap. These products had an additional advantage because a large portion of their sales was concentrated among a relatively small set of brands.

A similar process was used in deciding which rating scales to include. The criteria were diversity and popularity. Twelve scales plus brand awareness were chosen. Because awareness can also be scored in scalar fashion, it can be considered, in effect, the thirteenth scale. The scales are shown in Figure 3.4.

The sample consisted of 630 women over age 18 who were responsible for family grocery shopping. All interviews were conducted in person in the

[21] Haley and Case, "Testing 13 Attitude Scales."

homes of respondents. The sample was drawn from a single market, using city blocks as sampling units, and selecting households systematically, using a random starting point.

As is often the case in developing research designs for complex problems, this one was a compromise. Ideally, each homemaker would have rated each brand in each category on all 13 scales, but this was judged to be impossible. It would have required over 500 judgments from each respondent,

Scale	Structure	Subject	Scores*	
Scale 1 Acceptability	7-point verbal balanced	Brand acceptability	extremely acceptable (7) quite acceptable (6) slightly acceptable (5) neither one nor the other (4) slightly unacceptable (3) quite unacceptable (2) extremely unacceptable (1)	
Scale 2 Purchase Probability	11-point numerical and verbal	chance of buying brand next time product is purchased	100 absolutely certain 90 80 strong possibility 70 60 50 40 30 20 slight possibility 10 0 absolutely no chance	100 in 100 90 in 100 80 in 100 70 in 100 60 in 100 50 in 100 40 in 100 30 in 100 20 in 100 10 in 100 0 in 100
Scale 3 Six-point Adjective	6-point verbal unbalanced	Brand opinion	excellent (7) very good (6) good (5) fair (4) not so good (2) poor (1) "don't know" permitted (3)	
Scale 4 Paired Comparison	51 value positions, constant sum	brand liking	possible range of brand scores: 0 to 50. Sum of six brand scores: 150. (Each of the 15 brand pairs compared and rated by dividing 10 points between the two brands in that pair. A brand's score is the sum of points received in the five pairs where that brand appeared.)	

Figure 3.4.   Scales tested

Scale	Structure	Subject	Scores[*]
Scale 5 Brand Choice	3-point	brand choice if purchased tomorrow	first choice (2) second choice (1) no mention (0)
Scale 6 Ten-point Numerical	10-point numerical	brand opinion	1 poor 6 2 7 3 7 4 9 5 10 excellent
Scale 7 Thermometer	11-point numerical and verbal	brand liking opinion	100 90 excellent 80 like very much 70 like quite well 60 like fairly well 50 indifferent 40 not like very well 30 not so good 20 not like at all 10 terrible 0 where numbers represent degrees on a thermometer
Scale 8 Verbal Purchase Intent	5-point verbal unbalanced	chance of buying brand next time product is purchased	definitely will buy (5) very likely will buy (4) probably will buy (3) might or might not buy (2) definitely will not buy (1)
Scale 9 Agreement with Strongly Positive Statement	5-point verbal	brand opinion	agree completely (5) agree somewhat (4) don't know (3) disagree somewhat (2) disagree completely (1) (statement saying that brand "would be considered one of the best" was for each brand.)
Scale 10 Constant Sum	11 value positions, constant sum	brand liking	possible range of brand scores: 0 to 10. Sum of six grand scores: 10. (respondent divided 10 pennies among brands, giving more to brands she liked.)
Scale 11 Quality	7-point verbal balanced	brand quality	extremely high quality (7) quite high quality (6) slightly high quality (5) neither one nor the other (4) slightly low quality (3) quite low quality (2) extremely low quality (1)

Figure 3.4.   Continued

Scale	Structure	Subject	Scores*
Scale 12 Stapel Scale	11-point numerical	brand opinion	−5 poor 1 −4 2 −3 3 −2 4 −1 5 excellent 0
Scale 13 Awareness	5-point	awareness of brand names	top of mind (4), second unaided mention (3). other unaided mention (2). aided recall (1), never heard of (0)

*Scores assigned to verbal scales are indicated in parentheses.

Figure 3.4. Continued

and the interview would have been long, boring, and repetitive; there would likely have been dropouts, fatigue, and severe order effects.

The compromise chosen attempted to maximize the number of scales used by each respondent, because the problem of whether all scales are measuring the same thing might well be the most difficult one. Also the choice of this type of research design holds to a minimum the statistical confounding of differences in scales with differences in respondents.

Consequently, each person rated all of the brands with which he or she was familiar in two product categories, using six different rating scales on each. The interview was conducted in two parts, one in the morning and one in the afternoon, to minimize carryover effects and to permit rotation of the scales used.

To avoid dropout, respondents were told in advance that the interview would be split and that they would be given a gift when the interviewer returned for the second part.

Because the unaided awareness question must necessarily be asked first when it is used, it was asked in only three of the product categories covered. Each respondent used all 12 of the remaining scales however, and, although there are some imbalances in the design, within categories sets of six scales can be compared for six brands on a base of 35 respondents, sets of three on a base of 105, and pairs on a base of 210. Moreover, if product categories are combined as well as brands, the bases can be raised considerably.

Because the design was complex and involved 18 different interviewing formats, and because there were still some doubts about the questionnaire, it was extensively pretested. The FACT validation service was employed and the fieldwork carefully checked. Finally, all of the analyses suggested that the relationships among scales are particularly robust. The work within individual product categories strongly parallels results when categories are combined.

One way to determine whether all 13 scales are measuring the same thing is to look at the distributions of responses.

As shown in Figure 3.5, Scales 1, 3, 9, and 11 have similar distributions. These include the two balanced bipolar scales on acceptability and quality, the six-point adjective scale, and the agreement scale. All show a concentration of responses on the right-hand side of the scale, the side where the more favorable ratings are.

Scales 6, 7, and 12, also in Figure 3.5, are similar. These are the 10-point numerical scale, the thermometer scale, and the Stapel scale. They also show a preponderance of favorable ratings.

Scales 5, 10, and 13, in Figure 3.6, show a clustering of responses toward the left of the scale. Scale 5 is the brand preference scale, with the first choices on the right, second choices in the center, and all others on the left. Scale 13 is the awareness scale. Brands mentioned first and unaided are on the far right. Then come brands mentioned second, brands mentioned third, brands recalled on an aided basis and, on the far left, brands that were not known to the respondents.

The other three scales presented in Figure 3.7, are unique. Scale 2 is the purchase probability scale with both verbal and numerical answers. The

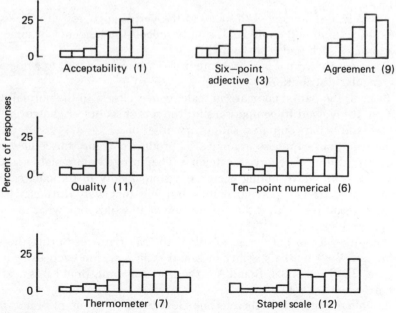

Figure 3.5.   Response distributions with many favorable ratings

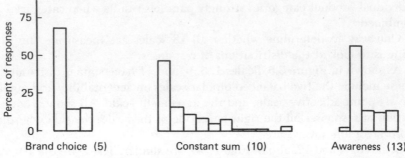

Figure 3.6. Response distributions with few favorable ratings

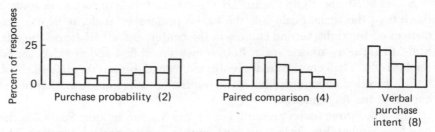

Figure 3.7. Balanced response distributions

lumps in its distribution correspond to the verbal anchors, with the exception of the lump in the middle. It simply reflects the tendency of some people to mark such scales in the middle.

Scale 8 is the verbal purchase intent scale. It is the closest to achieving a rectangular distribution.

Scale 4, the paired comparison scale, comes closest to the normal distribution. It involved 15 comparisons for the sets of six brands, however, with each brand being compared with every other one.

Distributions were also examined by product category to see how much they varied from category to category. They proved quite stable, and the only variation worth noting occurred systematically in the cola category where there are two popular brands and four that were distinctly less so. The net result was to shift the distribution of all scales somewhat to the left in that category.

Another way to determine whether all scales are measuring the same thing is to look at the stability of brand ratings within each category. In Figures 3.1 through 3.4, Brand A is the leader overall, Brand B is next, and so on.

In coffee (Figure 3.8), there is one clear leader, a group of brands in the middle, and two that trail.

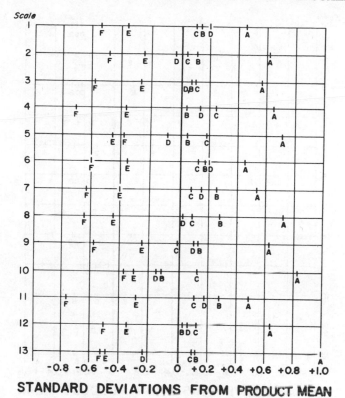

STANDARD DEVIATIONS FROM PRODUCT MEAN

Figure 3.8. Coffee brand ratings

In analgesics, there is a clear leader and a very clear trailer (Figure 3.9). The B on the buying preference scale is not a mistake; it is Alka-Seltzer. The question reads, "If you were going to buy a headache remedy tomorrow, which brand would you buy?" Alka-Seltzer is not perceived as strictly a headache remedy. Hence the understatement of its position.

In detergents, as shown in Figure 3.10, brands are seen as more similar. Even in this instance, however, F beats E on only one scale, and then barely.

Figure 3.11 shows toothpaste. Note that the second brand, Brand B, beats Brand A by a sizable margin on Scales 5 and 10, Brand C is a clear-cut third.

In toilet soap (Figure 3.12), A is clearly first, B clearly second, and F clearly last. And in colas (Figure 3.13), A and B stand out far above the remainder of the field.

The conclusion drawn from these product category charts is that there is a great deal of agreement among respondents about what these scales are measuring.

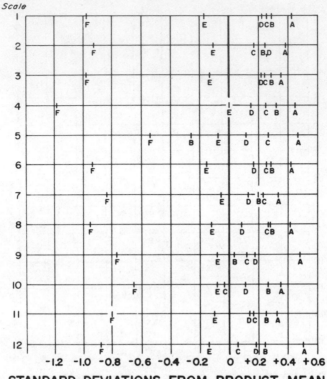

STANDARD DEVIATIONS FROM PRODUCT MEAN

Figure 3.9. Analgesic brand ratings

But are they all really measuring the same thing, or are there systematic differences among them? To test this, a 13 by 13 correlation matrix based on the maximum sample for each pair of scales was developed and factored. Table 3.2 shows the results.

Two factors were found. The first was by far the largest and accounted for nearly two-thirds of the total variance. The second accounted for another 10%. The first factor is clearly an evaluative factor. All scales show significant loadings upon it. The second factor appears to be a salience factor, with awareness being the key scale in it. To test the stability of the factor structure, each of the six product categories was factored individually. In every case a similar solution emerged.

Thus it was concluded that the answer to the first question, "Do all scales measure the same thing?," is that two factors underlie the scales that were tested—evaluation and salience. Three scales are associated with the second factor—awareness, brand preference, and, to a lesser extent, the con-

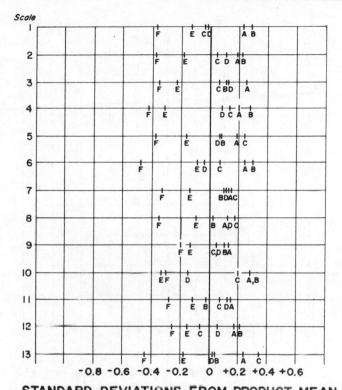

STANDARD DEVIATIONS FROM PRODUCT MEAN

Figure 3.10. Laundry detergent brand ratings

stant sum. The shapes of their distributions are somewhat different from the remaining 10 scales and, in some cases (e.g., toothpaste), their use results in somewhat different brand ratings.

Now consider the second question, "Which scales discriminate best among brands?" To provide insight into this question, the ratio of the variation among brands over the variation in reactions to individual brands was examined. On an overall basis (Table 3.3), two scales stood out as particularly good. The best discriminators appeared to be the awareness scale and the paired comparison scale.

Interestingly, there is substantial variation by product category. In coffee, awareness does particularly well. Verbal purchase intent is second. In analgesics, awareness information was not gathered, but the paired comparison does very well. The constant sum scale does less well, perhaps because of the confusing presence of Alka-Seltzer. In laundry detergents, the two leading scales do well, but so does the constant sum. In toothpaste, the

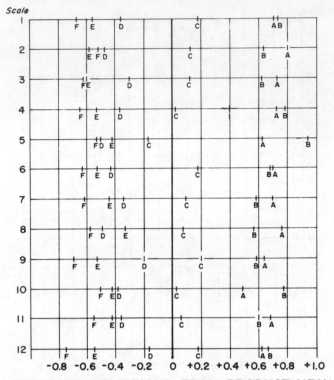

STANDARD DEVIATIONS FROM PRODUCT MEAN

Figure 3.11.   Toothpaste brand ratings

brand preference question shows good discrimination. In toilet soap, the constant sum again makes a strong showing. In colas, brand preference is second only to the paired comparison.

Summing up, awareness and the paired comparison discriminate well across the board. The constant sum also does well, particularly in lower variance categories. Note that these three scales are the ones that loaded on the second factor in the factor analysis.

The verbal purchase intent scale also looks quite good in higher variance categories, and the buying preference question discriminates well in two of the six categories.

The reason for the relatively high discriminating power of the scales just mentioned is not hard to determine. They all tended to have a higher portion of judgments on the left-hand side of the distribution of scale ratings.

On the basis of those findings, a number of conclusions were drawn. One of the central problems in the kinds of scales tested in this pilot study appears to be the relatively high proportion of positive ratings. These tend to

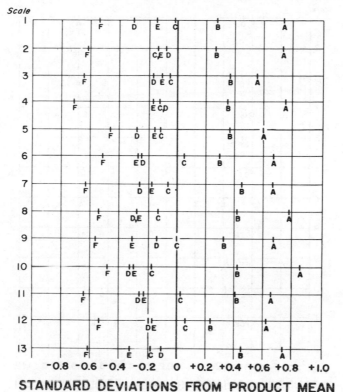

STANDARD DEVIATIONS FROM PRODUCT MEAN

Figure 3.12. Toilet soap brand ratings

cut down on the discrimination power of the scales and suggest one of several things:

Scoring procedures which give relatively great weight to differences at the upper end of the scale.

Greater use of unbalanced scales with more positive and fewer negative points on them.

Greater use of forced choice scales such as paired comparison, constant sum, brand awareness, and brand preference.

As another generalization, the use of scales having more than seven points tends to create clustering, areas of underuse, and, in general, lower discrimination. The purchase probability scale for one, appears to have these limitations.

The opinion scales, whether verbal or numerical, produce larger proportions of high ratings than we might like to see. This includes the bipolar ac-

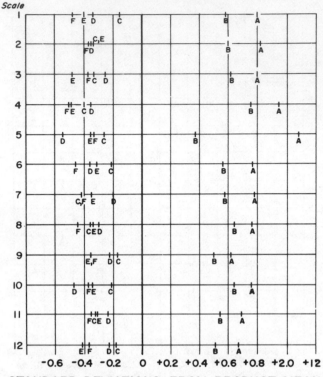

STANDARD DEVIATIONS FROM PRODUCT MEAN

Figure 3.13. Cola brand ratings

ceptability and quality scales, the six-point adjective scale, the 10-point numerical scale, the Stapel scale, the agreement scale, and the thermometer scale. This concentration of ratings in one area tends to reduce their ability to discriminate between brands.

Unless differential scoring of scale positions improves this situation, or unless a comparative measure can be developed by contrasting brands, the use of these scales is also likely to be less than ideal.

The remaining five scales are the awareness scale, brand preference, verbal purchase intent, paired comparison, and constant sum. Each is deserving of further consideration.

On the surface, the paired comparison scale has much to commend it. It yields an almost classic normal distribution, and it is a leading discriminator in every product category. But these advantages are at least partially offset by its cumbersome nature, its repetitiveness, and the difficulty in using it in telephone surveys.

TABLE 3.2　Factor Analysis of the 13 Scales (Grand Total)

Scale Name	Factor Loadings	
	I	II
Acceptability	0.80	−0.20
Purchase probability	0.86	−0.06
Six-point adjective	0.82	−0.13
Paired comparison	0.83	0.13
Ten-point numerical	0.87	−0.15
Thermometer	0.88	−0.14
Purchase intent	0.88	0.00
Agreement	0.82	−0.19
Quality	0.85	−0.17
Stapel scale	0.83	−0.20
Brand preference	0.61	0.62
Constant sum	0.74	0.36
Awareness	0.40	0.70
% of Variance	64.20	9.50

TABLE 3.3　Standardized Values of D by Scale and Product
(50 is Average, Standard-Deviation is 10)

	Six Products	Tooth paste	Colas	Anal-gesics	Toilet Soap	Coffee	Deter-gents
Awareness (13)	91				62	100	65
Paired comparison (4)	78	64	74	74	62	64	65
Verbal purchase intent (8)	56	44	51	54	60	70	44
Constant sum (10)	53	35	51	36	69	54	66
Brand choice (5)	52	66	64	38	38	52	52
Acceptability (1)	51	59	50	58	46	38	52
Ten-point numerical (6)	50	55	46	54	44	43	60
Purchase probability (2)	49	58	50	50	48	37	53
Six-point adjective (3)	48	52	51	55	40	41	52
Thermometer (7)	45	41	49	43	56	52	42
Quality (11)	42	36	41	43	53	59	38
Stapel scale (12)	39	49	39	51	35	44	40
Agreement (9)	36	42	36	43	47	45	34

DESCRIPTIVE ATTITUDE SCALES

Let us turn now to the category of descriptive scales and how they are best developed. It should be noted at the outset that interest in descriptive scales stems from the commonly held belief that our perceptions are likely to affect our evaluations. In other words, if you are able to change a consumer's perception of your product on a characteristic that he or she considers important, you have probably made the consumer like your product better and thus increased the probability of a purchase. Recent research suggests that for low involvement package goods, advertising only works in this manner some of the time. This model appears to hold better for more complex or high risk products, where information gathering activities play an important role in the purchase decision. Marketers continue to be concerned with image change, however, and as long as this interest persists, market researchers also will be interested in the best ways to measure brand images and image change.

Choosing the Descriptive Aspects to Be Measured

Traditionally, researchers have solved the problem of deciding what aspects of consumer attitudes should be measured by conducting some unstructured interviews or group sessions, by studying any past research that might be available, by talking with other people concerned with various aspects of marketing the product in question and, finally, by leaning heavily upon their own intuitions. The result of these processes is a list of items and phrases to be rated.[22] There appears to be a general feeling in research circles that any competent researcher can come up with a fairly good list of items to be measured. In other words, it is tacitly assumed that there are a limited number of things that we want to measure and that most analysts are likely to select much the same or similar items. Although that is a comforting hypothesis, experience shows the contrary. Let us recap a few experiments that prove it to be a very dubious hypothesis indeed.

In the first experiment seven analysts were involved; each was a professional researcher. The least experienced person in the group had been in the field two years. Most had been involved considerably longer, the average level of experience being about eight years. Also most had been working together in the same organization, and their viewpoints were expected to show a high degree of similarity. Certainly to the extent that market research is scientific, they should have shown reasonably high agreement.

[22] R. I. Haley, "New Insights into Attitude Measurement," in F. E. Webster, Jr. (ed.), *New Directions in Marketing—Proceedings of the 48th National Conference,* New York Hilton, New York City, American Marketing Association, June 1965, pp. 309–330.

To begin the experiment the analysts were asked to name the image areas that they would measure if they were to design an image study for the product in question. The product category involved was a familiar product category, one used regularly by about 80 percent of all homes.

Next some consumer research was done to find all of the consumer benefits and product attributes that could be developed for this particular category. This produced a list of about 150 items. Some, of course, were simply rephrasings of the same underlying benefits. Each benefit was expressed as a word or phrase and typed on a card.

The cards were then given to the analysts and they were asked to sort them into the categories they had named. If they felt that new or additional categories should be created during this sorting process, they were allowed to do so. No restrictions were placed on the number of categories that could be named.

Simultaneously with the intuitive sorting by the analysts, a sizable probability sample of consumers was contacted and asked to rate the desirability of each of the same 150 phrases on a six-point evaluative scale, ranging from "extremely desirable" to "not at all desirable." The ratings were factor analyzed and the resultant factors were compared with those chosen by the analysts. Two other experiments, essentially similar in design to this one, were conducted.

In the first experiment the analysts recommended that an average of 10 areas be covered in the image questioning. Recommendations ranged from a low of seven areas to a high of 13. Consumer responses indicated that 15 factors should be covered.

In the second experiment results were somewhat closer. The analysts identified an average of 11 areas with a range of from six to 16. The factor analysis of consumer responses indicated 13 underlying areas. In the third experiment the number of areas suggested by the analysts ranged from six to 17, whereas the factor analysis suggested 18. So, in general, the analysts did not do too badly in anticipating the number of factors to be covered in an image study. They perhaps chose too few, but this could presumably be remedied simply by asking them to make longer lists than their initial inclinations might suggest. No real trouble here.

However, the extent to which analysts agreed with each other was then examined. Considering only the single pair of analysts showing the *best* agreement with each other, in the first experiment one analyst named 12 areas and another 13. Nine of the factors looked more or less the same. In the second experiment, the best pair consisted of an analyst who named 12 areas and included in the listing the complete list of seven areas suggested by another analyst. And in the third experiment the best pair involved one analyst who named seven areas and another who named nine, with six in common.

Conversely, there were pairs of trained professional analysts who were thinking quite differently from one other. In the first experiment two analysts each named seven factors but had only two in common. In the second, two analysts each suggested 12 factors, but only three were the same. And in the third experiment, one analyst named 17 factors, another nine, with only four in common.

What this says, of course, is that if you were to have chosen different analysts to conduct these three studies, you would have gotten quite different studies. And all of these studies would be likely to meet the test of face validity!

Now let us look at how well the factors suggested by analysts matched the factor analysis of consumer reactions. In total over half of the factors suggested by the analysts appeared in the computer solution, 76% in the first experiment, 65% in the second, and 46% in the third. It will be recalled, however, that consumer reactions suggested *more* factors than the intuitions of analysts. Thus if we turn the question around and ask how many of the factors generated by consumer responses were anticipated by the analysts, the percentages drop to 51%, 55%, and 24%, respectively. Even the best analyst in each test was able to predict only two-thirds of the factors in the first two experiments and less than half of them in the third one.

All of this is a slightly roundabout way of saying that image studies as traditionally conducted are more an art form than a scientific endeavor. Results are likely to be predetermined by the instincts of the analyst. Fortunately, however, it is not necessary to live with this situation. All that is required is the careful construction of an image measurement tool. The next chapter reviews how that can be done.

FOUR

Constructing an Image Measurement Tool

Constructing an image measurement tool requires four separate but related steps—selecting the stimuli, conducting the first interview, doing factor analysis, and assigning importance weights to the resultant factors.

SELECTING THE STIMULI—EXPLORATORY WORK

The first step in compiling an image measurement tool is to make a comprehensive list of phrases covering every conceivable product attribute, consumer benefit, and user association. Potential sources for this material include:

Company research personnel
Company brand management personnel
Agency research people
Agency creative people
Agency account people
Past research
Past advertising for the brand and its competitors
New research

The new research normally consists of about 20 to 30 depth interviews with persons in the market target or, alternatively, of a series of group sessions. Sometimes both depth interviews and group sessions are employed. The main purpose of this research is to encourage people to talk about the product category of interest. Emphasis is placed on the benefits they expect to receive from the product of interest, reasons for using more or less of it, and the grounds on which they discriminate between and make choices among brands. General interviewing or moderator guides are usually preferable to a listing of specific questions. Tape recordings of depth interviews and group sessions have shown that some interviewers and some moderators have an unfortunate tendency to ask questions verbatim if they are stated explicitly in the interviewing or moderator guide.

The list of benefits and product attributes that is compiled from the sources cited above is likely to contain several hundred phrases. Consequently, one early task is that of screening the list down to manageable size. The definition of "manageable" depends to some extent on the complexity of the product category. Usually a list of from 50 to 75 items runs only a small risk of omitting a truly significant factor. This is particularly true if the list is reviewed by the project team before the next round of interviewing is begun. One useful method of reducing the list is the so-called Task Force Survey. In this approach items are first grouped judgmentally and then circulated to the project team. Each member is asked to vote for the 20 to 25 items he or she feels are important to include. When votes are tabulated it is usually found that quite a few items will receive *no* votes; these are automatically excluded. Other items will be found to have received support from a majority of the team members; these items are retained. The team can then be convened and a discussion can be focused on the remaining items, the marginal items that have received some support.

A few general rules may be helpful in deciding which items to keep and which to eliminate during the final screening process:

1. Screen out all advertising slogans. It is difficult for consumers to decide how well they apply to brands other than the one using them.

2. Use conversational words and phrases wherever possible. Erudite words (such as *erudite*) are often not in the average consumer's vocabulary. Although such words are likely to be screened out by the factor analysis, it is more efficient to eliminate them in this preliminary stage.

3. Make any phrases used as short as possible. To obtain meaningful responses it is necessary to communicate clearly with the consumer. The longer the sentences the more likely respondents are to tire of the rating game and to lose their willingness to discriminate between phrases. Furthermore, if the phrase is long, it is likely that some respondents will not take the time to read it completely. If they react only to the first few words of the description, their reactions may not be the same as they would have been had they understood the full content of the phrase.

4. Make sure that some phrases are included for each of the following areas:

The product physically—what the product is

The product at work—what the product does

Associations with the product—what kind of people use it, what kind of company makes it

Sensory benefits—stimulation of any of the five senses

Evaluative benefits—cognitive benefits

Emotional benefits—emotional feelings generated by buying, owning, or using the product.

5. Try to represent each basic idea by at least two separate phrases. Obviously this rule can only be followed in a general sense, because we cannot yet identify all of the basic ideas involved. If an item seems especially important, however, make sure it is stated in at least two different ways. It is desirable to use both general phrases (e.g., convenient) and specific phrases (e.g., easy to open the container) in order to simplify the problem of identifying and naming factors later on.

6. Use approximate syntax. When expressing consumer benefits, try to include the word *you* whenever possible in order to personalize the benefits. When dealing with areas such as product at work, no personal pronouns should be used. The focus should be on the product. In dealing with emotional benefits, try to talk about "people" rather than directing phrases directly at the respondent. Indirect associations avoid the problems of respondent "blocking" and attempting to give answers the interviewer will regard favorably.

7. Avoid expressing two ideas in a single phrase. For example, the phrase "smells and tastes good" should be separated into the two phrases "smells good" and "tastes good."

The analyst who will ultimately be responsible for interpreting the results, rather than the project team, should make the final judgement on the precise phrases to be used. In this way balance between the various types of phrases can be maintained.

CONDUCTING CONSUMER INTERVIEWS TO IDENTIFY KEY ATTITUDE FACTORS

The philosophy underlying the particular approach to attitude measurement summarized here is that we are more likely to obtain correct conclusions about consumer attitudes and motivations by asking people to react to a variety of stimuli and from their reactions to try to infer cause and effect, rather than by asking respondents to analyze themselves and report to us. People to be interviewed should be in the market target for the brand being researched. However, the approach used is relatively insensitive to sampling variations. Concessions to cost can be made in the area of sampling without undue risk to the research results. In fact, it can be argued that it is better to have respondents who are especially interested in the product category being studied than to have average consumers, many of whom are disinterested. Involved consumers are likely to make finer discriminations and consequently to generate cleaner factors in the factor analysis. A sample size of about 200 respondents is usually adequate for this phase.

For best results the phrases to be rated should be reproduced individually on printed cards. Respondents are given the rating scale to be used in the form of a board with squares large enough to permit each card to be placed at the appropriate point on the rating scale. Illustration cards, numbered on their backs, are shuffled from respondent to respondent to prevent order bias. It has been found that phrases which consistently appear next to each other can distort each other's meanings.

An alternative form for gathering these data is the self-administered questionnaire, which allows responses to be gathered more efficiently but sacrifices some discrimination. In this alternative about 20 phrases are listed down the left-hand margin of each page and the rating scale is written horizontally across the top of the page, with vertical lines extending down the page to identify the points on the rating scale and horizontal lines to separate the phrases from each other. Phrases are listed in a randomized order and pages are rotated from questionnaire to questionnaire. To reduce order effects the order of phrases can also be reversed from page to page.

A few other considerations are worth noting. The first concerns the use of a forced choice approach as opposed to allowing "no answer" responses. As mentioned earlier an attractive compromise is to provide a space for interviewers to record such responses but not indicate to respondents that they are allowable. This encourages more discrimination on the part of respondents, which is usually helpful. At the same time, if they insist on a completely neutral response, the interview is not derailed.

A second issue concerns the use of personal interviews rather than telephone interviews or mail panels. Although all three methods can be used successfully, personal interviews result in more respondent attention to the rating scales used and, consequently, in cleaner, more sensitive measurements.

A third issue concerns the arrangement of phrases when self-administered questionnaires are used. If phrases with similar content are grouped on the questionnaire, the grouping provides a more easily grasped frame of reference for respondents and permits them to draw fine distinctions between phrases that are similar. However, this gain in sensitivity is more than offset by the bias that grouping introduces into the factor analysis. Phrases that appear next to each other, or even near each other, are more likely to factor together than phrases that are far apart. Thus grouping phrases has a tendency to force reproduction of those groups in the factor analysis. In other words, it tends to make the factor analysis support the judgment of the analyst who decides upon the initial grouping of the phrases.

A compromise position is perhaps best here also, using three or four very broad groupings. For example, it is often deisrable to have separate groupings for emotional benefits and for user associations, allowing the remaining phrases to form a third broad group.

The issue of emotional benefits deserves special comment. If they are scattered throughout the group of phrases being rated, they are likely to drop out of the factor analysis entirely or they may all be classified into a single factor. This is partially because these items require a little more thought than straightforward items such as "good value" and "lasts a long time," and if they are mixed in a list, they are not given adequate attention. It is also, to some extent, attributable to the difficulty of adequately expressing emotions in a word or a phrase and to people's resistance to this sort of potentially revealing item. If emotional benefits are placed at the start of the interview, however, so that respondents rate them before they know that they have easier phrases to rate, results are at least better than if handled otherwise.

SCALE SCORING

Often this issue is ignored. Scales are simply scored with a sequential set of numbers. If a 10-point scale is used, the points are numbered from 1 to 10; if a six-point scale is used, the points are numbered from 1 to 6. This seems to work reasonably well for descriptive scales. However, there is considerable evidence that when this simpleminded approach is used with evaluative scales, it results in a loss in sensitivity. In other words, most evaluative scales are by no means "equal interval" scales.[1]

If, for example, the traditional five-point purchase intent scale (definitely will buy, probably will buy, might or might not buy, probably will not buy and definitely will not buy) is employed, a shift from "definitely will not buy" to "probably will not buy" is worth one point. A shift from "probably

[1] Haley and Case, Testing 13 Attitude Scales.

will buy" to "definitely will buy" is similarly worth one point. In the former instance, however, all that has happened is a slight lessening in dislike. The actual probability of purchase was low, and it remains low. In the latter case, however, a material increase in purchase probability has occurred.

It has been found that the probability of purchase goes up exponentially for almost all evaluative scales as ratings become more strongly positive. Therefore, some form of exponential scoring of the scale points would seem to be more appropriate.[2] Balanced against this theoretical consideration, however, is the complexity that necessarily accompanies the introduction of exponential weights. A compromise may be the so-called *top box* method of scale scoring.[3] This, in effect, scores the highest rating point as "1" and all other ratings as "0." This method is more sensitive than the conventional linear scoring, represents the most predictive way of dichotomizing the scale, and is easy for nonresearchers to understand.

FACTOR ANALYSIS

Factor analysis is an efficient technique for data reduction, and data reduction is an important problem at this point. It can be used to help to identify the key dimensions underlying consumer evaluations of the product of interest. It allows us to narrow our list of possible phrases to a very small number, and do it objectively, without losing much information in the process. This means that we can obtain reasonably accurate measurements of how people feel about our brand by obtaining reactions to that brand in just a few key areas. Factor analysis picks out the essential wholes among the influences at work. Thus it is invaluable in helping to identify the various product aspects and psychological aspects that may influence the purchase of a product.

Moreover, although arbitrary choices must be made in areas such as selecting values to go on the diagonal of the correlation matrix and in choosing schemes of rotation and selecting factor solutions, factor analysis is much more objective than simply relying on an analyst's judgment. It avoids an arbitrary choice of variables to measure and is relatively free of the bias associated with the "going in" hypotheses of researchers. The primary assumption implicit in factor analysis is that consumers are not making their ratings in a random fashion, and there is ample evidence to support that point of view.

---

[2] This problem also applies to descriptive scales, but in general it is less severe.
[3] For a fuller discussion of this issue see R. I. Haley and R. Gatty, "Adapting Attitude Measurement to Computer Processing," *Computer Operations*, Vol. 2, No. 2, April–May 1968, pp. 11–16.

In dealing with people—their likes, dislikes and motivations—we are presented with so many possible variables that we cannot measure them all efficiently unless we somehow systematically screen them down. Factor analysis points out for us the *minimum* number of dimensions on which measurements must be made if we wish to measure consumer attitudes. This does not mean that we cannot include, on judgment, things that do not show up in a factor analysis. Nor does it mean that every factor which appears must be carried in all subsequent measuring instruments. Factor analysis simply identifies a few basic and relatively independent dimensions along which consumers make judgments, and these dimensions are helpful in measuring image change.

It is beyond the scope of this book to review factor analysis itself. It is a common multivariate technique, however, and descriptions of its underlying assumptions, its use, and computational program are all readily available.[4] So let us assume that we have completed the factor analysis and identified the key attitude factors involved in consumer reactions to the product in question. We are now ready for the final step in the construction of the attitude measurement tool, the assignment of importance weights to the factors obtained,

ASSIGNMENT OF IMPORTANCE WEIGHTS

The factors obtained in the factor analysis quite clearly have diagnostic value. If it is assumed that overall evaluative attitudes are caused primarily by perceptions, however, they may have evaluative value as well. The problem is how best to weight and combine them. There are at least two schools of thought on this.

One holds that obtaining weights for the importance of each factor for each person in the sample adds no predictive power and thus is a waste of time. The importance weights, it is claimed, are already incorporated in the data on perceptions. Consequently, people in this school believe it is best to simply add everyone's judgments on each factor.[5]

A variant of this school calls for running a regression using overall attitudes as the dependent variable and individual factors as independent variables. However, this rests on the difficult twin assumptions of a homogeneous universe and a causal influence that flows only from the individual factors to the overall attitude and not vice versa. Additionally it as-

[4] H. H. Harman, *Modern Factor Analysis,* Chicago: University of Chicago Press, 1967.
[5] J. N. Sheth and W. Wayne Talarzyk, *Relative Contribution of Perceived Instrumentality and Value Importance Components in Determining Attitudes,* Urbana: Graduate School of Business Administration, University of Illinois, 1971.

sumes that individual differences in importance weights can be safely ignored.

A second school, stimulated by models postulated by people such as Fishbein, Rosenberg, and St. James, holds that importance weights must be obtained for each respondent and these, in the case of the simplest Fishbein model, multiplied by perceptions about the product, in order to arrive at a score for each person that predicts his or her likelihood of purchasing the brand in question.[6]

Within this school, however, there are substantial disagreements on how to go about obtaining individual importance weights. Some people believe that they can be obtained overtly, simply by asking the respondent to provide them via a rating scale; but this places the respondent in the role both of self-analyst and expert. In this role cognitive benefits always receive the highest weights. Emotional benefits and things like packaging regularly receive low weights—even in categories in which it can be demonstrated that they exert a major influence on purchase decisions.

For some respondents, ratings of individual image items on anchored adjective scales do not provide very high levels of discrimination between benefits. One way to avoid this problem (provided the benefit list is not too long) is to use a constant sum scale. This forces respondents to rate some items low if they want to rate any items high.

If the respondent has judged a number of brands both overall and on individual image dimensions, it is also possible to derive separate regression weights for each individual in the sample. With large samples, however, the process can be comparatively expensive, even when a large computer is readily available. Also it assumes that causation runs from the image items to overall ratings and not vice versa.

Other people in the school favoring individual weights believe that they are best obtained indirectly. Procedures for doing so have been explicated for tradeoff analysis[7] (which pits pairs of differing levels of two benefits against each other), for conjoint analysis[8] (which presents sets of benefits at varying levels), and for display board methods (which allow respondents to acquire information sequentially about the brands among which a choice is to be made).[9]

These approaches also have their drawbacks, however. For example,

[6] M. Fishbein and I. Ajzen, *Belief, Attitude, Intention and Behavior*, Reading, MA: Addison-Wesley, 1975.

[7] R. M. Johnson, "Tradeoff Analysis of Consumer Values," *Journal of Marketing Research*, May 1974, pp. 121–128.

[8] P. E. Green and V. Srinivasan, "Conjoint Analysis in Consumer Research: Issues and Outlook," *Journal of Consumer Research*, Vol. 5, September 1978, pp. 103–123.

[9] J. Jacoby, "Consumer Reaction to Information Displays: Packaging and Advertising," in S. DeVita (Ed.), *Advertising and Public Interest*, Chicago: American Marketing Association, 1974.

they do not handle emotional benefits well. Also the verbal descriptions of varying levels of an image element may be ambiguous (e.g., very strong, strong, mild, and very mild), and the ranges of the verbal anchors used may not be equivalent. And, finally, there is little support for the assumption that the kinds of decisions made in the game-playing situation parallel those that are made under actual purchase conditions[10-12] (e.g., how can the natural salience of image elements and the natural perceptual vigilance process of the respondent be simulated in an interview situation?).[13]

Indirect approaches are still relatively new, and some of these problems may well be solved within the next few years. However, tradeoff analysis, conjoint analysis, and display board methods are cumbersome to apply. So until their superiority is clearly demonstrated, the most practical choice would seem to be where lists are short constant sum measures and where they are longer anchored adjective scales. There is a larger base of experience with these approaches and their shortcomings are better understood. Moreover there is some evidence that results obtained in a direct fashion correlate highly with those obtained indirectly.

One closing comment may be appropriate with respect to the Fishbein and similar models, which assume that weighted perceptions together with other factors determine evaluations. It has been found that a large amount of the correlation which exists between overall attitudes and the weighted composite of image elements is attributable to the halo effect. In other words, causation flows from overall impressions about the brand to individual image elements rather than vice versa. If you like a brand, you tend to rate it highly on all image elements. If you dislike it, you tend to rate it low across the board. A comparatively recent article by Lehmann noted this relationship.[14] The 1966 Grey Validation study[15] showed that overall brand ratings obtained from a single evaluative scale were better predictors of be-

[10] F. Acito and A. K. Jain, "Evaluation of Conjoint Analysis Results: A Comparison of Methods," *Journal of Marketing Research*, February 1980, pp. 106–112.

[11] D. R. Wittink, L. Krishnamurthi, and J. B. Nutter, "Comparing Derived Importance Weights Across Attributes," *Journal of Consumer Research*, Vol. 8, No. 4, March 1982, pp. 471–474.

[12] P. Wright and M. A. Kriewall, "State of Mind Effects on the Accuracy with Which Utility Functions Predict Marketplace Choice," *Journal of Marketing Research*, Vol. 17, August 1980, pp. 277–293.

[13] Display board methods are perhaps less subject to salience distortions than conjoint and tradeoff methods, see *JMR*, February 1979, p. 61. See also, J. Jacoby, R. W. Chestnut, K. C. Weigl, and W. Fisher, "Prepurchase Information Acquisition: Description of a Process Methodology, Research Paradigm and Pilot Investigation," in B. Anderson (Ed.), *Advances in Consumer Research*, Cincinnati: Association for Consumer Research, 1975, Vol. 3, pp. 306–314.

[14] N. E. Beckwith, H. H. Kassarjian, and D. R. Lehmann, *Halo Effects in Marketing Research: Review and Prognosis*, Advances in Consumer Research, Vol. 5, 1978, pp. 465–467.

[15] New York: Grey Advertising, Inc., *How Advertising Works*, 1971.

havior than weighted composites of image elements. The implication is that models such as these should be used with caution.

VALIDATION EVIDENCE

It is evident from the foregoing material that the attitude measurement approaches suggested involve a heavy investment both financially and in terms of analyst time. It might well be asked whether all of that effort is required. What evidence do we have that people's predispositions do, in fact, help to predict their brand choices?

Sociologists have wrestled with this same question. How well do attitudes predict behavior? Some years ago Leon Festinger reviewed the literature and concluded that the link between the two had not been established.[16] The situation is not much different today. Although a few significant studies have been conducted on the predictive power of attitudinal information,[17] some of these have produced negative findings.[18] Consequently the link is still not completely understood. Most marketing people, however, are willing to take the link for granted. It has face validity and is strongly supported by what has been called the Grey Validation Study.

The Grey Validation Study was an attempt to establish a proven link between overall attitudes toward brands and subsequent purchase of those brands. It was designed by the author in the mid-1960s, and its results have been reported on numerous occasions.[19-22]

The basic research design called for three waves of interviews. The positive association between attitudes and behavior is a well-known phenomenon. However, association does not mean causation. It has been argued[23] that

---

[16] Leon Festinger, "Behavioral Support for Opinion Change," *Public Opinion Quarterly*, Vol. 28, 1964, pp. 404–417.
[17] C. DuBois, "Twelve Brands on a Seesaw," *Proceedings 13th Annual Conference*, ARF, New York, 1967, pp. 11–21.
[18] J. N. Axelrod, "Attitude Measures that Predict Purchase," *Journal of Advertising Research*, Vol. 8, No. 1, 1968, pp. 3–17.
[19] A. A. Achenbaum, "Knowledge Is a Thing Called Measurement," AMA Attitude Research Conference, January 21–27, 1966.
[20] R. J. Reiser, "Why New Products Fail, Why Old Products Falter," ANA Workshop on Advertising Planning and Evaluation, December 13, 1966, *How Advertising Works*, New York: Grey Advertising, Inc., 1971.
[21] A. A. Achenbaum, "Relevant Measures of Consumer Attitudes," Conference of the American Marketing Association, June 21, 1967.
[22] S. J. Ackerman, "How Advertising Works-A Study of the Relationship between Advertising, Consumer Attitudes, and Purchase Behavior," ARF Advertising Tracking Studies Workshop, New York, July 31, 1984.
[23] J. L. Ginter, "An Experimental Investigation of Attitude Change and Choice of a New Brand," *Journal of Marketing Research*, Vol. 11, February 1974, pp. 30–40.

behavior causes attitudes rather than vice versa, and undoubtedly behavior does affect attitudes. If people buy a brand and continue to use it, they are almost certain to feel more favorable toward it than people who do not buy it. However, the fact that behavior strongly affects attitudes does not preclude the possibility that attitudes affect behavior as well. The Grey study was designed to answer the question of whether attitudes determine behavior or whether behavior determines attitudes.

A minimum of three waves is necessary to establish the causal effects of attitudes on behavior. If only two waves of interviews are conducted and attitudinal changes are found to be correlated with behavioral changes, it would still not be clear whether the attitudinal changes had caused the behavioral changes or vice versa. With three waves, however, it was possible to relate attitudinal changes from period 1 to period 2 to behavioral changes between period 2 and period 3.

The full design covered three measurement areas:

Overall attitudes (measured several ways)
Brand purchase behavior (for 19 brands in 7 categories)
Media exposure patterns

It was hypothesized that period 1 to period 2 changes in exposure to brand advertising messages would precede and help to predict period 2 to period 3 changes in overall brand attitudes. A second hypothesis, the major hypothesis of the study, was that period 1 to period 2 attitude changes would precede and help to predict brand behavior changes between period 2 and period 3. Finally it was hypothesized that brand behavior changes between period 1 and period 2 would precede and help to predict attitudinal changes between period 2 and period 3 (see Figure 4.1).

A national probability sample of 3000 respondents was contacted during the first wave of interviews and each respondent was recontacted twice at six-week intervals. As expected there was some sample attrition; however, a total of approximately 2400 interviews was obtained, each respondent having been given an identical interview three times.

There was some concern that the first wave of interviews might "condition" respondents and somehow distort their responses in the second and third waves. Consequently, a "control" sample, a fresh sample of 1000 people, was contacted coincident with the second wave of interviews. Aside from one question[24] no significant differences in responses were found be-

---

[24] Unaided brand awareness was measured in the first wave and aided brand awareness was mistakenly asked as well. As might be expected, unaided brand awareness in the sample of people recontacted in the second wave was significantly higher than for the central sample. This was particularly noticeable for smaller brands.

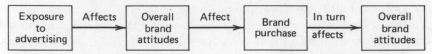

Figure 4.1. Hypothesized sequence of attitudinal and behavioral changes

tween the fresh sample and the recontacted sample. Accordingly, plans for drawing another fresh sample of respondents during the third wave of interviews were scrapped.

Results of this research confirmed that attitudinal changes do precede and help to predict changes in brand usage. Similarly, changes in the probability of exposure to advertising, as estimated from media exposure pattern data, did precede and help to predict changes in overall attitudes, although the effects were less strong than those of attitudes on behavior. However, no relationship was apparent between behavioral changes between period 1 and period 2 and attitudinal changes between period 2 and period 3. It was assumed that this was because the effects of behavior on attitudes were immediate (period 1 to period 2) rather than delayed.

FIVE

Developing Effective Communications Strategies

Although improving overall attitudes toward a brand of interest may be a legitimate advertising objective, the question remains as to how best to accomplish it. The answer lies in the development of an efficient and effective communications strategy. This requires providing the answers to three deceptively simple questions:

1. *Whom are you competing against?* How can the market for the product, brand, or service best be defined? Is the brand of interest most likely to gain sales by taking them away from similar competitors or from market expansion? If the latter, what kinds of products, if any, is it likely to replace?

2. *What should you say?* On what single buying incentive should the product focus its efforts? What should its primary cognitive appeal be and what should its personality, image, or "positioning" be?

3. *To whom should you say it?* On what group of people (market target) should communications efforts be concentrated? What is the best way to define the market target for a brand?

These questions need not be answered in any particular sequence. They are all interrelated. Decisions on the best answers for any one of them have a strong bearing on the most appropriate answers to the other two. Poor answers in any of these areas or—even worse—failing to address them at all, can result in the failure of the brand or, at best, in a huge waste of the money spent on communications.

This point cannot be overemphasized. The three question areas listed above are probably the three most important questions in marketing. The net sales response that results from accurate answers can easily justify a substantial research investment in assessing alternatives. This fact has been widely recognized and accounts for the continuing popularity of Segmentation studies or Market Strategy studies, as they are more commonly called today.[1] Grey Advertising has gone as far as to establish a subsidiary called Grey Strategic Marketing, Inc. to deal with problems in this area. Just what is involved in such studies will be reviewed in Chapter 8. In the meantime let us discuss the three key communications strategy areas in a little more depth.

MARKET DEFINITION

Proper definition of the market has important marketing implications. A premium-priced margarine brand defining its competition as all margarine brands may find its market share declining steadily over time. However, if, instead it defined its market as other high-priced brands of margarine, it might find its share to be stable or even increasing. A full understanding of submarkets defined by considerations such as diet, health, taste, and spreadability, as well as price, might suggest new products or line extensions in submarkets with attractive growth trends and perhaps additional investment of advertising and promotional funds in those submarkets.

Courts of law have also recognized the importance of proper market definition. In 1974 the manufacturer of Fleer bubble gum attempted to obtain a license from the Major League Baseball Players Association to sell satin patches picturing current players. They were turned down by the Association, however, because another firm, Topps, had contracts granting it exclusive rights to sell the pictures and names of baseball players alone or in combination with chewing gum or candy.

In 1975 Fleers asked Topps to waive its exclusive rights so that it might be granted a license to sell decals, stickers, and stamps showing major league players. Topps refused to do so and Fleers sued, claiming monopolistic practices.

In court, Topps argued that the relevant market for baseball cards was all gum and candy sold in outlets retailing primarily to children. Fleers argued that it was baseball cards alone or with bubble gum. There was no question of Topps being able to monopolize the market as Topps defined it. However, the court ruled that baseball cards were a legitimate submarket and that there was no acceptable substitute for them. Accordingly the Asso-

---

[1] D. K. Hardin, "10th Annual Survey of the Consumer Research Industry," Market Facts, Inc., Chicago, reported in *Marketing News*, May 27, 1983, p. 13.

ciation was ordered to consider applications other than that of Topps to market baseball cards and to license at least one additional firm in that submarket. So here the market definition hung on substitutability.

The objective in obtaining a clear market definition is to indicate explicitly the sources of short-term and longer-term potential growth. This can be obtained in a variety of ways:

> By taking sales from a single competitor (Avis versus Hertz), from a group of competitors (Yuban versus premium-priced coffees), or from all competitors (Coke versus all soft drinks).
>
> By broadening the market generically.
>
> Through bringing in new users (fire protection devices).
>
> By creating new use occasions (orange juice is not just for breakfast anymore).
>
> By increasing penetration of the market among current users.
>
> Through encouraging greater quantities of use per use occasion (McDonald's efforts to increase average check size).
>
> By reminding consumers of the variety of uses to which the product can be put (Fantastik can be used in both the bathroom and the kitchen).
>
> By simply reminding people of the attractive aspects of product use and thus encouraging more frequent use for the traditional use occasions. This is often a useful goal for products such as soup, Jell-o, and cranberry jelly, products that are already on the shelves of a large number of American households.

Markets can be viewed as a series of concentric rings (see Figures 5.1 to 5.4). In the center are the most immediate competitors, ones from which sales are most likely to be gained or to which sales are likely to be lost. In the next ring are important but less immediate competitors, and in the outer ring are still less direct competitors but ones that may take on greater importance over the longer term. The perils of ignoring this sort of competition have been memorably illustrated by Levitt in his classic article on Marketing Myopia.[2] For example, a premium-priced margarine may consider other premium-priced margarines to be its principal competitors, and therefore in the center of its market definition. In the next ring might be all

---

[2] T. Levitt, "Marketing Myopia," *Harvard Business Review*, September–October 1975, Vol. 53, No. 5, pp. 26–48.

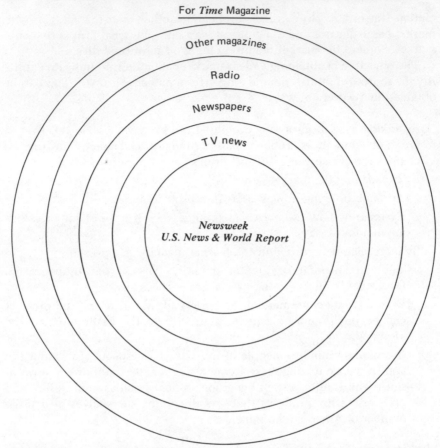

Figure 5.1. Possible definitions of competitive environment for *Time* magazine

other margarines. In the following ring might be butter. And beyond that might be other spreads such as peanut butter, jams, or jellies that could be used instead of margarine.

Once significant competitors have been identified it is important that all of their marketing activities be closely monitored—their communications, their pricing, their new product activities, and their distribution policies. Any significant changes need to be evaluated as rapidly as possible so that appropriate defensive actions can be taken immediately. Tracking systems (see Chapter 12) play a central role in this sort of monitoring.

The process of focusing attention on a limited number of key competitors reflects a basic principle almost invariably used by successful marketers. Efforts are concentrated where that concentration is likely to yield the

Figure 5.2. Possible definitions of competitive environment for General Motors

greatest rewards. In that way, not only is a substantial amount of waste avoided, but response per unit of effort is increased.

There are a large number of theories about how best to analyze market structure in order to identify primary competitors.[3] Economists have customarily defined markets in terms of cross-elasticity of demand. When changes in the price of one product are found to be correlated with changes in demand for another, those two products are said to be in the same market. Some brands so dominate their immediate competition (e.g., Campbell in the soup market) that they quite naturally look to other product types

---

[3] For a thorough discussion see George S. Day and Allen D. Shocker, "Identifying Competitive Product-Market Boundaries: Strategic and Analytical Issues," Cambridge, MA: Marketing Science Institute, 1976.

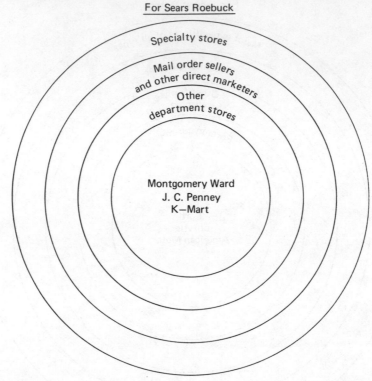

Figure 5.3. Possible definitions of competitive environment for Sears Roebuck

when they attempt to define their competition, testing cross-elasticities of their product and a wide variety of other products sold in supermarkets.

Most marketing people, however, use one of three approaches to market definitions:

Marketing judgment
Analysis of consumer purchase or usage behavior
Analysis of consumer perceptions and attitudes

The most common but also the most risky way to define markets is simply to use *marketing judgment.* The standard product categories and subcategories used in Nielsen and SAMI reports, as well as those used in Department of Commerce statistics, are examples of this method. Sometimes considerably more elaborate methods are used in reaching market definitions.[4] For ex-

[4] M. O. Stern, R. V. Ayres, and A. Shapanko, "A Model for Forecasting the Substitution of One Technology for Another," *Technological Forecasting and Social Change,* Vol. 7, 1975, pp. 57–79.

For Mazola Margarine

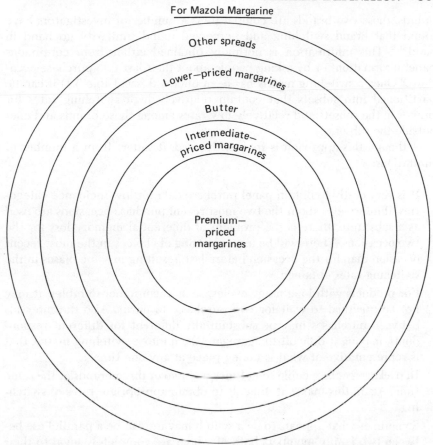

Other spreads

Lower—priced margarines

Butter

Intermediate—
priced margarines

Premium—
priced
margarines

Figure 5.4.   Possible definitions of competitive environment for Mazola

ample, one approach involves assembling a list of performance benefits, attributes, and occasions of use for the products considered to be potential competitors. Then experts are asked to rate the extent to which each product has each attribute and delivers each performance benefit for each occasion of use. By cross-multiplying importance by delivery, scores can then be developed to reflect the extent of competition for each occasion. Although this approach depends heavily upon the expertise of the people participating, and although it runs the risk of overemphasizing physical characteristics, it allows similar scores to be achieved by quite different routes. Thus it permits the inclusion of competitors and potential competitors that might be missed if only their similarity were to be considered.

Analysis of *purchase behavior* usually focuses on brand-switching behavior. It assumes that if a consumer switches back and forth between two brands, those two brands are competitors. A number of investigators have found that brand switching and perceived brand similarity go hand in hand.[5, 6] This information is normally obtained either from continuous panel information[7] or by asking people about their last two purchase occasions.[8] Once a switching matrix has been obtained (see Table 5.1) it can be partitioned into subsets that contain relatively high switching rates for brands in the subsets and relatively low rates among these brands and ones outside the subset.

Although this approach is frequently used, it suffers from a number of limitations:

It is very costly to obtain panel purchase data for low incidence categories. If interviews about the two most recent purchase occasions are used as a substitute, there is the problem of differential memory loss for the two occasions. There will be less forgetting of choices in the most recent occasion than for the occasion before last, resulting in some biases in the switching rates obtained.

For products with long usage cycles, such as consumer durables, it may not be practical to wait for two purchases to occur. Also the intervals between purchases may be substantially different for different respondents, making it difficult to aggregate them into a switching matrix that is representative of what is taking place at any one time.

In package goods, people sometimes buy two or three brands at the same time. Again this makes it difficult to obtain appropriate rates of switching.

Sometimes what appears to be a switch may instead be a parallel use between two family members both of whom are completely loyal to their own brands. Thus a husband may use Crest and his wife Colgate. If she does the purchasing, however, it will appear that she is switching back and forth between Crest and Colgate. Similarly products that might be considered competitive may be bought for different consumption occasions.

A homemaker may buy both Log Cabin syrup and 100% maple syrup. However, the former may be for family use, whereas the latter is used only when company is present.

---

[5] J. F. Donius, "A Perspective on Market Tracking of Established Brands," ANA Advertising Research Workshop, New York, Dec. 1981.

[6] V. Stefflre, "Some Applications of Multidimensional Scaling to Social Science Problems," in F. M. Bass, C. W. King and E. A. Pessemier (Eds.), *Multidimensional Scaling: Theory and Applications*, Vol. 2, New York: Academic Press, 1972, pp. 211–243.

[7] NPD Research, Inc. makes extensive analyses of switching patterns.

[8] Normally a method used in applying Hendry models.

TABLE 5.1 Main Dish Switching Matrix

Meal 1/Meal 2	Soup	Chicken	Veal	Pork	Beef	Fish	Tuna	Hot Dog	Rice	Tuna Salad	Salad	Pasta	Sandwich	Number of Users
Soup	417	58	5	20	103	20	10	26	2	15	27	35	266	1004
Chicken	44	287	3	172	275	82	3	24	10	18	24	87	65	1094
Veal	5	2	30	17	15	16	2	2	2	3	2	4	1	101
Pork	18	165	16	301	242	33	4	11	9	1	17	70	57	944
Beef	92	273	12	229	323	108	17	121	16	9	24	180	249	1653
Fish	19	76	14	30	101	62	2	3	11	1	1	2	49	371
Tuna	6	2	1	5	14	1	27	5	2	2	2	1	21	89
Hog dog	22	16	1	10	115	1	8	65	2	1	9	16	53	319
Rice	2	1	2	7	14	9	1	1	14	2	1	8	8	70
Tuna salad	16	12	2	0	10	0	2	2	1	26	1	8	23	103
Salad	25	17	1	14	15	2	2	7	2	2	111	19	87	304
Pasta	32	80	5	66	169	1	4	15	7	6	17	118	103	623
Sandwich	251	60	1	53	244	48	45	53	7	20	81	102	321	1286
Number of users	949	1049	93	924	1640	383	127	335	85	106	317	650	1303	7961

Out-of-stock conditions or lack of distribution can have strong effects upon switching rates. Even shelf location can determine switching to some extent.

When only purchase data are available it is difficult to separate complementary use from competing use. Peanut butter and jelly, purchased alternately, may be being used simultaneously or they may be competing directly on a "one or the other" basis.

Probably the most successful attempts to define competitive market structure have been those involving analysis of *consumer perceptions*. There are several ways in which this can be done,[9-11] but perhaps the most popular is perceptual mapping.[12]

Broadly defined, the term *perceptual mapping* refers to any method that yields a physical or graphical representation of the differences among brands, products, consumers or groups of consumers, companies or image characteristics. It has found a wide variety of applications, among them:

Spotting new product opportunities

Repositioning established products

Use as a projective technique to discover hidden associations

Before/after tests of copy, product, package, or name

New product tracking studies

Standard tracking studies on established products

Concept screening

Concept development

Concept testing

Mapping approaches are very attractive to marketing people because in many ways they parallel the ways in which marketing executives like to think about their markets. Perceptual maps show the competitive environment—where every brand stands in relation to every other brand. Moreover, they can superimpose consumers' "ideal points" on the map to indicate the directions in which a brand might be best advised to shift its

[9] J. H. Myers and E. Tauber, *Market Structure Analysis*, Chicago: American Marketing Association, 1977.

[10] V. T. Stefflre, "Market Structure Studies: New Products for Old Markets and New Markets for Old Products," in F. M. Bass, C. W. King, and E. A. Pessemeier (Eds.), *Application of the Sciences in Marketing Management*, New York: Wiley, 1968.

[11] R. I. Haley, *Positioning in Market Strategy Development*, New York: American Marketing Association, January 1973.

[12] The term *perceptual mapping* is intended to include the mapping of preferences as well as the mapping of perceptions.

image. And they can provide image signposts that suggest which characteristics should be modified and the ways in which they can be modified to move the brand position in the desired direction.

Finally, by representing highly complex situations in only two, three, or sometimes four dimensions, they drastically simplify (some would say "oversimplify") the marketer's world. Marketing people, of course, regularly attempt to do this in order to focus their marketing power on one or two critical elements that have enough leverage to cause favorable changes to occur.

There are, however, many different approaches to perceptual mapping. Both the research procedures used and the computer algorithms employed can differ significantly. Consequently, a few generalizations may be in order:

Some authors have concluded that the choice of algorithms is not important, that all algorithms give similar results. My own experience suggests that, as the number of dimensions necessary to describe the data increases, different algorithms are increasingly likely to produce different results. Unfortunately, there is little basis at present for choosing objectively among the varying maps that are produced by different algorithms. Face validity appears to be the best single criterion.

For low dimensionality *overall* results are similar. However, the position of an individual brand can vary substantially from technique to technique. This happens because every algorithm must make compromises in order to maximize the accuracy with which the graphical representation fits the overall pattern of data. It will sacrifice the fit of one brand if the *overall* fit can be improved. This is fine as long as the compromises are not made on the brand of central interest to the analyst. To guard against this possibility the raw distances between the items mapped should always be compared with the distances as represented by the map.

Environmental effects can be significant. In one study of national perceptions[13] it was found that when Russia and China were included with a group of European countries, the only dimension that emerged from similarity sorts was a very strong East/West dimension. When only European countries were included in the sorts, however, several meaningful dimensions between them appeared.

Maps frequently yield almost trivial dimensions, such as large/small or strong/mild. However, they often allow researchers to formulate hypotheses about market behavior that probably would not have been framed had the map not been available as a stimulus. They regularly help

[13] *A Survey of U.S. Attitudes Toward Germany and the German Language*, New York: Appel, Haley, Fouriezos, Inc., August 1971.

brands to redefine their competitive environments and to do so in particularly meaningful ways. They sometimes point to a factor in brand discrimination, the significance of which had been overlooked. They often provide clues to the analyst on where his or her analytic attention should be focused. When used in conjunction with a Market Strategy study, they frequently provide clues to potentially productive cross-tabs.

Mapping is not best used as a large sample technique. Different algorithms can produce different results, even with large samples. So some experimentation with different algorithms may be a good investment in a mapping project. For this and other reasons mapping is probably best used for diagnostic rather than definitive purposes. It can be used successfully with relatively small samples. It is not very expensive, and it can be very insightful.

One mapping approach that has worked quite well in studies designed by the author involves the following steps:

1. Exploratory work in which consumers who use the product of interest are asked about occasions of use—the purposes for and situations in which the brand is used. Once these are established the respondent is asked to name other brands or products that might be used for each of the purposes mentioned. Careful probing can produce a sizable list of potential competitors for the brand of interest.

2. The names of each of these products are placed on a white card. If the list is too long, it can be screened in much the same manner as lists of benefits are reduced in developing attitude measuring instruments (see p. 82).

3. A fresh group of respondents is asked to sort the cards onto a scale to measure their self-assigned levels of familiarity with each brand or product.

4. Cards representing brands with which respondents indicate acceptable levels of familiarity are then sorted by the fresh sample into groups in such a way that cards within a group represent items considered similar to each other. Respondents are told that there are no limits, either high or low, on the number of groups that can be made. In situations where there is more than one dominant consumption occasion, respondents can be requested to make several sorts,[14] one for each occasion.

[14] M. Wish and J. D. Carroll, "Applications of INDSCAL to Studies of Human Perception and Judgment," in E. C. Carterette and M. P. Friedman (Eds.), *Handbook of Perception*, Vol. 2, New York: Academic Press, 1974.

5. Respondents are then asked, for each group, what the members of the group have in common and what makes them different from other groups.

6. Image ratings are obtained, either by having respondents rate each brand, or where the number of brands is too large for this to be practical, a subset of brands on a preselected list of attributes. An alternative procedure is to have them deal a new set of cards, this time containing image items instead of brand names, onto the brand piles developed in step 4.

Several investigations have shown that sample sizes for these kinds of procedures can be quite small, even as small as $N = 50$, and still yield reasonably reliable results.[15] Several types of perceptual maps can be generated from the data obtained by the six steps listed above.[16] One of the most straightforward is to develop a simple space map such as shown in Figure 5.5. This involves submitting the pairs matrix (the number of times each pair of items has been placed in the same pile, expressed as a percentage of the maximum number of times it was possible for the items to be paired) to a computing routine such as KYST[17] and to a clustering program such as Johnson.[18]

The map that is generated has important marketing implications. Brands that are located in the same subsets are direct competitors and should design their information systems so that they can monitor, anticipate, and respond to marketing actions of their competitors. Other subsets represent opportunities for line extensions or new products.

The image ratings and reasons for grouping items provide diagnostic insights into consumer perceptions of the products under review. A variety of statistical procedures is available for superimposing image ratings on the map either as points (see Figure 5.6) or as vectors (see Figure 5.7).[19, 20] These help the analyst understand why the submarkets exist, and offer some guidance concerning repositioning possibilities.

[15] P. E. Green and F. J. Carmone, *Multidimensional Scaling and Related Techniques in Marketing Analysis*, Boston: Allyn & Bacon, 1970.

[16] P. E. Green, "Marketing Applications of Multidimensional Scaling: Assessment and Outlook," *Journal of Marketing*, Vol. 39, No. 1, January 1975, pp. 24–31.

[17] *Data Analysis Programs, Psychometric Laboratory*, Chapel Hill: University of North Carolina, January 1979, p. 5.

[18] S. C. Johnson, "Hierarchical Clustering Schemes," *Psychometrika*, Vol. 32, 1967, pp. 241–254.

[19] C. H. Coombs, *A Theory of Data*, New York: Wiley, 1964.

[20] J. D. Carroll and J. J. Chang, "PREFMAP," in P. E. Green and F. J. Carmone (Eds.), *Multidimensional Scaling and Related Techniques in Market Analysis*, Boston: Allyn & Bacon, 1970.

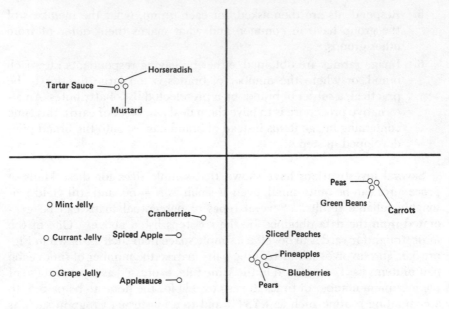

Figure 5.5.   Perceptual map of various food accompaniments

It should be pointed out that the types of maps mentioned thus far are *perceptual* maps. They are representations of the *descriptive* component of attitudes. That is one of the reasons that the procedures are robust and do not require large samples. Consumers tend to see brands quite similarly, at least in terms of their rankings on descriptive characteristics. For example, almost everyone familiar with Kent and Marlboro cigarettes considers Marlboro cigarettes stronger than Kents. This similarity of perceptual viewpoints is one of the reasons that brand images, once formed, are so difficult to change. The differences arise in the *evaluative* component. Although, as just noted, almost everyone considers Marlboro stronger than Kent, there is considerable disagreement about whether Marlboro is better than Kent. Some people feel that strength is affiliated with better flavor and is desirable. Others feel that mildness signifies less tar and nicotine and therefore is more desirable.

It is, of course, possible to develop *preference* maps as well as perceptual maps. Scaled overall preference or purchase intent ratings can be correlated, the correlations translated into distances, and the distances plotted on a map. Brands with similar preference patterns will then be grouped together on the map. Image data can again be superimposed for diagnostic help. However, preference maps appear to be less stable than perceptual

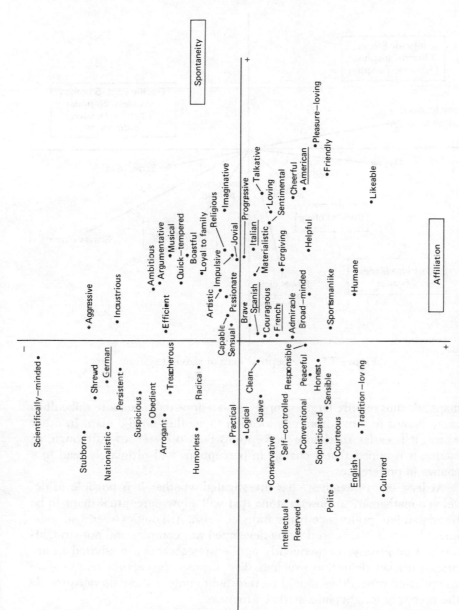

Figure 5.6. Perceptual map of country traits: affiliation versus spontaneity

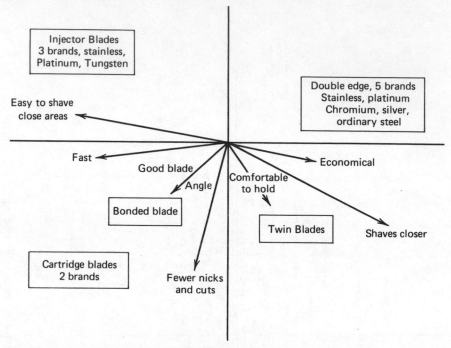

Figure 5.7. Perceptual map of shaving systems

maps and thus require larger samples. Also it appears to be more difficult to cause brands to move from one location to another on the map. In other words, it is easier to change perceptions than preferences—although, of course, it is hoped that a change in perceptions will ultimately lead to a change in preferences.

At least one researcher[21] has investigated whether it is possible to develop a mathematical Rosetta stone that will allow perceptual maps to be translated into preference maps and vice versa. Although Green had some limited success, the procedure he developed was complex and not straightforward intuitively. Consequently applied researchers are advised to approach market definition problems first through *perceptual* maps. More complicated procedures should be resorted to only if these do not provide the necessary insights into market structure.

Cluster analysis can be very helpful in deciding upon subcategories. As in the case of most multivariate techniques, a number of alternative algo-

[21] P. E. Green and F. J. Carmone, *Multidimensional Scaling in Marketing Analysis*, Boston: Allyn & Bacon, 1970.

rithms are available.[22-24] In instances where the results of one type of clustering are fuzzy, a second type is often worth trying, and sometimes even a third. No one algorithm is "best" for all configurations of data. To some extent there is safety in numbers. If several quite different clustering methods yield similar groupings, the analyst can be more confident about the results. Alternatively, split-half analyses can provide reassurance concerning the reliability of the solution. This involves randomly dividing the sample of respondents into two groups and applying the chosen clustering algorithm or algorithms to each separately to see if the same sorts of groupings emerge from both attempts.

Whatever the approach decided upon, it is likely that product class boundaries will be somewhat less than sharp and distinct. Consequently some judgment may be necessary in settling upon operational category definitions.

CHOOSING AN EFFECTIVE BUYING INCENTIVE

As mentioned earlier, one secret of effective marketing is concentrating efforts on high leverage points. At no time is this more critical than in the choice of a buying incentive. Effective communications are almost always what professionals call "single-minded." They focus on one key benefit to the exclusion of other benefits that the brand might reasonably claim for itself. There are several reasons for this:

A single focal point is likely to stimulate greater attention (see p. 154).

A single focal point is more likely to result in persuasion.[25]

People tend to stereotype brands as good for *one* particular situation or *one* type of person or as delivering *one* particular kind of benefit in a superior (or inferior way). Claims that the brand is good in several areas or, worse, good in every respect, are more easily dismissed as "just selling."

It is easier to support a single claim properly in a 30-second commercial than to attempt to deal with several simultaneously. Supported claims

[22] J. A. Hartigan, *Clustering Algorithms,* New York: Wiley, 1975.
[23] R. R. Sokal and P. H. A. Sneath, *Numerical Taxonomy,* San Francisco: Freeman, 1973.
[24] G. Punj and D. W. Steward, "Cluster Analysis in Marketing Research: Review and Suggestions for Application," *Journal of Marketing Research,* Vol. 20, May 1983, pp. 134–148.
[25] See J. G. Lynch, Jr. and T. K. Srull, "Memory and Attentional Factors in Consumer Choice: Concepts and Research Methods" *Journal of Consumer Research,* Vol. 9, No. 1, June 1982. pp. 18–37. They conclude that "Information about one attribute (A) has more effect on overall evaluations if it is presented alone than if it is accompanied by information about other attributes (B, C etc.)."

are less likely to be written off, especially if they are repeated consistently over the life of the brand.

Interest in the advertising of many products, especially package goods, is so low and people are bombarded by so much advertising that it is probably unreasonable to expect more than a single claim to register. This, of course, does not mean that focusing on a single benefit automatically guarantees effective communications, only that attemtping to cover several is likely to be self-defeating.

The term *benefit* is used here in the broad sense. The benefit can be a rational and cognitive one such as durability or an emotional or nonverbal one such as personality or lifestyle characteristics that are being expressed when the brand of interest is chosen. Benefits can be categorized into three general types:

1. What the product is. This concerns physical characteristics—what the product is made of, its ingredients, its color, its texture, its weight, and so on. Strictly speaking these are not benefits. When things such as these are emphasized in the advertising, however, it is usually because they imply benefits. Myers and Shocker have suggested that this category can be usefully subdivided into characteristics that can be measured on physical scales and those that require more subjective scaling (e.g., strong, spicy, all natural, inexpensive, etc.).[26]

Both types of product characteristics are descriptive in nature rather than evaluative. In other words, some people are likely to prefer presence of the characteristic and others are likely to prefer its absence.

Several systematic procedures, often involving correlations of benefit ratings and product ratings, have been developed for studying the links between physical characteristics and the benefits they imply.[27–30]

2. What the product does. This concerns the kinds of benefits delivered by the product in use—it is healthier, tastes better, lasts longer, acts faster,

[26] J. H. Myers and A. D. Shocker, "The Nature of Product-Related Attributes," *Research in Marketing*, Vol. 5, 1981, pp. 211–236.

[27] S. Young and B. Feigin, "Using the Benefit Chain for Improved Strategy Formulation," *Journal of Marketing*, Vol. 39, July 1975, pp. 72–74.

[28] J. H. Myers, "Benefit Structure Analysis: A New Tool for Product Planning," *Journal of Marketing*, Vol. 40, October 1976, pp. 23–32.

[29] H. Assael, *Consumer Behavior and Marketing Action, Attribution Theory*, Belmont, CA: Wadsworth, 1981, pp. 78–79.

[30] J. Gutman, "A Means-End Chain Model Based on Consumer Categorization Processes," *Journal of Marketing*, Vol. 46, Spring 1982, pp. 60–72.

dissolves more easily, and so on. Benefits are particularly relevant to "approach" products, products such as food and records that are bought primarily for their positive aspects.

Problem solving also fits into this category. Elimination of problems is a form of benefit delivery, although its proper measurement may require use of a different scale than the one used to measure benefits.[31] Problems are particularly relevant to "avoidance" products, products such as drugs and insurance where the focus is on eliminating negatives.

Occasionally what the product does is simply descriptive (e.g., makes lots of suds). In general, however, the performance benefits mentioned are ones everyone would like. Consequently they are evaluative in nature—the more the better—although with varying degrees of importance. Even in the case of descriptive performance (e.g., sudsing) the kinds of performances used in advertising are usually cues to related benefits.

3. How the product makes you feel. This category is intended to cover all sorts of emotional benefits. They are usually communicated nonverbally. This category has received far less attention historically than the two preceding categories. There are signs of increasing interest in nonverbal communications, however, and it is expected that this deficiency will be, to a large extent, remedied during the next decade or so.[32, 33] The work of Albert Mehrabian, although dealing largely with interpersonal communications, suggests that nonverbal communications are more important than verbal communications.[34, 35] It seems likely that we will discover this is true for advertising as well—that the messages communicated by the setting, the casting, the music, the colors, the pacing, and so on, are at least as important as the cognitive messages that have been the center of so much copytesting.

One form of emotional benefit is what has been called "sensory benefits"—sensations associated with the five senses—sound, sight, smell, taste, and touch. Strong sensations in each of these areas can be evoked by the sight, sound, and motion of television and by parallel mechanisms in other media.

A second form of emotional benefit is the way consumers feel when they

---

[31] E. E. Norris, "Your Surefire Clue to Ad Success: Seek Out the Consumer's Problem," *Advertising Age*, March 17, 1975, p. 43.

[32] J. Plummer and R. Holman, "Communicating to the Heart and/or Mind," American Psychological Association, Annual Conference, August 28, 1981, Los Angeles.

[33] R. I. Haley, "Benefit Segmentation—20 Years Later," American Marketing Association, Attitude Research Conference, Palm Springs, February 1983.

[34] A. Mehrabian, *Nonverbal Communication*, Chicago: Aldine, 1972.

[35] A. Mehrabian, *Silent Messages*, Belmont, CA: Wadsworth, 1971.

buy, use, or sometimes simply when they own the product of interest. These sensations are sometimes measured by adjective checklists,[36-39] which include adjectives such as secure, happy, carefree, proud, and so on.

Another subclassification under this category is what has sometimes been called "affiliative (or association) benefits.[40] These deal primarily with the reputation of the manufacturer or of the retailer, selling the product (e.g., Another fine product by GE; Babies are our business . . . our only business—Gerber; When you care enough to send the very best—Hallmark; Nobody undersells Gimbels; etc.). It can spill over to the way people feel about the company and, specifically, its advertising. If people admire it—its style and content—they are likely to retain these feelings to the point of purchase.

Finally, there is user imagery. Choice products that are consumed in social situations reveal something about the chooser. They help to reinforce self-images. Is he or she young, independent, hard working, intelligent, friendly, concerned with his or her family, devil-may-care, or what? Depending on the extent to which persons in the market target are concerned with favorable opinions of other people (other-directed) or dependent upon thinking well of themselves (inner-directed), advertising situations can be tailored to deliver the appropriate benefits.

CHOICE CRITERIA

Several criteria are helpful in making a choice between the many buying incentives that are available to a brand. Among the more helpful are:

Perceived Importance.   This can measured in a variety of ways (see pp. 87–90).

Supportability.   The advertised brand must be able to deliver the benefit around which the central buying incentive is built, preferably in a way that is superior to that of brands identified as primary competitors. One way in which the ability to do this can be determined is to compare the

[36] W. Wells, "EQ, Son of EQ and the Reaction Profile," *Journal of Marketing*, Vol. 28, No. 4, October 1964, pp. 45–52.

[37] W. Wells, C. Leavitt, and M. McConville, "A Reaction Profile for TV Commercials," *Journal of Advertising Research*, Vol. 11, No. 6, December 1971, pp. 11–17.

[38] C. Leavitt, "A Multidimensional Set of Rating Scales for TV Commercials," *Journal of Applied Psychology*, Vol. 54, No. 5, October 1970, pp. 427–429.

[39] C. Leavitt, C. Waddell, and W. Wells, "Improving Day After Recall Techniques," *Journal of Advertising Research*, Vol. 10, No. 3, June 1970, pp. 13–17.

[40] Sense and Nonsense in Creative Research, Grey Advertising, Inc., New York, June 1962, N. Kominik (ed.)

image ratings of regular users of the brand of interest with parallel ratings of regular users of the principal competitors. If ratings of the potential buying incentive are higher for the advertised brand than for its competitors, the claim is supportable. In other words, if people are led to try the brand on the basis of claimed superiority on a particular benefit, they will find that the claim is true and thus will be encouraged to continue to purchase the brand. The reverse also holds. If people try a product on the basis of an advertising claim and find that the claim is false, they are not likely to buy again. Moreover, they may complain to friends, retailers, or media, resulting in adverse word-of-mouth and publicity for the brand. Finally, once people have rejected a brand, it is extremely difficult to convince them to try it again.

Vulnerability.   Vulnerability is the opposite side of the supportability coin. It refers to the situation in which a leading competitor, often the leading brand in the product class, has an image area in which it is not particularly strong. Thus products that taste good may be vulnerable in the area of calories, soaps that clean the skin may leave it dry, appliances that are extremely durable may be extremely expensive, and so on.

Believability.   Believability refers to the compatibility of the possible buying incentive with the image of the product or company. Thus it is difficult for consumers to believe that Montgomery Ward can be a fashion leader, that Timex can be a leader in the premium-priced solid state watch market, and that wine connoisseurs find domestic wines superior to more expensive imports. Efforts to convince people otherwise are likely to be wasteful for brands with established images. Lack of believability is not always a negative, however; sometimes it can stimulate consumers to try the product just to check the claim. Whether or not they buy again then hinges on product performance.

Uniqueness.   This refers to the popularity of the claim among competitors. It is usually easier for the only brand making a particular claim to attract attention for its claim and for consumers to associate it with this brand. If all brands are saying much the same thing, it is easy for consumers to screen out the claim entirely, because it lacks news value. Even when it is screened in, processing activity is likely to be minimal and message recipients may be confused as to which brand is making the claim.

A related consideration is preemption. Sometimes a brand becomes so strongly associated with a particular claim that whenever anyone makes it, it is likely to be mistakenly attributed to the originator of the claim. Thus, for example, it would be extremely difficult for any brand other than Wisk to claim removal of rings around shirt collars without having a sizable portion of the audience thinking of Wisk, if not actually thinking that the advertising was being sponsored by Wisk. The claim has been preempted and is not available to other brands without an unaffordable cost and a great deal of time.

Leverage. Leverage refers to the extent to which the chosen benefit is related to overall attitudes toward the brand. For example, Figures 5.8 and 5.9 show two cross-tabulations of image characteristics with overall attitudes. In each figure the totals for the first row show that the number of respondents considering the product to be superior to competition on an overall basis is 40. This is because both figures are based on the same set of survey respondents. Consequently the number of people who do not consider it to be superior is 60 in both figures.

The column totals differ, however, because although both figures are based on the same respondents, Figure 5.8 shows their ratings of taste and Figure 5.9 shows their ratings of nutrition. Fifty people consider the brand

| | | Taste | | |
		Superior to competition	Not superior to competition	
Overall rating	Superior to competition	20	20	40
	Not superior to competition	30	30	60
		50	50	

Figure 5.8. Relationship of taste to overall rating

| | | Nutrition | | |
		Superior to competition	Not superior to competition	
Overall rating	Superior to competition	40	0	40
	Not superior to competition	0	60	60
		40	60	

Figure 5.9. Relationship of nutrition to overall rating

to be superior on taste, whereas only 40 consider it to be superior on nutrition.

From this it is tempting to conclude that, other things being equal, it would be better to emphasize taste than nutrition. However, the interior distribution of respondents in Figure 5.8 suggests that this would be a mistake. If the 50 people who do not consider the brand superior to competition on taste are examined, it is apparent that 20 of them feel the brand is superior to competition on an overall basis. In other words, among people who do not consider the brand superior on taste the probability of their preferring the brand overall is .40.

Now let us look at those who *do* rate the brand superior on taste. Again there are 50 of them and again 20 rate the brand superior overall. Thus the probability of rating the brand superior on an overall basis is also .40 among these people. Consequently the effort of convincing people that the brand has superior taste does not appear worthwhile. It seems that it would not improve overall attitudes and hence the likelihood that the brand would be purchased.

Now apply a similar line of reasoning to Figure 5.9. There are 60 people who do not believe that the brand is superior on nutrition. None of them believe the brand to be superior on an overall basis. In other words, the probability of their believing it to be superior overall is zero. Only 40 people believe the brand to be superior on nutrition. All of them believe the brand to be superior overall, however, a probability of 1.00. Thus the effort to change people's attitudes toward the brands' nutrition appears to be well justified. The probability of liking the brand overall would be increased from .00 to 1.00. Nutrition has leverage, whereas taste does not. Therefore, on this criterion at least, and assuming that one attitude can be changed as easily as another, nutrition is a better choice than taste.

Leverage in this sort of figure can be calculated simply. If the cells are labeled as in Figure 5.10, the formula is simply $L = \dfrac{(AD - BC)}{(AD + BC)}$ and the resultant numbers will have a range of from +1.00 to −1.00.

For scales of more than the two points into which responses are divided in this example, the correlation coefficient and/or the partial correlation

A	B
C	D

Figure 5.10.   How to calculate leverage.

coefficient can also be used as measures of leverage (as can still other measures of association[41]).

Although leverage appears to be a simple concept, a word of caution is necessary for those who are considering employing it. Leverage analysis is a correlation approach. It relates aspects of the brand image to a criterion measure such as buying intent, overall attitude, purchase, or purchase frequency. It is normally assumed that the higher the correlation between, for example, an image characteristic and the criterion measure the more important that characteristic is in influencing the criterion. In other words, it is assumed that causality extends from the individual characteristics to the criterion measure.

Although this may be true most of the time, it is not always true. Sometimes causation extends from the overall evaluation back to the individual characteristics. An example will serve to illustrate this sort of situation.

Let us assume that we would like to apply leverage analysis to the choice of a buying incentive for a pvesidential candidate. In other words, we would like to know what kinds of issues are having the most impact on whether or not people are favorably inclined toward our candidate. To do this we have decided to survey prospective voters using an "excellent" to "poor" scale, with "overall opinion" as our criterion measure.

First we ask people to rate the domestic policies of our candidate and, if our candidate is well known, respondents are able to do this without difficulty. Next we ask them to rate his foreign policy. Again, no trouble. Now we ask the respondents to rate how well he treats his children. This time they are not sure. If they like our candidate, they will probably assume that he treats his children well and give him a high rating on that characteristic. If they don't like him, they will tend to rate him correspondingly lower.

When the leverage analysis is conducted, correlating ratings in each of these areas with the overall rating of the candidate, results may well suggest that the way the candidate treats his children has more effect on whether people are favorably inclined toward him than his stands on domestic or international issues.

Admittedly this is an extreme example, but the principle that it illustrates is valid. When brand images are measured, people's overall attitudes inevitably affect their ratings of individual charcteristics to some extent, the so-called *halo effect*. Of course, how they feel about individual characteristics affects their overall opinions as well. The problem is how to avoid being misled by reverse causal influences.

One useful rule relates to the extent to which consumers can be assumed

[41] R. R. Jones and L. R. Goldberg, "Interrelationships among Personality Scale Parameters: Item Response Stability and Scale Reliability," *Educational and Psychological Measurement*, Summer 1967, pp. 323–333.

to have enough information at their disposal to make rational judgments. When they do not have information, people in an interview situation are very likely to guess. And their guesses are strongy colored by their overall attitudes.

How then can we be sure that the concept of leverage has relevance to the choice of a buying incentive? One way is to examine the extent to which leverage scores correlate with straightforward "importance" or "desirability" ratings of benefits. Although we would not expect a perfect correspondence between generic importance ratings and leverage scores (if there were we would certainly not use both measures), it is reasonable to assume that there should be broad similarities between them.

To test this idea, 10 studies were selected for examination. Image items were factor analyzed in each study and the ranking of the generic importance scores of each factor was compared with the corresponding leverage scores for those factors. Results were as follows:

Shampoo Study. Five of six factors show good agreement. The exception was the "cleaning" factor, the factor with the highest importance score. Because cleaning is a basic requirement for the existence of a brand, the variance associated with that item was relatively low. Other factors showed more brand discrimination and were more likely to be choice criteria.

Phonograph Record Study. Although the top leverage score also got the highest importance rating and the second ranking leverage factor ranked third in the generic set, agreement was looser here. An emotional factor had a high generic rank but showed little leverage. Presumably this is because record labels are not differentiated in this area.

Cigarette Study. Genrally good agreement. The exception was packaged appearance, which had a low importance rating but high leverage.

Salt Study. Here the leverage scores were not significantly different from one another. It was felt that images of salt brands were not sharply differentiated, salt being viewed mainly as a commodity.

Facial Tissue. Virtually complete agreement between leverage scores and generic importance ratings all the way down the line.

Laxative Study. Not much agreement. High leverage items tended to be in the middle of the generic importance rankings. This was attributed to a lack of brand differences on higher rated generic items.

Hair Preparation Study. Good agreement. The exception was the "not harmful to hair" factor. This had high importance but low leverage. No brands were seen as harmful to the hair.

First Gasoline Study. Generally good agreement. Top generic factors are also top leverage points. However, "clean stations" has more leverage than generic importance. This is intuitively plausible.

Second Gasoline Study (two years later).   Good agreement. In line with first study, suggesting that both generic importance and leverage are slow to change.

Stockings.   Five of six factors agreed on the basis of ranks. The sixth is "fit." Again brand variance on fit was comparatively low.

Summing up, in eight of the 10 studies leverage scores and importance ratings were found to be significantly related to each other. In the remaining two studies results could be rationalized with little trouble.

Several factors appear to have a bearing on leverage scores. For them to be high on a particular factor, people must discriminate on that factor and their discrimination must be related to their overall evaluations. Low scores can result either from lack of discrimination or from the fact that the discrimination which does occur is not systematically related to the criterion measure.

Low leverage scores by no means rule out the choice of an item as the buying incentive. They simply reflect respondents' *current* perceptions. If low leverage is coupled with high generic importance, it suggests tlat a major opportunity exists if R&D can come up with a readily perceivable product advantage in that area. This, of course, is doubly true if there is also evidence of customer dissatisfaction in the area under review.

In attempting to apply the foregoing criteria for choosing a buying incentive, it becomes apparent that they do not always point to the same choices. It is normal for some to indicate that one buying incentive is likely to be superior and for others to suggest other choices. So in this, as in all marketing decisions, marketing judgment comes into play. Some criteria must be given more weight than others. And market conditions not reflected by the criteria must be taken into consideration. It is advisable to review data relating to this decision with the entire communications team before a final choice is made. Especially in situations where the choice is not clear-cut the enthusiasm of creative people for one alternative over another can be the most important factor in market success. The importance of choosing the perfect buying incentive can easily be superseded by the likelihood of achieving superior executions and follow-through.

SELECTING A MARKET TARGET

We have emphasized that one key to successful marketing is finding areas of high potential responsiveness and concentrating effort upon them. Targeting is clearly one of the areas to which this principle applies most strongly.

It is easy to be wasteful and to invest communications dollars in areas that are unlikely to be productive. Even today many companies believe that they are aiming their communications efforts at the entire market. What they are really saying is that they do not know who is likely to respond, but that they hope that someone will. Proper research is an investment that no large company can afford to ignore.

It is apparent that all markets are segmented. A company can, if it wishes, ignore that fact. However, this does not change the situation; it only means that the company is willing to waste money. This is not necessarily vitally damaging, especially if all of its competitors are looking at the market similarly. Moreover to some extent good products can overcome inefficient marketing policies and find their own markets.

The situation changes significantly, however, when one company knows and understands the major segments that exist in its market and develops its marketing strategy on the basis of that understanding. Then the firm that blithely assumes it is marketing to everyone is highly vulnerable. Segments, the existence of which had not been suspected, can form the base for successful new campaigns. And as a result of communications that speak directly to them and that cater to their needs, other segments can shift their purchase patterns to brands which seem to offer the kinds of satisfactions they are seeking. Attrition can be sudden or gradual, but the end result is the same. Brands that do not understand their markets and that do not anticipate and keep pace with the changes which, given enough time, always take place, will inevitably lose share when more knowledgeable and astute competitors become interested in their markets.

Particularly dangerous is the tendency to think in terms of an average consumer and to try to design a product to fit his or her needs. For example, it is obvious that iced tea is a very popular drink. Hot tea is also a popular drink. Using total market logic, then, the perfect product should be a lukewarm tea! Of course, in many markets the structure is not quite this obvious. It is even true that in quite a few markets a product that fits the average pattern of consumer wants and desires also meets the needs of a sizable market segment. Even in these markets, however, segmentation opportunities often exist for brands that can be content with less than a dominant market position. They can leave the center of the market to the leading brand and profitably dominate a smaller market segment, one whose needs are not well met by the leading brand.[42]

In many markets it is difficult to guess the nature of the important market segments from knowledge of the total market. For example, one study of the gasoline market done a number of years ago is summarized in Table 5.2.

---

[42] C. Y. Woo and A. S. Cooper, "The Surprise Case for Low Market Share," Vol. 60, No. 6, *Harvard Business Review*, November–December 1982, p. 106ff.

TABLE 5.2 Importance of Gasoline Benefits, by Segment (average importance = 100)

Factor	Total Market	Segment 1 "Everything"	Segment 2 "Gasoline Performance"	Segment 3 "Location"	Segment 4 "Reassurance"	Segment 5 "Brand"	Segment 6 "Price"
Gasoline performance	237	144	784	262	69	363	148
Convenient location	186	153	55	621	144	147	160
Personal reassurance	165	129	160	52	469	76	102
Friendly attendants	156	130	117	190	283	162	136
Clean station appearance	142	178	101	123	67	63	69
Car repair	136	162	69	26	226	13	69
Well-known brand	114	115	23	38	23	601	67
Conscientious service	69	93	39	20	56	9	42
Know owner	69	92	12	39	66	11	27
Price	66	94	18	46	23	11	519
Giveaways/games	50	59	55	38	28	13	74
Charge cards	48	68	32	28	11	0	26
Availability of TBA	30	42	11	14	18	11	17
Gasoline additives/ingredients	26	33	24	3	12	20	38
Tire value	6	8	0	0	5	0	6

It shows the profile of benefits sought by each of six major market segments. Had a gasoline advertiser decided that his market target was the entire market, and had the foregoing profile of the benefits sought by the total market been available to him, he might have decided to focus the advertising copy on gasoline performance with supporting information on his many convenient locations. In doing so he would be likely to miss all six market segments.

The "Everything" segment is best addressed in terms of the cue of clean station appearance. Car repair is perhaps not a compatible benefit. The "Gasoline Performance" segment should attend messages emphasizing that benefit but is not likely to be persuaded by them unless they are presented in an environment involving personal reassurance. The "Location" segment is interested in the same two benefits that are at the top of the "Total Market" rankings, but in reverse order. Consequently, convenience should be the primary message communicated to this segment.

The "Reassurance" segment wants personal reassurance and friendly attendants. The "Brand" segment wants a well-known brand whose gasoline can be counted upon to perform well. And the "Price" segment, as the label suggests, is primarily interested in obtaining a relatively low price. So a combination emphasizing gasoline performance with secondary emphasis on convenience is not perfectly tailored to any segment. Although such messages would undoubtedly be seen by some people and could favorably influence their behavior, they are likely to be less efficient than messages that are custom tailored to the known interests of one of the six segments.

Lack of knowledge of underlying segmentation can be damaging in other ways. For example, one brand of freeze-dried coffee got off to a fast start only to find its leading competitor rapidly overtaking it. When they had fallen behind by a share ratio of 10% to 14% for the competitor, they made an all-out effort to ascertain the basic causes of their problem.

Their first hunches were that there might be some crucial weakness in the product itself. However, the product had been developed from a series of very careful taste tests and appeared, at worst, to be a parity product. Moreover, thousands of respondents had been tested subsequent to the introduction and they too suggested that the product was not the cause of the failure of the brand to meet sales goals.

Their next thought was that the trouble might lie in the advertising. But heavy pressure had already been brought to bear on the agency, the campaign had been changed significantly several times, and no sales strength had been observed following copy changes.

Pricing, sales promotion, and distribution were fully competitive, and although there was some speculation that the package might be a weak spot, no one felt that the observed sales differences could be caused by differences in package design.

At this point the results of a major segmentation study became available and four segments with quite different patterns of wants were uncovered. When the next taste test was conducted, respondents were coded into the four segments identified by the segmentation study.[43] One of those segments was the obvious target for the new product. It was not price conscious (the new product was premium priced), preferred stronger coffee (the new product was above average in strength), and in general had a benefit profile that was in line with what the product could reasonably be expected to deliver. In this segment, however, the taste of the product was judged to be significantly inferior to that of the competitor. The loss in the key segment was counterbalanced by wins in other segments, making the product, in total, look like a parity product. However, the probability of purchasing the product was notably lower in the segments other than the target segment. In other words, if people were weighted by their probability of purchase, the reason for the 14/10 share shortfall became clear. The product, as then formulated, was, in fact, an inferior product.

In another case an extensive concept test was conducted for six new product concepts. One of these was a product for which the marketing team had high hopes. Consequently, it was tested at two price levels. The research design, therefore, called for seven monadic cells of 500 respondents each. In other words, each respondent was exposed to one and only one concept.

When the results of the test became available, the marketing group was amazed to find that the sales potential for the product tested at two price levels was greater at the higher price level than at the lower. Rationalizations were quickly developed around the hypothesis that price was an indicator of quality. It was hypothesized that there was a larger market for a premium-priced product than for one priced at the level of the average product on the market.

Fortunately, benefit profiles had been measured in the course of the research, and so it was possible to develop benefit segments and to analyze the market from that perspective. When the segments were tabulated, an obvious target for the product emerged. The product offered important health benefits and one segment was clearly health conscious. It was apparent, however, that the segment of interest was not evenly distributed across the seven monadic subgroups. One contained substantially more of these people than the remaining six. Unfortunately, the subgroup with the superabundance of health-oriented people was also the one that had evaluated the higher-priced health concept. In fact it contained fully 50% more health-oriented people than the sample which had evaluated the lower-

---

[43] One by-product of a segmentation study is formulas for classifying new respondents into the segments identified in the study (see p. 352).

priced concept. When the samples were corrected[44] for this imbalance, it was seen that the lower price level actually had greater potential than the higher price level, a result that was in line with the anticipations of the marketing staff before the research had been launched.

A final example may be helpful in highlighting the risks of looking at total markets or "average" consumers. It concerns the Corning Glass Works and their highly successful introduction of the Corelle and Expressions lines of dinnerware, especially the pattern selection problem.

Obviously patterns are a crucial element in the sales success of any dinnerware line. To obtain measures of the relative appeal of possible patterns, Corning had regularly exposed candidate patterns to the large numbers of consumers touring the Glass Center in Corning, New York. To avoid regional biases, people were weighted according to their places of residence. Thus because there were fewer of them, the opinions of visitors from California were given greater weight than the opinions of those from New York State. Consequently the sample used was balanced geograhically to approximate the national distribution of consumers.

The evaluation procedure was straightforward. Visitors were shown several designs and asked about their preferences, and the patterns that received the most favorable ratings were chosen as the ones to be manufactured. Initially four different designs were offered for sale as a result of this kind of selection process.

To make the problem clear let us assume that eight designs were under consideration and that only two of them could be made. The original Corning procedure would involve submitting the eight designs to its sample of respondents and manufacturing the two winners. This design is intuitively logical and frequently used.

Now, however, let us assume that a study has been made of pattern types and pattern preferences. To keep things simple let us assume that two basic pattern types have been discovered, and let us call the two types "formal" and "informal." Additionally, let's assume that two-thirds of the population prefers formal dinnerware patterns and only one-third prefers informal patterns. Moreover, let us assume that each segment—those who prefer formal designs and those who prefer informal designs—has strong preferences. Under these circumstances, Corning might have greater sales volume from marketing the patterns ranking second and fourth of the eight tested rather than marketing those ranking first and second. This is *not* intuitively obvious; however, it may very well be correct.

If all respondents are forced to evaluate all patterns, the informal patterns will never be chosen. Only one-third of the population prefer that style and they will always be outvoted by the two-thirds who prefer formal

[44] Sample balancing program; Marketmath, Inc., 1860 Broadway, New York City.

patterns. But the problem is even more serious. When the people who prefer informal patterns are asked to evaluate formal patterns, they are likely to rate the most informal of the formal patterns as the most attractive. However, this is *not* likely to be the pattern preferred by the segment who will actually buy formal designs. They prefer very simple designs. In fact, they are likely to consider pure white as one of the best alternatives available.

When the votes of the people who prefer formal designs are combined with those who prefer informal designs, the winning designs are compromise designs that are not completely satisfactory to either segment. Thus if the formal segment prefers the design that ranks second in the combined vote, and if the informal segment prefers the design that ranks fourth, those two designs (when only two designs can be offered) are almost certain to generate more sales volume than would be generated by offering the designs ranking first and second.

Returning to real-world situations, the original Corning design testing procedure had produced four Corelle designs which were very similar, differing primarily in terms of their colors. Although these were popular designs and sold very well, they were all what is known in the trade as "rim designs" (see Figure 5.11), which consist of borders of small flowers or lines

Figure 5.11. A typical rim design

Figure 5.12. An "Expressions" design

around the rim of plates. Thus the tastes of people preferring patterns that extend across the entire plate were not being served.

Research showed that, not only was this latter group a sizable group, they were willing to pay premium prices for designs that matched their wants. Accordingly a second line of four designs called "Expressions" was introduced (see Figure 5.12) and it has been highly successful. Sales goals have been met and because they carried larger profit margins, overall profit margins were increased. Moreover by extending their offerings to a segment not previously covered, Corning lines were made less vulnerable to new product introductions by competitors.

As a result of the segmentation research, design testing procedures were also modified. Consumers are now screened for the types of designs they prefer and are asked to evaluate only designs of types that are reasonable purchase possibilities. In other words, people are segmented by design preferences and shown designs that are compatible with their preferences.

CRITERIA FOR SEGMENT SELECTION

Once a segmentation study has been conducted and the segments have been enumerated and described, the first step in selecting an appropriate market target is to array alternatives possibilities and to assess the relative assets and liabilities of concentrating efforts on each. Alternative modes of segmentation have already been discussed. In general, causal segmentation schemes (segments based on benefits sought, problems experienced, occasions of use, or category beliefs) are likely to be more successful means of uncovering potentially responsive subgroups, and thus more attractive targets, than are descriptive segmentation schemes (segments based on demographic or behavioral characteristics). Schemes based on lifestyles or values are likely to fall somewhere in the middle. Lifestyles are less proximate than benefits but generally more relevant than demographics. However, no generalities hold completely; each case must be judged on its own merits. Sometimes demographics are an effective mode of segmentation,[45] and it is often discrete to segment the market in several ways before making a final decision as to the best target available.

It may be well to comment upon one frequent misconception before proceeding with the discussion of criteria for segment selection. Many people believe that selecting a target segment means foregoing the possibility of obtaining sales from other segments, but this is by no means true. Even when message segmentation is done perfectly there will be substantial spillover in message delivery from the target segment to other segments. This is likely to stimulate sales among those people to some extent, even if only through increasing brand salience. Also, although segments are often treated as though they are discrete and mutually exclusive, this is done only to simplify the analysis. In point of fact, segments almost always overlap, especially when they are defined by more than a single variable, as is usually the case. Thus any marketing effort aimed at one segment will necessarily draw sales from other segments as well. The purpose of targeting is not to limit sales to people in the target segment, but rather to maximize response to a fixed amount of marketing effort by concentrating it in areas where responsiveness is likely to be highest and accepting lower responses in areas where generating response is relatively difficult.

Returning to the criteria for selecting the best possible targets, the principal ones are size considerations and the probability of generating sales. Each of these is discussed below.

Size Considerations

Other things being equal, larger segments are more attractive than smaller ones. Size in this context is measured by volume of consumption rather than

---

[45] For example, age is one of the most effective variables for segmenting the market for popular music. Each age group appears to have developed its own unique musical tastes.

by head count. A related concern is the size of the core group of the segment. It is common practice to assign all members of the population to one of the segments being analyzed. As in the case of overlapping segments this is done as a convenience—to simplify the analysis rather than to provide a perfectly accurate description of the population. The result of this procedure is that some segment members are prototypical, whereas others are assigned to the segments simply because they bear a stronger relationship to the members of that segment than to members of other segments.

Prototypical segment members are called the "core group." Theoretically at least, the members of the core group can be reached simultaneously by a message perfectly tailored to their needs and interests. Segment members who are not in the core group are presumably less likely to respond to the message because their needs and interests are less homogeneous. They are more accessible to messages aimed at the core group of their segment, however, than to messages aimed at the core groups of other segments. Some analysts have suggested that measures of segment homogeneity are also measures of core group size.[46]

Because the interests of segments overlap, and because the extent of overlap varies, it is also desirable to estimate the spillover of messages aimed at one segment to others. Sometimes the choice of one segment as the market target makes it possible to include compatible supplementary messages in the communications, and thus broaden the reach to other segments without diluting the impact of the central message. The message and the interests of the segment interact. Consequently, the idea of broadening the reach of the message can be pursued either inductively (from research on the segments to assumptions about reactions to the message) or deductively (from standard copy research on reactions to the message to assumptions about segment appeal based on knowledge of the market segments).

Probability of Generating Sales

Segments vary in the extent to which they can be expected to provide incremental sales to the advertised brand. Two questions are involved: (1) How likely are they to attend to the communications and (2) given that they attend the communications, how likely are they to change their buying behavior? The answers to these questions are, to a large extent, subjective. Fortunately, in many cases the problem of selecting a target segment is a simple one because one segment is obviously preferable to the others. Where there is a question between two or more segments, each of which is

[46] D. Chittenden, "Simigraph: A Fresh Approach to the Definition and Description of Market Segments," *Journal of the Market Research Society*, Vol. 13, No. 1, January 1971, p. 1–7.

attractive, the following information can be helpful in the selection process:
With respect to attending to the message:

1. The brand image profile will document the kinds of buying incentives that are supportable.
2. Profiles of benefits sought, problems experienced, occasions of use, beliefs, lifestyles, and/or values are indicative of the kinds of executions that will cause members of a segment to turn on their minds.
3. The higher the level of category involvement the greater the likelihood of attending messages concerning it. Involvement can be measured directly, by asking people about their levels of interest, or indirectly. Indirect measures include volume of usage (higher levels usually signify greater involvement), the number of benefits desired (people who are involved in the category regularly indicate interest in a greater range of benefits than those who are not), and perceived level of brand differences (people who consider all brands the same are likely to be uninvolved).
4. The more favorable people are to the advertised brand, product, or service, the more likely they are to attend messages relating to it. Favorability can be measured directly via attitude rating scales or indirectly through measures of awareness trial and usage.

With respect to the probability of changing buying behavior, just as there are a number of measures that are indicative of attention to the message, so too there are a number of measures that relate to the likelihood of a behavioral change.

1. Persuasibility is a research topic of long standing in psychology. Some studies[47] suggest a U-shaped relation between measures of self-confidence and persuasibility. People with low self-confidence are not persuasible because of concern that they will be fooled. People with high self-confidence like to make their own decisions and, similarly, are difficult to persuade. Consequently people with moderate levels of self-confidence represent the most attractive targets. Measures of risk-taking styles may also be helpful in identifying persuasible segments.

2. A more relevant set of measures is those relating to brand-switching behavior. Segments in which people tend to buy the same brand over and

---

[47] J. A. Barach, "Self-Confidence and Reactions to TV Commercials," in D. F. Cox (Ed.), *Risk Taking and Information Handling in Consumer Behavior*, Boston: Division of Research, Graduate School of Business Administration, Harvard University, 1967.

over are less likely to be persuaded to make behavioral changes than segments that exhibit a considerable amount of switching behavior. To some extent, however, this can be offset by behavior after they try the brand of interest. People who were loyal to their old brand may be inclined to be relatively loyal to the new brand as well, whereas people who regularly switch brands may be very difficult to retain once attracted. A number of measures of brand loyalty and brand switching are available. One of the best has been suggested by Moran.[48] The constant sum scale can also be used for this purpose, as can the simple expedient of asking people the brand bought last and the brand bought the time before that.

Another measure relating to the probability of behavioral change is the firmness with which current attitudes are held. This can be estimated by checking reliability of overall attitudes measured at different points in the interview, by estimating halo effects,[49] or by bombarding attitudes with competing messages and seeing how much they change.[50]

An alternative approach is to compare profiles of current users with those of members of the segments under consideration. The assumption here is that the more similar prospects are to current users, the more likely they are to be converted. Ogilvy & Mather, for example, has formalized a procedure utilizing the logistic function for scoring individuals in terms of their similarity to current users.

Still another approach is one called "Directed Targeting," recently developed by the author. If it is in fact true that (1) every advertisement selects its audience by the way in which it is constructed, and (2) the benefits communicated by the advertisement are the single most important factor in determining which individuals are likely to turn on their minds when exposed to the advertising, then, given the availability of a Benefit Segmentation (Market Strategy) study, it is possible to:

Do a competitive "double difference"[51] analysis to identify a few benefits that are important and which the brand of interest can support better than, or at least as well as, competing brands.

---

[48] W. T. Moran, "Consumer Nondurables: A New Chapter Opens," The Conference Board Record, November 1975, pp. 57–60.
[49] Beckwith, Kassarjian and Lehmann, "Halo Effects in Marketing Research."
[50] S. B. Shiller, "Accelerated Attrition," *Journal of Advertising Research*, Vol. 21, No. 1, February 1981, pp. 51–57.
[51] Double difference analysis consists of, for the image element under consideration, first computing the difference between the brand rating on that element versus the average rating of all elements. This is done for competing brands as well. Then the resultant scores for competing brands on the key image element are subtracted from the score of the brand of interest to obtain the double difference score.

Through cross-tabs identify the individuals who are interested in the indicated set of benefits.

Reduce the size of the segment by eliminating people who are not favorable to the brand of interest.

Examining the resulting segment to assess its attractiveness.

If the segment is attractive, it is almost certainly available. If not, the preceding process can be repeated with a somewhat different set of benefits and the results again evaluated.

SIX

Conducting Attitude Segmentation Research

By the time this book appears in print it will be well over 20 years since the first full-scale Benefit Segmentation was conducted.[1] The methods that have been employed, and their extensions into lifestyles, beliefs, problems, values, and other universes of content have followed the classical learning curve. A few pioneering studies were done in the mid-1960s, largely by advertising agencies. There was a sharp upsurge in interest in the approach in the late 1960s and in the number of studies done. By the early 1970s the statistical segmentation of markets using scaled ratings had assumed a fad status. Almost without exception all major advertisers had done one or more segmentation studies and were attempting to use the results to improve their market situations. For many reasons this was frequently a disappointing and frustrating experience. Some companies concluded that the method was not worth the investment of time and money that it required, and abandoned it. Others, however, continued to use the general approach, although perhaps conducting such studies at a reduced rate. As recently as 1980 an informal poll showed that 18 of 20 leading companies had conducted at least one segmentation study in the preceding 12 months.[2] And still more recent polls[3] show that market strategy studies are once again on the rise. So, this seems an appropriate time to take stock of the approach

[1] R. I. Haley, "Experimental Research on Attitudes Toward Shampoos," unpublished paper, New York, Grey Advertising, 1961.
[2] Workshop Group, Conference on New Research Techniques, Sarasota, Florida, February 17–20, 1980.
[3] "Inflation Adjusted Spending is on Rise for Consumer Research," *Marketing News*, May 27, 1983, p. 13.

131

and assign it to its proper place among other useful marketing research approaches.

One way of accomplishing this is to examine the reasons for past failures so that they can be avoided in future attempts to apply the Benefit Segmentation approach to the problem of developing effective communications strategies. The problems can be grouped under:

Failure to organize properly for the study

Failure to define objectives clearly

Unrealistic expectations concerning the nature of the study and its results

Technical research shortcomings

Incorrect interpretation of results

Inadequate follow-through

Each of these will be dealt with in the following sections.

ORGANIZING FOR A SEGMENTATION STUDY

When segmentation studies were introduced, they were considered to be almost wholly within the province of the research department. They involved a variety of multivariate techniques, and most brand managers and account executives had neither the training nor the inclination to deal with them. Consequently, aside from some negotiations about cost, which affected both questionnaire length and sample size, and attempts to shorten time requirements (usually six to nine months), responsibility for conducting and interpreting the study lay totally with research departments. A team of from two to five analysts was assigned to the project, and when results were available they were presented with great fanfare and highly professional charts, often in slide form, to a mixed audience of client and agency executives. Presentations took between 4 and 8 hours, culminating in the conclusions and practical implications of the study as seen by the research department. Questions from the floor were entertained and there was a substantial amount of discussion concerning the changes in creative strategy that were inevitably suggested by the findings. Because they were so carefully orchestrated, the presentations of research results were almost invariably considered successful. Then for the research team it was "on to the next study," while the marketing and creative executives were left with the task of implementing the agreed-upon implications of the study. It was assumed that once the creative strategy had been decided upon the job of delivering advertising executions that incorporated it was fairly straightforward.

This turned out to be an incorrect assumption for a number of reasons. Most creative people are not trained to work with data. Segmentation studies always produced huge and threatening quantities of data, too much to permit creative people to make an independent review of the process leading up to the recommendations. Moreover in many agencies, the creative people are not in frequent contact with the research people and thus had no friendly expert to consult when questions arose. When they didn't understand the implications of the research or when they lacked emotional conviction that the research was pointing them in the direction of better advertising, their natural tendency was to forget about the research and to return to their customary intuitive approach to copy development. As a result a large number of segmentation studies ended up on the shelves of research departments and marketing people and were largely unused. Not surprisingly these people tended to feel that the major investment of time and money which had been made was largely wasted. Accordingly segmentation studies began to get, and in some quarters still have, a reputation for being worthless.

The presentation format was of little help to creative departments. They were often reluctant to ask questions for fear of appearing ignorant of the value of modern research, and when they did have the courage to raise objections they were often overwhelmed by the better prepared and more numerically oriented research and marketing people. In retrospect one of the problems that creative people had with segmentation studies was the strong cognitive bias of such studies. They generally overemphasized logical appeals and overlooked the emotional factors that creative people instinctively knew to be so important to the creation of successful advertising.

Theoretically, copy testing should have filled the gap. It should have been possible to determine objectively whether the communications strategies suggested by segmentation studies were, in fact, better than current strategies. However, copy testing measures (see Chapter 11) also tend to emphasize the cognitive aspects of copy and have never really been accepted by copy people as measures of good advertising.[4]

For whatever reason, it was apparent that with few exceptions segmentation studies were not really addressing creative people and thus were not being utilized. While creative people liked the concept of obtaining the promised types of information about the people whom they were trying to persuade,[5] the actuality of the study itself usually fell far short of fulfilling their needs.

As studies piled up on shelves, it became apparent that something special

---

[4] S. Kurnit, "The Impact of Creative Research on Creativity," Advertising Research Foundation Conference, October 1979.

[5] R. DeLuca of Kenyon & Eckhardt, Inc., New York, called it "the most valuable technique research has come up with to help creative people."

would have to be done to communicate the import of the research findings to the creative people. The question was, what? One agency marketing research executive, who felt he had a full and complete cognitive and emotional understanding of the results of a large segmentation study, actually moved his office to the center of the creative department. He reasoned that if he could communicate with the creative staff on a regular basis and could share the creative development process with them, effective advertising would result. He felt that, although he couldn't create appropriate advertising himself, he could recognize it when he saw it. The result was a complete failure, and was highly frustrating both to the creative people and to the research executive involved.

Another more successful approach was to attempt to communicate the nature of the discovered segments through artwork. It was reasoned that because this was a frequent approach to communicating between artists and copywriters, it might be an appropriate mode for communicating research findings as well. Figures 10.2 to 10.6 represent segments found in a study of the cruise market.

In the late 1970s, William Wells at Needham, Harper, and Steers went so far as to hire professional actors to play the roles of prototypical segment members. They were briefed by the research department on their roles and, according to Wells, did an excellent job of assimilating the research findings. Once they had done so to the satisfaction of the research department, they were turned over to the creative department. Thus copywriters were able to write ads and obtain immediate feedback from the types of people they were trying to influence.

Today the most common procedure for handling this problem is to form a research team or task force at the start of the project. This normally consists of a diverse set of members, with their own areas of expertise, who can ask the right questions, analyze the research results fully, and develop effective plans for implementing the research implications. Although groups vary with the nature of the company and the interests of key executives and middle-management people, the project team normally includes representatives from:

Marketing

Sales

The account groups of the agency

Marketing research, both agency and client

The creative department of the agency, usually including the copywriter in charge of developing copy executions

Research and development, especially when new product opportunities are an important area of interest

Often a variety of outside consultants is included—less frequently members of Finance, Accounting, or the Media department of the agency. It is extremely important to have the active participation of at least one influential member of the top management of the marketer—the President, Chairman, Executive Vice-President, or Vice-President of Marketing. This gives the project an authentic stamp of importance and insures that team members will be motivated to put forth their best efforts. It also increases the odds in favor of successful follow-through activities. One relevant review of reasons for new product failure found that failure to generate high level support early enough in the project was a key factor.[6] And one leading U.S. consultant, W. Edwards Deming, goes so far as to refuse to become involved in projects unless the chief executive of the corporation attends the meetings that he attends.

The project is normally announced by way of a meeting notice indicating who the members of the team will be, underlining the importance of the project to the corporation, and giving time and place. Meetings usually last for about 2 hours. They cover: (1) A general outline of research plans and the timetable. The logic underlying Benefit Segmentation is carefully explained and examples of successful applications from other industries are given. (2) Team members from the company and agency review industry history, current marketing plans, current advertising and the rationale supporting it. (3) The roles of team members are defined and various tasks are assigned to individual members (e.g., rounding up past research reports and marketing plans, gathering tear sheets of past advertising of the client and its competitors, assembling available sales data, etc.). (4) A list of preliminary hypotheses about the market is read and discussed. This is normally prepared by the research people directing the project and it is supplemented during the meeting.

Following the meeting it is customary to conduct a series of interviews with key executives lasting perhaps a half hour to an hour. These are aimed at identifying the types of information which each executive feels would be most helpful in conducting his or her particular activity. They are also used to supplement the growing list of hypotheses about the factors that are driving the business.

Research and development people and new product groups, if they exist in the client organization, are interviewed about new products that are under consideration or in development. Arrangements are made to reduce the ideas judged to be most promising to concept boards.[7]

A Benefit Segmentation study normally involves three phases—an ex-

[6] J. O. Eastlack, "Top Management Involvement with New Products," *Business Horizons*, December 1971.
[7] Standard concept boards are the size of a magazine page. They have an illustration, a one line headline, and about 75 words of body copy.

ploratory phase, a data reduction phase in which the large amount of information that has been gathered is reduced to manageable size, and a quantitative measurement during which the final questionnaire is exposed to a projectable sample of respondents. The project team is consulted on the design of each phase, on the analysis of results, and on the marketing implications of the findings. Meeting reports and progress reports are issued regularly so that the team members continue to feel involved in the project and continue to contribute to it. By the time the project has been completed, everyone more or less believes in it, is looking at the market from similar perspectives, and has ideas as to how this new understanding of the market can best be translated into improved marketing actions. Consequently, follow-through activities tend to be better coordinated than might otherwise be the case and to be synergistic in their effects.

It has been suggested, perhaps facetiously, that the kinds of cooperation and communications fostered by the project would result in marketing improvements, even if the planning decisions were not based on research. Whatever the reason, a large number of marketing successes can be traced back to a carefully organized study of the sort just described.

DEFINING OBJECTIVES

Large market studies, whether they are called segmentation studies, benchmark studies, strategy studies, or attitude and usage studies, are often done with no clearly stated objectives—more in the hope that they will find something that will be helpful and will justify their cost than with a clear understanding of what can and cannot be accomplished. Very often the brands from whose budgets the research is underwritten are experiencing sales declines or have not met recent sales goals. It is recognized that help of some kind is needed, and it is hoped that a careful study of what consumers are thinking and doing will somehow provide it. When the huge volume of data produced by such studies arrives, however, there is likely to be a considerable amount of confusion over what should be done with it. Often it is simply tabulated and presented without an integrated point of view. The hope is that the people exposed to the findings will see a clear, understandable pattern running through the many tables of possible interest.

It is unusual for this kind of understanding to emerge from a presentation that itself has no clear-cut structure. Instead the initial presentation is often followed by a series of new tabulations designed to provide the necessary overall understanding of the market. When these also fail to do the job, it is concluded that the fault lies with the research approach. Brand managers and account executives who are familiar with this kind of confusion are understandably reluctant to go through another similar experience. Consequently, these studies have been written off as useless in some quarters. Even in research circles there have been arguments about their utility.[8-10] However, much of the trouble stems from situations in which the nature of such a study has not been clearly understood and objectives have not been made explicit.

Benefit Segmentation research has one overall objective—to provide an in-depth understanding of the market in question—an insight of sufficient depth to allow substantial improvement in the formulation of the communications strategy. As indicated earlier, this involves answering three research questions:

1. What is the best way to define market segments? Alternative modes of segmentation have been spelled out in Chapter 1.
2. How can the market for the product and the submarkets within it best be defined? Again alternative possibilities must be allowed for in developing the questionnaire. (See Chapter 5.)
3. How can consumer attitude structure and perceptions best be summarized? (See Chapter 5.)

Well thought out answers to these questions, together with the supplementary information normally available from segmentation studies, allow answering the three crucial marketing questions:

1. Whom am I competing against?
2. On whom should I focus my marketing efforts?
3. What should my primary buying incentive be?

These are legitimate objectives for a segmentation study. They should be stated as such in the research proposal prepared before the research is authorized. Conclusions relating to them, together with suggestions as to their marketing implementation, should be drawn in a highly specific manner in the summary that is written when the research has been completed.

A fourth objective that is usually included in segmentation studies is new product development and evaluation. Because the overall study objective is

---

[8] E. M. Tauber, "Editorial: Stamp Out the Generic Segmentation Study," *Journal of Advertising Research*, Vol. 23, No. 2, April/May 1983, p. 7.

[9] K. Clancy, "Another Kick at a Dying Horse," *Marketing Review*, Vol. 28, No. 9, May 1973, pp. 21–22.

[10] L. E. Ott, "Don't Throw Out the Baby with the Dirty Bath Water," *Marketing Review*, Vol. 29, No. 2, October 1973, pp. 18–21.

to obtain a complete picture of the market, it is natural to want to search for unmet needs and to test new product concepts in the course of the research. Experience has shown, however, that the segmentation study is a somewhat cumbersome tool for this purpose. In fact if interest in new products is the primary reason for doing the research, a segmentation study is a less effective vehicle than the more direct concept/product test and market modeling approach. This is true for several reasons:

> Understanding current market segments and current structure is critical for established brands. Because they are familiar to many people and have been tried and stereotyped, their goal is normally to shift brand perceptions in a more favorable direction and thus gradually experience increased sales. It is most unusual for established brands to cause changes in market segmentation or even to experience sharp sales gains as a result of changes in their communications strategies. New brands, however, especially if they are genuinely new, can cause major market upheavals. Segment sizes can change sharply and new segments can emerge. However, such developments are extremely difficult to forecast from a segmentation study. Insights can be obtained concerning what to say about the product and what it is likely to be competing against, but the segmentation information itself cannot be regarded as a rigid structure.
>
> Segmentation studies are not efficient vehicles for discovering unmet needs. For example, the first Benefit Segmentation conducted dealt with the shampoo market.[11] Although it showed plausible segments, it did not show one whose primary concern was dandruff. Yet several dandruff products were successfully introduced shortly after the study. Although some unsuspected needs are usually uncovered during first phase qualitative research, the intended areas of coverage are too global to be well suited to the kinds of intensive probing required to discover, flesh out, test, and execute a good new product idea.

Thus although it is tempting to treat segmentation as though it were a productive method of generating and evaluating new product ideas, it is not. Moreover this misconception is one of the reasons that academic researchers have not explored the method more fully—that and the limited opportunity to work directly and extensively with major advertising agencies. Although the situation is gradually changing, major agencies remain largely concentrated in New York, Chicago, and a limited number of other cities. No more than two or three of the 25 largest agencies are outside of

[11] R. I. Haley, "Experimental Research on Attitudes Toward Shampoos," unpublished paper, New York, Grey Advertising, 1961.

New York and Chicago. Thus major agencies and their communications problems are often inaccessible to the more highly dispersed academic community, which has resulted in a lack of communications between academics and agency researchers.[12] However, as will be demonstrated, Benefit Segmentation is a highly effective approach to evaluating and refining the communication strategies of established brands. Although the last thing needed by the research industry is more terminology, it may be more appropriate to call Benefit Segmentation studies Communications Strategy studies than to call them Market Strategy studies. Perhaps had this been done earlier in the evolution of the approach it might have more quickly assumed its rightful and proper place in researcher's collections of useful techniques.

WHAT A SEGMENTATION STUDY CAN AND CAN'T DO

Some marketing people, approaching a Benefit Segmentation study, consider it to be a fixed set of methods. As will be shown in the next section, nothing could be farther from the truth. Although the types of input are fairly well standardized, a wide variety of multivariate techniques is available for processing the input. As anyone who is familiar with multivariate techniques knows, each multivariate method involves a few important but subjective choices. Findings are anything but automatic. Therefore, marketing people who expect an automatic data processing procedure with very obvious marketing implications are bound to be disappointed.

Successful application of Benefit Segmentation research requires the ability to shed some traditional ways of thinking about markets. The data that emerge are more like radar than like a high-fidelity satellite photograph. They identify the general contours of the market, but they are concerned with what the statistician calls "fuzzy sets." The definitions of submarkets of competing products are probabilistic rather than precise; so are the definitions of market segments. Segmentation patterns are likely to be subtle rather than obvious. If they were obvious, marketing people would have recognized them and acted upon them. The attitude factors underlying overall attitudes are similarly imprecise. Multivariate techniques are useful in spotting patterns of response that are buried in the data. These patterns, once recognized, often have significant marketing implications. In the last analysis, however, Benefit Segmentation, despite its use of sophisticated multivariate methods, is as much an art form as any form of

[12] A. J. Kover, "Careers and Noncommunication: The Case of Academic and Applied Marketing Research," *Journal of Marketing Research*, Vol. 13, November 1976, pp. 339–344.

market research. Its successful application depends heavily upon having a realistic set of expectations about the kinds of findings it can produce. One major package goods manufacturer, wishing to experiment with Benefit Segmentation, commissioned a large study for his flagship brand. The situation was somewhat unusual in that the brand whose market was under investigation was the leading brand in its category, and its sales were growing steadily and satisfactorily. This brand was the "cash cow" for the corporation, however, and it feared that any successful attack upon the brand would do material harm to the category.[13] Accordingly one of their goals was to anticipate the kinds of communications strategies that might be used against them. If they found they were vulnerable in any respect, they hoped to be able to employ "inoculation" techniques[14] or other marketing defenses to prevent significant damage.

When the results of the research became available, the reasons for the underlying strength of the brand became apparent, together with one or two weak spots which could best be handled by new products or line extensions. At the same time some unexpected opportunities for modest growth were discovered. The product was consumed at the highest rates in households with children, yet neither the brand in question nor its primary competitor ever showed children in their television commercials.

The addition of children to their commercials, together with some fine tuning in their positioning, resulted in some clear short-term sales gains. The competitor, however, responded by adding children to its commercials shortly thereafter, and the initial advantages of the research sponsor were largely neutralized. Sales patterns returned to those experienced before the research.

The client, although satisfied with the results of the research, expressed some disappointment that it had largely reaffirmed things he was already doing. He had been hoping that "new and radically different" directions would be uncovered for his brand. However, he was sufficiently pleased to commission a second study for one of his smaller brands—one that had been experiencing declining sales and market share.

Again the study clarified the reasons for the weakness of the brand. Major surgery was indicated and a radical repositioning was recommended, together with suggestions as to how it could be accomplished. Although the client was intrigued with the analysis, and agreed that "major steps of some sort" were required, the plan was ultimately rejected as "too radical a de-

---

[13] *Cash cow* is a term associated with the Boston Consulting Group (see their publication "Perspectives on Experience"). It refers to mature brands that are providing funds for work on new products and other brands elsewhere in the corporation.

[14] W. J. McGuire, "A Vaccine for Brainwash," *Psychology Today*, Vol. 3, No. 9, February 1970, pp. 36–39ff.

parture from our current communications." Not too surprisingly, sales of the brand have continued to slide. The marketing director remains enthusiastic about the potential contributions of Benefit Segmentation to his brands, however, and has conducted several additional studies on his businesses.

In fairness it should be added that, because drawing implications from Marketing Strategy studies is an art form, there is no assurance that the somewhat radical direction suggested would have "worked" had it been accepted. In cases of doubt, however, a compromise solution can be reached by subjecting proposed directions to additional research. Both copy tests and market tests can be used effectively to avoid the "opportunity cost" associated with failure to take advantage of potential opportunities to increase sales.

One way of looking at Marketing Strategy studies is that they must begin simply and end simply but that they can legitimately become as complex as necessary in the middle. In other words, it is essential to decide *before the study is begun* how the research findings will be used to improve marketing judgment. Problem definition is properly a group effort, involving people with diverse backgrounds and holding positions with diverse responsibilities.

Once the marketing problems have been adequately defined, the research professionals become the key participants. It is their job to determine the most efficient, reliable, and valid research methodology within given cost limitations. They then oversee every phase of the study to make sure that it is conducted in accordance with the highest research standards.

At the analytic stage, despite the employment of sophisticated mathematical tools, it is vital to the success of the study that the marketing implications of the research be stated in clear, unambiguous, understandable *marketing* language. Moreover they should be tied directly and explicitly to the objectives of the research.

The conduct of a Benefit Segmentation study is discussed in greater detail in Chapter 8.

SEVEN

Benefit Segmentation Premises

HOW ADVERTISING WORKS

The conceptual model that underlies the Benefit Segmentation approach is based on a number of premises, most of which were discussed in Chapters 5 and 6. Here is a succinct review of them and of the evidence and/or logic supporting each one.

> Advertising works through gaining attention and then by means of persuasion and/or increased brand salience. Practitioners generally believe that advertising achieves its results through gaining attention, registering a persuasive message, and making message recipients more favorably predisposed to the advertised brand. This belief is reflected in the popularity of recall and purchase intent as copy testing criteria. Brand salience, although not currently having the general acceptance of recall and purchase intent, is among the measures experiencing increasing interest.[1-4]

---

[1] A. S. C. Ehrenberg, "Repetitive Advertising and the Consumer," *Journal of Advertising Research*, April 1974, Vol. 14, No. 2, pp. 25–34.
[2] H. Krugman, "Processes Underlying Exposure to Advertising," *American Psychologist*, Vol. 23, No. 4, April 1968, pp. 245–253.
[3] M. L. Ray, "Psychological Theories and Interpretations of Learning," in *Consumer Behavior: Theoretical Sources*, S. Wood and T. S. Robertson (Eds.), Englewood Cliffs, N.J., Prentice-Hall, Inc.
[4] N. K. Dhalla, "Causal Influences in Attitude Research," American Marketing Association Conference on Attitude Research, Las Vegas, 1977.

Attention is gained through the promise of information, entertainment, or emotional reinforcement. Although it also can be gained through technical tricks, unless they can be linked to a consumer benefit of some sort, this is generally less effective.

It is a common belief that the primary consumer benefits of advertising are information and entertainment. The importance of emotional reinforcement, an unstated benefit, is attested to by the fact that recall scores are usually found to be higher among users of the advertised product than among nonusers.

Attention is selective and depends upon the interests of the person exposed to the message. Ample evidence in support of this point was presented in Chapter 2. Because this is true, each advertisement in effect selects its audience by its contents and the way in which it is constructed.

Benefits, because they deliver both information and (if the message recipient is a user of the advertised brand) reinforcement, are important predictors of attention.

AN EXPERIMENT ON THE RELATIONSHIP BETWEEN BENEFITS AND ATTENTION

The Benefit Segmentation model has been used frequently and successfully in a real-world marketing environment. Because that environment involves so many variables it is difficult to determine how much of the success is the result of the use of an accurate model of the consumer information processing process and how much is due to the coordination that is virtually forced onto marketing teams who are making full use of the Benefit Segmentation approach. For this reason the author designed and conducted a laboratory experiment aimed at examining the role that benefit interest plays (if any) in message registration.[5]

Previous research had documented the importance of variables such as color, size of advertisement, amount of copy, and size of illustration on recall levels.[6] To test the hypothesis that the benefits included in an advertisement would allow us to predict which individuals would recall which ads, it was necessary to attempt to hold mechanical variables as constant as possible. It was hoped that the perceptual screening that occurs whenever people see an ad would relate more to the message content of the ad than to

[5] Dissertation, R. I. Haley, "Effective Communications: With Application to Marketing and Social Marketing," Union Graduate School, 1974.
[6] Rafael Valiente, "Mechanical Correlates of Ad Recognition," *Journal of Advertising Research*, Vol. 13, No. 3, June 1973, pp. 13–18.

mechanical factors. Message seeking and avoidance was also virtually eliminated through use of the laboratory setting and forced exposure to the advertising.

It was hypothesized that (1) even though all people would be physically exposed to all themes, themes would be selectively retained, and (2) it would be possible to predict which individuals would retain which themes through knowledge of the benefits each person considers important.

Five types of advertising messages were investigated—airline messages (service), automobile messages (product), corporate advertising, public service messages, and insurance messages. The latter category was included because of its well-known tendency to generate low recall scores. Public service messages were included to allow investigation of noncommercial messages and their relationship to consumer values.

As noted earlier it is believed that effective communication involves knowing enough about those in the target audience to be able to design messages that will, in effect, select them from the physically exposed audience and cause them to turn on their minds. Thus a great deal of information was needed from each respondent.

The research itself involved four steps: (1) selecting the message and designing the advertisements to be tested; (2) designing the questionnaire and planning the multivariate analysis; (3) exposing respondents to messages and measuring their reactions; and (4) measuring residual effects from the communications.

SELECTING THE MESSAGES AND DESIGNING THE ADVERTISEMENTS

Three of the categories of commercial advertising were chosen for testing the hypothesis that different themes would select different respondents from the physically exposed audience—automobiles, airlines, and corporate advertising. To ensure that the messages to be tested would be reasonably representative of the kinds of advertising being used in each of these industries, a content analysis was conducted on the advertising. In all 233 ads were reviewed and their primary claims coded. The results are shown in Table 7.1.

This material was reviewed at a meeting attended by research and creative people. The benefit themes indicated were selected as those likely to be of interest to different types of people. At the same time a predictor phrase was chosen for each theme, a phrase that, if rated important by respondents, would indicate their interest in the chosen theme. Thus a high rating should predict retention of the advertising message once the respondent

TABLE 7.1 Content Analysis of Airline, Auto, and Corporate Advertisements

Category	Central Benefit	Number of Advertisements
Airlines	Big (many flights to many places)	20
	Economical (flights, tours, packages)	17
	Friendly in-flight service	15
	Destination	15
	Good for business travel	10
	Dependable/safe	7
	Fun to fly on[a]	6
	Value for the money	6
	Knowledgeable about trip planning[a]	5
	Comfortable/relaxing	5
	Trouble-free flight	4
	Ground services	3
Autos	Luxury/elegance	22
	Economy/savings	21
	Handling	17
	Beauty/appearance/style	16
	Comfort	15
	Value for money	13
	Durability/dependability/reliability[a]	9
	Sportiness/speed	9
	Smooth ride	8
	Resale value	8
	Spaciousness	7
	Prestige/pride of ownership[a]	6
	Warranty	6
	Quiet	6
	Power/performance	4
	Safety/security	4
	Uniqueness/distinctiveness	4
	Variety of models	3
Corporate	Informative/responsive (gives address/number to call)	10
	Diversified	8
	Concern for people	8
	Concern for environment[a]	8
	Technologically advanced	7
	Concern for future/our children	6
	Innovative/creative	6
	Concerned with conserving energy	5
	Efficient/thorough	4

146

TABLE 7.1   Continued

Category	Central Benefit	Number of Advertisements
Corporate	Large/growing	4
	Quality/dependable	4
	Service	4
	Employee-oriented[a]	3
	Cultured	2
	Knowledgeable/expert/specialist	2
	Well-established/experienced	2

[a] Category selected for the experiment.

TABLE 7.2   Areas Covered in the Experiment

Category	Theme	Predictor Phrase
Airlines	Fun/friendly	Friendly service
Airlines	Vacation planning help	Airline vacation planning
Autos	Prestige	An automobile that you can be proud to own
Autos	Durability	Automobile reliability
Corporate	Jobs	Fair employment opportunities offered by large corporations
Corporate	Ecology	Corporate concern with the environment

giving the rating had been exposed to it. Table 7.2 summarizes the categories, themes, and predictor phrases included in the experiment.

It has been shown that the way in which a message is expressed, its execution, is at least as important in involving a respondent in the advertising as is the underlying message or theme.[7] Thus to obtain some insight on the effects of different executions on reception of a theme, the two themes within the auto, airline, and corporate categories were each randomly assigned to two different creative people. All creative people were briefed simultaneously on the intent of the central theme and were asked to execute the themes with as little superfluous material as possible. To neutralize graphic effects to some extent, size of illustration was held constant, headlines were restricted to one line, and the creative people were asked to use

[7] Russell I. Haley and Ronald Gatty, "The Trouble with Concept Testing," *Journal of Marketing Research*, Vol. 8, May 1971, pp. 230–232.

only about 75 words in expressing the themes assigned to them. To allow some creative latitude, this last guideline was not tightly enforced. However, body copy turned out to be of roughly equivalent length from execution to execution. Formatting was similar as well (see Appendix A).

DEVELOPING THE QUESTIONNAIRE

Two questionnaires were developed, one designed to measure factors considered to be potentially predictive of message retention and the other to measure message responses to which respondents were to be exposed. Among the factors included in the first questionnaire were attitudes toward companies represented in the messages and (to limit respondent sensitization) toward companies *not* represented; interest and behavioral patterns relating to both topics and products (to avoid focusing respondents on products); benefit ratings for benefits related and not related to the advertised products; personality and lifestyle measures; demographics, and values.

Value items were included in the questionnaire because it was thought that they might be predictive of selective attention to public service messages in much the same way that lifestyle measures sometimes help to predict attention to commercial messages. A literature search was conducted to review past work with value instruments and this was supplemented by a survey of leading practitioners and academics on current work in that area.

After careful consideration the "terminal value" section of the value instrument developed by Milton Rokeach[8] was selected as most appropriate for the purposes of the research. It had the advantage of being compact, easily understood and quickly completed by respondents, and well documented by past usage. Moreover, firsthand experience had been gained with a modified version of the technique.[9]

Another area hypothesized to relate to public service advertising responses was attitudes toward alternative societal goals. A search for instruments in this area revealed a paired comparison method used in a study of preferences for societal goals among Los Angeles families.[10] The areas covered, brevity of the instrument and availability of data on past use were factors in its choice for inclusion.

---

[8] *The Nature of Human Values,* New York: Free Press, 1973.

[9] "A Survey of U.S. Attitudes Toward Germany and the German Language," Appel, Haley, Fouriezos Inc. New York, August 1971. In this variation respondents were asked to use a 10-point constant sum scale instead of the normal ranking procedure.

[10] J. R. Bettman and R. B. Andrews, "Social Marketing and Consumers' Preferences for Social Consumption," unpublished article.

Finally a measure of social responsibility was desired. It was found, however, that the term *social responsibility* had not been consistently defined in the literature. As a compromise the eight-item measure developed by Berkowitz and Lutterman was chosen, although the authors point out that it measures only one form of social responsibility.[11]

EXPOSING RESPONDENTS TO MESSAGES AND MEASURING REACTIONS

The seven creative people participating in the study provided a total of 14 print advertisements, four for each of the three major product categories plus two insurance advertisements. Additionally two public service ads were made available by Doyle Dane & Bernbach, Inc. One of these was for a project called LEAP School, aimed at contributions to help educate high school dropouts, and the other concerned Aid to Biafra. The Biafra ad was formatted in a manner judged to be similar to the other test ads, whereas the LEAP School ad contained about twice as much text.

To provide a semblance of media context, 19 articles from old issues of consumer magazines were selected and reproduced in slide form together with 16 advertisements. The criterion for choice was simply that they deal with themes of continuing interest.

The research design called for obtaining attitudinal information from respondents via a self-administered questionnaire, then exposing them to a simulated magazine in the form of the 35 slides and, finally, obtaining recall information. For the latter purpose, and to make the exposure situation more realistic, it was necessary to add brand names to the executions supplied by the creative people. However, a brand name itself can be a powerful stimulus, conjuring up a host of associations. Thus it was necessary to rotate brand names systematically across executions. Accordingly, the advertising was assigned a set of fixed positions within the context of the 19 filler stories, and the design was counterbalanced to minimize positional biases among competing themes within product categories.

Similarly, each of the three categories in which competing themes were to be tested was assigned four fixed positions in the 35-slide sequence, two early in the sequence and two in its latter part. Combinations of brands and copy executions were systematically varied within those positions in accordance with eight rotational patterns. Slides other than the 12 in the

[11] L. Berkowitz and K. Lutterman, "The Traditional Socially Responsible Personality," *POQ*, Summer 1968, pp. 169–185.

three product categories of primary interest occupied fixed positions in the sequence.

Approximately 25 respondents were exposed to each of the eight rotations. It should be noted that each rotation contained all of the test messages and all of the brand names, although messages and brand names were coupled differently from rotation to rotation. Thus all respondents were physically exposed to all messages.

Respondents were recruited by telephone from the area surrounding the central location in which the tests were conducted. After filling out their self-administered questionnaire, they were seated individually in front of a screen and given a button with which they could advance the slide projector. They were told that the slides represented a simulated magazine and that they could proceed through them at their own pace, reading as much or as little as they wished.

Because screening activities were of interest as well as message retention, a Biometrics eye-movement monitor was used to measure scanning and reading of the 35 slides. It was hypothesized that the number of times a person's eyes stop on an advertisement might be related to, and thus be predictive of, message retention.

The Biometrics eye-movement monitor employs two invisible pulsed infrared light sources in conjunction with phase-sensitive infrared detectors mounted on a pair of spectacle frames. The pulsed infrared light source illuminates the iris with invisible light. Two infrared detectors were focused on the right and left boundaries between the iris and sclera of the right eye. Both eyes, of course, move in concert. As they do, the infrared detectors pick up the differential reflectivity between the dark iris and the white of the eye. Vertical eye movements are obtained by monitoring lower eyelid movements. The signals are amplified and converted into output signals that are directly related to the eye movements. These were recorded on a two-channel recorder on heat-sensitive paper. In appearance the results resemble those of an electrocardiogram.

One other type of signal was obtained. As each new slide was projected by the respondent, the operator of the eye-movement monitor triggered a manual signal marker that identified the start and completion of the viewing of each slide.

Although eye-monitor equipment looks rather imposing, the respondents reported that they were not bothered by it. The spectacles are very light and the sensors in no way impede the respondents view of the slide. As an insurance policy, however, and to be sure that respondents were as much at ease as possible, uniformed off-duty nurses were engaged to calibrate the equipment for each new respondent. Also because the exposure was individual, respondents were ushered into the laboratory one at a time. None saw the preceding respondent with the spectacles on.

MEASURING COMMUNICATIONS EFFECTS

Immediately following exposure to the simulated magazine, respondents were given a standard recall interview. Unaided recall was obtained for all 16 advertisements. Then a category prompt was given for all but the public service ads and additional recall was obtained. Finally, a brand prompt was given and still more recall data were obtained.

Recall scores were generally in line with expectations. The automobile category received the highest level of message recall, whereas the insurance category registered the lowest scores of the four commercial categories (see Table 7.3). The level of message recall was higher than the level of visual recall, suggesting that the experimental efforts to neutralize the normally large visual effects of print advertising had been for the most part successful (see Table 7.4). Finally no order effects of appreciable magnitude were evident with the exception of the vacation planning theme, which was more memorable in the later position (see Table 7.5).

Public service messages scored notably lower than brand or corporate advertising. The lower levels are accentuated by the fact that both public service ads were *finished* ads. Moreover they were created by an advertising agency that has won more awards for creativity than almost any other agency. The remaining 14 messages were "roughs" (see Appendix A) developed by the Time Inc. creative staff. Although other explanations are possible, a reasonable hypothesis is that people are more adept at screening out public service advertising than commercial advertising.

Brand recall was approximately double the level of message recall, which means that about half the people who recalled having seen an ad for

TABLE 7.3 Immediate Recall: Unaided Category Recall (Base: All Respondents, $N = 203$)

Base	Total (%)
Airlines	93
Automobiles/cars	93
Corporate (paper/business machines)	89
Insurance	62
Public service/charity	24
Other	19

TABLE 7.4 Unaided Recall (Base: All Respondents, $N = 203$)

Theme	Immediate Message Recall	Visual Recall
Friendly (net)	51%	23%
fun and friendly	20	14
"Dullsville"	14	9
Other friendly	25	—
Planning (net)	41	20
Name your dream	16	12
Time and money	14	10
Other planning	15	—
Prestige (net)	47	32
Envy of neighborhood	15	16
Arrived	34	28
Other prestige	7	—
Durability (net)	53	30
1978	30	20
Prescotts	28	19
Other durability	14	—
Jobs/People (net)	39	23
Job	23	15
Neighbor	17	11
Other job/people	5	—
Ecology (net)	68	42
Tree	47	34
Waste	34	24
Other ecology	15	—
Retirement (net)	44	25
Easy way	24	18
Save $20	18	12
Other retirement	10	—
Public service (net)	14	11
LEAP school	5	4
Biafra	11	9
Other public service	0	—

TABLE 7.5   Unaided Message Recall (By Position in Slide Series)

	Position			
	1	2	3	4
Airlines				
Fun and friendly	23%	—	15%	—
"Dullsville"	11	—	14	—
Name your dream	—	9%	—	22%
Time and money	—	10	—	16
Automobiles				
Envy of neighborhood	15	—	15	—
Arrived	41	—	35	—
1978	—	30	—	27
Prescotts	—	23	—	30
Corporate				
Job	17	—	26	—
Neighbor	15	—	8	—
Tree	—	45	—	48
Waste	—	34	—	33

a brand could remember nothing other than the brand name. Message recall levels averaged 22%, which is generally in line with accepted norms for copy testing scores.[12] In other words, in this research almost three out of every four people who were exposed to advertising messages immediately screened them out. This is in line with the experience of the British Market Research Bureau (see p. 43).

The analysis to be summarized here centers on people who can supply related recall, people who can play back, as a minimum, the brand name and the general theme with which it was linked. However, it may be desirable first to comment upon the eye camera measurements gathered during the experiment. The two primary types of measurements made were time spent on the ads and fixations, the number of times a respondent's eyes stopped on the ad.

In one respect the eye camera tapes were reassuring. They showed that more time was spent with the stories included as filler material than with the test advertising, a pattern that doubtless exists under real-life reading conditions. It had been anticipated, however, that fixations and/or time spent would show a strong relationship to related recall. Had this been the

---

[12] The Burke all-category norm for day-after recall from on-air copy tests was 21 percent at the time of the experiment.

case, the fact that they are behavioral measures rather than questionnaire measures might have represented a significant advantage.

Interrelationships among time spent, fixations, and recall, however, did not support this hypothesis. The two eye camera measures showed a reasonably strong relationship to each other ($r^2 = .691$). An analysis of situations in which these measures pointed in different directions suggested that time spent is a function both of the complexity of the message and the level of interest in the topic. Fixations, on the other hand, are strongly influenced by copy visuals, especially by the number of centers of interest in the illustration.

Surprisingly the measure of related recall showed a slight but significant negative relationship to the two eye camera measures[13] when correlations are based on the 16 advertising messages. If correlations are analyzed by person instead of by message, however, the correlations obtained are slightly positive.[14] Other investigators have discovered this seeming anomaly.[15] The most likely explanation involves how people process messages. Memorable messages are ones that can be synthesized quickly and the page turned. Messages that are confusing or that require a substantial amount of effort to grasp require more time from the reader but are less likely to be remembered. The slight positive association when looked at by individuals rather than by ads simply reflects the fact that people who recall more advertising are inclined to spend more time with advertising messages and those who do not recall much are likely to skip a lot of advertising.

On the whole the use of the eye camera was rather disappointing. It was difficult to use, and those who wore eyeglasses had to be excluded from the experiment. Also the camera itself had to be calibrated to reflect the scanning patterns of each respondent. Sometimes this can be done quickly; at other times from 5 to 10 minutes were required. This had the net effect of increasing the cost of the fieldwork substantially. Also because only one camera was available for the experiment, the number of days required to complete it was substantially larger than had been anticipated.

Processing the heat sensitive tapes used to record the behavioral information was also troublesome. About 40 of the 200 tapes had to be examined inch by inch by hand. This required perhaps an hour per tape and even then a few were unsalvageable. Fortunately, later generations of eye cameras have largely solved the mechanical problems and programs can be developed to precode output and deliver it directly to a computer.

One difficult problem remains, however—the learning that is likely to

---

[13] Recall was correlated −.437 with time spend and −.405 with fixations.

[14] Recall was correlated +.276 with time spend and +.288 with fixations.

[15] H. E. Krugman, "Processes Underlying Exposure to Advertising," *American Psychologist*, Vol. 23, No. 4, April 1968, pp. 245–253.

take place during the exposure sequence. Eye calibrations made at the end of the sequence were often different than those done at the start. Moreover both exposure time and the number of fixations showed significant decreases as the test progressed. Slides positioned early in the sequence received significantly more attention than those placed later in it. Although the positions of individual slides were rotated from respondent to respondent to counterbalance these effects, they nevertheless inject a sizable amount of "noise" into the analysis.

This is not to say that eye cameras have limited value. Many investigators have found their best use to be in conjunction with standard questioning techniques rather than as replacements for them.[16] And at least one organization has been offering copy evaluations, based heavily on eye camera data, for more than 10 years.[17]

Returning to the analysis of results from the laboratory experiment, an immediate question is whether the basic unit of analysis should be themes or individual copy executions. It will be recalled that each theme was represented by two executions. Historically, most marketing strategists have emphasized themes and have left executions to copy testing. The author has maintained elsewhere[18] that executions are probably more important than themes. This is probably because executions are the stimuli to which consumers are exposed. Every advertisement is a unique message, and seemingly minor changes in words, models, or settings can cause major differences in consumer responses. Furthermore the nonverbal aspects of messages are just beginning to receive the kinds of attention they deserve from advertising researchers. And it seems likely that they will turn out to be more important than the cognitive aspects on which most advertising research has centered (see Chapter 11).

The criteria used in the experiment did not allow this question to be answered definitively. If immediate recall is accepted as the primary criterion, executions explain more variance than themes in autos. For corporate advertising, however, the job and ecology themes show larger differences than executions within themes. The airline case is indeterminant.

In terms of relevance to this book the key aspect of the research was how well the questionnaire items were able to predict recall scores and, in particular, how well the predictor phrases reflecting benefit interest were able to predict recall on a person-by-person basis.

As noted earlier, levels of recall tend to vary from respondent to respon-

[16] J. E. Russo, "Eye Fixations Can Save the World: A Critical Evaluation and a Comparison Between Eye Fixations and other Information Processing Methodologies," *Advances in Consumer Research*, Vol. 5, 1978, pp. 561–570.

[17] *Perception Research Services*, Englewood Cliffs, NJ.

[18] R. I. Haley and R. Gatty, "The Trouble with Concept Testing," *Journal of Marketing Research*, Vol. 8, May 1971, pp. 230–232.

dent because of factors such as reading styles, memory, and interest in the laboratory experimental situation. Similarly, differing response styles may cause people to use benefit rating scales in somewhat different ways. This difference in respondent levels of response, if ignored, can make the problem of predicting individual responses an extremely difficult one. One way to reduce problems of differing response styles is to use comparative rather than absolute measures. Other researchers have found that comparative ratings are generally better predictors than absolute ratings.[19-21] Accordingly, recall information was scored comparatively for purposes of testing ability to predict. Respondents were scored "two" if they recalled both executions of a given theme, "one" if they recalled one of the two executions, and "zero" if they could recall neither. Then, to obtain comparative ratings, within each of the three categories where respondents were exposed to two themes the score for the second theme was subtracted from the score for the first. Benefit predictor phrases were handled similarly. Each pair of predictors within a product category was first scored individually in a linear manner (6,5,4,3,2,1). Then the score for the second predictor was subtracted from the first to create a new comparative score.

An analysis of variance shows significant ability of the benefit predictors to predict recall. Moreover, their predictive power is related to the variance between themes. In the corporate area where it is highest, the F ratio of the predictor is also high ($F = 9.2$) (see Table 7.6). In airlines, where the variance is second highest, the F ratio of the predictor is also substantial ($F = 3.9$). In autos, however, the variance within themes is greater than the variance among themes, and in this instance the power of the predictor drops to nonsignificant levels ($F = 0.77$).

To put these F ratios into context an additional 77 variables were chosen from the questionnaire as possible predictors, and F ratios were computed to measure their predictive ability. Results are ranked in the same table. The F ratio for the corporate predictor ranked second of the 80 variables tested and the airlines predictor ranked fifth in its category. In autos, where executional variations dominate theme variations, response to themes cannot be predicted well from the benefit predictors. The F ratio ranked thirty-fifth of the 80 F ratios derived. This again documents the difficulty of separating executions from themes. Despite the care taken in this experiment to reduce the effects of executional variables in the auto category, responses were determined primarily by executional variables.

[19] J. N. Axelrod, "Attitude Measures that Predict Purchase," *Journal of Advertising Research*, Vol. 8, No. 1, 1968, pp. 3–17.
[20] G. D. Hughes, "Distinguishing Salience and Valence," Workshop on Attitude Research and Consumer Behavior, University of Illinois, Urbana–Champaign, December 3–5, 1970.
[21] G. D. Hughes, *Attitude Measurement for Marketing Strategies*, Glenview, Ill.: Scott, Foresman, 1971.

TABLE 7.6   Summary of Predictive Ability of Benefit Importance Ratings

Category	F Score	Rank Among 80 Predictors
Corporate advertising	9.16[a]	2
Airlines	3.87[a]	5
Autos	0.77	35

[a] Highly significant.

As a footnote in the public service area, the items in the modified Rokeach instrument predicted fairly well, the national priorities measures less well, and the Berkowitz and Lutterman measure not well at all.

The principal conclusions to be drawn from this experiment are as follows:

Benefit predictors do predict recall of themes centering on those benefits.

It is more difficult to choose good benefit predictor items than might generally be supposed. Relying on a single item is risky unless that item has been used previously and validated. Consumers do not always respond to items in ways that seem to be suggested by their superficial meaning. For example, people who are durability oriented may interpret the item "a car you would be proud to own" as indicating a durable car, because that is the type of car they prefer and would like to own. Similarly, reliability and durability, although in one sense related, might in another be quite different. Reliability may refer to the way the engine starts and runs, whereas durability may concern the body and the number of years a car can be used without having to be replaced.

Although benefits are important predictors, a great many variables, especially executional variables, are involved in the way a consumer responds to an ad. Responses to different executions of the same theme were far from homogeneous. In the auto category, where variation within themes was particularly large, it appeared that the use of emotional appeals (prestige) and nonverbal communications was largely responsible. Levels of recall, considered by themselves, can be quite misleading. For example in the automobile category the themes of durability and prestige had roughly equivalent levels of immediate recall. It might be assumed, therefore, that the primary factor in tuning into either of the commercials was interest in automobiles and that the audiences of the two commercials were otherwise equivalent. If so, the choice between them, assuming that a choice had to be made, would presumably be made on persuasion measures. This might not be an ideal decision process, however. There is a tendency for people who tune into one of the themes not to tune into the other. Of those recalling automobile executions, only 42% recalled an execution from each theme, 28% recalled only durability executions, and 30% recalled only prestige executions.

In airlines the selective process is even more apparent. Only 24% of the people who recalled any airlines advertising recalled both themes. And in the corporate category, of the people who recalled that type of advertising only 34% recalled both themes. The alert reader will have noticed that, although variance among themes was greatest for corporate themes, the recall overlap among them is not the lowest of the three categories in which theme comparisons were made. This is because the levels of recall for the ecology ads were so high that they virtually assured overlap with the ads centered on jobs.

The amount of overlap between recall of themes would not be of much concern if the people who tuned into one theme were much the same as those who tuned into another. However, this does not appear to be the case. For example, the majority of the people who recalled only the vacation planning theme were men, whereas most of the people recalling only the fun/friendly theme were women. Similarly just 8% of those recalling the durability theme for autos were in the upper income category; however, 36% of the people recalling only the prestige theme fell into the upper-income category. Finally almost half the people who were exclusive recallers of the ecology ads were 35 years of age or under, whereas less than a third of those recalling only the job ads fell into the youngest age category.

Executions also appear to draw differing audiences. For example, of people who recalled the fun/friendly theme for airlines, only 9% recalled both executions; 91% recalled only one of the two. Similar percentages of overlap were obtained for the two vacation planning executions. In the automobile category the overlap of executions within themes was somewhat higher, 18% for the durability executions and 27% for the prestige executions. In the corporate area overlap was high for the well-remembered ecology theme (40%) but was only 11% for the copy executions on the job theme.

The material summarized in the preceding paragraphs supports the theory that each message selects its own audience both by its theme and by the way in which it is constructed. Thus it is difficult for a marketer to make a strategy choice among themes or a tactical choice among alternative executions unless he or she has done a very careful job of defining the market target or targets. An ideal copy testing or market testing approach to selecting executions and/or themes would be one in which the probability of a behavioral response could be estimated both before exposure to the advertising and again afterward. The sums of the changes in those probabilities are the desired measure of advertising effectiveness. The state of the art has not yet advanced to the point where these can be accurately estimated, if indeed it ever becomes possible. In the meantime the best alternative appears to be to test only among target groups and to define targets in terms of measures that relate to potential responsiveness.[22]

Knowledge of people's attitudes, and especially the benefits they seek allows researchers to predict whether an individual will or will not recall a theme and to be correct in this assessment three out of four times. For individual executions, attitudinal information alone allows the correct prediction of whether or not a person will remember an ad about 70% of the time.

WHEN PERSUASION IS EFFECTIVE

Persuasion is most effective when favorably inclined people are addressed in areas of interest to them.

Benefit segmentation theory rests heavily on a hypothesis (advanced by Lazarsfeld and Merton in 1949) that the effectiveness of mass media depends upon, among other things, the presence of an existing attitudinal or emotional base for the feelings that the institution is trying to communicate to its public.[23] In other words, people are most likely to accept and act upon messages that are in line with their natural inclinations. They called this process *canalization*. It is believed that this idea extends to advertising as well. Viewed from the perspective of canalization, the principal function of advertising is that of a catalyst—to trigger existing predispositions. To be effective it must be delivered to people with the appropriate attitudinal or emotional base. For established products the bases have been built up over time from personal experience, advertising, publicity, word-of-mouth, and other market factors. For new products, advertising has the advantage of being "news," especially if it addresses people in terms of their interests.

Interests have great stopping power. As John Caples once said, "You see a headline that arouses your curiosity. You read the copy if you have time. You see a headline that offers you something you want. You *make* time to read the copy." Although that statement referred specifically to print advertising, it is no less true for broadcast. People will willingly turn their minds on for benefits they want—information, entertainment, and or emotional reinforcement. Copy testing, market testing, and campaign tracking

[22] Some weighting of individuals within target groups, other than equal weighting for each respondent, may also be a practical short-range possibility.

[23] P. F. Lazarsfeld and R. K. Merton, *Mass Communication, Popular Taste and Organized Social Action,* Urbana: University of Illinois Press, 1949, pp. 459–480.

studies provide abundant evidence in support of this viewpoint. First, consider a product category in which there are three clear-cut segments. The pattern of benefits sought by one attractive segment suggested that it would be particularly responsive to a theme emphasizing traditional values. A second segment showed mild support for traditional values and a third showed very little interest, largely rejecting them. A laboratory-type copy test was designed in which four groups of respondents were exposed to four copy treatments of the theme. Three of the copy executions dealt with the central theme with differing levels of intensity. One was a control commercial that addressed a benefit which the segmentation research had shown was not of particular interest to anyone. Results of exposure are shown in Table 7.7.

The data shown are product interest ratings as measured by a verbally anchored six-point rating scale. They were gathered immediately after exposure. The top two categories on the rating scale ("Excellent" and "Very Good") have been combined to make results parallel with those obtained by this client for other commercials.

All four commercials succeeded in arousing the interest of the first segment, the target segment, to some extent. However, the highest level of in-

TABLE 7.7 Relationship Between Interest in Theme and Level of Interest Aroused

	Interest Score
Commercial 1	
Favorable	71
Acceptant	71
Uninterested	46
Commercial 2	
Favorable	75
Acceptant	83
Uninterested	19
Commercial 3	
Favorable	84
Acceptant	77
Uninterested	17
Commercial 4	
Favorable	92
Acceptant	50
Uninterested	2

TABLE 7.8   Relationship Between Interest in Theme and Attention Level

	Attention Value Score
Ad with Child Oriented Theme	205
Control Ad A	103
Control Ad B	88
Control Ad C	72
Control Ad D	68
Control Ad E	64

tensity did the best job of generating interest and was selected for the campaign that followed.

The second experiment was also a laboratory experiment, this time with print advertising. In this case a CONPAAD measure of attention and involvement[24] was obtained for six alternative themes. Testing was done only among members of a target segment that Benefit Segmentation research had indicated would be particularly responsive to advertising with a child-oriented theme. People in the target group were parents, were heavily involved in family activities, were concerned about the health and nutrition of their children, and were heavy consumers of the advertised product. Although attention and involvement are not equivalent to persuasion, there is evidence that involvement may be a necessary condition for persuasion to occur.

Results of the tests are shown in Table 7.8. The child-oriented theme generated almost twice as high an involvement score as the second highest scoring theme.

The next example is also a test of print advertising, but it was done as an in-market test. Independent samples of readers of the publication in which the advertising was run were interviewed before and after the campaign had been run.

A Benefit Segmentation study had identified a segment of fashion-oriented people as the logical target for the client. The brand of interest was the second largest brand in the product category. It had an awareness problem even in its target segment, although that segment was comparatively favorable to the brand. Its primary advertising goal was to correct that situation, but it hoped that its advertising, which dramatically featured fashion merchandise, would be persuasive as well. In this instance both awareness and persuasion were measured. The results are shown in Table 7.9. The campaign had little effect in segments other than the target seg-

[24] R. I. Haley, "Beyond Benefit Segmentation," *Journal of Advertising Research*, Vol. 11, No. 4, August 1971, pp. 3–8.

TABLE 7.9 Comparative Responsiveness of Target Segment

	Before	After	Difference
Awareness among target segment			
Industry leader	100	100	
Our brand	77	86	+9[a]
Awareness among other segments			
Industry leader	100	100	−1
Our brand	67	66	−1
Attitude shift			
Target segment	4.8	5.5	+0.7[a]
Other segments	4.7	4.6	−0.1

[a] Significant at .05 level.

ment. Nevertheless it was highly successful both in terms of improving brand awareness and in improving overall brand ratings as measured by a six-point "Excellent" to "Poor" rating scale. The table shows average ratings, scored linearly, as was the custom for this particular client.

The next example is an on-air television test. In this instance the market consisted of five Benefit Segments. For each a measure of interest had been obtained for the benefit on which the commercial was focused. Telephone interviews were conducted 24 hours after the commercial had been aired. The fact that people had been in the viewing audience when the commercial was shown was established and recall information was obtained. Table 7.10 shows a strong relationship between theme interest levels across segments and recall levels for the test commercial. Again this is recall rather than persuasion, but it does show that perceptual screens can be penetrated by choosing subjects of interest to intended recipients.

TABLE 7.10 Benefit Interest and Attention Levels, by Segment

Segment	Interest	Attention
1	17	43
2	12	35
3	12	23
4	10	25
5	8	27

TABLE 7.11 Comparative Responsiveness, by Segment

Segment	Unexposed	Exposed	Shift
1 (Target)	9	21	+12
2	5	8	+ 3
3	11	11	0
4	3	5	+ 2

A final example should cement the point. This one concerns a test in a product category which Benefit Segmentation research had shown had four segments. One had been chosen as the primary market target. It consisted of a group of young people with contemporary values and relatively high levels of interest in taste benefits. The test commercial presented these in a commercial involving a series of fast cuts to the accompaniment of a rock jingle.

The research design was a single exposure test involving a group that was exposed to the commercial and a matched group that was not exposed. Because the client wanted to measure persuasion not only in the target segment but in other segments as well, interviews were conducted among a sample of the general population. The information necessary to code respondents into segments was gathered from both the exposed groups and the unexposed groups. The criterion measure was attitude shift. A six-point rating scale was used to measure attitudes. The scores in Table 7.11 are the so-called top-box scores,[25] the percentages of people who rated the brand at the highest possible point on the rating scale. Once again the target group shows the greatest responsiveness.

On one level these case histories are not surprising. They simply indicate that people are more likely to look at, remember, and be persuaded by things in which they are interested than things in which they are not. On another level, however, they tell us that the use of attitude rating scales, so predominant in consumer research today, is a productive direction in which to continue to work. They also suggest that the kinds of multivariate techniques used in Benefit Segmentation research are useful in classifying people into groups whose responses to messages can, to some extent, be anticipated. Once creative people understand these groups in depth, they are able, as has been shown, to develop advertising that can effectively and efficiently reach the group at which it is aimed.

[25] R. I. Haley and R. Gatty, "Adapting Attitude Measurement to Computer Processing," *Computer Operations*, Vol. 2, No. 2, April–May 1968, pp. 11–16. (The term *top-box score*, now in common use among practitioners, was first used in this article.)

GENERAL CONCLUSIONS ABOUT THE COMMUNICATIONS PROCESS

The one-way model of communications, which remains the model in most widespread use in the communications industry today, is inadequate. Communications is clearly a two-way process. As has been noted in earlier chapters, the sender may design a message and deliver it, but the intended recipient in effect decides, consciously or unconsciously, whether or not to receive the message. If the person does receive it, he or she can distort it, take pieces of it out of context, discredit the spokesperson or the source, or possibly add to it or interlace it with aspects of his or her own experience and attitudes. If, after all of this information processing activity, the person does not value the message, he or she can forget it. The recipient is by no means a passive target.

The playback obtained in the experiment described earlier in predicting attention shows a substantial number of distortions and additions to messages which had intentionally been made as simple, clear, and unequivocal as possible. Moreover the amount of actual distortion is undoubtedly much larger than was observed. The research procedures used were designed to measure correct recall rather than distortion. To minimize the risk that some correct recall would be missed, doubtful cases were scored as correct. Thus playback that was broadly related to a given theme but which also could have been obtained from other print ads in the given category, was scored as correct.

That experiment also suggests, as other investigators have suggested,[26] that obtaining attention is a two-step process: (1) attracting attention to the physical aspects of the message, and (2) attracting attention to the content of the message. To have meaningful impact the advertisement must carry the person exposed to it through both of these steps. If it only carries the customer through the first step, the consumer will supply his or her own preconceptions in place of the message content. In other words, the feedback aspects of the two-way model will overwhelm the message and prevent its registration.

Another factor strongly supported by the experiment is importance of the synergistic effect of the elements in an effective advertisement. It is the gestalt of the advertisement that is important. Researchers who are soundly grounded in principles of experimental design may be tempted to separate key elements of an advertisement, such as the illustration and the body

---

[26] H. Krugman, "Why Three Exposures May Be Enough," *Journal of Advertising Research,* Vol. 12, No. 6, December 1972, pp. 11–14.

copy, to rotate them from ad to ad, and to try to measure their individual effects. In doing so, however, the integrity of the advertisement is destroyed and its effects are diluted. Developing an ad, even a rough ad for testing purposes, is a creative act. The copywriter and artist, working together, fit all of the parts together so as to maximize the impact of the total impression created by the ad. It is that total impression which is important rather than the individual pieces. Similarly it is important that message elements be compatible. When they are, they multiply each others' effects. For example, Knapp has shown that nonverbal support for a message adds more to its ability to communicate than repetition of the message.[27] This topic will be treated more fully in Chapter 11.

The fact that advertising can work through a triggering effect also seems well established.[28] There are at least two types of triggering. In the first instance the intended message recipient is already using the product or service and the function of the advertising is to reinforce the user so that he or she will continue to use it. If the respondent is emotionally rather than cognitively oriented, the mere presence of the advertising may be sufficient to provide the needed reinforcement—signifying that the brand is still popular and is being supported by its manufacturer. If the person is inclined to use cognitive choice processes, the advertising helps to reinforce him or her by providing cognitive reasons, often rationalizations, that support his or her choice. Of course, the presence of the advertising is a supportive cue as well.

In the second situation the intended message recipient favors the product or service because of some benefit that he or she believes the product to impart. This person need not be a current user of the product in question. In such a case the function of the advertising is to trigger the person to act in a way in which he or she is already inclined to act.

From a practical standpoint the two situations are compatible. Users generally have favorable attitudes toward their products and, by definition, nonusers who represent the most attractive targets for communications do also. Therefore, it is often possible to accomplish simultaneously the reinforcement and the triggering functions.

Persuasion intended to change behavior rather than simply reinforce desirable behavior is a more difficult proposition. Rokeach[29] has identified

---

[27] *Nonverbal Communication in Human Interaction*, New York: Holt, Rinehart & Winston, 1972.
[28] Vaseline Petroleum Jelly, after an advertising hiatus of a number of years, was found to be quite responsive to increased advertising weight. Similarly, Campbell soup found that even a mature product could be responsive when the right theme (Soup Is Good Food) was found.
[29] M. Rokeach, *The Nature of Human Values*, New York: Free Press, 1973.

three circumstances under which attitude change, and presumably behavior change as well, can occur:

1. Through exposure to information about the cognitions or behavior of a "significant other" that is discrepant with his own cognitions or behavior. The popularity of spokespersons as an advertising device goes back to this principle.

2. Through inducing a person to engage in behavior that is discrepant with his cognitions. New product sampling is a good example of the application of this principle.

3. Through making a person consciously aware of contradictions in his belief system that exist below the level of awareness. Most advertising attempts to do this but it is usually a slow process, the first step of which is an in-depth understanding of the belief systems of potential prospects.

RULES OF THUMB FOR COMMUNICATORS

At this point we are ready to sum up the implications of this discussion, in the form of some general rules for communicators. To plan effective communications the communicators must keep uppermost in their minds the concept of selective processes. Choice of different themes, and even of different executions, means selecting different audiences for the communications. Some audiences are invariably better than others. Physical exposure to messages is not enough to insure impact. The standard media reach and frequency calculations, routinely supplied by all advertising agency media departments, are at best crude indicators of message receipt. Through selective processes each execution seeks out its own audience, determining the nature of that audience both by how it is constructed and by what it says.

In planning campaigns it should be kept in mind that if the sales performance of the brand is reasonably satisfactory, reinforcement is much easier, and, in the short run, probably more productive than launching a new theme. A common belief among agency people is that advertisers are likely to tire of their campaigns before those at whom they are aimed. Perhaps because of this, campaigns are frequently changed before the product or service they feature can establish a strong position in the minds of consumers. Changing themes without a good reason for doing so prevents people from crystallizing their perceptions about the role a brand plays—in effect, its reason for existence. The result is a blurry image, the worst kind of image—worse in many respects than a negative image. People most readily absorb messages about a brand that are in line with their preconceptions about it. For example, a Volvo automobile *is* durable; persuading people that it is also extremely stylish would be an uphill fight and probably a waste of money.

However, there are also some risks in a single-minded reinforcement strategy. After a few exposures the message may be learned and additional exposures screened out. Similarly, if the message is too trivial, it may be screened out immediately. Unsupported claims of "good service" for an airline, "good taste" for a food product, or "cleaning ability" for a soap fall under this general heading. Effective communications involve well-targeted executions and a continual flow of fresh executions all revolving around a believable and important theme. The highly successful Miller Lite beer campaign involved about 15 new commercials a year with a large cast of sports celebrities. Similarly, the widely acclaimed James Garner/Mariette Hartley Polaroid campaign involved as many as 40 different commercials in a single year. Of course, both of these campaigns made heavy use of humor, and humorous commercials may well have faster rates of wearout than conventional commercials.

To avoid excessive waste, messages should be targeted at people who are likely to receive them. One of the most receptive targets is current users of the product or service. People are generally open to reinforcement of activities in which they are already engaged. Brand usage is an activity that can efficiently be extended and reinforced through appropriate advertising. When advertisers find themselves in the frequent position of not having anything new and significant to say about their brands, one safe policy is to aim their advertising at their current users and those like them.

Having detailed research information about market targets is always important, but its importance varies somewhat with the size of the market and the breadth of reach of the appeal being used. For corporations marketing a single brand which is the leading brand in a product category with high incidence of usage, such information may be a little less important. Such cases are exceptions, however. Most companies either market several brands or market one that is not the category leader. Smaller brands tend to generate lower advertising recall scores than larger brands because they have fewer users and, as mentioned before, users are particularly receptive to messages about their brands. When the characteristics of the people who recall messages having low recall scores are analyzed, it is apparent that the lower the recall of a message the more likely it is that the group recalling it will be unusual in some respect. But there is a saving grace: The more unusual the group is the easier it is to identify them.

Some basic advertising principles have been reaffirmed by Benefit Segmentation research and related laboratory experiments. Although many of these principles were originally established in the early days of advertising, they are today too often honored in the breach. For example, the experiments clearly show the great importance, in print advertising, of synthesizing the essence of the message into the headline. If the headline by itself does not communicate, the ad is not likely to do so either. Also dominant illustrations must tie directly and unequivocally into the sales message; otherwise people are likely to make up messages of their own.

Clever ads are likely to be confusing because of the way in which people absorb messages. If the normal sequence is "What is it?" and then "What of it?" an inability to answer the first question without undue effort is likely to prevent the message from going any further. Its recipients will tune out at the first step in the attention process.

Upscale audiences, depending upon the product category and levels of involvement, are generally better addressed through cognitive rather than emotional appeals. Longer messages with high information content are particularly appropriate for this audience. In general, effective advertising is advertising that contains one or very few ideas, can be quickly synthesized, and is designed so as to penetrate the perceptual screens of the prime prospects.

Experience in working with creative people indicates that it is highly undesirable to attempt to lock them into inflexible rules, restrictions, and prohibitions. The loss in advertising effectiveness that resulted from dismembering ads and rotating their pieces clearly demonstrates that it is the totality of the advertisement which is most important. The sum of the parts does not necessarily add up to the whole. Thus it would seem wise to give creative people no more than general directions initially. This allows their creative skills full rein and puts the burden of integration where it is likely to be handled best. Copy testing can then be used to make sure that unanticipated problems are not encountered in consumer reactions to the creative executions.

Media implications can also be drawn from the experimentation. The extensive confusion of messages that was observed when several products in the same category had ads near each other argues strongly for the doctrine of "dominance." This holds that an advertiser should select media vehicles so as to insure that the brand of interest is the largest advertiser in the product category in that vehicle. If another brand is a larger advertiser, according to the argument, confusion will operate to its advantage. In other words, it is believed that the leading advertiser in a particular vehicle is likely to get credit not only for his ads but for some of the competitors' ads as well. Thus other things being equal, it may be better to be the leading advertiser in a magazine with a slightly higher cost per thousand than to be the second or third largest advertiser in a magazine with a somewhat lower CPM. Best of all, of course, would be to appear as the *only* advertiser in the product category, provided the media environment was appropriate.

Another media implication involves reach. Reach, in media department terminology, refers to the percentage of an intended audience that receives (physically) at least one message in a given campaign. If the media strategy is to obtain maximum reach, as it often is, it would be wise to create as large a pool of commercials as is economically feasible and to vary executions substantially around the central theme. Because each ad could reasonably be expected to reach a somewhat different audience, a large pool of diverse executions should deliver the desired extensive reach.

EIGHT

Benefit Segmentation Methodology

TYPES OF INFORMATION GATHERED

Benefit Segmentation research is an extension of the large traditional studies that used to be called benchmark studies. It involves gathering information in the following standard research areas:

Brand awareness and knowledge
Brand purchase
Brand usage
Brand preference
Brand image
Media habits
Demographic data

In addition, information is gathered on:

Perceived importance of product attributes and consumer benefits
Problems experienced and their frequency and troublesomeness
Perceived similarity among brands or products in the category
Frequency of product use and of individual brands for consumption occasions, purposes, or situations.
Category beliefs, defined as attitudes involving the product category.
Other psychographic measures, defined as personality, lifestyle, and value measures.

171

Benefit Segmentation has achieved its popularity because it is an easy concept to understand. It relies primarily upon that traditional tool of market researchers—cross-tabulation. However, the cross-tabulations are aided by advanced statistical tools, heavily supplemented by marketing judgments.

In the kinds of benchmark studies conducted in the 1950s, researchers were satisfied with cross-tabulating the responses to their questions by demographic variables, frequency of purchase, and/or usage and similar variables. But, especially in high-volume, similarly priced, mass-marketed, packaged goods products, they often did not discriminate between consumers. Moreover, they did not explain why some people chose one brand and others different brands. And because reasons for current behavior were not well understood, predictions of responses to marketing actions were notoriously uncertain.

One of the most popular procedures was to identify heavy users as the target for the brand underwriting the research. This procedure was often misleading, however, because these consumers, although they were heavy users of the product category, were not necessarily potentially heavy users of the brand of interest. Demographic and volumetric segmentation merely *described* behavior without *explaining* it. For this reason they were inefficient predictors of responsiveness to advertising. On the other hand, there is evidence that attitudinal changes often precede and help to predict behavioral changes,[1] that changes in perceptions of a brand's ability to deliver a benefit can lead to changes in overall attitudes toward that brand,[2] that benefits predict behavior better than personality and lifestyle measures or demographics,[3,4] that benefits predict behavior better than product attributes,[5] and that the perceived benefit is the most significant dimension in print advertising.[6] Thus benefits almost surely are a better area for concentrated attention than the demographic and volumetric alternatives.

Past Benefit Segmentation research has demonstrated that the variables

[1] Alvin A. Achenbaum, "How Advertising Works: A Study of the Relationship between Advertising, Consumer Attitudes, and Purchase Behavior," New York, Grey Advertising, 1968.
[2] M. J. Rosenberg, "Cognitive Structure and Attitudinal Affect," *Journal of Abnormal and Social Psychology*, Vol. 53, November 1952, pp. 367–372.
[3] W. D. Wells, "Seven Questions About Lifestyle and Psychographics," *American Marketing Association Conference Proceedings*, Series No. 34, Spring & Fall 1972, pp. 462–465.
[4] D. R. Lehmann, "Television Show Preference: Application of a Choice Model," *Journal of Marketing Research*, February 1971, pp. 47ff.
[5] Author unknown, "Product Attributes Versus Benefits in Preference Research," submitted to *Journal of Marketing Research*, May 1983.
[6] J. Hornik, "Quantitative Analysis of Visual Perception of Printed Advertisements," *Journal of Advertising Research*, December 1980, pp. 41–48.

which best determine brand choice fall into one or more of the following universes of content:

Benefits or problem solving

Occasions or situations of consumption

Category beliefs

Lifestyles, personalities, or values

Because it is difficult, if not impossible, to guess on an a priori basis, which of these orientations is likely to be the best entry point for market segmentation, current Benefit Segmentation methodology calls for covering each of them. The market is then segmented on the basis of each orientation and then testing is done to determine which does the best job of discriminating segments on criterion measures, such as brand preference, product-type preference, and volume of consumption. This process will be covered in some detail in the technical section that follows. It can be noted at this point, however, that on the basis of some 34 studies in which the benefit belief and lifestyle areas were covered and significant differences were observed, in 17 cases benefits did the best job of discrimination, in 14 beliefs did the best, and in 3 (liquor, cigarettes, and clothing) lifestyles showed the most discrimination. It should be added that, with a few exceptions, these cases involved packaged goods.[7]

The primary advantage of Benefit Segmentation studies is that they provide a great deal of guidance in the development of a communications strategy. They identify the consumers and occasions offering the most promising source of business and describe them in meaningful and actionable terms. They indicate whether a brand can best grow by attracting new users into the category, by increasing sales among current users, or by attracting users of other brands. They delineate the buying incentive with the greatest potential for the brand of interest and provide guidance to appropriate advertising tonality, visuals, spokespersons, nonverbal appeals and choice of promotions, media types, and vehicles. Finally, they provide criteria that can be used to test alternative advertising executions and to track results once campaigns have been released in the marketplace.

Inferences can also be drawn from Benefit Segmentation research concerning new products, distribution, and pricing. As noted earlier, however, the primary payoffs are in improved communications.

Benefit Segmentation procedures group consumers into segments in terms of their patterns of interest in the kinds of benefits available or po-

[7] Anthony J. Adams, "Why Lifestyle Research Rarely Works," 13th Annual Attitude Research Conference of the American Marketing Association, February 8, 1982.

tentially available in the product category under study. Interest in each benefit is measured by equal interval rating scales. It is the total configuration of responses that is important, not ratings on any one scale. Sometimes, however, one or two scales turn out to be the key discriminators and it is easiest to think of a segment in terms of its responses on these few scales. Segment names attempt to capture the flavor of the segment in a single phrase (e.g., Creative Cooks).

Statistically the procedures group people so that differences in response patterns of the members of a segment are minimal, whereas differences in response patterns between groups are maximally different. However, segmentation patterns and the dimensions along which markets can be segmented tend to be subtle rather than obvious. Where they are obvious, as for example in the case of the strength dimension in the cigarette market (also identified as taste/health in some studies), marketers have seized upon them and proliferated products at all levels on the dimension. Thus we have large numbers of "mild" cigarettes, currently the desirable end of the dimension and fewer, but several, choices of "strong" cigarettes.

Differences need not be large to have marketing significance. If two products have concentrated their attention on the same segment and one of them is perceived to offer a slightly greater amount of the key benefit sought by that segment, it may well find itself with double or triple the share of the second brand. If all other benefits of the two products are considered to be equivalent, there is no reason to choose the second brand. In such a case it is possible, theoretically, for the first brand to capture the entire market despite a very slight difference in its favor. In real life, of course, differences among brands are likely to be perceived on several dimensions. Packaging graphics communicate different feelings about brands, and prices are likely to vary. Consequently, brands have both assets and liabilities. Nevertheless, advantages on one key dimension are ardently sought and, once gained, can have a significant impact on sales and brand share.

Once Benefit Segments have been identified and the nature of each has been well understood, it is normally possible to select one or more segments that offer superior marketing opportunity to the brand of interest in terms of its future promotional development. Before exploring the ways in which segmentation research results can be used it, however, may be helpful to review attitude segmentation methodology in some detail.

OVERALL STUDY DESIGN

Chapter 4 described the methods by which attitude measurement tools can be constructed. Those largely parallel the procedures that will now be reviewed in greater detail in the context of Phases I and II of a Benefit Segmentation study. Benefit Segmentation studies are normally conducted in three phases. The first phase is exploratory; the objective is to gain insights into the perceptual and evaluative processes of consumers and, in particular, to gather exhaustive lists of items in the major universes of content. The second phase attempts to build effective and efficient measurement approaches through reducing the long lists generated in Phase I to manageable size, while retaining representative coverage of each universe of content. The third phase involves application of the measurement approaches developed in Phase II to a large probability sample of consumers. Results of the third phase are then used for the ultimate purpose of the research—the development of an effective communications strategy.

Phase I—Exploratory Research

The goal of the first phase is a thorough review of the product category. It attempts to ensure that nothing of any possible marketing significance has been overlooked. The research team begins by developing a series of hypotheses about the market. These may be based on little more than hunches, or they may have been developed from past marketing experiments. This list is supplemented by material drawn from a thorough review of available research, both proprietary studies done on behalf of the client and relevant research in the public domain. Professional and trade literature, publications of associations, and speeches or proceedings of public meetings are all helpful sources.

Existing personality and lifestyle inventories are reviewed and factors and items that are judged to be relevant are culled from them. Where needed, new items and factors are constructed. In addition, content analyses of past advertising are conducted, available research is reviewed, and information on current sales trends and marketing activities is assembled.

When secondary sources have been culled and summarized, the primary research begins. This usually consists of group sessions, depth interviews, and/or observational sessions. However, both formats and areas of coverage are highly idiosyncratic to the research team responsible for the study.

Group sessions are probably the single most popular device because they allow a skilled moderator to review the hypotheses assembled by the team, so that choices can be made about which are worth pursuing further. The exploratory phase inevitably generates more material than it is economically feasible to carry into subsequent phases, so that some method for screening out the most promising material must be found. Reactions of group session attendees, although obviously not fully projectable, are used as one of the screening devices.

A number of exploratory devices can be incorporated into the group session framework. For example, the Kelly Repertory Grid,[8-10] normally a one-on-one technique, can be used to gain insights into the perceptual and evaluative dimensions that people use to discriminate between brands and product types. Types, in this sense, refer to generic categories, such as roll-on, spray, stick, and cream deodorants or injector, double-edge, band, and twin-blade razor blades. As in the version employed in individual interviews, the first step is to prepare a deck of cards and to place on each card the name of one of the brands or types of interest. The cards used should be large enough so that when held up by the moderator, they will be visible to all members of the group.

The interview procedure also parallels that of the individual interview situation. The moderator shuffles the cards and deals out three of them. He or she then singles out one of the group session members and asks which of the three products this person sees as most different from the other two and why. This, of course, identifies one dimension of discrimination. If, for example, the dimension is strength and the "different" product is stronger than the other two, the moderator follows with a question of whether it is better for a product to be strong or mild. This interjects evaluative aspects into the discussion. The choice as to which is better is followed by a discussion of why that is true. This, in turn, provides evidence on the kinds of cues people use to judge product performance.

At this point the moderator selects another group member or asks the group as a whole whether they all agree that the product chosen by the first respondent is actually the most different of the three products being discussed. Other group session members will often see another product as more different and when asked why will identify other dimensions of discrimination and evaluation. When no further useful material is forthcoming from the group discussion, the moderator deals out a fresh triad of cards and the discussion continues. New triads can be dealt until the discussion becomes redundant. Triads need not be random. Some that are of special interest to the research team can be purposefully selected from the deck by the moderator and exposed to the group for comments.

Similar decks of cards reproduced on smaller cards and sorted by individual respondents can be used to generate maps (pp. 106–108), reflecting market structure. Similarity sorts yield perceptual maps; sorts onto an eval-

[8] G. A. Kelly, *The Psychology of Personal Constructs*, Vols. I and II, New York: Norton, 1955.

[9] P. Sampson, "Common Sense in Qualitative Research," *Commentary*, Vol. 9, No. 1, July 1967, p. 161ff.

[10] ———, "The Repertory Grid and Its Application to Market Research," American Marketing Association, Attitude Research Conference, Mexico City, 1970.

uative scale yield preference maps. And paired comparisons and image ratings can be used to construct joint space maps. Usually these data are gathered from each participant as he or she arrives for the group session. One effective procedure is simply to ask people to sort the cards into groups while they are waiting for the group discussion to start, seal each group in a separate envelope, and write on the outside of the envelope the things that the cards in it have in common. This prevents respondent perceptions from being contaminated by the perceptions of other group members. Also it prepared them to some extent to contribute to the subsequent moderator-led discussion of triads.

Triads can also be used to uncover perceptions of user characteristics or use situations. Usually this is best done on a group basis. The group is asked to think about the kinds of people who use the various brands or product types. The three cards are then dealt out and group members are asked which brand users are likely to be most different and why.

Similarly, in the case of occasions, group members are asked to think in terms of occasions of use. The three cards are dealt and the group is asked which product is most likely to be used under circumstances that differ from those under which the other two products would be used. The term *occasion* is itself somewhat ambiguous, and this procedure can be helpful in developing a typology of occasions. It will also indicate whether occasions are best defined in terms of times of day, people present, mood, or some other criteria. The descriptive labels on the previously mentioned envelopes can also indicate whether *occasion* is a useful way of looking at the market.

Another useful function of groups is to clarify consumer semantics in key areas. Consumers are often asked to look at products and describe their appearance, to smell them and describe their sensations, and, if appropriate, to taste them and describe their taste characteristics. Sometimes they are asked how they would describe a brand to someone from a foreign country who had never heard of it. If this is done before the product itself is shown, its most salient characteristics quickly become apparent. Consumers are also asked about terms that are in frequent use in an industry. For example, in the deodorant category they might be asked what terms such as wetness, strength, and irritation mean to them.

Groups can also be used to study the decision process. Students of consumer behavior have identified a number of differing routes by which consumers arrive at brand choice decisions. One such decision process is called "lexicographic." It applies to situations in which a series of decisions is made rather than a simple brand choice. For example, if a woman intends to buy a new dress, she may first decide on which store or stores she will visit. If one of the stores is a department store, her second decision may be whether to shop upstairs or in a bargain basement. If she decides to look upstairs, she may still have to choose between regular priced and sale merchandise. Then she may decide on what sizes she will examine. Next color may come into play. Then, perhaps, price. And, finally, brand name. Of course, consumers are likely to have different decision sequences. However, alert marketers will want to understand common sequences and how their products gain or lose by the choices that are made at each stage in the sequential decision process. J. R. Bettman[11] and others have developed procedures for studying individual sequences, called decision networks or decision nets for short.

Another decision process thought to be in common use is the compensatory process. When this process is used, the assets and liabilities of each brand are weighed and an overall attitude toward the brand is formed. The brand with the most favorable overall attitude rating is then chosen and bought. This process has been modeled via the Fishbein model. He defines a person's attitude toward a brand as a function of the strengths of his beliefs about that brand and the evaluative aspects of those beliefs.[12]

Still another model is the conjunctive model. It posits that a brand will be considered acceptable if it meets minimum standards on each of the key dimensions of evaluation in the product category of interest. In other words, it assumes that people "satisfize," whereas the compensatory model assumes that they "optimize," weighing alternatives and picking the best brand.

Finally, there is the disjunctive model. In it people start with the single most critical dimension and try to find the single brand that performs best on it. Thus a price buyer would focus on price and would buy the least expensive brand. If two brands were to be equally low in price, the consumer, using a disjunctive decision process, would move on to the second most critical dimension, compare the two brands on it, and make a choice. If the brands were again tied, the consumer would move on to the third dimension and continue in this manner until a choice was possible.

There is little evidence in the literature to indicate whether people always use the same decision process or use one decision process in one situation and shift to other processes in other situations. It seems likely, however, that the latter is the case. In any event, group sessions can shed considerable light on the types of decision processes being used.

The process itself is not the only issue. Where more than one family member takes part in the decision, it is important to know the kinds of roles

---

[11] *An Information Processing Theory of Consumer Choice*, Reading, MA: Addison-Wesley, 1980.
[12] Martin Fishbein, "Attitude and the Prediction of Behavior," in *Readings in Attitude Theory and Measurement*, M. Fishbein (Ed.), New York: Wiley, 1967.

y different family members. If, for examp...
...en are particularly concerned about econo...
...concerned about styling, it suggests that differ...
...be needed in men's and women's magazines. It m...
...different emphasis on questionnaires for men an...
...ents in the quantitative phase of the research. And in ...
cases of some products (e.g., dinnerware), group sessions may be useful in...
assessing the risks involved in interviewing *only* women in the quantitative
stage.

Depth interviews serve many of the same functions as groups do. However, they have advantages in several situations:

When the topic is one that requires extensive individual probing.

When the product is one bought largely for individual consumption and the decision is made without having discussed the product category with others.

When deep psychological motivations are thought to be related to brand choice and use of a trained psychologist for interviewing consumers is considered desirable.

In depth interviews the intent is to get behind surface reactions to "true" motivations. Interviews often last for 2 or more hours. To break the monotony and retain respondent interest in the interview situation, a variety of game-playing aspects are customarily introduced into the interviews.

In a number of consumption situations consumers maintain inventories of products with overlapping functions. To fill laundering needs people keep soaps, detergents, bleaches, and softeners on hand. Moreover each of these products is available in a variety of forms—liquid, powder, solid, and spray. Consequently, the possible number of combinations that can exist in consumer inventories is staggering. It is not surprising, therefore, that there is considerable confusion among marketers as to subcategory definitions. This in turn makes it difficult to develop successful new products. Can two functions such as cleaning and softening be combined successfully in a single product or are they best handled separately? What brands are currently competing with each other? And how would the introduction of a new product change the way in which products are seen to compete with each other?

To answer questions like these it is necessary to understand how consumers view categories and subcategories. Perceptual mapping can be helpful in this regard. An alternative technique might be called the "ideal product inventory." Respondents are told that they have just moved to a foreign country and no familiar products are available. Without referring to any

they are asked to describe, one by one, the kinds of pro
vant in order to cover their needs. To refresh their memorie
ir past week's cleaning activities, a technique similar to the "cam-
e" method developed by Yoell[13] is used. This involves a lengthy in-
ew and a moment-by-moment reconstruction of every action taken by
he respondent during a specified recent time period (e.g., yesterday).

After inventing the products they will need, consumers are asked the smallest number that they could get by with if all of their desired products were not available to them. This procedure usually shows that quite different perspectives on the market are held by different consumers. Some prefer a few general purpose products—often the fewer the better. Others are only comfortable when they have a different product for each specific need. If this tendency is clear-cut, as it often is, it may call for different marketing approaches to these segments—making different products for people with different market perspectives, identifying one as the target, and focusing on it, or, at least, recognizing these different orientations in communications efforts.

The "ideal product inventory" method works well in product categories such as food, family health, hair care, and cleaning—wherever inventories of products are maintained to cover a set of related needs.

A less frequently used but equally helpful approach is observational sessions. The objective here is to understand how people go about buying and using products. One such approach is that of gathering verbal protocols.[14] Respondents are recruited for both a home interview and a shopping trip. They are given money for a purchase of the type of interest and asked to provide a running commentary on their decision processes as they plan and carry out their shopping trip. The interviewer records this material and accompanies the respondent on the shopping trip.

A second observational approach is to assemble product users at a central location and ask them to use the product while under observation. In one instance deodorant users were asked to apply deodorants of various kinds while behind a screen. Sinks and towels were also available to each respondent behind his or her screen. Respondents were asked to provide a verbal protocol on the process they were using and on their reactions to the products being used. A spray deodorant was of central interest, and the manufacturer of the product considered it to be the ultimate form of product development. He was aware of no problems associated with its use, having received no complaints about it. Respondents, however, found that the product form had a number of liabilities. For instance, the mist from the

[13] Behavior Research Institute, n.d.
[14] Bettman, *Information Processing Theory.*

deodorant occasionally got in their eyes or up their noses. Als\
quently complained that it was cold on first contact with their sk.

Still another form of observational interview is the purchase obser\
Most interviews are conducted, either in person or by telephone, ir
homes of respondents. Unfortunately interviews are weak tools for reco
ering the details of purchase situations. So much is done by habit that respondents are largely unaware of what they actually do. They will attempt
to cooperate with interviewers, but in many cases it is impossible to recap-
ture the details of what occurs at the point of sale. Because consumers make
so many brand decisions in such a short time in a supermarket visit, individual purchases leave little impression on their memories unless something
unusual happens in the course of the purchase situation. But it is the usual
that is of primary interest to manufacturers.

One way to avoid this problem is to videotape people unobtrusively
while they are shopping, and then play back the videotape for them and ask
what was going through their minds while they were behaving in various
ways. Often when people see themselves in action, especially when the actions took place only moments prior, they can recall in great detail what
they were thinking about.

In a recent study for a complex package goods product category, several
buying styles were identified, the existence of which had not been appreciated before the research. One style was to walk by the large display area
and, almost without pause, to select a product and continue on. When interviewed, it became apparent that these people were largely repeat purchasers who were simply identifying the brand they wanted and putting it
into their carts. Many were regular customers of the store and knew exactly
where to find the brand they wanted in the large display area.

A second buying style was to stop in front of the display and to scan the
display carefully and extensively before making a choice, often selecting
items from the display, looking at them, and returning them to the shelves,
sometimes even moving off and returning to the display before a choice was
made. These people tended to be those who had no specific brand in mind
and who were trying to assimilate the available choices or those who were
not familiar with this particular store's display pattern.

A third buying style involved picking up a product and holding it in the
purchaser's hand while continuing to scan the display. These people were
generally looking for special price opportunities or products considered
equivalent or for possible new products.

In addition to identifying differing buying styles, the exploratory work
cast doubt on some of the "conventional wisdom" of the industry. For example, it was commonly believed that few people paid any attention to the
information on the product label. In the stores in which the observations

, however, this was not the case. Almost half the people referred
...el. When asked why they did so, they usually indicated that they
...necking whether or not the product contained one or two elements
...ecial interest to them (e.g., calories, sugar, preservatives, chemicals).

Phase II—Refining Measuring Instruments and Hypotheses

At the completion of the exploratory phase, the research team is thoroughly inundated in data. Lists ranging from about 50 to perhaps several hundred items have been assembled for each of the universes of content potentially useful in understanding and predicting consumer behavior. It will be recalled that these are:

Consumer benefits and problems, including product characteristics that relate in some way either to benefits or problem solving

Category beliefs relating to product performance and to tradeoffs between benefits

Occasions or situations of consumption defined in a variety of ways

Lifestyles, personalities, and/or value items and factors

In addition there will be a number of possible alternative ways of defining boundaries of product categories and subcategories, hypotheses about forces driving the market, ideas about consumer decision processes, and so on. This huge accumulation of data raises the question of how best to reduce it to a more manageable size without losing valuable ideas.

The traditional method is to leave the decision to one or two people—often the market researcher in charge of the project, subject to the review of the person paying for or sponsoring the study. As pointed out in Chapter 4, however, such judgments are likely to differ substantially from person to person. So the traditional method runs a high risk of turning what purports to be an objective research process into an art form. The results, therefore, are only as good as the artist.

In some respects this is an acceptable procedure, provided it is clear that results do depend upon the right questions having been asked and that the choice of questions is subjective rather than objective. Certainly much research has been successful because of the artistry of the people involved. However, on any individual study it is hard (*in advance*) to separate the true artist from the self-styled artist. Afterward it is too late. Most researchers believe themselves to have excellent judgment in selecting the right questions.

Also the traditional approach has the important advantages of saving time and money. Everyone is anxious for the research results to become available for use. Thus there is a great deal of pressure to move directly to the final wave of interviews. Yet one of the reasons for the failure of communications strategy studies is exactly this sort of pressure. If ambiguous items are included in the questionnaire and, most important, if key questions are left unasked, there are no ways to make up for these deficiencies at the analytic stage. As a general rule it is usually wise to invest between 30 and 40% of the total budgeted to the project to work *before* the final large-scale field phase is begun. Time spent in generating meaningful hypotheses and in developing reliable and valid measuring instruments is an excellent investment.

Now let us examine the tools that can help us select the best items and to retain the most meaningful hypotheses. Some are logical and systematic; others are primarily statistical.

As noted in Chapter 4, one simple but effective tool is the Task Force Survey. To illustrate its use, let us assume that we have developed a list of some 300 benefits of possible value to consumers. Clearly that is too many to carry to a national probability sample, especially when similar "laundry lists" of items from the other universes of content must also be considered, in addition to standard behavioral and demographic questions.

In the early days of Benefit Segmentation the procedure was to assemble the Task Force and review the items, item by item, discussing what attitudinal dimensions they were assumed to be tapping and arguing for or against inclusion of each one. Such meetings frequently turned into day-long, highly frustrating situations. The Task Force Survey was developed in the hope that it would speed the selection process.

About 10 days before the meeting each team member is sent a full listing of the items to be considered. For example, each member would receive a listing of all 300 Benefit items, and is asked to check off 50 or fewer items that he or she believes should be included in the final questionnaire. Results from individual team members are added together and each item is classified into one of three groups—for example, a group receiving more than two votes, a group receiving one or two votes, and a group of items that did not receive a single vote.

The groups are used to simplify the screening process. Items that have received a majority of team member votes are automatically included without discussion. Those receiving no votes can usually be disposed of with a minimum amount of discussion. The review can then be centered on whether or not the marginal items are worth inclusion.

Modified Delphi techniques are applicable at this point. The original Delphi approach was developed to pool the judgments of experts, each of whom had the opportunity to modify his or her judgment after having seen a frequency distribution of the judgments of other participating experts.[15] Modified Delphi approaches attempt to speed up the feedback process and to allow the completion of more judgment cycles. In a typical session the team members, each an expert in his or her own area, are equipped with pushbutton voting devices. These allow a secret vote and prevent one dominant individual from giving the impression that his or her views are widely shared. After each team member has registered a vote, often by a dial or button located under the edge of the meeting table immediately in front of his or her chair, results are displayed in the form of a frequency distribution. One impressive device for recording and displaying votes is called a Consensor (Applied Futures Corporation, Greenwich, CN). It produces a lighted bar chart showing the percentage of the team members who support a given position. General Electric has a permanently installed Consensor in its boardroom and regularly uses it to reach consensus viewpoints. In Benefit Segmentation studies it can be used to screen rapidly all of the material under consideration for inclusion in the final questionnaire. At the same time people holding minority viewpoints have a chance to express the reasoning behind their opinions and to convert other team members to their positions.

Modified Delphi sessions have another advantage. On occasion, team members will find that they have virtually no differences of opinion and that they are all looking at their market in similar ways. When substantial unanimity exists as to the best courses of action for the company, it is sometimes possible to design a highly focused research project to test the effectiveness of those courses of action. In this way time and money can be saved and the process has an early payout. And at the very least the cooperation that is forced upon team members by team discipline has important fringe benefits. The amount of work done at cross-purposes is invariably reduced.

It will be recalled that the primary purpose of Phase II is efficient data reduction, particularly in the areas of benefits and problems, beliefs, personality and lifestyle measures, and occasions. The most effective means of accomplishing this is to gather consumer response data from a limited number of consumers, normally 150 to 200, and to process them with a variety of multivariate statistical techniques. The output from these can be helpful fodder for the research team. Once it is apparent how the individual items group, how they discriminate among important subgroups of consumers, which benefits consumers consider most desirable, and what kinds of potential centers of consumer interest exist, the choice of items to be included in

[15] N. C. Dalkey and O. Helmer, "An Experimental Application of the Delphi Method to the Use of Experts," *Management Science*, Vol. 9, No. 3, April 1963, pp. 458–467.

Phase III becomes much more straightforward and, accordingly, it is much easier to reach consensus among team members.

Phase II questionnaires consist primarily of rating scale information. They normally cover:

Benefits (rated on a scale ranging from "extremely desirable" to "not at all desirable").

Problems (rated on both a frequency of occurrence scale and a troublesomeness scale).

Personality and lifestyle measures (rated on a "very much like me" to "not at all like me" scale). Values, when included, are rated on a desirability scale or a constant sum scale.

Beliefs (rated on an agree/disagree scale).

Occasions of use (rated on a frequency of occurrence scale).

Additionally information is usually gathered on volume of consumption, brand preference, brand usage, and demography. Interview length is typically about 1 hour.

One of the techniques for narrowing the lists of items to a manageable size is already discussed in the context of constructing an image measurement tool (see Chapter 4). Representative sections from Phase II questionnaires are presented in Figures 8.1 and 8.2. Each universe of content is normally factor analyzed. Thus separate factor analyses are run on benefits, problems, beliefs, occasions, and lifestyles.

Some analysts prefer to combine universes, run fewer factor analyses, and thus save on computer costs. However, because different universes frequently call for use of different rating scales, combined analyses risk the loss of sensitivity and clarity. Often a major component of the factors they produce is simply attributable to differences between the universes that were combined. In other words, they frequently "discover" the original universes of content. Also they tend to lump into a limited number of factors the items within universes. When universes are tackled one at a time, more and clearer factors are likely to emerge.

Factors are, in effect, groups of items with similar meaning. Thus it is comparatively safe to eliminate items that clearly belong in a given factor but which show lower factor loadings than other items in the same factor.

A second technique that is helpful in choosing the items to be carried over into Phase III is discriminant function analysis.[16] This shows the power

[16] D. G. Morrison, "On the Interpretation of Discriminant Analysis," *Journal of Marketing Research*, Vol. 6, May 1969, pp. 156–163.

	Extremely	Very	Quite	Rather	Slightly	Not At All	
		D	E	S	I R A B	L E	
	1	2	3	4	5	6	
You can always find a parking space near the store							48-
It's easy to get to							49-
It is an attractive store to shop in							50-
It's easy to get around the store							51-
It is air conditioned in summer—well heated in winter	1	2	3	4	5	6	52-
It is well lit so you can easily see the merchandise							53-
It's a busy, active store							54-
The store is kept very clean							55-
It's a convenient place to shop in							56-
People who shop there are middle-income people							57-
Its customers are mostly older people							58-
Most of its customers are men							59-
It's a working-man's store							60-
Its customers are sophisticated people							61-
It's a national chain store	1	2	3	4	5	6	62-
It has many self-service sections							63-
It is open at convenient times							64-
It has a mail-order desk in the store							65-
It has an advisory service for such things as clothing, layettes, and college fashions							66-
It has fitting rooms for trying clothes on							67-

Figure 8.1. Retail Store Benefit Desirability Rating Page

186

of each individual item to discriminate between significant subgroups of the population surveyed. The definition of significance is left up to the analyst. Normally, however, the most significant groups are considered to be groups such as:

Users of major brands including, of course, the brand of interest

Users of different product forms (e.g., spray, aerosol, cream, pad, and roll-on deodorants)

Users of differing quantities of the product category being researched

Other groups may be specified, depending upon the product category under investigation and the marketing situation of the brand sponsoring the study.

Discriminant function analysis provides a discrimination ratio for each item. The denominator is an estimate of the level of random variation associated with the item of interest. This is obtained simply by computing the variance of the ratings of each subgroup of respondents around the mean rating of their subgroup and cumulating across subgroups. In analysis of variance,[17] this is called the "within-group" variance.

The numerator is a measure of the extent to which the subgroup means differ from the grand mean, commonly called the "between-group" variance in analysis of variance. Thus a ratio level of 1.0 means that the between-group variance in responses to a given item is no larger than the presumably random within-group variance. Obviously items at this level or lower are not strong candidates for inclusion in Phase III. However, it is not unusual to find items with scores of 100.0 or higher, depending upon the choice of subgroups and the nature of the items themselves.

Incidentally, one use for discrimination scores is to compare universes of content for segmentation relevance. If, as often happens, benefit items show consistently higher discrimination scores than lifestyles, it suggests that more benefit than lifestyle items should be carried into Phase III.

It should be noted that, for a negligible additional expense, discriminant function analysis runs can be extended to provide discriminant maps. These provide a visual representation of how subgroups are discriminated from each other, and often stimulate hypotheses about market structure and the kinds of segments that are likely to emerge in Phase III.

A third multivariate technique that is sometimes applied in Phase II is regression analysis. It is helpful to understand how the various items in the Phase II questionnaire are related to criterion measures such as frequency of usage of the brand of interest, purchase intent toward that brand, and constant sum allocations among major brands in the product category.

[17] B. J. Winer, *Statistical Principles in Experimental Design*, New York: McGraw-Hill, 1962.

	Extremely	Very	Quite	Rather	Slightly	Not At All	
	\- I M P O R T A N T						
	-6	-5	-4	-3	-2	-1	
Provides pep and energy							4
Helps develop a strong body							5
Is good for a change of pace							6
Tastes good							7
Has a strong chocolate flavor							8
Does not have a chalky or powdery texture							9
Has a very sweet taste							10
	-6	-5	-4	-3	-2	-1	
Has a malt flavor							11
Comes in an unbreakable container							12
Comes in a container which opens and closes easily							13
Is available in a large size							14
Comes in a powdered form							15
Comes in a container that can be used for a toy after use							16
Is unsweetened							17
	-6	-5	-4	-3	-2	-1	
Has vitamins and minerals added							18
Comes in a container that is easy to hold							19
Comes in a container that is easy to keep clean							20
Is a pure cocoa product							21
Is easy to mix							22
Dissolves completely so you don't have any lumps							23
Doesn't thicken or harden after it's opened							24

	-6	-5	-4	-3	-2	-1	
It is not difficult to control the amount you are using							25
Stays fresh							26
Can be used for cold drinks or hot drinks							27
Can be used in many different ways							28
Covers up the taste of milk							29
Is not fattening							30
Makes milk thicker							31
	-6	-5	-4	-3	-2	-1	
Is made by a well-known company							32
Is made by a company that makes other chocolate products							33
Is widely available in many stores							34
Is economical							35
Is made especially for children							36
Has recipes on the label							37
Can be used any time of the year							38
	-6	-5	-4	-3	-2	-1	

Figure 8.2. Drink Mix Benefit Importance Rating Page

189

Regression is a technique for measuring the relationship between a dependent variable such as those listed in the preceding paragrpah and one or more independent variables. When several independent variables are analyzed simultaneously, the process is called multiple regression. Several conditions must be met before it is appropriate to apply regression to a data set. For example, it is usually assumed that a causal relationship exists between the independent variables involved and the dependent variable, that the relationship can be described by a line (usually a straight line), that the scatter around the line of relationship is evenly dispersed (homoscedasticity), that the relationship can be explained in terms of variance around the line of estimate, and that the independent variables are, in fact, independent. In attitude measurement it is unusual for the independent variables to be independent, which makes it difficult to interpret the coefficients in the regression equations. If two "independent" variables are related, both of their coefficients are likely to be unstable and highly sensitive to sampling error.

There are at least two ways to avoid this problem. One is to run separate regressions for each independent variable. The other is a special form of regression called "Principal Components Regression."[18] This is, in effect, a combination of factor analysis and regression. The algorithm first factors the independent variables, creating new variables that meet the independence requirement. These are then regressed on the dependent variable.

Assuming that the conditions required for regression are met reasonably well, the higher the coefficient the stronger the association between the independent variable and the criterion measure, and the more powerful the evidence supporting inclusion of the independent variable in Phase III.

Still another statistical technique that is helpful in selecting items from Phase II responses is called, appropriately, "item analysis."[19] This is normally used in conjunction with factor analysis in choosing the best items to represent a factor. It examines the intercorrelations of the ratings of items tentatively classified into a factor (see Table 8.1). This table, suggests that item C is a much better representative of the factor than, say, item G.

Finally, some form of cluster analysis may be helpful in pointing out the types of items that might best be preserved.[20] Cluster analysis differs from factor analysis in that cluster analysis is primarily a data organization technique, whereas factor analysis is primarily a data reduction technique. It should be pointed out that many analysts consider factor analysis as a data organization technique as well. If the goal of the analysis is to identify atti-

---

[18] BMDP Biomedical Computer Programs, P-Series, 1977.
[19] D. R. Lehmann and K. E. A. Britney, *Determining an Appropriate Measure of Reliability for Psychographic Measures in Contemporary Marketing Thought,* Chicago: American Marketing Association, 1977.
[20] Cluster analysis references cited in footnotes 22, 23, and 24, Chapter 5 above.

TABLE 8.1   Item Analysis Correlations

Item	A	B	C	D	E	F	G
A	—	.800	790	.855	.729	.684	.531
B		—	.853	.788	.902	.846	.590
C			—	.905	.788	.824	.693
D				—	.529	.703	.669
E					—	.885	.416
F						—	.727
G							—

tudinal segments, however, factor analysis suffers definite limitations. These will be discussed in the forthcoming section on Phase III of the research.

In Phase II cluster analysis is employed as a sort of preview of coming attractions. Once the factor structure of each universe of content has been decided upon, a cluster analysis can be run on the selected factors. There are perhaps 100 different clustering algorithms. In general, most of these can be classed into three types: aggregation algorithms, disaggregation algorithms, and bump and push algorithms.

Aggregation algorithms in general search for the two respondents whose pattern of ratings is most similar. These become the center, sometimes called the "node," of the first cluster. Then the computer checks to see if it can find a third respondent who is more similar to the first two respondents than another two new respondents are to each other. If the third respondent is closer to the first pair than the two new respondents are to each other, he joins the first pair, making it a trio. If not, the computer starts a new cluster. This process continues until every member of the sample has been assigned to a cluster. One popular aggregation algorithm is that of Johnson.[21]

Disaggregation approaches work on the basis of successive splits. The computer first attempts to divide respondents into two groups in such a way that the groups are maximally different (e.g., the ratio of between-group to within-group variance is at a maximum). It then splits one of the two groups into two parts, testing each possible split and choosing the one that results in maximum differentiation. The computer proceeds in this manner until the sample of respondents has been completely decomposed. One popular disaggregation approach is the AID algorithm developed at the University of Michigan.[22]

[21] S. C. Johnson, "Hierachical Clustering Schemes," *Psychometrika*, Vol. 32, 1967, pp. 241–254.
[22] H. Assael, "Segmenting Markets by Group Purchasing Behavior: An Application of the AID Technique," *Journal of Marketing Research*, Vol. 7, May 1970, pp. 153–158.

"Bump and push" algorithms are iterative. In other words, they attempt to reduce some preselected criterion to minimum levels. Popular examples are Howard-Harris[23] and Singleton-Kautz.[24] The Singleton-Kautz algorithm is designed to group observations, which in the case of Benefit Segmentation studies are people's response patterns, into clusters in which the within-cluster variance is at a minimum. In more technical language, we are trying to minimize trace W, where W is the within groups covariance matrix.

The algorithm works in the following manner:

All respondents are assigned to one large group and the centroid of that group is located.

The respondent farthest from the center is selected as the first member of a second group.

All respondents are tested, one at a time, to see if reassignment to the second group will reduce the sum-squared error. If it will, the reassignment is made.

This process continues until it is no longer possible to reduce the sum-squared error by reassigning any single respondent to the second cluster.

The number of clusters is then increased to three by selecting the respondent who is farthest from the centroids of the first two clusters. As in the previous split, respondents are tested to see whether reassignment further reduces the statistic being minimized.

The cycle of steps repeats until the number of clusters reaches some maximum set by the analyst before beginning to run the program. In the case of Benefit Segmentation studies this number is usually set at six, seven, or eight.

When this limit is reached, the procedure is reversed and the number of clusters begins to be systematically reduced. This is done by combining the two clusters that minimally increase the sum-squared error. If, for example, the limit has been set at eight and the reduction reduces the number of clusters to seven, the variance of the seven-cluster solution resulting from contraction is compared with the seven-cluster solution generated earlier on the way up to the maximum.

The computer retains solutions that are attractive and iterates the process of increasing and decreasing the numbers of clusters until it can find no further way to reduce the sum-squared error at any level. At this point the process terminates.

[23] N. Howard and B. Harris, "A Hierarchical Grouping Routine, IBM 360/65 FORTRAN IV Program," Philadelphia: University of Pennsylvania Computer Center, 1970.
[24] "Singleton-Kautz Clustering Program," Stanford Research Institute, Palo Alto, CA, 1968.

Singleton-Kautz, like most minimum-variance partitioning techniques, is based on the assumption that the goal is to group respondents into relatively homogeneous segments. Homogeneity is determined by some measure of distance from the cluster average or centroid. It makes no explicit distributional assumptions.

It works most efficiently with variables that are relatively uncorrelated. Consequently although it is possible to use original items, it is preferable to use orthogonal factor scores from R-mode factor analysis. Alternatively an item analysis can be conducted to insure that the benefits chosen for clustering purposes are indeed relatively independent of each other.

Another caution for prospective users is that the algorithm is sensitive to changes in the scaling of the original variables and the variability of their variance. Thus it is desirable to standardize the data before applying this technique. It is invariant with respect to orthogonal transformations of the data. But the effectiveness of the clustering can be reduced by outliers. Thus consideration should be given to eliminating any individual respondents whose responses are quite different from those of other people.

Singleton-Kautz is what has been called a "hill-climbing" technique. As has been indicated it minimizes the squared error variance, starting from a variety of positions and selecting for each set of clusters the lowest value of the squared error found in its various tries. The user need input only the maximum number of clusters to be found. Output includes the cluster assignment for each observation in each cluster set, cluster mean vectors, squared error within clusters, and other useful statistics.

The clusters produced by bump and push algorithms tend to be more stable in split-half reliability tests—both as to composition and as to size.[25] AID, in particular, appears to require larger sample sizes in order to produce reliable results. One source[26] suggests that a minimum of 1000 respondents is required before a stable structure can be counted upon. For this reason bump and push programs are preferred when they are available. Once attractive clusters have been generated, discriminant analysis can be employed to identify the items that best discriminate among them.

An analyst who has followed *all* of the suggestions contained in this section will at this point find himself or herself suffering from information overload. The analyst will have at his or her disposal:

Mean or top box desirability ratings (for benefits only)

Factor loadings

[25] R. Johnson, "Techniques of Market Segmentation: Cluster Analysis versus Q Analysis," 1969 International Marketing Congress, American Marketing Association, June 1969.
[26] H. J. Einhorn, "Alchemy in the Behavioral Sciences," *Public Opinion Quarterly*, Fall 1972, pp. 367–378.

Item analysis results
Discrimination ratios (between significant subgroups)
Regression coefficients
Discrimination ratios (between clusters)
Frequency of occurrence data (for occasions only)

Needless to say these criteria will often point to the retention of different items. There are several systems for dealing with this complexity. Among the more popular are:

1. Determine approximately how many items it will be feasible to include in the Phase III questionnaire, prioritize the criteria, and select items until the target number has been approximated.

2. Make up a grid, such as that shown in Table 8.2, to give a visual impression of which items are supported by two or more criteria and which criteria support them.

3. Assign the research member or members of the team the task of developing a preliminary list of recommended items together with the supporting logic for each. The list is reviewed in a team meeting and modified to some extent. However, its availability gives the meeting a running start.

4. Include everything suggested by one or more criteria. Although it is easy to get agreement when this procedure is used, it often generates

TABLE 8.2   Summary of Benefit Choice Criteria

Benefit Number	Top Box Desirability	Factor Marker and Number	Brand Discrimination	Volume Discrimination	Type Discrimination
1	H	3	H	H	H
2		7	H		
3	L			H	
4		3			
5	H	3	L		
6	H			H	H
7		1			
8		1	H		
9	H	5	H		H
10	L				
etc.					

H = high
L = low

a long list and thus can be self-defeating. The purpose of Phase II is data reduction. Unless around two-thirds of the items considered are eliminated, the result is likely to be an extremely long Phase III questionnaire, respondent fatigue, and fuzzy research results.

Obtaining effective and efficient item lists depends upon the judgment and skill of the project team, especially that of the team coordinator. And the difference between good and bad results can mean the difference between a successful and an unsuccessful study. Although this is still largely an art form, the structure outlined in the preceding pages will materially improve the odds favoring success. Having some team members who are thoroughly experienced in attitude segmentation studies is also helpful in producing successful studies. Attitude Segmentation research projects are as complex as any type of marketing research extant. Consequently it is to be expected that the second, third, and fourth segmentation studies will be better executed and more productive than the first one attempted.

Phase III—Measuring the Market in Detail

The result of a well-done second phase is a series of carefully developed measuring instruments. These have value not only for their primary purpose—input into Phase III—but for the multitude of secondary uses to which they can be put. These include all future concept tests, product tests, package tests, copy tests, and tracking studies. If consumer behaviors are to be understood and consumer responses to advertising accurately predicted, it is usually necessary to measure benefits sought and delivered, lifestyles, beliefs, and occasions of consumption. This is just as true for copy testing, product testing, and tracking studies as it is for attitudinal surveys. Thus the large costs normally associated with communications strategy studies can be amortized across a variety of projects.

Phase III has as its objective providing a full and detailed picture of the market of interest and of the major consumer subgroups within it. Because this picture forms the basis for the brand communications strategy, it is vitally important that the research is done well. Cutting corners on research costs is usually false economy. Any savings that result, such as using a mail panel in place of a national probability sample, will be outweighed by the risks involved. Although a mail panel may provide substantially the same results as personal interviews in the homes of a national probability sample of respondents, the number of instances where this has not been so make the risk unaffordable.[27]

[27] A *National Study of the Laxative Market,* New York: Grey Advertising, Inc., 1963.

Cold Beverage Study
June 1984
ID#

Answer Booklet

Respondent's Name_____
City_____ State_____

Figure 8.3. "Answer booklet" cover page

Areas of coverage are extensive. Benefit, problem, occasion, belief, and personality and lifestyle items are carried over from Phase II. Often they are incorporated into an answer booklet and given to respondents in an "attended self-administered" format (see Figures 8.3 and 8.4). In this process the respondents are asked to fill in the rating scale booklet while the interviewer waits nearby to answer any procedural questions that may arise.

Various methods have been tried to obtain the necessary ratings information without wasting the time of the interviewer. The obvious expedient of leaving a stamped envelope with the respondents and asking them to

Name_____ Phone No._____
Address_____ City_____ State_____
Interviewer_____ Metro Area_____ Date_____

Dear Consumer:

As your interviewer told you, you have been scientifically chosen to take part in a survey being conducted among a specially selected sample throughout the United States. Your opinions are *very important to people in the music industry so they can make products you will like and want.*

Your interviewer has left this questionnaire for you to fill out. She will return shortly to pick up the questionnaire. This questionnaire contains several short, easy to fill in parts. Listed here are statements and phrases that various people have made to us in describing their attitudes and opinions in general, as well as about music. There are no right or wrong answers, since different people have different attitudes, feelings, and opinions.

Please make sure to fill in *every* question in each part. We care about all of your opinions and are very much interested in everything you have to say. Please answer *all* questions if you can. We have shown this booklet to many people like yourself (some even in your area) and most found the experience interesting and entertaining. Of course, all of your answers will be confidential.

Please disregard any numbers in the right-hand margin. They are for office use only.

In appreciation of your cooperation in filling out the entire questionnaire you will receive your choice of one of a list of records as a "thank you" gift.

Thank you again for your help.

Sincerely yours,

Figure 8.4. Answer booklet instructions.

drop the booklet in the mail once it has been completed does not work very well in practice. Nearly one-third of the respondents do not return their booklets under such conditions. Moreover those who do not return their booklets often are quite different from those who do return them. This causes serious problems in interpreting cross-tabulations of attitudinal and behavioral data.

Another approach that works reasonably well is to leave the booklet with respondents and return at a later time to recover it. Because most fieldwork involves callbacks and thus the necessity for an interviewer to work several days in the same area, the callback recovery method is fairly efficient. Stimulated by the promise of a "lovely gift" when the interviewer returns (at an agreed upon time), recovery rates normally are about 90 percent.

The choice between the "attended self-administered" and the callback approach depends primarily upon the average amount of time required to complete the booklet. If it takes a half hour or less, the attended self-administered approach is superior. On the other hand, if it requires an hour or more, it is probably better to call back. In the interest of making the interview somewhat more enjoyable, and thus making the task of the next interviewer to approach the respondent a little easier, it is suggested that the average time requirement of the booklet be held to at about a half hour.

The question often arises as to how many rating scales a respondent can handle before fatigue and boredom set in and adversely affect the quality of the data. Little work has been published on this subject. The only known study was conducted at Grey Advertising in 1964.[28] In an experiment involving benefits it was hypothesized that, as the number of ratings increased the variance among ratings would decrease and the mean level of ratings would increase. In this instance individual benefits were represented by phrases on cards. Respondents were asked to sort the cards onto a rating board to reflect their opinions about the desirability of each benefit. The rating board contained six degrees of desirability ranging from "Extremely Desirable" to "Not at all Desirable."

In all, 132 benefits were rated by each respondent, and these were divided into three random groups. A latin square design was set up to control the sequences in which the three sets would be presented to respondents. As noted previously it was hypothesized that fatigue would be reflected in two ways. First, if fatigue was present, it was assumed that people would show less discrimination from benefit to benefit—that people would tend to place more cards in the same box. Second, it was assumed that people might be-

---

[28] "A Study of Respondent Fatigue in the Administration of Attitude Scale Ratings," New York: Grey Advertising, Inc. (unpublished study), 1964.

come less critical and rate most of the benefits presented late on the list as important.

Neither of these hypotheses was substantiated. No evidence of fatigue was found, not even directional evidence. Consequently, it was concluded that it was safe to go as far as about 150 ratings and perhaps farther. The limits imposed by fatigue are not known but they undoubtedly exist at some level. And many of the answer booklets used with attitudinal segmentation studies appear to press whatever limits exist.

Some indirect evidence bearing on fatigue is also available. On occasion the same item has been included at two separate points in phrase lists, ranging from 100 to 300 items. It is reassuring to report that when factor analysis is employed, these two items invariably appear in the same factor and have similar factor loadings. It is less so to observe that the direct correlations between them average only .8.

In addition to the material carried over from Phase II, the answer booklet normally contains brand ratings for the brand of interest and its principal competitors. The items rated parallel the benefits and occasions identified as worth carrying over from Phase II. In other words, brands are rated on product characteristics, on benefit delivery, and on their suitability for various occasions, activities, times, or purposes. Overall brand ratings are also included.

Sometimes it is not practical to ask each respondent to rate every brand on every image item, particularly when the product category contains many brands and the list of image items to be rated is imposing. There are several ways to circumvent this situation:

Respondents can rate only a fixed set of two or three leading brands, including, of course, the brand that is sponsoring the study. Although this approach is appealing in its simplicity, it has some significant drawbacks. For example, some respondents may be loyal users of a fourth brand. If this brand is excluded from the set to be rated by the respondent in question, it may be almost impossible to interpret the remaining ratings.

Respondents can be asked to rate a randomly selected set of two or three brands. With traditional methods of interviewing this may pose problems of field administration. However, if Cathode Ray Tube interviewing[29] is used and the appropriate programming is available, it may not be too difficult to accomplish.[30] Nevertheless, the problem remains the

[29] CRT interviews involve the use of a microcomputer and the telephone. The interviewer reads the questions appearing on the screen to respondents and types in the answers of the respondents.

[30] S. Dutka, "The New Technologies and Tracking Studies," ANA Advertising Research Workshop, New York, December 9, 1981.

same. Unless respondents rate their favorite brand or brands, their responses may be hard to interpret.

One solution is to have respondents rate only their own brands and the brand of interest. If their favorite brand *is* the brand of interest, they are asked to rate their second favorite as well. This procedure provides a solid basis for analyzing user ratings. It does not provide nonuser data for major competitive brands, however, and this limits the possible analyses.

A compromise approach is to include one or two major competitive brands in all interviews while making sure that each respondent rates his or her own brand and the brand of central interest as well.

Although the answer booklet and the carryover material from Phase II represents an important portion of the Phase III interview, a great deal of new material is added to the Phase III interview. Typically this includes measures of:

Awareness (top-of-mind,[31] unaided evoked set)

Brand usage (past month, past year, ever used, used most often)

Circumstances of use (people present, time of day, location, purpose, accompanying products)

Brand switching (brand used the time before last)

Brand purchase (family members involved, store type, sizes bought, number of units bought per purchase, frequency of purchase, timing of purchase)

Perceptions of brand similarity (sorts or paired comparisons)

Brand preference and choice (family members involved, monadic purchase intent, constant sum allocation of next 10 purchases)

Media habits (magazines read regularly, favorite television program types, types of radio stations listened to, newspapers read regularly)

Demographic characteristics (age, sex, education, family size, marital status, employment status, occupation, race, city size, geographic location, income)

Responses in these areas are usually obtained by direct questions. Interview length for this portion of the study averages about 45 minutes, making the total amount of respondent time required about 1¼ hours. Because this places a considerable burden on the respondents, it is customary to offer them a small incentive to express appreciation for their cooperation. This

---

[31] Top-of-mind refers to the proportion of the time a brand is mentioned *first* when the unaided awareness question is asked.

can range from something as simple as felt-tip pens to something as complex as a catalog which allows each respondent to choose one of a number of alternative gifts.

The timing of the gift offer varies among research firms. Some researchers prefer to mention the gift at the outset, believing that it minimizes the level of refusals and thus provides a more representative sample of respondents. Probably a larger group prefers to use the gift in conjunction with the self-administered portion of the interview. This is particularly true when the callback research design is used and the answer booklet has to be recovered with a second visit to the respondent.

Some marketers like to distribute samples of their own products as gifts for cooperation, believing that this gives them added value for their research dollar. In such a case, of course, it is necessary to conceal the brand name of the gift item until complete survey information has been obtained from the respondent. Another limitation is that the gift may break the competitive security of the research project. Questionnaires are usually carefully constructed so that respondents cannot tell which of the brands in the product category is sponsoring the study. Often the "double-blind" procedure is employed. Neither the respondent nor the interviewer knows the study sponsor. This prevents either cooperative bias or reverse bias from coloring survey results. If a product manufactured by the study sponsor is used as a gift, however, the interviewer will be aware of who is underwriting the research. Moreover the respondent may talk to neighbors and friends about the kinds of questions he or she has been asked, and word that research is being conducted may find its way back to important competitors of the study sponsor. This is considered undesirable because although research results are fresh, the sponsor presumably will have a competitive advantage in that his information will be more up to date than that of competitors. Once the word is out that someone in the field is conducting a major study, however, other firms may be stimulated to do something similar and the competitive advantage will be lost.

Direct disclosure to employees of competitors is usually avoided, at least partially, by asking a screening question to ascertain whether the person being interviewed works for an advertising agency, market research firm, newspaper or magazine publisher, or a manufacturer or governmental agency connected in any way with the product category of interest. If they say that they do, they are not interviewed. Of course, a competitor may well be aware that this is common practice and so may avoid being screened out of the interview.

One more area of coverage may well be inserted into the Phase III questionnaire. Because a national probability sample of households has been contacted, or at least a larger or more carefully drawn sample than for the usual research project, it is tempting to incorporate a concept test or a concept/product test into the basic research design. This allows not only a measure of the level of interest in the new product ideas under consideration but provides direction both for targeting the new products and for strengthening the basic concept. Several concepts and/or products can be tested monadically in this manner by assigning different subsamples of respondents to each concept/product. For example, with a national sample of 1000 respondents it is possible to test five concepts, exposing each concept to 200 different respondents. More complex designs can be used when exposing people to more than a single concept. Using the segmentation study as a vehicle for concept testing is especially efficient when the new products are ones with narrow appeal. In such cases it can be prohibitively expensive to attempt to evaluate them individually with standard new product procedures.

When product/concept tests are added to studies of communications strategy, concepts are usually exposed to people at the end of the interview. In the callback design they are exposed at the point at which the self-administered questionnaires are picked up. If a product test is involved, the product is left with respondents at the same point. In the latter instance, after a suitable period of use (often a week), respondents are recontacted by telephone and their reactions to the product are obtained.

Adding concept tests, and especially concept/product tests, runs the risk of overcomplicating the research and detracting from its basic objective of developing a superior communications strategy.

When the priorities on learning about new products are strong enough to override this risk, the question sequence is usually as follows:

Overall rating of purchase interest in the concept/product without price

Ratings of perceived similarity to existing products

Ratings of anticipated strengths and weaknesses

Perceived suitability for various image occasions or purposes

Responses can, of course, be integrated with those obtained in other sections of the questionnaire, thus providing a complete picture of the potential prospects for the new product, the products from which it is most likely to draw sales and, in general, how it might be effectively positioned.

ANALYSIS OF PHASE III RESULTS

If the framework for the project has been constructed in accordance with the suggestions made thus far, the structure of the analysis is reasonably clear. The basic goals of developing an operational definition of the market and the brands competing within it, of identifying the best prospects, and of gaining insights into how best to communicate with those people must be met. Additionally a number of hypotheses about the market and driving forces within it will have been raised and the grounds for accepting or rejecting these have been provided. However, the data themselves may generate new hypotheses. In any survey research project perhaps two-thirds of the most relevant questions can be raised in advance. The remaining questions and the answers to them, or the need to gather further information relating to them, come from the body of data gathered.

The favorite analytical tool of marketing researchers has been and continues to be cross-tabulation. Although multivariate tools have advantages in winnowing out subtle differences and in analyzing overall response patterns, most marketing tools are not precise enough to take advantage of minor differences in attitudes or behavior. Then, too, the questionnaire method of research has definite limitations, and sampling error is a continual concern. Are survey differences real and will they predict how consumers will respond to changes or innovations in marketing practices? The larger the differences the more meaningful they are likely to be, and if they *are* large, they will almost invariably be uncovered by a thorough program of cross-tabulation.

In attitude segmentation studies it is common practice to handle the cross-tabulation problem by constructing "banners" and cross-tabulating them with all of the information gathered in the survey, question by question. A banner consists of a number of subgroups of possible interest to the analysts who will be reviewing the findings. Typically the subgroups consist of:

Demographic subgroups (sex, age, income, etc.—see Table 8.3)

Behavioral subgroups (heavy users of the category, brand-loyal people, people who remember seeing advertising, users of selective competitive brands, people who purchase in particular outlet types, people who consume on specific occasions, etc.—see Table 8.4)

Attitudinal (psychographic) subgroups (segments defined by multivariate methods. These will be discussed in the following section)

The banner approach to cross-tabulation produces huge books of tables. Although many of the tables they contain are unnecessary, the procedure itself is more efficient than attempting to specify each table individually. The books can be indexed and they serve as reference volumes for questions that may arise long after the study has been analyzed and findings have been presented. But a few supplementary tables may have to be produced indi-

TABLE 8.3 Demographic Banner

Brand A	Sex — Male	Sex — Female	Age — <30	Age — 30–55	Age — >55	Income — <$15,000	Income — $15,000–$25,000	Income — >$25,000	Total
Excellent	58 14.5	156 16.6	46 19.2	152 24.0	16 4.2	24 15.2	106 19.1	82 13.6	214 16.0
Very good	180 45.0	418 44.5	108 45.0	308 48.6	158 41.8	60 38.0	242 43.7	286 47.5	598 44.6
Good	92 23.0	220 23.4	60 25.0	122 19.2	120 31.7	46 29.1	122 22.0	132 21.9	312 23.3
Fair	48 12.0	98 10.4	18 7.5	38 6.0	64 16.9	20 12.7	60 10.8	66 11.0	146 10.9
Poor	22 5.5	46 4.9	6 2.5	14 2.2	20 5.3	6 3.8	24 4.3	36 6.0	68 5.1
Don't know	—	2 0.2	2 0.8	—	—	2 1.3	—	—	2 0.1
Total N	400	940	240	634	378	158	554	602	1340
%	100.0	100.0	100.0	100.0	100.0	100.0	100.0	100.0	100.0

TABLE 8.4 Behavioral Banner

Ratings of Brand A	Usage Level Heavy	Other	Number of Purchases Out of Last 10 10/10	6-9	1-5	0	Advertisement Exposure Saw	Didn't	Brand Usage A	B	Other Majors	Total
Excellent	122 22.1	178 22.8	50 27.2	84 27.1	32 26.2	94 20.3	140 23.1	160 22.0	60 26.5	12 13.3	226 24.1	300 22.4
Very good	174 31.5	268 34.3	50 27.2	88 28.4	36 29.5	174 37.7	218 36.0	220 30.2	84 37.2	30 33.3	314 33.5	444 33.1
Good	182 33.0	264 33.8	68 37.0	108 34.8	40 32.8	142 30.7	188 31.0	262 36.0	60 26.5	28 31.1	328 35.0	450 33.6
Fair	44 8.0	50 6.4	8 4.3	20 6.5	10 8.2	36 7.8	46 7.6	48 6.6	14 6.2	16 17.8	40 4.3	94 7.0
Poor	6 1.1	4 0.5	2 1.1	4 1.3	—	2 0.4	4 0.7	6 0.8	—	—	6 0.6	10 0.7
Don't know	24 4.3	18 2.3	3 3.3	6 1.9	4 3.2	14 3.1	10 1.7	32 4.4	8 3.6	4 4.4	22 2.4	42 3.1
Total N	552	782	184	310	122	462	606	728	226	90	936	1340
%	100.0	100.0	100.0	100.0	100.0	100.0	100.0	100.0	100.0	100.0	100.0	100.0

vidually. However, the number required is not likely to be large. Most needs will be met by the banner tables.

Another simple but effective tool that every researcher uses is graphics. Sometimes when data are plotted it is possible to see relationships that are difficult to spot in tabular form. One such approach is called *quadrant analysis*. It consists merely of plotting image ratings against importance ratings. Image data are usually expressed as top-box scores and are plotted on the horizontal axis with the higher scores to the right. Importance scores similarly are top-box scores with the higher scores toward the top of the page.

The name *quadrant analysis* comes from the fact that both horizontal and vertical medians are computed and are plotted on the graph; dividing the plotted data into four quadrants (see Figure 8.5). In the upper right-hand quadrant are image items that are important and on which the brand scores relatively well. If the ratings being plotted are those of brand users, the image items in the upper right-hand quadrant are considered to represent supportable claims.

Image items that appear in the upper left quadrant are ones rated important but below average in terms of the performance of the brand of interest. This area is usually fertile ground for ideas for new products, line extensions, and/or product improvements. Occasionally a brand can be rated below average because of consumer misperceptions. However, this is more likely to occur among the total sample than among experienced brand users. When it does occur it may be possible to correct misperceptions by a

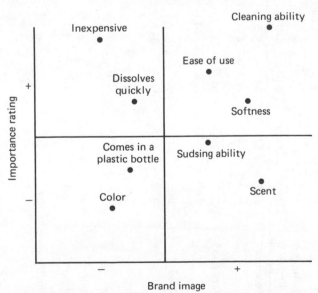

Figure 8.5.   Quadrant analysis for cleaning product

campaign focused on the issue in question. For example, for a number of years the name Mazola was considered by users and the general public alike to have Spanish connotations. Unfortunately consumer preferences were moving steadily toward lighter foods, and Spanish foods were perceived to be on the heavy side. Accordingly a campaign to stimulate associations with maize and thus with the healthy and light corn oil ingredient was launched and was successful in achieving the desired objective.

The lower right-hand quadrant represents an area in which the product has strength but where the characteristics are perceived as below average in importance. Here the goal suggested is agenda setting—increasing the importance attached to the characteristics on which the brand is highly regarded. The fourth quadrant (low importance and below average importance) is generally disregarded.

Quadrant analysis has been employed in a variety of ways. Various samples of consumers can be plotted, of course. And in situations such as the cola market where Pepsi and Coke each focus efforts on the other, *differences* between brand images can be plotted on the horizontal axis.

Various forms of importance scores can be plotted on the vertical axis (see Chapter 4). Also it is desirable that *the same people* who consider a brand strong on a given attribute also consider that attribute important. This is not necessarily true in the first form of quadrant analysis described. If 30% of the people consider Listerine strong on breath freshening, and 30% consider that benefit extremely important, the crucial question is whether or not they are the same people. If this point is not checked, it is possible for one group to consider the brand as superior in a given area and for an entirely different group to consider that area important. The latter group may even consider the brand to be inferior on that image aspect.

To avoid this problem, weighted image scores (image rating times importance rating) can be computed for each respondent and averaged across respondents. When these scores are plotted on the horizontal axis, high scores signify a concurrence of both importance and brand delivery.

Another simple tool is the spine chart (also called the butterfly chart). One way in which these are used is in comparing the brand image of the sponsoring brand with the images of the leading competitors. This is normally done one brand at a time, using ratings. The "spine" that runs down the middle of the chart is the point at which the two brands being compared are equivalent in top-box image ratings. Bars to the right of the spine represent image items on which the sponsoring brand is superior, and bars to the left of the spine show where the competitior excels. Image items are usually shown in rank order of importance with those appearing high on the page considered more important than those shown lower on it. Thus it is possible to identify at a glance areas on which the brand of interest is superior and which, at the same time, are important (see Figure 8.6).

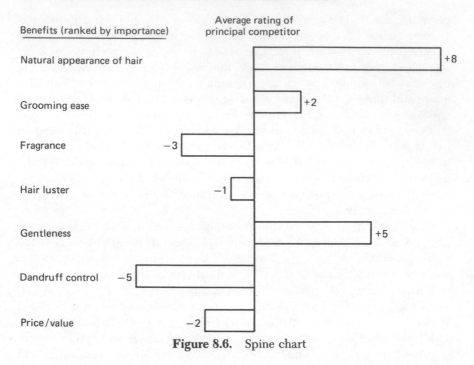

Figure 8.6. Spine chart

Another use of spine charts is in understanding segments. In this application the spine represents either differences from the total sample or differences from total sample less the segment of interest. Using spine charts it is possible to tell quickly which characteristics best distinguish the segment of interest from the remaining segments.

METHODOLOGICAL TRICKS AND TRAPS

This section is intended as a nontechnical review of a highly complex area and one that recent research has tended to make even more complex. A large number of marketing research practitioners feel that the professional literature, as typified by the *Journal of Marketing Research*, the new *Journal of Marketing Science, Consumer Behavior*, and even the *Journal of Marketing* has become more technical than necessary—what Leo Bogart calls the "increasingly autistic literature." The open question is how far multivariate techniques and mathematical modeling can carry us. Some believe we are trying to fly before we have learned to walk. A great many practitioners feel that topics such as sampling, questionnaire design, fieldwork, attitude measurement, copy testing, market testing, product testing, tracking studies,

resent a full range of benefits, may discourage respondents from fully absorbing the content of each set and making accurate cognitive comparisons from set to set. Data from conjoint studies suggest that this may be true even when respondents attempt to cooperate fully with the interviewer.

Emotional benefits are extremely difficult to represent in conjoint studies. As noted earlier this is also a problem for more conventional approaches. The problem is much more severe for conjoint research, however, where the number of stimuli is smaller and emotional and cognitive benefits have to be pitted directly against each other. Consequently, emotional benefits are usually ignored entirely in these studies.[37]

As most frequently employed it assumes that the essence of the benefit can be captured in a phrase on a card. This limitation has been appreciated and recent work is shifting toward heavier use of visuals (e.g., people are given a simulated ride on an airline while their evaluations are obtained) and more frequent evaluation of physical products (e.g., tasting foods). Although these steps represent improvements, they introduce the possibility of giving false cues to people, either nonverbally or through the artificial mechanisms necessarily associated with any laboratory test. Also, although results are weighted to reduce sampling problems, it is unlikely that the weighting actually eliminates the problem.

Similarly, point-of-sale benefits are often ignored—the effects of the package display and in-store promotions. This is by no means a problem unique to conjoint analysis, yet it does affect its ability to predict behavior.

Changing the ranges of values for a given benefit can greatly affect its importance relative to other benefits. Thus when the goal is to find a buying incentive, it is extremely important that the ranges used in the conjoint experiment accurately reflect the marketplace. Similarly, there may be some bias operating in favor of factors with larger numbers of levels.

Although the inclusion of product profiles on cards makes it appear as though respondents would use a compensatory decision process in making their choices, this does not appear to be the case. Because of the large amount of information usually presented to respondents, they are likely to adopt a lexicographic decision process. In other words, they first look for differences on a key benefit such as price. If differences exist on this item, they become the basis for the choice. If they do not, the respondent

[37] Benefit Segmentation studies also have limitations in this area. See "Benefit Segmentation—20 Years Later," *Journal of Consumer Marketing*, Vol. 1, No. 2, January 1984, pp. 5–13.

proceeds to the benefit he or she has decided to use as the next choice criterion. If differences exist, there they become the basis for this choice. If not, the respondent proceeds to the third ranking benefit. Although this may be an efficient way for the respondent to play the game, it is an open question as to whether this is how he or she makes choices in an actual purchase situation. In short, the method is biased toward lexicographic processes.

The ordering of benefits and attributes on cards can introduce significant biases. Although it is possible to build order controls into the process, this usually means that respondents will have to deal with more cards. And the more cards the more likely that respondents will employ a lexicographic decision process, no matter what process they might use in real life.

If one benefit at a particular level is ranked higher than any alternative profile, which includes that attribute at other levels, the estimates of utility values are not unique.

Some combinations of benefits and attributes may not be believable (e.g., a $3000 car that gets 50 miles per gallon and can do 100 miles per hour). Including these can cause respondents to decide that the research isn't very serious and thus to be less involved in the game being played.

Where there is more than one decision maker, the decisionmakers may need to be interviewed as a single unit. Again this is not a problem unique to conjoint analysis.

In summary, conjoint analysis appears to be a technique that is still undergoing substantial development. Despite its general availability since about 1970, it is rarely used where the primary purpose of the research is the development of a *communications strategy*. Although some of the reluctance to adopt it can be attributed to lack of familiarity with the method among practitioners, part of this reluctance can be traced to knowledge of or experience with some of the aforementioned limitations.[38] For the time being, at least, it seems safest to use conjoint analysis in *product development* applications where the product or service is realistically decomposable into a set of highly specific, nonsubjective attributes. It has limited value in communications studies, and it is most effective when the number of product characteristics to be evaluated is small and when each alternative can be clearly and unambiguously understood by every respondent.

Tradeoff Analysis, similar in philosophy to Conjoint Analysis, was devel-

[38] It is interesting to note that the Wharton group which pioneered the conjoint or Full Profile approach is now primarily using the Tradeoff approach, whereas the developer of the Tradeoff approach is now placing primary emphasis on the Full Profile approach.

% of Beverage Made from Fruit Juice

Price	50% fruit juice	40% fruit juice	30% fruit juice
59¢			
69¢			
79¢			

Figure 8.7. Tradeoff Chart

oped by Richard Johnson[39] in 1974. Instead of presenting Benefit Bundles, however, benefits, each at two or more levels, are presented to respondents two at a time (see Figure 8.7) and respondents are asked to "trade off" the levels of one benefit against levels of the other. For example, in the Figure respondents are asked to number the cells of the nine-cell matrix in the order of their preference. Assuming that fruit juice is a desirable ingredient, everyone should rank the upper left-hand corner first. In other words, everyone should prefer the maximum amount of fruit juice at the lowest possible price. The choice of the second ranking cell forces a tradeoff, however. The respondent can elect either to give up some fruit juice or to pay a little more to retain the maximum amount of fruit juice.

Tradeoff Analysis falls midway between Conjoint Analysis and simple scaled importance ratings of benefit sets. It cannot promise to avoid turning people into experts, as does Conjoint Analysis. Nor can it cover the diverse

[39] R. M. Johnson, "Trade-off Analysis of Consumer Values," *Journal of Marketing Research*, May 1974, Vol. 11, No. 2, pp. 121–127.

range of benefits that use of simple importance ratings allows. But it does feature a very sensitive measure of a limited set of alternatives.

In practice, respondents (especially downscale respondents) often have trouble with the concept of numbering the cells in the matrixes that are given to them. Also the number of benefits that can be handled is sharply limited. And the "game" that respondents are required to play becomes cumbersome and repetitious as the number of comparisons mounts. As in the case of Conjoint Analysis there is doubt that consumers will behave in real life as they do in the game situation. This is especially true of the price tradeoffs. It is strongly suspected that people are more willing to "pay" additional amounts of money for added benefits in an interview situation than they are in an actual purchase situation. As in the case of Conjoint Analysis, emotional benefits are not well handled and are customarily ignored in Tradeoff studies. And from a purely technical standpoint, Tradeoff Analysis has been criticized because it does not allow the measurement of interactions among combinations of benefits and attributes as does Conjoint Analysis.

Although Tradeoff Analysis offers limited possibilities in studies of communications, it offers the same kinds of advantages in product design problems that Conjoint Analysis does. Parenthetically, still another design, the "build-your-own" design, should be mentioned in conjunction with product design. This method establishes how much the respondent usually pays for products in a particular class, gives him a number of chips equivalent to that amount (dollarmetric scaling), and then asks him to allocate those across features to indicate their relative value to him.[40]

Putting the alternatives for obtaining benefit importance ratings into perspective, Conjoint Analysis and Tradeoff Analysis are best suited for situations in which the number of benefits to be evaluated is relatively small and where each benefit can be expressed in an objective and unambiguous manner. This is often true of product development problems where the number of variables that can be manipulated is limited and the variables are physical characteristics with levels that can be expressed explicitly.

As the number of variables increases and the number of subjective variables with imprecise levels increases (e.g., tastes good, convenient to use, lasts a long time, etc.), these techniques are suspect. When the number of benefits is large and each one can be expressed in a variety of ways, simple rating scales are the preferred choice. When the final set is moderate in size, say 20 or fewer, constant sum scales, which themselves force tradeoffs, are

[40] For a comparison of the multiattribute, dollarmetric, and constant sum approaches, see D. J. Reibstein, "The Prediction of Individual Probabilities of Brand Choice," *Journal of Consumer Research*, December 1978, pp. 163–168.

worth considering. And where the stimuli include physical characteristics with objective levels, the choice is among:

Including a statement relating to each level and rating each statement individually.

Using principles of experimental design and obtaining a series of constant sum ratings over varying sets of items.

Separating physical items from the more subjective benefits and analyzing benefits in two groups—a group of objective items and a group of subjective items.

In this case, if the set of objective characteristics is not too large, Conjoint Analysis or Tradeoff Analysis may be practical possibilities.

DETERMINING THE BEST METHOD FOR SEGMENTING A MARKET

Segmentation can be achieved in a forward or a backward manner.[41] In other words, an analyst can start with a set of factors that he or she believes to be causal, segment the market or them, and see how well the segments developed are discriminated in terms of their *behavior*. Alternatively the analyst can group people in terms of similarity in their behavior and work backward to try to discover the reasons for the similarity. The latter procedure is called "Backward Segmentation."[42] Although backward segmentation is useful where only behavioral data exist and the analyst would like to infer causes,[43] there are problems with backward reasoning. Principal among them is the fact that the same behavior can arise from different causes. As the advertising claims, some people buy Millers Lite beer because it tastes great and some because it is less filling. If the goal is to understand and predict consumer behavior, then it is preferable, wherever possible, to reason from cause to effect. Of course in some situations both behavioral and attitudinal data are available in detailed form.[44] In such situ-

[41] R. Haley, "Benefit Segments: Backwards and Forwards," *Journal of Advertising Research*, February/March 1984, Vol. 24, No. 1, pp. 19–25.

[42] W. Wells, "Backward Segmentation" in Johan Arndt (Ed.), *Insights into Consumer Behavior*, Boston: Allyn & Bacon, 1968, p. 85.

[43] L. Alpert and R. Gatty, "Product Positioning by Behavioral Life Styles," *Journal of Marketing*, Vol. 33, April 1969, p. 67ff.

[44] R. I. Haley, "Benefit Segments: Backwards and Forwards," *Journal of Advertising Research*, February/March 1984, Vol. 24, No. 1, pp. 19–25.

ations the analyst has the option of segmenting the market both by attitudes and by behavior and of crossruffing the two modes of segmentation.

It has also been pointed out that it would be preferable to segment on the basis of response elasticities where they are available.[45] The problem is that the kinds of databanks which would be required for developing elasticities for differing advertising themes are rarely affordable as a continuous research project. Even on a single study basis (as opposed to a tracking study) at least three waves of interviews are needed if lead/lag relationships are to be fully investigated.[46] So, given cost limitations the procedure used most frequently is to mount a large study covering promising universes of content and to use cross-sectional analyses of those universes as a substitute for time series analyses. Although it is recognized that this procedure can be slightly misleading, it seems reasonable to believe that the rank order of segment attractiveness is not badly distorted by this compromise.

For purposes of discussion let us assume that the results of a major communications study are available for multivariate analysis. For purposes of simplicity let us also assume it covers three universes of content—benefits, beliefs, and lifestyle measures. (The procedure when "problems" and "occasions" are included is directly parallel.)

One question is whether the search for attractive segments should *simultaneously* embrace all three universes or whether one universe should be chosen as the primary basis for segmentation, with the other universes used primarily as cross-tabulations to give added depth to the segments defined on the basis of the first universe.

Logic would seem to favor dealing with the maximum amount of data that can be handled and to do so simultaneously rather than in stepwise fashion. Among the procedures, both stepwise and simultaneous, that have been and are currently being used are the following:

Develop factor scores from R factor analysis for each universe of content and cluster people into segments on the basis of their factor scores.

Develop segments for each universe separately, construct for each respondent a vector of dummy variables (zeros and ones) to reflect membership in the segments of each universe, and cluster on the basis of that vector.

Use Q factor analysis.

Use canonical correlation.[47]

[45] H. Assael, "Segmenting Markets by Response Elasticity," *Journal of Advertising Research,* Vol. 16, April 1976, pp. 27–35.

[46] "How Advertising Works," Grey Advertising, Inc.

[47] Ronald Frank and Charles Strain, *Journal of Marketing Research,* Vol. 9, November 1972, pp. 385–390.

Use Componential Segmentation.[48] This method attempts to extend conjoint analysis to include usage, demographic characteristics, and other universes of content that can be described categorically. Separate utilities are computed for each level in each universe of content. These allow the user to play "what if" games between segments and alternative positionings. However, the earlier mentioned limitations of conjoint analysis apply here. Consequently, the model seems more appropriately applied to product problems than to communications problems.

Use the Benemax method—one of the newest models. Evidence on its performance was fragmentary at the time of publication. It purports to find optima in six areas, including the optimum combination of benefits to be communicated in advertising. It appears to downplay the importance of salience and selective perception, however, assuming that it is just as easy and just as effective to communicate two benefits or three benefits as to communicate one.

Experience with these models in a communications setting suggests that their mathematical sophistication does little to provide clearer segments or ones with more exciting marketing implications. Instead, by forcing the data to fit the model and by including so many different types of variables, they tend to blur the distinctions between segments and to confuse the marketing and advertising people who attempt to use their output. As a result they continue to receive most of their support from the academic community.

An allegory may be appropriate at this point. A baseball player was having trouble with his hitting. He asked a management scientist (who happened to be a mathematical psychologist) and a marketing researcher to analyze his problem. Both people videotaped his batting style, coded what they saw, and analyzed the results. The management scientist's recommendations on the basis of his model were:

"Drop your left shoulder one and one half inches."
"Rotate your left foot approximately 30° more to the outside."
"Turn your chin to the left until it touches your collarbone."
"Lower your right elbow until it points directly at the ground."
"Count to two before you begin your swing."

The market researcher said, "Try pulling a little more to the left."
The reader can decide which recommendation was likely to be more

---

[48] P. E. Green, D. G. Carroll, and F. J. Carmone in Y. Wind and M. Greenberg (Eds.), *Moving A Head with Attitude Research,* Chicago: AMA, 1977, pp. 9–18.

helpful, which was most likely to be accepted, and which analyst was called the next time the batter had a slump.

In the case of segmentation research, segments based on a single universe of content tend to be clearer than those based on fancier models, and they are certainly easier to communicate to the marketing people involved. If all three universes are used simultaneously, it is likely that some segments will be best identified by the benefits they are seeking, some by their lifestyles, and some by their beliefs about the product category. If the first segment described at the unveiling of research findings is identified by one or two key benefits, the audience is likely to be dissatisfied with a description of a second segment that focuses on lifestyles. They will want to know how the second group differs from the first in terms of its needs. On the other hand, if a single universe of content is chosen as the entry point for segmentation, this problem is largely avoided. All segments will be defined from a common framework. If benefits turn out to be the most viable basis for segmentation, all segments will be differentiated in terms of their patterns of benefits sought. The question then is not the best way of covering all universes of content simultaneously but rather in our hypothetical example, how to decide whether benefits, lifestyles, or beliefs are a more appropriate basis for segmentation.

There are several ways of answering this question.[49] One of the most straightforward is to use canonical correlation to test the degree of association among selected criterion measures (e.g., volume of consumption, brand preference, type preference) and segments derived from alternative universes of content.

Canonical correlation is similar in many respects to multiple regression. Instead of developing an equation relating a series of independent variables to *one* dependent variable, however, it develops several equations (canonical vectors) relating a series of independent variables to a *set* of dependent variables. In this application the dependent variables are the criterion measures. It is usually best to choose a small set, each of which is important in its own right. Frequently included criterion measures are volume of category usage, usage of the clients brand, usage of one or two key competitors and, where different product types exist, type usage. Often these are coded as dummy variables with "1"s for usage and "0"s for nonusage. For volume of category usage a "1" can be assigned to the consumption level called "heavy usage."

[49] P. E. Green and F. J. Carmone, "Segment Congruence Analysis, A Method for Analyzing Association Among Alternative Bases for Market Segmentation," in D. W. Scotton and R. L. Zallocco (Eds.), *Readings in Market Segmentation*, Chicago: AMA, 1980. See also K. J. Clancy and M. L. Roberts, "Toward an Optimal Market Target: A Strategy for Market Segmentation," *Journal of Consumer Marketing*, Vol. 1, No. 1, Summer 1983, pp. 64–73.

The independent variables are segment membership, again coded as dummy variables. Observations are individual respondents. Thus if a given universe of content produces five segments, there will be five independent variables, one of which will be coded "1" and the remaining four zero.

Canonical correlation can produce several significant vectors, but the first of these is usually given the greatest attention. In most cases it does discriminate between the alternative segmentation bases. Output provided by standard statistical packages such as SPSS and BMDP also gives some preliminary insights into the probable nature of the segments should they be chosen as the primary entry point for segmentation. An analyst can see which segments are related to which criteria. This allows judgment to enter into the choice process—an important ingredient in any successful approach. One caveat may be appropriate when dummy variables are employed. The levels of association may look abysmally low to analysts accustomed to working with continuous data, but this is to be expected.[50, 51] It does not mean that subsequent cross-tabulations will not show discrimination.

One limitation of canonical correlation is that, as in the case of regression, linearity is assumed. Although this means that the canonical vectors may not fit the data very precisely, the rank orders of universe attractiveness are not likely to be materially affected by this lack of precision.

DERIVING THE SEGMENTS

Let us assume that we would like to develop the best possible segments from the ratings of 50 individual benefits. Some analysts favor immediate use of Q factor analysis. This is a highly efficient approach from a cost standpoint, but it has a number of problems.[52] First, the segments are strongly affected by the input. If half of the 50 items deal with a single factor such as "taste," then the segment solutions are likely to emphasize taste distinctions. As has been shown, however, until the results of R factor analyses are available, it is normal for analysts to disagree about the underlying

[50] F. M. Bass, Unexplained Variance in Studies of Consumer Behavior, Paper No. 339, Nov, 1971, Herman C. Krannert Graduate School of Industrial Administration, Purdue U., Lafayette, Indiana.

[51] D. G. Morrison, "Evaluating Market Segmentation Studies: The Properties of R^2," *Management Science*, Vol. 19, July 1973, pp. 1213–1221. See also *Educational and Psychological Measurement*, Summer 1967, p. 323ff.

[52] S. J. Arnold, "Desirable Conditions in an Optimal Lifestyle Clustering Procedure," Series 37, *1975 Combined Proceedings*, pp. 211–215.

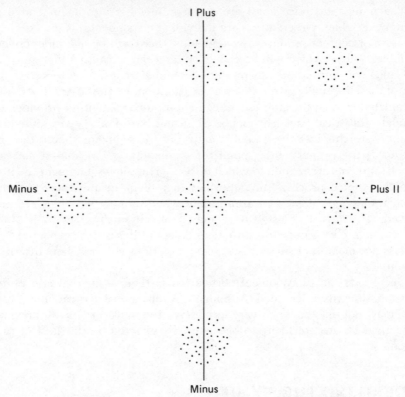

Figure 8.8. A situation with clearly visible clumps

factors being tapped by individual items. For this reason a second school of analysts believes in first conducting an R analysis to identify the factors involved and then clustering respondents on factor scores or on combinations of items selected to represent each factor.[53]

The second procedure is considered preferable to the first for a number of reasons. First, Q analysis assumes that consumers can be aligned along vectors in multidimensional space. However, many product categories show consumer benefit interest to be grouped into several clumps in multidimensional space. Second, the Q model is inefficient when clumps exist. In situations where several visual clumps clearly exist, the Q model will miss some clumps. For example, if the data in (Figure 8.8) are subjected to Q analysis, the result is likely to be two bipolar factors. The clump in the cen-

[53] A few analysts follow R analysis with Q analyses. However, this practice tends to produce "mirror segments," pairs of segments that are direct opposites of each other.

ter of the chart and the one in the northeast corner will be missed. Third, some Q "segments" are bipolar. The vector that identifies the segment contains people with both high positive and high negative factor loadings. In other words, they are opposite types rather than members of a single Q segment. Although these segments can readily be split in two, it seems preferable to use methods that will identify segments directly.

In one review of clustering alternatives, Q analysis is specifically ruled out of bounds. In the words of the author, "Q factor analysis is often a principal tool employed in market segmentation studies. Its use has continued despite repeated criticisms and its disappointingly poor record of reliability. The use of Q factor analysis for the identification of segments or types is one of the paramount abuses of factor analysis."[54]

Even after the R factors have been developed and clusters have been run, the analyst must decide on the number of segments he or she wishes to develop. Several criteria are helpful in reaching this decision.

The scree diagram, referred to in the earlier discussions of factor analysis, has a counterpart in most cluster analysis programs. It shows the rate at which the total variance of the universe is being reduced by the process of systematically extracting one cluster at a time. (See Figure 8.9 for such a diagram, this one suggesting a four cluster solution.)

Cross-tabbing each successive cluster solution by the preceding solution. Thus, for example, the five group solution should be cross-tabbed by the four group solution. This will show whether the fifth group is a "new" group, drawn from several of the four previous segments, or whether one of the four groups has simply been split into two pieces to form the required five groups. Early clusters tend to be "new" clusters, but as the clustering process breaks the universe down into smaller and smaller segments, split clusters become more likely. Thus one stopping criterion is the appearance of the first split clusters.

The cluster size of the smallest cluster obtained is another consideration. At some point clusters begin to lose their marketing significance. Most communications strategy studies look for groups of substantial size, recognizing that no brand can convert *all* of the members of any group. Also as sample sizes decline the interpretation reliability of the nature of the segment decreases.

Split-half reliability tests attempt to identify segments that are likely to be discovered among fresh samples of respondents. One problem with small segments, even if their character seems to be clear, is that they may

[54] D. W. Stewart, "The Application and Misapplication of Factor Analysis in Marketing Research," *Journal of Marketing Research*, Vol. 18, February 1981, pp. 51–62.

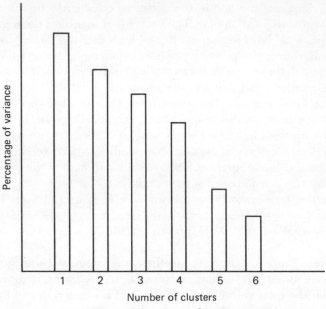

Figure 8.9.   Scree diagram

be unique to the sample obtained in the survey. In other words, the segment may exist in the sample but not in the world at large. Split-half research reduces the chance of this. It can be accomplished in a number of ways.[55] One of the simplest is to separate the sample into two subgroups using questionnaire numbers as a guide. Even-numbered questionnaires are classified into one group and odd-numbered questionnaires in the other. Because questionnaires usually arrive in bunches from individual interviewers or from field supervisors and are numbered sequentially, this procedure balances the two subsamples fairly well by geographic area and by interviewer.

Separate cluster analyses are performed on each subsample. Then, assuming that the analysis was conducted on benefit desirability ratings, the profiles of benefits sought by each segment of the first sample are correlated with the benefits sought by each segment of the second sample. Table 8.5 shows a correlation matrix of this sort. Note the benefit ratings of segment 1 in a sample A correlate to the extent of .9976 with the benefit ratings of segment 1 in sample B. Similarly, the benefit ratings

[55] W. E. Deming, "On Simplifications of Sampling Design Through Replication with Equal Probabilities and Without Stages," *Journal of the American Statistical Association*, March 1956, pp. 24–53.

TABLE 8.5 Split-Half Reliability Test of Segments

Second Half Sample (B)	First Half Sample (A)					
	Segment 1	Segment 2	Segment 3	Segment 4	Segment 5	Segment 6
Segment 1	.9976	.2950	-.2151	-.1817	.0347	-.0477
Segment 2	-.0998	.2887	.9490	-.0583	.0335	.3443
Segment 3	.3753	.9034	-.3673	.0105	.0703	-.0237
Segment 4	-.1848	-.1315	-.1710	.9829	-.0155	-.2972
Segment 5	-.0888	.1272	-.1113	-.2112	-.6165	.5091
Segment 6	-.0492	-.2787	.0076	.0135	-.3244	.0160

of segment 2 in sample 1 correlate to the extent of .9034 with the benefit ratings of segment 3 in sample B. However, the benefits sought by segment 5 of sample A correlate no higher than .6165 with any segment of sample B. Similarly, segment 6 of sample A does not correlate higher than .5091 with any segment of sample A. Thus it appears that there are four reproducible segments in the market to which these tabulations relate.

Cross-tabulation by criterion measures can show whether adding segments increases the probable marketing utility of the results. As in the choice between universes of content, criterion measures are typically brand usage, type usage, and volume of consumption.

In the last analysis the final choice as to the number of segments rests heavily on the judgment of the researchers making the decision. However, the judgment can be aided substantially through use of the foregoing criteria.

Normally this procedure results in the selection of between three and seven segments, the most frequent numbers being four, five, and six. Although it is, of course, a simple matter to generate additional segments, the point of diminishing returns is reached quite early in the process. Partly this is because of the sample degeneration just noted. From a pragmatic standpoint, however, it has been found that marketing teams have difficulty in keeping more than about six segments clearly in mind. A frequency distribution for the results of 118 studies in which the author has personally been involved is presented in Table 8.6.

TABLE 8.6 Numbers of Segments Typically Obtained in Benefit Segmentation Research

Number of Segments Obtained	Number of Studies
Three	11
Four	54
Five	35
Six	18
Total number of studies	118

NINE

Interpreting Segmentation Study Results

Each of the segments produced represents a potentially productive focal point for communications efforts. In the case of Benefit Segmentation each is automatically identified by the benefits it is seeking. However, it is the total configuration of the benefits sought that differentiates one segment from another, rather than the fact that one segment is seeking one set of benefits and another a totally different set. Individuals benefits are likely to have appeal for several segments. Most consumers want all the benefits they can get. But the *relative* importance they attach to individual benefits can differ and, in communications can be used to position brands so that they have special appeal to a known target group.

It should be emphasized that the interpretation of attitude segmentation research requires a somewhat unorthodox approach to survey research data. It is necessary to oversimplify the research results in a number of ways in order to develop a marketing strategy. In the real-world situation, because all consumers want all benefits, the differences between attitudinal segments are not black and white. A parallel from topographical geography is perhaps a reasonably analogous way of viewing the real-world situation. Picture a series of mountain peaks rising from a plain. Each of the peaks represents one segment of the market—a group of people seeking a similar combination of benefits. Toward the top of each mountain are those people who best represent the segment. On the very peak are a few who are virtually perfect representatives of their segments. There are relatively few of them because there isn't much space on mountain peaks.

Down the sides of the mountains are people who are less typical of the other members of the segment. The farther down the mountain they are the less typical they are. If they share the desires of people on a neighboring mountain, they are on the side of their mountain that faces it.

People who share equally the characteristics of two segments are in the valley between the two mountains representing those two segments. And there aren't too many people located in the valleys because if there were, and if they shared interests with each other, they would form hills of their own.

This sort of situation can be represented very well mathematically. For example, Q factor analysis, used in the early years of attitude segmentation studies, yields a number of scores that can be used to represent factors and provides a factor loading for each respondent on each factor. These data cannot be incorporated into the normal market research cross-tabulation process, however, unless some sort of categorization is superimposed on them. The usual procedure in Q analysis before the 1960s was to create factor scores for each factor and then to divide these arbitrarily into terciles, quartiles, quintiles, or some other subdivision considered to be appropriate to the problem. But this was a cumbersome procedure because it involved several scores for each individual, and thus it was seldom employed in market research.

The breakthrough occurred at Grey Advertising in 1961.[1] It was a relatively simple concept, like many important advances. It involved ignoring the reality of overlapping segments and simply coding each respondent into one and only one segment. This allowed segmentation to be handled as a standard cross-tab in much the same way that an ordinary demographic such as geographic or race would be handled. Several conventions for assigning people to segments were tried. One was to set a fixed minimum level of factor loadings as a requirement for segment membership. Respondents who did not meet that level for any segment were assigned to a "miscellaneous" segment, a procedure also suggested by Ziff in 1971.[2] Where a respondent qualified for membership in more than one segment, the person was assigned to the one for which he or she had the higher loading.

Under this approach the higher the required level for group membership the fewer the members assigned to each segment; however, the larger the "miscellaneous" group. Because the group is a legitimate portion of the market, the assignment convention that evolved was in the opposite direction. Namely it became common practice to assign all respondents to

[1] R. I. Haley, "Experimental Research on Attitudes Toward Shampoos," Unpublished paper, New York: Grey Advertising, 1961.
[2] R. Ziff, "Psychographics for Market Segmentation," *Journal of Advertising Research*, Vol. 11, April 1971, pp. 3–10.

segments regardless of the levels of their factor loadings. They were simply assigned to the segment for which they had the highest loading. This simplifies the process and solves the problem of how the miscellaneous group should be treated. Some analysts employ discriminant function analysis after respondents have been assigned to segments in order to "purify" the segments. Equations that predict group membership are developed, and respondents are assigned to segments on the basis of those equations. This causes some changes in the assignments obtained from direct factoring, but, these are not likely to change the overall character of any of the segments.

When cluster analysis is used, respondents are usually automatically assigned to segments by the clustering algorithm so that the problem of how to assign respondents to segments is arbitrarily bypassed. As we pointed out in the earlier discussion of cluster analysis, however, differing clustering algorithms may well give different results.

Once respondents have been classified into segments, the next job is to try to understand each segment in as much depth as possible. This means cross-tabbing the segments against all of the information gathered in the survey. One effective way to understand a segment is to contrast its responses with those of the remaining segments. This is a principle often employed in psychological testing. Responses that are in line with average or typical responses are not given much weight, whereas unusual responses are studied closely for the clues that they may give *because* they are unusual.

Of course, this process is not guaranteed to work all of the time. In World War II, servicemen about to be discharged were given a Rorschach test. The inkblots in this test have no inherent meaning, but people read meaning into them, and their interpretations give clues as to the state of their emotional health. Thus some people see the red blots as blood and others stroke blots that appear fuzzy. A carefully constructed manual has been developed to help psychologists interpret the responses of those whom they test. In one particular instance the soldier being interviewed was giving standard responses such as "flower," "butterfly," and "dog" to successive inkblots. Suddenly he was presented with an inkblot that reminded him of a Pacific island that he had been stationed on, and he said so. He spent the next 20 minutes answering questions about how happy he had been on the island and whether anything unusual had happened to him there. Later he obtained a copy of the test and checked the blot in question against the map of his island. They were virtually identical! So even such well-validated procedures have limitations.

Table 9.1 shows how contrasting one segment with the remaining segments can provide insights into the nature of the segment. The same information presented in tabular form is not nearly so insightful. For example, the sensitivity of the segment to price appeals shows up clearly on a relative

TABLE 9.1 Segment Contrasts to Pinpoint Unusual Interest Levels

	% Considering Benefit Extremely Important				
Benefit	Total Sample	Segment 1	Segment 2	Segment 3	Segment 4
Tastes good	55	53	56	56	55
Nutritious	42	42	50	38	37
Attractive appearance	33	36	31	37	28
Pleasant scent	32	36	29	36	31
Good price/value	25	35	22	21	23
Filling	18	18	19	17	17
Easy to prepare	17	16	16	16	18

Contrast between Segment 1 and Total Sample	
Benefit	Difference from Total Sample
Good price/value	+10%
Pleasant scent	+4
Attractive appearance	+3
Nutritious	-0-

basis. On an absolute basis, however, several appeals look as though they might be stronger. Although absolute levels of desirability should not be ignored, relative levels are also useful predictors of response. This is true because relative measures to some extent correct for the scaling response styles[3] that different types of items may evoke. Thus in an interview situation cognitive items usually receive higher desirability ratings than emotional items. However, if one segment rates an emotional benefit as considerably more attractive than other segments do, it is safe to assume that the people in it will be more responsive to that claim also.

Perceptual mapping can also be helpful in understanding segment differences and differences in brand positionings. DFA maps can be constructed for each universe of content, using segment membership as the category definition. Thus segments can be discriminated pictorially by:

Benefits sought (see Figure 9.1)

Problems experienced

Category beliefs

Occasions of consumption

Personality and lifestyles

[3] G. D. Hughes, "Selecting Scales to Measure Attitude Change," *Journal of Marketing Research*, Vol. 4, February 1967, pp. 85–87.

Similarly, charts can be produced to show how brands are discriminated from each other in terms of benefit delivery (image) or perceived suitability for differing occasions of consumption.

Receptivity to new product ideas can also provide insights into the nature of the segments. To some extent this is predictable from the nature of the benefits sought by the segment. For example, if a new product concept board focuses on the stylishness of the product, the segment that is most style oriented, assuming that there is one, should indicate higher purchase intent than other segments. If it does not, one of several things is likely to be true:

(a) The concept board does not communicate the concept properly, (b) the product is not considered stylish, (c) the price, if included on the concept board, is a deterrent, or (d) the nature of the segment has not been properly interpreted.

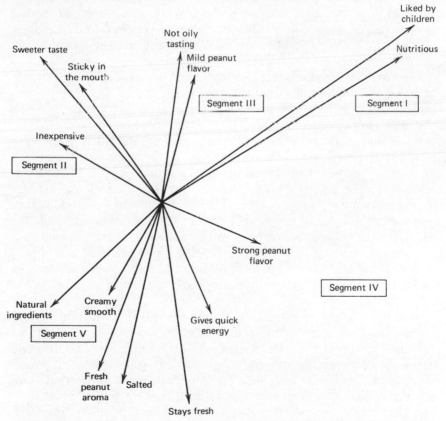

Figure 9.1. Map illustrating how segment differences can be depicted

In any event the research is likely to generate greater understanding of the interactions among consumers, communications, and the product. The evaluation of the product idea may be positive or negative. But in either case the joint involvement of the team members in analyses of this kind is beneficial. At the very least new hypotheses about the market will be developed and tested and these can result in significant learning.

In the early 1970s bourbon marketers recognized that they were facing a serious problem. Per capita sales of bourbon were showing steady declines. It was apparent that people's consumption patterns were shifting toward vodka, gin (the so-called white goods), and toward lighter alcoholic beverages such as beer and wine.

The bourbon industry's response to this environmental threat was to create a new whiskey type with relative low proof but with a bourbon flavor. The product was called *light whiskey* and a substantial industrywide advertising campaign was planned for its introduction. First, however, the produce had to go through the aging process. While aging was taking place there was adequate time for a major attitude segmentation study, one of the goals of which was to identify the most attractive market target for the product.

The marketing team, thinking in traditional demographic segmentation terms, expected the product to have particularly strong appeal to younger drinkers and to women. The possibility that an attractive attitude segment existed was left open to the research.

When study results became available, it was apparent that the product did *not* have special appeal for younger drinkers or for women (Figure 9.2). Moreover no segment with special potential was uncovered in the course of the analysis. The research team concluded that the product was likely to fail and advised the study sponsor of that fact. Because of the substantial investment in the aging process and in inventory, however, management felt that it was committed to moving ahead aggressively, so the planned campaign was launched. The product received low rates of trial, as had been predicted, and after several years of attempts to find a viable position for the product, it was withdrawn from the market, a sort of negative validation for the research.

In addition to the product concepts tested explicitly, attitude research generates new product hypotheses in a variety of ways. One is simply to analyze the "ideal brand" profile of each segment is represented by the benefits sought. This profile can be compared with the profiles of brands currently on the market and "gaps" in the offerings can be spotted. Similarly the "problem" information can be used to identify significant problems that might be solved through the introduction of appropriately designed new products.

The Concept:
There are several categories of liquor such as scotch, bourbon, blends, and Canadians. As of July 1, 1972, a whole new category is being introduced—a *Light Whiskey* category. This whiskey, to be brought to market by leading U.S. distillers, will be produced by a method never before used in the United States. It will have a light amber color and will bring you a lighter whiskey flavor than ever before experienced. It will cost about the same as popular brands of blends and bourbons.
The Response:

% Who Said They "Will Definitely Buy"

Characteristic	%
Age	
Under 35	13
Over 35	15
Sex	
Males	15
Women	14
Race	
White	14
Black/non-white	19

Figure 9.2. Results of light whiskey concept test.

Finally, the quadrant analyses mentioned earlier in this chapter can provide new product guidance. In particular the "consolidated own-brands" analysis is helpful. This plots on the horizontal axis the combined performance ratings of respondents, each of whom is rating his or her own brand. On the vertical axis, of course, are the traditional importance ratings. So the upper left-hand quadrant highlights items that are considered important but where brands on the market are relatively weak. This is worth examining for new product possibilities.

BENEFIT SEGMENTATION PRINCIPLES

Returning to the analogy from topographical geography, a number of principles of attitude segmentation—those with important marketing implications—can now be stated. The *first* of these is that every marketer, whether or not he or she cares to acknowledge it, is faced with a market segmentation situation. There are very few topographical maps with only one mountain. It is hard to conceive of any consumer markets where all consumers are seeking exactly the same set of benefits. People have different needs, wants, and circumstances of use. They are unlikely to see all products as equally compatible with these. Manufacturers can if they wish—and many do—claim that they are trying to sell their products to all customers in a market. They are deluding themselves, however. As soon as the brand assumes a definite position in the market (and this cannot be avoided) there will be people to whom the position is not appealing. And because of this they will prefer to buy other brands. Successful communications planning involves understanding exactly how your market is divided into segments and how your brand is positioned by consumers in relation to competing brands.

A *second* principle is that in marketing communications applications it is almost always easier to take advantage of market segments that already exist than to try to create new ones. Some marketing organizations emphasize product differentiation without regard to segmentation.[4] Using this approach, the marketer tries to make his or her product significantly different from those of competitors. The difference can be physical, psychological, or a combination of the two. The hope is that the product will appeal to a sizable subgroup of the market and that by pleasing them it will obtain a solid and unassailable position in the market place. This is a "push" strategy; it attempts to force consumer demand in the directions desired by the marketer.

Success for this approach depends heavily upon the types of marketing tools that are to be employed. If the marketer is prepared to pull out all of the stops—to introduce new products or make significant modifications in current offerings, to launch new advertising, to modify prices if necessary, and to use promotions tailored to the new strategy—then this approach can be successful. However, the marketer must be prepared to make sizable investments and to be patient for substantial periods of time. The Miller High Life campaign is a case in point.

The success of the Miller Brewing Company in the 1970s was legendary; they sold approximately 5 million barrels of beer. In 1978 sales had risen to 31 million barrels. During that time the industry grew at the rate of about 5% a year. Competition had been becoming increasingly severe, and the number of breweries had dropped in 35 years from about 400 breweries to 40. Accompanying this trend was a sharp movement away from regional brands and toward national brands. The regional brands share of total consumption dropped from 55% in 1970 to 35% in 1978.

The highly visible Miller Lite Beer campaign has deservedly been given

[4] J. Trout and A. Reis, "The Positioning Era Cometh," *Advertising Age*, April 24, 1972 (pp. 35–38) May 1, 1972 (pp. 51–54), May 8, 1972 (pp. 114–116).

a great deal of the credit for the surge in sales that propelled Miller from the eighth largest brewer in the United States to the second largest. When Phillip Morris Inc. acquired Miller, however, they launched a comprehensive restaging program. This involved a new management team, reorganizing the sales force, modernizing breweries, and reviewing their distributors from the standpoint of their inventory levels, their use of sales aids, and their independent advertising efforts.

In the product planning area they not only identified a need for new products, the stimulus for the development of Lite Beer, but they found a pressing need to revitalize their flagship brand, High Life. Research in 1970 showed that High Life had 8% of users but only 4% of volume. The advertising theme at that time was "The Champagne of Bottled Beer."

The new communications strategy targeted on the heavy beer drinker with the announced objective of "moving the product from the champagne bucket to the lunch pail." The copy initially focused on blue-collar people drinking High Life, but it was found that this campaign was not believable to blue-collar consumers. It was clear that revitalization would require time.

Research was done to uncover potentially productive directions. It was found that the heavy beer drinker does a disproportionately large portion of drinking between 4 P.M. and 7 P.M., using the product to relax with friends. The copy strategy decided upon, therefore, was to create a special time, called "Miller Time," in much the same way that Phillip Morris had created a special place called "Marlboro Country." The supporting cue became the setting sun, a blue-collar trigger to beer-drinking time.

In the first year of the campaign the goal was to neutralize the champagne image which, from the standpoint of the blue-collar target, was a liability. This was done by focusing on the product and the jingle ("If you've got the time we've got the beer"). Intentionally no people were shown.

In the second year the advertising brought in people, but largely in silhouette. For example, it showed silhouettes of fishermen relaxing with the product as the sun set and the jingle played in the background. No detectable sales response had occurred up to this point.

Next they began trial-oriented promotions, pushed the use of distributor aids, and introduced a 7-ounce size (which by 1978 accounted for 15% of sales). At the same time they more than doubled the number of breweries. Sales now showed a 10% gain.

Subsequent copy emphasized the activity aspects of work in romanticized work situations. It continued to employ sunsets and music (as a tension release) and began to show product users. Research was conducted to find an appropriate masculine voice. Gene Barry's voice was selected from a set of 150 candidate voices and was used in subsequent commercials.

The media strategy involved outspending competition on a per barrel basis, concentrating in one medium (98% of the budget went into television) and focusing on sports programming. It was the only type reaching more men than women and it was 25% cheaper than prime-time television. Local sports programs received special emphasis. Sports were considered an attractive media environment, the goal being to provide a "locker-room atmoshpere" for the commercials.

The media dollars for sports programs were committed a year in advance on an "exclusive" basis, meaning that no other breweries could advertise on sports programs on which High Life advertising was scheduled. This had the effect of forcing competition to more expensive prime-time slots.

The rest of the record speaks for itself. The overall program was tremendously successful. The brand image in 1978 was sharply different from the image in 1970. However, the changes occurred gradually and over a period of years.

When advertising is the primary marketing tool, and no new product or significant modification is involved, the chances for a successful intuitive campaign that attempts to carve out a new market segment drop sharply. Occasionally a marketer and his or her advertising agency will strike it lucky and will produce an intuitive campaign that happens to match the interests of a sizable segment of the population, and that has unquestioned impact upon the sales of the advertised brand. Occasionally advertising is even picked up by television comedians and is discussed on talk shows. This sort of publicity is guaranteed to multiply the effects of the campaign. However, successes in this vein only go to illustrate the fact that "all you have to do to win in marketing is to be right—you don't have to use sophisticated multivariate analysis." Marketing judgment is still a powerful tool.

The kinds of creative insights that produced the Miller Lite advertising, the Mean Joe Greene Coca-Cola commercial, and the "Reach out and touch someone" AT&T campaign will succeed regardless of whether Benefit Segmentation research is conducted. On the other hand, some campaigns whose success is attributed to the creativity of the advertising are successful not because they created new segments, but because, by good fortune, they tapped benefit segments that already existed.

Offsetting a few notable successes are the cases of innumerable advertising campaigns that had no measurable impact on their markets and quite a few new products and product "improvements" which, according to the engineers and laboratory technicians who spawned them, were important technological breakthroughs. Among products still waiting for their markets to emerge are the picture phone, Corfam (the synthetic product that was to replace leather as synthetic fibers had largely replaced natural ones), Pringles (the uniform potato chip), Kraft Imitation Mayonnaise (fewer calories), instant movie cameras, Palmsweet (a hand lotion with a deodorant), flavored ketchup, an 8-hour pain reliever, and vitamin E deodorant. In most of these instances consumers did not enthuse over what they were being offered. Responses were especially poor at the repeat purchase level for those products where the unasked for "improvement" was accompanied by a price increase.

People who make full use of the attitude segmentation concept and all of its implications are likely to make fewer costly errors than those who rely strictly on their intuitions. So, to repeat the principle, it is much easier to capitalize on an understanding of the market as it exists than to try to force it into new and different shapes. And a corollary is that it is easier to reshape markets with new products than with new advertising messages.

A *third* principle is that no brand can expect to appeal to all consumers. The very act of focusing communications on one or two primary groups may alienate other groups. At the very least communications are likely to be screened out by a large proportion of the people to whom they are not tailored. It is sometimes possible for a brand to appeal to more than a single group by using the marketing tools at its disposal differently. For example, it is possible for a brand to appeal to one segment through the use of contemporary advertising themes and to another through a low in-store price. Or to one because of its high-quality ingredients and to another because of its good taste. Usually, however, the advertising does best to focus on a single benefit, leaving product performance, packaging, and in-store factors to communicate additional benefits. It is important, however, that when the communications strategy calls for the communication of multiple benefits, those benefits be compatible with each other and each of some interest to those in the target segments.

It would be unwise, for example, to attempt to communicate a modern image to one segment and an old-fashioned image to another; or to communicate a high-status image to one segment and an image of being well suited to the working class for another. It is even difficult to communicate simultaneously "good taste" and "good for your health" with food products or to convey both cosmetic and therapeutic benefits in the beauty aid category.

Because an advertisement is a complex stimulus it is at least theoretically possible to create ads which, through selective processes, will communicate one and only one benefit to a given segment and a different benefit to another segment. In other words, one segment may screen out the portions of the message that are irrelevant to it, and another, viewing the same advertisement but using quite a different perceptual screening process, may receive quite a different message. There is evidence in most copy testing that this happens fairly frequently. At our present level of expertise in using message differentiation, however, this is rarely planned and executed successfully. More often attempts at double message delivery result in above average screening activities. When two messages are received, they usually relate to compatible benefits and they are usually received by the same person.

A *fourth* principle of attitude segmentation is that brands from the same marketer need not cannibalize each other heavily. This holds for line extensions as well as for individual brands. Rates of cannibalization depend upon the extent to which the products are positioned against the same market segments. For example, generic grocery products cut more deeply into the shares of private label brands than into national brands. This is because both generics and private labels are positioned against the same segment, the price segment.

A *fifth* principle is that a perfect communications campaign is one that fits *exactly* the mental set, needs, and lifestyles of the target segment of the market. The phrase "communications campaign" in this context refers to the advertising, the sales promotion, the packaging, the public relations and publicity, the way in which the sales force handles itself, pricing, the outlets and types of displays in which the product is sold, and even the design and performance of the product itself—every major and minor medium of communication. All should be telling the best prospects that the product is more compatible with their needs than any other product available—verbally and nonverbally.

In other words, the communications campaign should be aimed at the people on the peaks of the mountains referred to earlier. In that way close misses will still engage a substantial number of people. They will scatter down the hillside—the misses not the people.

It is a truism in marketing that "You've got to get *someone* to buy your product before you get *anyone* to buy it." A substantial group of people must be interested in the kinds of benefits that a brand projects before it can make progress in a market. Yet there is a continuing temptation for a brand to try to be all things to all people. Brands that attempt to do so, however, are likely to end up in the valleys between the segments. Instead of having good, clear, distinctive images, they are likely to end up with bland personalities—no outstanding weaknesses but no outstanding strengths either. And their sales will suffer as a result. Two of the worst sins in marketing communications are to have a fuzzy image or to have one which, although distinctive, does not appeal to a sufficiently large group of consumers.

Another tenet among faithful market segmenters is that marketers who believe in and fully implement a segmentation program have a distinct competitive edge. The existence of particular benefit segments is often not obvious because there are a great many ways in which segment structure can be hypothesized. Thus if a marketer discovers through segmentation research a benefit segment that is seeking a set of benefits which (perhaps with some repositioning) his brand can offer, he can almost certainly dominate the purchases of that segment.[5] Moreover, if his competitors are viewing the market in terms of the more traditional demographics or behavioral segments, they may be unaware of the existence of the benefit segment on which he has chosen to concentrate his efforts. And if they are ignorant in this sense, they will be at a loss to explain the steady growth of a brand that has properly calibrated its appeal to market demand. It naturally follows then that, because they do not understand the reasons for the brand's success and have not properly perceived what its customers have in common—the sets of benefits sought—they will find it very difficult to counter the growth of the brand and, once it has realized its full potential, to attack its market position successfully. Once the brand begins to grow they will, of course, hypothesize reasons for that growth. However, their hypotheses are likely to involve global tools such as media choices, advertising weight, pricing, promotion, or the overall appeal of the new sets of advertising executions that follow analysis of the research and the implementation of the new communications strategy. And their competitive responses are likely also to involve global tools and to have limited effectiveness.

On the other hand, a segmentation study can be a potent defensive weapon. An understanding of the market and of the benefit segments that exist within it can clarify the reasons for any new trends that develop within the market, whether they be generic trends or competitive trends. For example, if per capita consumption within the category begins to drop as, for example, in the coffee market, the marketer can ask himself whether the decline is an across-the-board decline or one that is disproportionately rapid in some segments.

Equal across-the-board change are extremely rare. The changes usually occur more rapidly in some segments than in others, and the nature of the segments in which the more rapid changes are taking place can provide valuable insights into the reasons behind the change itself. Thus in the coffee market the long-term decline in per capita consumption shows up in a relatively rapid decline in the consumption of regular coffee among the "health-conscious" segment. To a large extent this has been offset by *increases* in per capita consumption of decaffeinated coffee within the same segment.

In 1977 the coffee market experienced sharp declines in per capita consumption. Declines were far greater than the overall decline among the "price-sensitive" segment. This was not unexpected, however, because cof-

[5] According to Chester Kane in *Advertising Age* (October 4, 1982, p. 60), Ultra-Brite toothpaste appealed to less than 10% of the entire dentifrice market, yet its appeal was so strong within this segment that it generated a dollar share in excess of 7%.

fee shortages resulting from disastrously low crop yields in South America had forced large price increases. Once prices returned to more normal levels, so did the consumption of this segment.

The impressive success of international coffees, as well as the "choose your own blend" coffee shops, was explained by the disproportionately high positive reactions of the "venturesome" segment to these ideas. Reverse reasoning would suggest that new and distinctively different coffee products must do exceptionally well in these segments if they are to succeed in the marketplace.

Segmentation studies can also be used to understand the reasons behind competitive product successes and to decide upon appropriate countermeasures. For example, in 1975 Kraft introduced a mayonnaise product called Kraft Imitation Mayonnaise. Some felt that the word *imitation* doomed the product from the start.[6] But CPC International, the marketeers of the Hellman's, Best Foods, and Spin Blend brands viewed the product as a potentially serious threat to their business. In support of this view the product performed very well in blind product tests.

Fortunately a major Benefit Segmentation study was available to help evaluate the damage that the new product could be expected to cause. Close examination suggested that the benefit set offered by Kraft Imitation Mayonnaise was more likely to cannibalize Miracle Whip, another Kraft brand, than to cut into Hellman's and Best Foods, the CPC flagship brands. The situation was complicated, however, by sharp differences in regional sales patterns. The strength of the Hellman's/Best Foods brands was concentrated in some regions, whereas the Miracle Whip/Kraft brand were stronger in others. Obviously the new Kraft product, nicknamed KIM, was being introduced first in areas where the Hellman's/Best Foods brands were most strongly entrenched.

Given the knowledge provided by the Benefit Segmentation study, CPC was able to develop effective countertactics involving not only defense in the threatened area but attack in areas of Kraft strength, and the threat posed by KIM was successfully turned aside.

Generalizing from this sort of experience, when a competitor introduces a new product or, in effect takes any important marketing action, a company with a Benefit Segmentation orientation toward the market can determine how the product is being positioned by consumers and assess the likelihood that the product will make inroads into segments of primary interest. The decision as to whether counteraction is needed can then be taken. If the new product is poorly conceived in terms of marketplace fit (or its ability to restructure the market), the company can relax and watch it

[6] For legal reasons any mayonnaise-type product containing less than a specified percentage of oil must be labeled "imitation."

flounder. If it seems to be approaching the top of one of those mountain peaks, however, it can introduce a new brand or line extension of its own, modify the physical properties of its current brand, change its communication strategy, or take any of a number of possibly effective marketing actions. In cases of doubt or high risk, it can even test alternatives, measure the responses of the various segments, and make an appropriate choice.

COMMUNICATIONS AND OTHER MARKETING IMPLICATIONS

Now let us turn to some specific market situations to illustrate how Benefit Segmentation research can be used to guide the development of effective communications strategies. One useful analytic device is called the Segmentation Grid. Segmentation studies typically generate a superabundance of data, and for this reason it is difficult for the marketing team to get a firm grasp on the key facts relating to each of the segments identified. To avoid this problem they are customarily summarized in a shorthand table, or segmentation grid, such as that shown as Table 9.2, presented in part in the original article on Benefit Segmentation.[7]

The toothpaste market is one with which we are all more or less familiar. Although the Benefit Segmentation that is illustrated was done in the late 1960s, aside from more concern about breath, the toothpaste market has shown relatively little change. The market consists of four major segments—one particularly concerned with decay prevention, one with brightness of teeth, one with the flavor and the appearance of the product, and one with price. A great deal of supplementary information is available from the Benefit Segmentation research on each of these segments, enough to make some very good guesses as to how best to communicate with each of them. The decay prevention segment, for example, contains a disproportionately large number of families with children. They are seriously concerned about the possibility of cavities and show a definite preference for toothpastes that contain fluorides. The concern is reinforced by their personalities. They tend to be slightly hypochondriacal and, their lifestyles are less socially oriented than some of the other groups.

These are the key facts about the segment. Now judgment, and to some extent creativity, come into play. It is desirable to give the segment a name. Of course, it could simply be called Segment I, but that would not function as a very effective reminder of the nature of the segment. What is needed is

[7] Russell Haley, "Benefit Segmentation: A Decision Oriented Tool," *Journal of Marketing*, July 1968.

TABLE 9.2   Toothpaste Grid

Segment Size:	25%	26%	33%	16%
Segment name	The Sensory Segment	The Sociables	The Worriers	The Independents
Principal benefit sought	Flavor, product appearance	Brightness of teeth	Decay prevention	Price
Personality	High self-involvement	High sociability	High hypochondriasis	High autonomy
Lifestyle	Hedonistic	Active	Conservative	Value oriented
Behavioral characteristics	Use spearmint flavor	Smokers	Heavy users	Heavy users
Brands favored	Colgate, stripe	Macleans, Ultrabrite	Crest	Brand on sale
Demography	Children	Teens, young people	Large families	Men

a label that will capture the essence of the segment. And proper labeling is worth considerable thought, because if the label is not accurate, it can be misleading at a later point when the detailed findings become slightly blurred in the minds of team members. At that point the label more or less *becomes* the segment. In this instance the segment was named the Worriers.

The second segment, comprised of people who show above-average concern for the brightness of their teeth, and more recently about their breath as well, is quite different. It includes relatively large numbers of teens, singles, and young marrieds. People in this segment are likely to be above-average smokers. They are strongly social and their lifestyle patterns are very active. At the time the Segmentation Grid was prepared they were most likely to be users of Macleans, Ultra-Brite, or other brands emphasizing whitening. More recently Close-up and Topol have made their greatest penetration in this group. This segment was named the Sociables.

It should be noted that the second segment is *not* exclusively interested in white teeth and pleasant breath. They would like to guard against cavities as well. However, when they make tradeoffs, as they invariably do when faced with a variety of brands from which to choose, they place special emphasis on teeth whitening.

The third segment is one that is particularly interested in product characteristics, especially flavor and appearance, although they are also interested in decay prevention. Brand deciders are more likely to be children here than in any other segment. Use of spearmint-flavored products is well above average. People in this segment are more ego-centered than other segments and their lifestyle is outgoing but not to the extent of the Sociables. Because of its flavor Colgate had done well in this segment before it was repositioned. The success of Aim is also attributable to its appropriateness for this segment. It was called the sensory segment. Note that although the primary dimension determining the segments was in this case the benefits sought, segment names are sometimes couched in benefit terms and sometimes in lifestyle terms—whichever is considered best for capturing the essence of the segment.

The fourth and final segment is the price-oriented segment. At the time of the original segmentation this was the smallest of the segments. Given an increase in price consciousness among the population as a whole, however, it seems likely that this segment has grown somewhat in size. Historically the segment was predominantly male, although recent research suggests that sex differences have evened out along with the increases in working women. People in this segment are slightly above average in terms of toothpaste usage. They have large, evoked sets of acceptable brands, and see few meaningful differences among brands. Thus it is not surprising that they switch brands more frequently than do other segments. They also seek out sales and frequently buy brands when they are on sale. In terms of personality they are cognitive and they are independent. They like to think for themselves and to make brand choices on the basis of reasoned judgment. They were called the Independent segment because the central communications problem seemed to be how to get a group of independent people to think in a similar manner and to make similar purchase decisions. In retrospect they could just as easily have been called the Price/Value segment.

The nature of the categories used to summarize markets via the Segmentation Grid approach may vary from product category to product category. Examples of several of the formats that have been used successfully will be given shortly. Even in instances where there are no data, however, the Segmentation Grid can be a useful training device. It is often difficult for marketing executives who are accustomed to thinking in terms of demographic or behavioral segments to reorient their thinking to attitudinal segmentation. College students, both undergraduate and graduate, have many of the same problems. A useful exercise for improving the understanding of marketing people is presented in Appendix B.[8]

Another use of such grids occurs at the beginning of an attitude segmentation study. Members of the Research Team are asked to fill out blank grids of the sort presented in Appendix B. This serves two purposes: (1) It helps to insure that major potential dimensions of market segmentation are

[8] See also, G. Miaoulis, R. I. Haley, and J. T. Sims, "An Experiential Exercise in Product Benefit Segmentation," in *Proceedings of the Association for Business Simulation & Experiential Learning*, April 1978.

thoroughly covered in the course of the research, and (2) it provides a base against which learning from the study can be measured. This point will be covered more fully in the section on presenting the results of an attitude segmentation study.

Returning to the toothpaste market grid, it is quite evident that both copy directions and media choices will be sharply different, depending upon which benefit segment is chosen as the market target—the Worriers, the Sociables, the Sensory segment, or the Independents. For example, the tonality will be light if either the Sociable or the Sensory segment is to be addressed. It will be more serious if the copy is aimed at the Worriers. And if the Independent segment is selected, it will probably be desirable to use rational, two-sided arguments and, where possible, to support them with demonstrations. In fact, in order to talk to this group at all it will be necessary to have either a price edge or some kind of demonstrable product superiority.

The depth of sell reflected by the copy will also vary, depending upon the segment which is of interest. It will be fairly intensive for the Worrier Segment and for the Independent Segment, but much more superficial and mood-oriented for the Sociable and Sensory segments. User imagery and nonverbal appeals are likely to play a more important role with the latter two groups.

Differences in depth-of-sell will also be reflected in the length and structure of advertising messages as well. For the Worrier and Independent segments, longer and more complex messages would be appropriate, whereas for the other two segments shorter messages, single-minded messages, and higher frequency are indicated.

Similarly, settings and casting will vary. Advertising aimed at the Sensory group will focus on the product, emphasizing its appearance, taste, and perhaps even its smell. Scenes of people enjoying use of the product would be compatible. Socially oriented situations are needed for the Sociables. Groups of people should probably be shown, although a single presenter with a reputation for sociability would also be suitable. For the Worriers, family scenes and/or statistics on cavity rates would be desirable. And for the Independents, comparative advertising should be effective.

Media choices also would be quite different. Of course, the media types with above-average exposure would be favored provided their cost-per-thousand figures were not out of line. Thus newspapers and news programs might be favored for the Independents, television for the Sensory segment, television and magazines for the Worriers, and radio for the Sociables. Demographic information and preferences for individual media vehicles would also be taken into consideration. Given a few facts about the media exposure patterns of any segment, most media professionals can make accurate guesses as to other media vehicles that would be effective in reaching them.

Media environments would also have a bearing on the final choices. They would be tailored to the segment or segments chosen as targets. Vehicles with more serious environments would be used for the Worrier and Independent segments, and those that project a more youthful, modern, and active environment would be chosen for communications aimed at the Sociable and Sensory groups. In terms of media types the environments provided by broadcast media might justify a larger portion of the advertising budget aimed at the Sociables and Sensory segments, whereas print usage might be relatively high for the more cognitive Worriers and Independents.

The information in the Segmentation Grid also has implications for choice of consumer sales promotions. Clearly price promotions, whether coupons or price-offs, would be especially well suited to the Independents, a booklet on tooth care would be appropriate for the Worriers, premiums with sensory qualities for the Sensory segment, and premiums with a tie to personal appearance for the Sociables.

Packaging implications can also be drawn from the grid. For example, it might be appropriate to have colorful packages for the Sensory segment, perhaps aqua (as a cue to indicate fluoride) for the Worrier segment, gleaming white for the Sociables because of their interest in bright, white teeth, and a simple, functional no-nonsense package for the Independents.

By now it should be apparent that the kinds of consumer information normally obtained in the course of a Benefit Segmentation study have a wide range of marketing implications. Sometimes they even suggest physical changes in a product. For example, one manufacturer in the dentifrice market found that his product was well suited to the needs of his chosen market target with a single exception in the area of flavor. Working indirectly in the area of scent, he was able to make a relatively inexpensive modification in the product and thereby strengthened his market position within his target segment.

The new product implications of Benefit Segmentation work add to its advantage. The benefit sought by each segment can be directly compared with the benefits delivered by each product currently on the market via Quadrant Analysis. Needs that are not being well met by brands on the market can be discovered and guidance can be given to the new product people as to those areas on which they might most productively focus their attention. As pointed out earlier, new product directions are normally not the primary payoff for Benefit Segmentation research; however, they are an attractive fringe benefit. In one Benefit Segmentation study of the dinnerware market, conducted for Corning Glass, profits from the discovery of the need for a coffee mug alone more than paid for the cost of the research.

Although most Benefit Segmentation research has been concentrated on package goods, it has value in other areas as well. The following Segmentation Grid, taken from a Benefit Segmentation study conducted for a major retailer, illustrates this point (see Table 9.3).

Once again there are four segments. The group labeled "Store Loyal" favors one or two stores and patronizes them regularly. Because this group is older, we can presume that they have patronized these stores for a long time and that they are fairly satisfied with them. They are conservative and do not try new stores very often. In fact it is doubtful that anything short of a friend's recommendation or a store with high-quality merchandise opening in an especially convenient location would persuade them to try a new store. Even the decor would have to be appropriate to someone accustomed to shopping in old, established stores. These people are quality conscious and can afford to pay for it. This segment is the second largest of the four.

TABLE 9.3 Retail Grid

Segment Size:	29%	18%	15%	38%
Segment Name	Store loyal	Convenience shopper	Compulsive shopper	Price buyer
Principal benefit sought	High-quality merchandise	Fast shopping	Recreation	Good value
Personality or life style	Conservative	Sociable	Hedonist	Cognitive
Behavioral characteristics	Shops predominantly at one or two stores	Shops at stores near home	Shops in a wide variety of stores	Usually tries several stores
Stores favored	Old established stores	Stores with ample parking and fast service	New stores	Discount stores
Shopping frequency	Medium	Low	High	Medium
Demography	Older/upscale	Middle class	Young married	Upper education
Print media	*Vogue, Atlantic Monthly*	*Reader's Digest*	*Cosmopolitan, Modern Romance*	*Consumer Report,* heavy newspaper

Next we come to a segment called Convenience Shoppers. Shopping is really a necessary evil for them. They are active socially and are likely to have full calendars and busy schedules. Being able to get into and out of stores quickly is of central interest to them. They dislike long or slow checkout lines and like wide aisles and efficient layouts so that they can quickly and easily locate the merchandise of interest to them. They are likely to have shopping lists or to know what they are going to buy before they enter the store. They tend to shop near home, and easily accessible parking space is a factor in their choice of shopping areas. They are not distinguished from other segments demographically. Their primary discriminator is the benefit they are seeking—fast shopping.

The third segment, Compulsive Shoppers, is the smallest of the four segments on a head count basis. They are active shoppers, however, and spend considerably more on a per capita basis than the Convenience Shopper. For them shopping is a form of recreation. They enjoy the experience of being exposed to a wide variety of merchandise. Not surprisingly, they shop in a wide variety of stores. As soon as a new store opens anywhere within their shopping range, they will visit it. Their shopping ranges are far larger than those of the Convenience Shopper (the smallest) or the Store Loyal segment, and even a little larger than the segment still to be discussed, the Price Buyer. For them shopping is a social occasion and they often shop with friends. They are susceptible to buying on impulse. Demographically they are especially likely to be young married people (and the wife of the author, for her an aspirational group). In terms of personality they are hedonistic, enjoying sight, sound (music), textures, scents, and, in the case of food stores, taste.

The final segment, and the largest of the four, is the Price Buyer. Contrary to what some might expect, the Price segment does not consist of poorer people forced to economize. On the contrary, the most discriminating demographic characteristic is education. The more education a consumer has the more likely he or she is to be a Price Buyer. Price Buyers normally try several stores before making purchases. The higher the price of the item to be purchased the more stores will be visited. This segment does not necessarily buy the lowest-priced merchandise. They are looking for good value—a lot for the money. Of course, if the same item is priced differently in different stores, they will buy at the lowest price. Unlike the Compulsive Shopper this segment is highly cognitive. They gather information as they shop and attempt to make rational choices. Discount stores are favored for small-ticket items, and as a shorthand way of ensuring good value.

Now let us examine some of the implications of these findings. If the study sponsor is a national chain of department stores, as was the case, a national target is desirable. Some variations may be necessary from store to store, however, if some of the stores are in newer suburbs whereas others are in older downtown areas. So before any final decisions are made at the individual store level it is necessary for the store to define its trading area and to estimate the incidence of each segment within it. In actuality, this need was anticipated. Before the study was begun the trading areas of each store were defined and probability samples were drawn within those areas. This allowed stores to be categorized into groups in such a way that the market characteristics of all of the stores in a given group were similar. And this in turn allowed management to develop a marketing strategy that took local conditions into consideration to some extent without sacrificing the value of a corporate umbrella.

It was felt that the offerings of this particular chain could not meet the needs of the Store Loyal segment. Its stores did not fit the "old established" mold and its merchandise emphasized price/value rather than high quality. Fortunately, however, the Store Loyal segment did not dominate the trading areas of any of the existing stores. Had it done so it is unlikely that the store would have strong performance, and the evidence of limited potential would have made it a candidate for closure. Management believed that it could market successfully to any of the three remaining segments.

Where the incidence of Convenience Shoppers was sufficiently high, they planned extensive renovations. Aisles in stores were to be widened so that customers would flow through them more freely. Special studies were made of store layout, again to speed traffic. A new type of shopping cart was introduced, one that moved more easily and was more maneuverable. Additional checkout locations were installed so that customers had more flexibility in their direction of exit. And coverage procedures for manning the checkout locations were revised to insure against customer lines of more than a specified length. Where possible, additional parking spaces were provided and entry and and egress was made easier. Finally clerks were given training on how to serve customers quickly and efficiently, and these clerks who did the best jobs in this respect were given special recognition for their efforts. Local advertising emphasized ease of shopping and price value.

Relatively few changes were required in areas where price buyers dominated. Specials were run more frequently as were price promotions (e.g., lotteries where consumers receive discounts of from 10% to 30% on purchases). Price value remained the central theme in local advertising, but comparative claims were used more frequently.

In the few areas where Compulsive Shoppers were a dominant force, breadth of assortment was increased substantially. Special attention was given to displays to make them useful and exciting. Store decor and lighting were also revised to provide an atmosphere of venturesomeness, and window displays were used to reinforce this feeling. Local advertising emphasized the fact that the store was the best place to go to see all of the latest styles and models. Arrival of new merchandise was announced frequently Underlying all advertising, however, was the continuing theme of price/value.

Note the parallels and differences between the application of attitude segmentation research by package goods marketers and by retailers. Package goods brands customarily choose a single market target as a focal point, taking into consideration the value of potential spillover to secondary targets.[9] Retail chains, on the other hand, try to service a number of segments simultaneously. In the example just given the retailer in effect was saying that he had three different products, as defined by store characteristics, competition, and market characteristics. However, these products were separated geographically in that each is offered in a different set of markets. Therefore it is practical to have somewhat different messages in the different sets of markets, because the local advertising in one set of markets is likely to have little overlap with the advertising in other markets. Thus each market can have a message more or less tailored to local conditions without the risk of creating a fuzzy image by having differing messages coming from a single source. The only problem is the one associated with population mobility. People who live in one area and become familiar with the way in which a store has been positioned are likely to move to other areas and find the store positioned differently. This potential problem is mitigated, in this instance, by the underlying theme of price value. So when people move from one area to another, the transition from one branch of a chain to another is not difficult. And favorable images and patronage built up in one area can be transferred to others.

Banks are much like retail stores in this respect, and the use of attitude segmentation research is similar. Industrial marketers have a slightly different problem.[10] They too make use of a unifying corporate theme or corporate umbrella under which their individual products or services can cater to the markets they serve. However, when customers that are business firms are segmented by their needs—grouped into segments seeking homogeneous sets of benefits—the resultant segments usually turn out to be different types of businesses and/or different sizes of business. Where they

[9] Firms marketing several brands do, of course, choose a target for each brand. Where brands compete the targets are sometimes the same.
[10] R. T. Moriarty and D. J. Reibstein, Benefit Segmentation: An Industrial Application, Marketing Science Institute, Cambridge, MA, 1982.

are different types of businesses, it is frequently true that each business type has its own trade publications. Thus an aluminum manufacturer may have among the various publics whom he would like favorably disposed to his product:

Architects

Stockholders

Prospective employees

Engineers

Oil field equipment manufacturers and suppliers

Metal-working industries

Fabricators

Container manufacturers

Distributors

Because there is comparatively little overlap between the trade publications of these groups it would, theoretically at least, be possible to beam a message of progressiveness to the first three groups, durability and strength to the next two, versatility to metal-working industries and fabricators, cost to container manufacturers, and service to distributors. In other words, it would be possible to view the market as a five segment market with different messages tailored to each. Also because the sales force is such an important aspect of marketing for industrial marketers, it is possible to tailor sales forces to serve individual segments. For example, AT&T has one sales force for marketing consumer products and another for marketing products to businesses. Where this is not practical, where salespersons necessarily contact all segments, it is possible to train them to ask questions that will identify the type of person with whom they are dealing (i.e., segment classification) and then to tailor their sales presentations to fit the segment with which they are dealing. Xerox does something akin to this when they train their sales force to recognize customers primarily interested in gains and willing to take risks to achieve them, as opposed to customers who are trying to avoid losses and do not want to risk making mistakes. The former segment is "sold" on the benefits of the new equipment and what it will allow him to do; the latter on possible cost savings and the minimal risk in view of support he can count on from Xerox. Sentry Insurance at one point, having just completed a Benefit Segmentation study, set up a questioning sequence that allowed a salesperson to identify to which of four segments the small business owner to whom he or she was talking belonged. This allowed a custom presentation of the benefits most likely to be persuasive.

EXAMPLES ILLUSTRATING THE VERSATILITY OF THE BENEFIT SEGMENTATION METHOD

To illustrate the versatility of the Benefit Segmentation method, segmentation grids are presented for the following categories:

Wine

Sports

Car repair

Cereal

Tires

Hosiery

Airlines

Snacks

Automobiles

Cocktail mixes

Welfare clients

Fast food

Banking

Soft drinks

Liquor

Dinnerware

Recorded music

Gasoline

Cruise

Soluble coffee

These grids are included for illustrative purposes only. See Appendix B. Dates on which the studies were conducted are not shown, nor are segment sizes. Some are recent, whereas some, like the toothpaste study, go back to the early 1960s. In several cases the studies presented have been updated and thus are superseded by more recent data.

In addition to providing insights into the markets represented and demonstrating the versatility of the Benefit Segmentation approach, these grids show that the sort of information customarily obtained can be extremely useful in the development of communications strategies and tactics. The key to the value of any study is its ability to provide helpful marketing directions. Unfortunately action implications do not spring from the grids automatically, although some implications are fairly obvious. Moreover, the ability to draw useful implications from Benefit Segmentation grids improves with practice. The samples included should allow the reader the opportunity to speculate on appropriate implications without the expense and time required for a full-scale study. The first Benefit Segmentation study conducted can be an overwhelming experience; sometimes so overwhelming that the experience is not repeated. For those who know how best to handle these kinds of data, however, it can be both rewarding and productive. So if you have not yet been involved in an attitude segmentation study, the following material should show you what to expect and give you practice in interpreting it. If you have done segmentation studies, you may want to compare your own segmentation grids with the ones presented here to see if there are ways of extracting still more useful information from them.

GENERALIZATIONS

One question that arises quite frequently in relation to Benefit Segmentation is the extent to which it is possible to generalize about the types of segments that are likely to emerge from Benefit Segmentation studies. Unfortunately the ability to generalize is limited because in the best Benefit Segmentation studies benefits are custom tailored to the product category being investigated. If the desire is to generalize across categories, then lifestyles are probably a more appropriate segmentation tool than benefits. However, if an incisive segmentation instrument in a specific category is desired—one much more likely to be related to brand choice in that category—then benefits generally represent a superior analytical tool.[11] Generalizations about benefit segments yield a broad inventory of human needs.

In the original article on Benefit Segmentation[12] six groups that had appeared two or more times were enumerated. These were:

The Status Seeker—a group very much concerned with the prestige associated with brands or products purchased.

The Swinger—a group which attempts to demonstrate through its brand choices that it is up to date and modern.

The Conservatives—a group that prefers to stick to large successful companies and popular brands.

[11] W. L. Willkie and J. B. Cohen,"An Overview of Market Segmentation: Behavioral Concepts and Research Approaches," Marketing Science Institute Working Paper, June 1977.
[12] Russell I. Haley, "Benefit Segmentation: A Decision Oriented Tool," *Journal of Marketing,* Vol. 32, July 1968, pp. 30–35.

The Rationalists—a group seeking cognitive benefits such as economy, value, and durability.

The Inner-directed—a group especially concerned with self-image and viewing themselves as honest, independent, and having a sense of humor.

The Hedonist—a group concerned primarily with sensory benefits.

Obviously the need to generalize steered the group labels toward lifestyles. Now that more than four times the number of studies have been completed it is possible to identify related benefit sets that have defined segments in five or more studies. They are:

Price/value, economy
High quality, prestige
Convenient, fast, easy
Taste, flavor, scent
Durability, longevity
Styling, appearance, beauty
Health, diet, nutrition
Comfort, feel
Protection, risk, worry, or pain reduction
Love, affection, respect
Well-known or popular company or brand

Some of these appear in one form or another on most segmentation grids. Others are obviously applicable only for some product types. (The scent segment for automobiles is rather small.)

Does a review of the preceding segmentation grid suggest any items that might be added to this list? If it does, or even if you're sure it doesn't, you are thinking correctly in order to understand and use benefit segments.

GENERALIZED BENEFIT SEGMENTS

Before leaving the topic of generalized benefits, it should be noted that there are no real obstacles to determining these segments directly. In at least one instance, exactly that was done. Generalized benefit segments were developed for the consumption of all foods and beverages. The study referred to is one designed by the author for NPD Research, Inc. and reported in the *Wall Street Journal* (February 3, 1984, p. 25) and in the *Jour-*

nal of Advertising Research (February/March 1984, Vol. 24, No. 1, pp. 19–25).[13] The data involved represent in-home consumption of individual products and brands in 52 food and beverage categories. This information is used to generate estimates of market size, frequency of use, heavy user profiles, occasions of consumption, and a variety of other market statistics. Most major food and beverage companies are subscribers.

Anyone involved in the marketing of foods and beverages today must be aware of the upsurge of interest in diet, health, and nutrition that has occurred in this country during the past few years. This has been accompanied by an increase in weight watching, exercise, and in the avoidance of a variety of food substances and ingredients thought to be undesirable. All that has to be done to verify this trend is to check the current *New York Times* list of nonfiction best-sellers, which usually includes several books related to health and fitness.

As might be expected, this heightening of interest in health has been accompanied by a variety of behavioral changes. Typical among them have been:

Reduction in consumption of items high in saturated fats and oils

Substituting fish, poultry, and lean red meat for fatty red meat

Increase in consumption of fiber foods

Substituting margarine for butter

Substituting unsweetened or artificially sweetened foods and beverages for high-sugar products

Substituting skim or low-fat milk for whole milk

Substituting whole wheat bread for white

Substituting decaffeinated products for products containing caffeine

Substituting low-salt products for those higher in salt

Any revolution of this sort is bound to cause extensive segmentation. Some people change and some do not. Then, too, some people are strongly *taste*-oriented and believe that any compromise in the direction of *health* is likely to detract from what to them is the number one benefit of food—its taste.

The objective of the study described here is to identify some of the larger market segments that are emerging from the many changes in eating habits that seem to be occurring. The overall research design selected is the basis for the title of the *Journal of Advertising Research*, "Benefit Segments: Backwards and Forwards." The "forwards" aspect refers to the normal approach to benefit segmentation. Overgeneralizing a bit, this involves a three-step process:

[13] See also USA today, Dec. 4, 1984, p. 1, and New York Times, Dec. 5, p. C6.

Phase I.   Exploratory research to develop a complete enumeration of benefits of possible value in segmenting the market of interest.

Phase II.   Scale development work to evolve sensitive and reliable measures of major attitude dimensions.

Phase III.   Quantitative measurement of the market. This usually involves a national sample. Respondents are clustered by their attitudes and individual clusters (or segments) are described in terms of their behavior, lifestyles, demographics, and other relevant characteristics.

Under this approach segments are maximally discriminated by their *attitudes* and differences in *behavior* are analyzed through cross-tabulations.

The backwards approach begins with behavior. Respondents are clustered on the basis of their behavioral patterns, and the behavioral clusters (or segments) are described by their attitudes, lifestyles, demographics, and so on. In other words, segments are maximally discriminated by their *behavior,* and differences in attitudes are analyzed via cross-tabulations.

Which is the better approach? Is it best to start with attitudes and look for reflections of those attitudes in behavior, or to start with behavioral differences and try to explain those by looking for differences in attitudes? It's hard to say. Is it better to have segments that think differently or segments that behave differently? Ideally an analyst would like both. There are, of course, algorithms that purport to provide both—to maximize differences in both attitudes and behavior simultaneously. Experience with them, however, suggests that they generally discriminate less well on attitudes than approaches which focus specifically on attitudes, and less well on behavior than methods which focus specifically on behavior. So what is necessarily an average may not be the best approach either. Someone has remarked that there is a large market for hot tea and a large market for iced tea, but that the market for lukewarm tea has yet to develop.

If it is necessary to choose between behavior or attitudes, which is the better starting point? That bears similarity to the long-running controversies over the tradeoffs between reliability and validity. Would you rather have a research method that gives a reliable estimate or one that gives a valid estimate? Ideally, you would like both. But if you were forced to make a choice, you would like to know first how much reliability you would have to give up to have a valid measure and vice versa, so that is what the project team decided to do. It was decided to approach the problem both from the behavioral standpoint and from the attitudinal standpoint to see what might be gained and lost with each approach.

Starting with behavior, of course, does not mean that the problems of developing sensitive and reliable measures can be ignored. Behavior can be measured in many different ways, and not all of them are equally effective.

Before going further it may serve well to review the overall research design employed. First, the project team opted for the standard three-phase design: Phase I, Exploratory Research; Phase II, Scale Development Work; and Phase III, Quantitative Measurement.

Because it had been decided to proceed both backwards and forwards, however, the standard design was modified so that it looked more like that shown in Figure 9.3.

Now let us proceed, one phase at a time. Returning to Phase I, as the guideline suggests, a considerable amount of time and effort was invested in up-front work. The exploratory phase in this instance consisted largely of two extensive reviews—one, of all of the products included in the NET data base of in-home consumption of foods and beverages; 156 behavioral items were chosen that we hypothesized might be related to nutritional segmentation of one sort or another.

Next material from both public and private sources was reviewed, and special attention was given to attitudinal factors that had been developed in the course of more than 30 segmentation studies focused on foods. This resulted in the selection of 270 attitudinal items.

The second phase (as per recommended procedure) was the scale development phase. This involved two parallel streams of research—the behavioral stream and the attitudinal stream. In the behavioral stream the first step was to select a sample of 975 households which had participated in the NET service for two successive years. Two separate factor analyses of the consumption patterns of those households were then run—one based on consumption patterns of the most recent year alone and the other based on the past two years.

The two-year analysis accounted for a larger portion of the total variance in consumption behavior of the households involved than did the one-year analysis. Also the factors that it produced had somewhat greater face validity. Consequently the final choice of behavioral factors is based on the two-

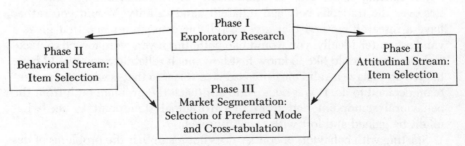

Figure 9.3. Research design.

TABLE 9.4   Sampling of Product Sets

Rabbits

Salad dressings: regular

Salad dressings: low-cal

Vegetable (tossed) salads

Scratch Bakers

Frosting: total

Total extracts

Layer/loaf cakes: from mix

Cookies and brownies: homemade

Baking sweets: total

Luncheon Heroes

All other lunch/process meat

Hot dogs: total

Total condiments

Bologna: total

Sausages: total

Sandwiches with meat/lunch meat

Soda Poppers

Carbonated soft drinks: regular

Carbonated soft drinks: diet

Meat and Potatoes

Pork (e.g., ham and bacon)

Beef roasts: total

Potatoes: boiled/steamed

Gravies/marinades

Italian Oriented

Total sauces

Spaghetti: total

Italian cheeses

Pizza

Bread and Cheese Boards

Total rye/pumpernickel bread

Total bagels

Total cream cheese

Swiss cheese

Lil' Ol' Pie Makers

Total dough, crusts, shells

Pies: homemade

Blue-Collar Drinkers

Beer: regular/no specific type

Beer: light

White-Collar Drinkers

Plain/mixed alcoholic drinks

Wine

Pilgrims

Stuffings/dressings

Turkey: total

Fruits

Fruit salads: total

Fruit juices

Calorie Counters

Skimmed/low-fat milk

Margarine: diet/low-cal

TABLE 9.4   *(Continued)*

Lumberjacks	Health Enthusiasts	Convenience "Bakers"
Pancakes/waffles/French toast	Natural/granola RTE (ready to eat) cereal	Layer/loaf cakes: commercial RTE frozen
Total syrups	Bran/fiber bread	
	Grains/wheat germ/sprouts	Pies: Commercial RTE
Kids' Lunches	Total wheat bread	Pies: Commercial frozen
Sandwiches without meat	Yogurt	
Total peanut butter	Seeds/nuts oil	**Dieters**
Total jelly	Rice: brown and long grain	
		Weight loss/gain products
Candy Lovers	**Soup-ers**	Total granola/Non-granola bars
Chocolate candy	Soup: cream-style (commercial)	
Candy bars: total	Soup: all other (commercial) types	**Synthetic Sympathizers**
Nonchocolate candy	Crackers: regular/soda	Total sugar substitutes
		Egg substitutes

year source. A sampling is shown in Table 9.4 (with apologies for some of the names). As those who have done this sort of analysis know, naming factors and naming segments allows people who have been overwhelmed by all those statistics to exercise a little creativity.

As a next step respondents were clustered on their overall patterns of food consumption, using factor scores as input. To ensure that the segments we discovered were not unique to the sample from which they were derived, a split-half reliability test was conducted. In other words, the sample was randomly divided into two equal subsamples, and separate cluster analyses were done on each. Comparisons of the two sets of solutions verified the fact that five segments could be produced reliably. Their profiles are shown in Table 9.5.

Now let us turn to the attitudinal stream. The sample of 975 families was asked to indicate the extent to which they agreed or disagreed with each of the 270 attitudinal statements. Because most of these items came from previous factor analyses, the behavioral work was not immediately paralleled

TABLE 9.5   Profiles of the Five Food Consumption Segments

Segment I—Child Oriented

Food preferences
  Sandwiches with lunch meat
  Hot dogs
  Bologna
  Soda pop
  Fruit drinks/ades
  Spaghetti
  Pizza

Demographic descriptors
  Larger households (children)
  Younger
  Female head less likely to be employed
  More high-school graduates
  More blue collar
  From smaller towns

Segment II—Diet Concerned

Food preferences
  Skim milk
  Diet margarine
  Salads
  Fresh fruit
  Sugar substitutes

Demographic descriptors
  Lower income
  More two-person households
  Older
  Fewer children
  More likely to be out of work force
  More nonwhites

Segment III—Meat and Potatoes

Food preferences
  Whole milk
  Pork
  Roast beef
  Boiled potatoes
  Gravy
  Pies

Demographic descriptors
  Below-average income
  Above-average age
  Fewer professionals
  More non-SMSA
  More nonwhite

Segment IV—Sophisticated Consumers

Food preferences
  Wine
  Mixed drinks
  Beer
  Butter
  Rye/pumpernickel bread
  Bagels
  Swiss cheese

Demographic descriptors
  Upper income
  More one-person households
  Fewer children under 18
  More female heads employed full time
  More college grads
  More professionals and white collar
  Larger cities

TABLE 9.5 *(Continued)*

Segment V—Natural Food
Enthusiasts

Food preferences	Demographic descriptors
Fresh fruit	More upper income
Rice	More one-person households
Natural RTE cereal	More younger people
Bran/fiber bread	More college grads
Wheat germ	More professionals
Yogurt	More people from Pacific region
Granola bars	

---

by repeating the factor analyses. Instead several criteria were used to select a reduced set of items to be added to the final phase. First a discriminant function analysis was run against the five behavioral segments to see which items were the best discriminators. Next reliability checks were made on individual items. Then some consideration was given to items which had been factor markers in previous studies; and, finally, allowing some latitude for marketing intuition, we chose a set of 56 items to be carried into the third and final phase.

At this point we were ready to launch that phase. Here we were blessed with a sample of approximately 13,000 households. Each was sent a questionnaire containing the sets of behavioral and attitudinal items derived from the Phase 2 work. Completed returns were used to classify all households back into the five original behavioral segments. Then the attitudinal information was searched for reliable and meaningful benefit segments. The 56 attitude statements were factored and the interrelationships between individual items (as shown by the factors obtained and by the correlation matrix used as input) were studied. After reliability checks on individual items, a subset of 11 items and factors was chosen. A sampling is shown in Table 9.6.

Respondents then were clustered on these factors, split-half reliability tests on the resulting segments were run, and four reliable attitude segments were found to be present. The segments themselves are not surprising; however, they do have face validity. There is a taste segment, an exercise and nutrition segment, a sophisticated segment that enjoys alcoholic beverages and, finally, a segment of avoiders—people who avoid calories and other unwanted elements in their foods and beverages.

TABLE 9.6   Subset of Factors and Items Within Them

Avoidance of Unwanted Elements

- Preservatives
- Additives
- Salt
- Fat
- Cholesterol
- Sugar
- Caffeine

Nutritional Involvement

- I know more about nutrition than most people.
- I carefully plan my household meals to be sure they are nutritious.
- I often read labels to be sure the foods I buy are nutritious.

Adult Beverages Encouraged

- Wine
- Beer
- Caffeinated coffee

Quality/Taste

- The best-known brands are likely to be the highest-quality products.
- Almost everything that is very good for you doesn't taste very good.
- The most important things about food are that it look good, smell good, and taste good.

Avoidance of Bad Eating Habits

- I try to avoid snacking entirely.
- I try to avoid fried foods.

Popular Youth Foods Encouraged

- Pizza
- Tacos

259

TABLE 9.6 *(Continued)*

- French fries
- Fried chicken
- Lunch meat
- Hot dog sandwich

Dieting

- I would like to lose at least 20 pounds.
- My doctor gives me advice on my diet.
- I'm always conscious of the calories in the meals I serve.

Finally the two streams of the research—the backward (or behavioral) stream and the forward (or attitudinal) stream—were merged and cross-ruffed.

At this point, a sizable variety of alternative targeting possibilities are available to users of the data base. There are five behavioral segments, four attitudinal segments and, if the two are cross-ruffed, there is the possibility, at least, of 20 "combination" segments. Of course, substantial overlap between some of the behavioral and some of the attitudinal segments occurs (see Table 9.7).

It is also possible to return to the 34 original behavioral factors to develop factor scores for each individual factor for each household, and to choose as a target for a given manufacturer the households who score highest on that factor; or, the same thing could be done with the 11 attitudinal factors.

Which is the best way to select your target? Again there is a forward and a backward approach. The forward approach is to incorporate brand image and other relevant information into the Phase III questionnaire; analyze positioning information; examine alternative targeting possibilities, their behavior, lifestyles, and their interests; and make a reasoned choice. The backward approach is to expose your copy to a large diverse sample and see who salutes. Once the segments among whom you presumably have the greatest chance of increasing your net sales have been established, it is possible to zero in on a responsive target because so much will be known about the people in it, and to refine the advertising copy so that it is tailored even more precisely to that segment.

The real payoff for a Benefit Segmentation study is how the segmentation information is used once it has been obtained. To receive full value it should

TABLE 9.7 Cross-ruff of Attitudinal and Behavioral Segments (Average representation = 100)

Behavioral Segments	Attitudinal Segments			
	Nutritionally Fit (24.3%)	Taste (25.9%)	Avoiders (24.1%)	Urbanites (19.7%)
Kids around (21.3%)	109	128	102	56
Diet conscientious (20.9%)	71	49	159	124
Meat and potatoes (25.2%)	65	154	105	72
Sophisticates (17.0%)	94	105	53	159
Naturalists (15.5%)	38	38	63	108

be incorporated into a continuous information system. The world changes, and no matter how well a segmentation study may have been done at one time, and no matter how accurate the picture of the market obtained at that time may have been, a strategy study allows no more than an informed guess to how people are likely to respond to any marketing actions you may decide to take. Then, too, there are competitors. The marketing actions that they take can have almost as much influence on your sales, share, and profits as your own actions. So virtually the only practical option for an intelligent marketer is to monitor his or her market continuously. Try something, see how it works, observe which segments react in what manner, learn from your mistakes, and gradually improve your batting average. That is what marketing is all about. And whether it is done backwards, forwards, or sideways, as long as it is done well, Benefit Segmentation can be enormously helpful in learning how to anticipate accurately the responses of the customers in your market.

TEN

Presenting Results and Beginning Follow-through Activities

Segmentation grids are a shorthand way of summarizing a segmentation study. However, they are usually prepared more as a reminder of study contents than as the primary presentation device.

The presentation of results itself is a carefully organized and thorough review of the highlights of the study, together with its practical implications. Usually a preliminary presentation is prepared for the research team by the analyst primarily responsible for the interpretation of the findings. This normally takes a full day, during which changes are made in the sequence in which points are presented, charts are revised for clarity, points are added and deleted, and alternative interpretations and implications are considered. This preliminary presentation is scheduled far enough in advance of the formal presentation to allow time for any needed changes to be made and to allow the research team to reach consensus.

The formal presentation is a critical aspect in determining the extent to which the study will be accepted and acted upon. The temptation to show the audience "everything" should be firmly resisted. The result of "data overload" is more likely to confuse the audience than to impress it. There is always time to go back at a later point to pick up some of the finer points which, if covered in the formal presentation, may detract from its main thrust.

The importance of the charts themselves cannot be overemphasized. If the charts are professional in appearance, they indicate to the audience that the study has been professionally done. If they are sloppy, even a carefully prepared analysis may be discredited. Misspellings are particularly serious, because they suggest both carelessness and lack of intelligence. So the entire committee should watch for small errors of any kind. One common

263

error occurs in columns of figures that are supposed to represent percents of the total but which do not add up to 100%. Either these numbers should be forced so that they do add exactly to 100% or it should be pointed out that rounding errors can cause the column to be a point or two off. The former procedure is probably preferable; no one ever asks why every column adds up to *exactly* 100%.

Charts should be largely simple bar charts and pie charts; overly complex charts should be avoided. Clarity and a factual aura are more important than artistic value if tradeoffs have to be made. The data presented should be legible from the last row of the audience. As a rule of thumb each chart should make a single point. This can be checked by writing a "flow statement" for each chart summarizing the point it makes. If the presentation has to be repeated at a later date by a presenter who is not as familiar with the material as the original presenter, these flow statements can be set in type and interspersed with the charts. In this mode the statement is shown first, followed immediately by the chart with the data supporting it. Presenters who are thoroughly familiar with their material can dispense with the flow statements and, in doing so, give the presentation more spontaneity.

The choice between hand-drawn charts, overhead transparencies, and slides depends both upon the personal preferences of the presenter and the size of the audience. One desirable objective is to try to maintain personal contact between the presenter and the audience. Hand-drawn charts usually accomplish this best if the audience is not too large.

PRESENTATION FORMATS

Presentation formats must vary to fit individual audiences, but one that is usually effective with large heterogeneous audiences is the following:

    I.   A "Menu" is presented showing the types of information to be reviewed and the sequence in which it will be covered.

   II.   Background and objectives—A series of statements recapping the reasons for conducting the study, the uses for which it is intended (Marketing Objectives), and the kinds of information sought (Research Objectives)

 III.   Method
          Respondent definition
          Sample size, design, and location
          Dates on which the survey was conducted
          Method by which the interviews were conducted
          Question areas covered

IV. Detailed findings

    Market boundaries—statistics based on the total sample

        Incidence of qualified respondents

        Demographic description of sample interviewed

        Awareness and knowledge

        Behavioral characteristics of the sample (brands used, quantities consumed, brand switching)

        Decision process and purchase influences

    Brand user analysis—differences in demographic characteristics, volume of consumption, etc.)

    Heavy user analysis—demographics, occasions of use, brands used, benefit sought, etc.

    Brand image and positioning analysis

        Perceptual maps

        User/nonuser contrasts

        Leverage analyses

        Quadrant analyses

    Segmentation analysis

        Method of segmentation selected

        Number of segments found and size (head count)

        Segment sizes in terms of volume of consumption

        Segment I (versus remainder of market)

            Attitudes (brand awareness, brand preference, benefits sought, beliefs, etc.)

            Behavior (occasions of use, brands and quantities used, place of purchase, media habits, etc.)

            Characteristics (demographics, personality, and lifestyles)

        Segment II (versus remainder of market)

        Segment III (versus remainder of market)

        Others

    New product analysis

V. Conclusions and practical implications

    Market definition

    Market target selection

    Buying incentive

    Copy execution

    Media selection

    Other marketing suggestions (promotion, packaging, pricing, distribution)

    Opportunities for new products, line extensions, and/or product modifications. (A sample "presentation outline" chart is shown in Figure 10.1.)

I. National Data
   A. Objectives of the Research
   B. Method
   C. Validity Checks
   D. Definition of Terms
   E. Market Boundaries
      1. Product types
      2. Volume of consumption
      3. Brand penetration
      4. Occasions of use
   F. Benefit Segments
   G. Conclusions and Practical Implications
      1. Source of business
      2. Buying incentive
      3. Market target
II. Regional Differences
   A. Regional Differences
   B. Regional Tactics
III. Line Extensions
IV. New Products

Figure 10.1. Typical presentation outline.

Several points in the preceding outline require clarification. First you will notice that segments are reviewed one at a time rather than all at once. Experience has shown that asking an audience to assimilate information about several segments simultaneously throughout a series of charts places too great a burden upon them. It is more reasonable to go through a single segment in great detail, contrasting that segment with the total of the remaining segments[1] and gradually understanding the nature of that segment. To cement that understanding it is customary to complete the review of what is sometimes called an ABC chart (Attitudes, Behavior, and Characteristics). This is normally a single page, similar to one column of the segmentation grids presented earlier. At the conclusion of the ABC summary page the suggested name for the segment is introduced for the first time. As noted earlier the purpose of the name is to capture in a single phrase the essence of the segment. Often the ABC summaries are placed on separate charts and pinned to the walls of the conference room in which the presentation is being given, so that the audience will be able to remember the characteristics of the early segments as later segments are presented.

When all of the segments have been covered, segmentation grids can be passed out. These serve as reminders of study highlights long after the study has been completed. They have been enlarged and turned into wall displays

---

[1] Sometimes for the sake of convenience, or to show how marketing to a single segment would be different from attempting to market to all consumers, contrasts are made with the total sample.

in the offices of brand managers in some instances and, in at least one case, were photo reduced, laminated, and turned into a wallet card for handy reference.

The term "Conclusions and Practical Implications" is carefully chosen. Conclusions in this context are factual summaries drawn from several charts. For example, "The higher the social status of a family the more likely they are to use Brand A" is a conclusion drawn from several demographic cross-tabs. Similarly, "greatest competitive advantage of Brand A is its unique taste" is a conclusion drawn from a number of brand image and leverage tables with, perhaps, perceptual maps considered as well.

The term "Practical Implications" is used in preference to the term "Recommendations" to indicate that information beyond the scope of research must be considered before firm recommendations are made. For example, although the segment chosen as the market target may favor one particular type of television program, both its cost and its availability must be considered before it is recommended for inclusion in the media schedule. Similarly, although the research may reflect favorably upon a new product idea, its potential profit margin must be weighed in relation to alternative uses the company may have for the funds required to launch it before a firm recommendation can be made to market the product.

In preparing the implications section, it is wise to return to any documents issued during the planning and hypothesis generation stages of the study to make sure that every possible analysis has been conducted to answer the questions that were raised at that point. Similarly, to the extent possible, the hypotheses suggested with respect to how the market operates should be accepted or rejected on the basis of the newly available data. Of course, no single piece of research can answer all of the questions which have been raised by the marketing team. And, similarly, good research often raises almost as many questions as it answers. However, if the study is part of a continuous decision support system (as it should be) hopefully the more important questions will be answered over time. Only slight improvements in communication efforts are necessary to justify the cost of the research. The leverage of informaiton per dollar invested is usually higher than that of alternative investments, such as advertising weight. This is especially true when a Benefit Segmentation study is being conducted for the first time.

COMMUNICATING WITH THE PROJECT TASK FORCE

As a verbal introduction to the section on implications it is usually pointed out that there are two stages for any research project. The first stage is to ensure that an accurate picture has been obtained of the market and of the consumers in it. That is largely a market research matter; it requires asking the right questions, asking them in a way that reveals people's true perceptions, attitudes, and behavior, asking them of a representative sample, and tabulating them in a meaningful way. The second stage involves deciding how to reshape the situation in ways that will be favorable to the brand underwriting the research. In this area brand managers, account executives, and creative directors are often more skilled than marketing researchers (although good marketing researchers, to be effective, should consider themselves as good marketing people first and good researchers second). Consequently, the implications are presented deferentially—as representing the best combined thinking of the project team but as points for discussion rather than as firm and final conclusions about what should be done.

Good notes should be taken during these discussions so that any agreements that are reached and actions decided upon can be formalized. Often agreement and subsequent action can best be accomplished by holding a preliminary discussion at the initial presentation, distributing copies of the study so that those most concerned will have time to review the findings in detail at their leisure, and then holding an informal work session, perhaps a week after the original presentation. The work session is then focused on selective issues of importance, frequently covering them in more depth than originally. At the same time, information bearing on questions raised but not covered during the initial presentation is reviewed. Again good notes are taken and a memorandum summarizing the results of the meeting is circulated. Although this helps to stimulate action, further follow-up activities are desirable later to make sure that those responsible for implementing the results of the study do not get so bogged down under the pressure of day-to-day activities that they simply revert to doing things the way they did them before the new information became available. Follow-through activities will be discussed in more detail in Chapters 11 and 12.

Returning to the formal presentation, there are a few tactics that the project team can use to its advantage in attempting to get study findings accepted and used. There are a variety of reasons for studies being rejected or, worse, simply ignored. Among the more frequent are:

Resistance to change, for a variety of reasons

Feeling nothing new was learned

Not trusting the research—evidence of lack of thoroughness

Not trusting the analysis or the analyst

Not understanding the import of the findings

Resistance to change may be simply a reflection of personality or it may have a rational foundation. Sometimes marketing executives expect that the research will rubber stamp the communications strategies which have been selected on judgment for the brand. When the research suggests that the current strategy is off track, they feel that their judgment is being called into question—that the research, if accepted, will prove that the point of view for which they may have argued vigorously in the recent past is wrong. In such circumstances attacks on the research are quite natural. To avoid them the focus of the research should be upon future gains. It should be pointed out that past decisions may well have been appropriate at the time, given the limited amount of information available. With the new insights provided by the research, however, it seems that the best approach is to proceed in the directions indicated. Sometimes people resist change simply because it is easier not to change. In such cases the prospect of significant gains for the brand in question, together with the financial and nonfinancial rewards that accompany marked sales or share improvement, can sometimes be an effective lever in getting the cooperation of those needed to make the new strategy a success.

Sometimes resistance to change can arise from a genuine fear that the risks of failure are too great to make the suggested change. In such cases it is sometimes possible to compromise on a test of the new campaign in a few markets or regions. If the new strategy represents a significant improvement over the old one, and generally it does, the results of the test will do the rest.

One tactic sometimes used by those opposed to the research is to say that nothing new was learned from the research, that all of the facts gathered were already known. For example, at one point early in the author's career, he had been the project director for a large study for a client of Grey Advertising. Having completed the analysis, he was looking forward to reviewing the findings with the client. A presentation date had been set, the charts had been prepared, and the presentation had been rehearsed. At the last moment the then research director, Richard S. Lessler, announced that he had decided to make the presentation himself. (He was later Chairman of the Board of Grey Advertising and Vice-Chairman of McCann Erickson.) He said that in his opinion the audience to which the study was to be presented was not likely to receive it with open minds. To the contrary, the client's marketing and salespeople had already decided to veto any suggestions that changes should be made.

The presentation was made to a group of perhaps 20 marketing and sales executives. As the charts were successively reviewed, audible comments could be heard. They centered around a single theme—"We knew that." "Nothing new there." "Same old story."

Finally after looking at a chart showing image strengths and weaknesses, a client sitting in the front row said "We knew all that." Mr. Lessler stopped, looked him in the eye, and said, "Did I hear you say that you were familiar with the information on this chart?" The salesman said he was. Mr. Lessler commented, "As I've been going through this presentation I've heard comments that you people are already aware of the information on these charts. Is that right? For example, does everyone agree that there is no news on this chart?" A general murmur of agreement was heard, "Yes, nothing new there."

"All right," said Mr. Lessler, "this chart shows three critical weaknesses. What did you do about them?"

Dead silence.

In a loud and aggressive voice, "You mean to tell me that the entire marketing team was aware of these weaknesses and you didn't *do* anything about them?"

More silence.

"Well, if it was my company, some heads would roll. But let's get on with the presentation."

The rest of the presentation was made without audible comments from the audience. At its conclusion several people came up and complimented Mr. Lessler on the study and said that they felt it would be very helpful to the company. The recommendations of the study were accepted and carried out.

Where it is anticipated that there may be questions as to how much learning the study has occasioned, the problem can sometimes be avoided by what has been called a "mini-questionnaire." This contains between five and 10 questions which, in effect, ask members of the audience to guess at the outcome of the survey. The mini-questionnaire is distributed at the outset of the meeting, and it is explained that it is for the private use of the attendees only. It is not to be collected at any point. Rather it is a personal measure for the amount of learning that has resulted from the research. Each person is to fill it out and then compare his or her answers with the facts as they are revealed.

As the presentation proceeds the completed questionnaires have a tendency to be folded and tucked into notebooks and pockets. No participant has yet come forward with a mini-questionnaire saying, "Look, I got everything right!" And comments about lack of new information have completely evaporated.

Occasionally suggestions are rejected because, "We tried that X years ago and it didn't work." Larry Light, Executive Vice-President at Ted Bates, had a fairly brutal way of dealing with that sort of objection. He would respond by saying, "Fine, if you're willing to assume that the world doesn't change."

The problem of suspicion that the study was not carefully and thoroughly done can largely be dealt with by investing in professional charts and through rigorous proofreading. A nonverbal device that is helpful in this respect is to bring all of the tabulations that were generated by the study to the presentation (a Benefit Segmentation study generates quite a few) and pile them in the center of the table in the conference room. This is both tangible evidence of the effort expended and it permits immediate answers to questions that can be answered by looking up data in a table.

Lack of trust in the analyst may be generated by his or her attitude during the presentation. The analyst should avoid projecting superiority and an attitude of "I have all of the answers," and should field all questions courteously, admitting lack of knowledge when necessary and offering to look up and report back on issues to which the research is relevant but which have not been covered by the presentation. Some people like an informal atmosphere and indicate their willingness to answer questions at any point. Others prefer that questions be held until the discussion period at the end of the presentation. To some extent the choice depends upon the amount of time available for the presentation. The former approach can take substantially more time. One compromise is to allow questions for purposes of clarification of the data but to hold discussion questions. In other words, if a member of the audience does not understand the data, this person is shown he or she is free to interrupt. If, however, the person would like to discuss the *implications* of the data, he or she is asked to wait.

Usually it is a good idea to have the project team dispersed throughout the room during the presentation rather than concentrated in one area. In that way if the study comes under attack at any point, it is difficult for opponents to concentrate their attack. If the project team believes in the study, as they usually do, support will seem to come from all directions.

In larger companies it is not unusual to have a special foreshortened presentation of perhaps an hour for the top executives of the corporation. Usually, however, this can be prepared simply by abstracting portions of the full presentation.

COMMUNICATING WITH CREATIVE PEOPLE

Because the creative people are most deeply involved in the follow-through activities relating to Benefit Segmentation research, it is particularly important that they absorb the research, not only intellectually but emotionally. One way of making progress on this front, as was mentioned earlier, is to attempt to represent the members of each segment with a line drawing. Figures 10.2 through 10.6 show artists' renderings of the five benefit segments discovered in the cruise market (see also, p. 439 for the grid).

Figure 10.2.   Representation of Segment III, cruise market

Figure 10.2 represents Segment III, the Personnel-Oriented Cruiser. As you can see from the drawing, they enjoy contact with the staff, being waited on, and the quality of the food.

Figure 10.3 represents Segment II, the Formal, Nightlife, Excitement Seekers. The woman is likely to be the key decision influence in this segment. She loves to dress up and have a good time and her partner keeps her

Figure 10.3.   Representation of Segment II, cruise market

company. In this instance they are at a formal ship's dance. Note that the man has a little gray hair, there is no gray in hers.

Figure 10.4 shows Segment IV, the Ship-Oriented Comfort Seekers. For them the ship is an end in itself; they don't care where it goes. They just want to sit on deck and be waited on. This segment is predominantly male.

Figure 10.5 is Segment I, the Informal Social Vacationers. Cruise passen-

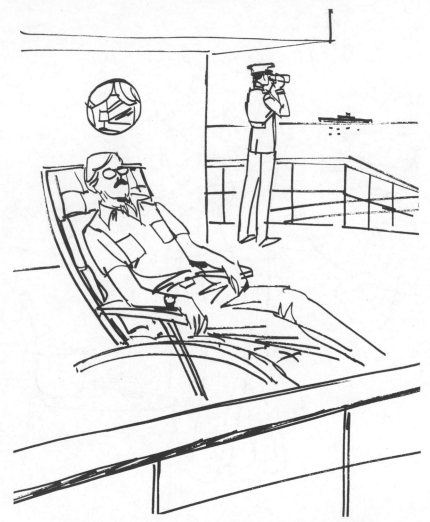

Figure 10.4. Representation of Segment IV, cruise market

gers in general are older than the average for the remainder of the population, as can be seen from most of the drawings. This is the youngest of the
five segments. As in the case of Segment II they like excitement and entertainment, but their preferred form of entertainment is quite different. It has
to be informal; they hate to get dressed up. And, of course, their music preferences are much more likely to be rock and country western than
Lawrence Welk or Lester Lanin.

Figure 10.5. Representation of Segment I, cruise market

The final segment, the Price/Value Sightseers, is also younger than the average cruise passenger. They see the cruise ship as a floating hotel. They are adventurous; the more ports the ship visits the better they like it. Unlike the Comfort Seekers they go ashore in every port and explore. Figure 10.6 shows them exploring an old fort. (Unfortunately it looks as though the guns in this particular fort were mounted so as to prevent a land attack rather than an attack by sea.) A copywriter, after studying this illustration and having been exposed to the data that generated it, will be able to write copy that is much more appropriate for the segment than if she simply let her imagination ramble.

That, of course, is the objective of all these drawings. They are an at-

Figure 10.6.   Representation of Segment V, cruise market

tempt to personalize the communication situation, to acquaint the copywriter with the market target in detail. Then instead of saying, in effect, "Hey, all of you out there, you ought to try a cruise, you'll like it," a copywriter can address prospects in ways that are fitting and can talk to them about benefits that are virtually guaranteed to interest them. In this way the copywriter can get the right people to turn on their minds for the advertising messages. And the net result will be much more impact per advertising dollar invested.

TYPES OF FOLLOW-THROUGH REQUIRED

A properly handled segmentation study is the beginning of a carefully controlled marketing program, not merely the completion of an extremely am-
bitious research program. The market now stands out in clear definition.
The most attractive market targets have been defined in detail, primary
competition and potential sources of business have been identified, and desirable brand images and primary buying incentives have been specified. In
short, the communications strategy is complete. All that remains to be done
to realize the promised returns on the investments in time and money made
thus far is to make sure that every marketing effort is coordinated and focused on the explicit strategies that have been set forth.

As has been mentioned previously, a large share of the value of a segmentation study comes from improved communications with consumers.
Groups of people who are relatively homogeneous attitudinally can be
reached efficiently by copy designed with knowledge of the composition of
those attitudes, certainly more efficiently than groups with heterogeneous
profiles.

Hopefully the continuous involvement of the creative people on the
project team throughout the course of the study and the presentation will
have resulted in an in-depth understanding of the market target, and thus
allow these people to use their normal creative processes to develop copy
which is particularly appropriate for it. It is likely that they have been
thinking about the best copy approaches from the point at which relevant
information began to emerge. They should know which visual settings,
types of casting, copy tonality, and depth of sell (cognitive or emotional) are
most suitable, and through their intuitions they should be able to supply
nonverbal cues that heighten the intensity of the appeals they use. And this
should allow them to capture the attention of the best prospects and to address them in an empathetic and persuasive tone about things that are likely
to interest them. But how can we be sure that they are accomplishing what
they intend to?

Copywriters themselves try to make sure that their ideas are on track by
a considerable amount of up-front work. In fact one of the strongest trends
in copy development over the past 10 years has been the increase in the
amount of qualitative research being done by the creative groups in advertising agencies and their clients. For example, in a review of "Recent, Significant Trends in the Use of Research to Evaluate Advertising" early in
1981,[2] Calvin W. Gage, Director of Research for the Leo Burnett Company,
one of the nation's leading advertising agencies, cited "increasing use of

---

[2] Unpublished paper. Burnett has an active unit, called the Copy Research Workshop,
which they employ specifically for this purpose.

preproduction research by clients for decision making"; Gage mentions that more than half of the copy testing by the major TV testing services is now on preproduction copy. Use of focus group sessions and depth interviews has also been flourishing. Creative people make heavy use of them to obtain feedback on their ideas at a stage early enough to allow for substantial changes in the directions being taken.

Usually, however, before the final decision is made on whether or not a specific copy execution is to be used, some sort of formal copy testing procedure is employed. And because this plays such an important role in determining what consumers do or do not see, it is worth covering in some depth.

ELEVEN

Copy Research Follow-Through

Copy research has been called the weakest tool used by marketing researchers. It is frequently attacked by leading creative people in advertising agencies[1] and its weaknesses are all too well known to marketing research professionals.[2,3] At a meeting of the New York Copy Research Council, Paul Gerhold, then president of the Advertising Research Foundation, suggested that the statement in Figure 11.1 be read before the presentation of all copy testing results. Although this was offered mostly in jest, it struck closely enough to home to mute the laughter in his audience.

STATE OF THE ART OF COPY TESTING

At a conference on advertising held by the Marketing Science Institute in 1981, the following were identified as important gaps in our knowledge:

Sales effects of advertising copy

Reliability and predictive validity of recall and recognition

Number of exposures required to stimulate action

[1] S. Kurnit, "The Impact of Creative Research on Creativity," and B. Manning, "Advertising Research, Crutch or Tool?" ARF Silver Anniversary Conference, New York, October 21–23, 1979.

[2] J. R. Andrews, "If Recall's Not the Answer What's the Question?," 26th Annual Conference of the ARF, New York, March 17–19, 1980.

[3] W. B. Miller, "Don't Blame Me—The Agency/Client/Research Killed It," AMA Western Advertising Conference, Rancho Mirage, CA, May 7, 1982.

Results of interaction of commercial types and formats with various programming types and formats

Wearout

Intermedia comparisons

Differences in how advertising functions for packaged goods, durables, services, and so on

Whether advertising works differently on users and nonusers

How to measure reinforcement

Relationship of advertising to positioning

Most of these relate either directly or indirectly to copy testing. And as recently as June of 1982, Mike Naples, president of the Advertising Research Foundation, issued a plea for "research experiments, studies, or papers" relating to 25 topics. One of these was copy research and almost half of the remaining topics were in some way related to copy testing.

The confusion extends to the methods used to evaluate the effectiveness of copy. A 1982 ART survey of current practices showed a wide divergence of methods and measures among firms.[4]

In the face of substantial criticism of copy testing and its frequent misuse, the top 21 agencies, led by a steering committee of Sonia Yuspeh of J. Walter Thompson, Dr. Ted Dunn of Benton & Bowles, and Joe Plummer of Young and Rubicam, issued a position paper announcing that the leading advertising agencies had agreed on nine basic principles of copy testing.[5] These maintained that a good copy testing system:

1.   *Provides measures which are relevant to the objectives of the advertising.* The implication here is that advertising can accomplish a variety of objectives. Therefore, before a piece of copy can be evaluated there must be a statement indicating what it was expected to do. Most large companies do have "copy platforms" that summarize their copy goals. Figures 11.2 through 11.6 provide a few examples.

2.   *Requires agreement about how the results will be used in advance of each specific test.* This is frequently termed "action standards." For example, one major corporation sets their copy testing standards so that if a commercial receives a recall score of 26 or higher[6] it will automatically be

---

[4] B. Lipstein and J. Neelankavil, "Television Advertising Copy Research Practices Among Major Advertisers and Advertising Agencies," Advertising Research Foundation, New York, September 1982.

[5] *Advertising Age*, January 25, 1982, p. 71.

[6] A score of 26 means that 26 percent of those exposed to the copy are able to play back enough about it to prove that they have seen it.

This statement should be read aloud before each presentation or discussion of test results.

This modest study was designed to provide fast and affordable clues on some aspects of this advertising.

　　However—

　　This is not a measure of how sales of the brand were or will be affected by the advertising.

　　It does not show how people reacted over time, or the response to the ad after repeated exposures.

　　It has not measured performance of the advertising in the media vehicles that are likely to be used, nor was it conducted among a representative sample of the total audience to which the advertising would be exposed.

　　It does not reflect the ability of competitive campaigns, or of brand availability, or product performance to nullify or augment this advertising.

　　It does not predict performance for other possible ads from the same campaign.

　　It does not show absolute accomplishment, and relative comparisons are based on other brands with other aims and problems, at other points of time.

In the past, retests have produced conflicting evidence on the stability of results in studies using this method.

In general, whatever it is that this test measures, the value of the results is probably commensurate with the time and budget expended.

Lots of luck!

(Strike out inapplicable statements, if any.)

Figure 11.1.   Universal all-purpose statement on validity and relevance for standard copy testing procedures

used. On the other hand, if a commercial scores below 16, it will be scrapped. Commercials that score between 16 and 25, a range that includes most of the commercials tested, will be evaulated in terms of their persuasion scores and other criteria. Still another type of action standard is shown in Table 11.1. This attempts to provide guidelines for various configurations of results for three criteria—persuasion, recall, and attitude change on a key benefit.

　　3.　*Provides multiple measurements because single measurements are generally inadequate to assess the performance of an advertisement.* This attempts to torpedo the "magic number" school of copy testing. Most re-

1. *Source of Business*

Will additional sales for our brand come *primarily* from expanding industry volume or from taking sales from competitors?

a. If from industry expansion, what will be the most important source of growth?

New users?

New use occasions?

More frequent use for same occasions?

More quantity per use?

b. If from competitors, which competitors represent the best potential source of business?

One competitor? (If so, which one?)

A group of competitors? (If so, how is the group defined?)

All competitors?

2. *Market Target*

Is it best to attempt to appeal to all consumers or to appeal to a selected segment of the market?

If segmentation is desirable, how is the target segment different from other segments?

What benefits are of special interest to this segment?

Is this a heavy user group?

How is the segment described demographically?

What are the important personality characteristics of this segment?

3. *Buying Incentive*

What claim is most likely to attract potential users to our brand?

a. Is the claimed benefit of particular importance to the market target?

b. Can the brand fully support the claim?

4. *Media Selection*

Which media will most effectively reach our market target?

a. What kind of media environment is desirable?

b. How much depth of sell is required to communicate the buying incentive?

c. How important is reach relative to frequency?

d. How desirable are demonstration and color?

e. What are trade merchandising requirements?

5. *Copy Execution*

How can we best communicate our buying incentive to our market target?

a. What tonality is most likely to attract people in the market target?

b. What format is most appropriate?

c. What kind of settings and casting are desirable?

Figure 11.2. Strategy statement questionnaire.

1. Objectives:
   Sales or share_____
   Advertising goals_____
   _____

2. Primary source of business_____
   _____

3. Market target:
   Benefits of greatest interest_____
   Consumption habits_____
   Demographic characteristics_____
   Personality and lifestyles_____
   _____

4. Buying incentive_____
   _____

5. Copy execution:
   Tonality_____
   Depth of sale_____
   Setting_____
   Casting_____

Figure 11.3. Strategy statement

1. Specific advertising objectives_____
   _____

2. Target audience:
   Demographics_____

   Attitudes and lifestyles_____

   Behavioral characteristics of product use_____

3. Unique benefit our product delivers best_____

4. Supporting point that will make consumers believe our message_____
   _____

5. Source of business_____

6. Desired brand image_____

7. Competitive strategic leverage_____
   _____

Figure 11.4. Copy strategy

The product's key benefit:
 —Does what?_____
 —For whom?_____
 —On what occasions?_____
_____

Why is the key functional attribute beneficial?_____
_____

Why does our brand do it better/cheaper/easier?_____
_____

What symbolic associations can be developed with:
 —The benefit?_____
 —The beneficiary?_____
 —How the benefit is achieved?_____
_____

 —The occasion of the benefit?_____

Figure 11.5.   The selling package

To convince users and purchasers that (NAME) is the one brand of (CATEGORY) that (BUYING INCENTIVE).

They can believe this because (DEMONSTRATION/SUPPORT).

Target:_____
_____

Sources of volume:_____

Figure 11.6.   Copy strategy

searchers believe that the effects of advertising are too complex to be summarized in a single number such as a recall score or a persuasion score.

 4.   *Is based upon a model of human response to communications—the reception of a stimulus, the comprehension of the stimulus, and the response to the stimulus.* The three-step model of receipt comprehension and response is the most widely accepted model of the advertising process in advertising agencies. But some people would argue that a message does not have to be understood in order to affect attitudes and, subsequently, behavior. However, the argument can quickly become semantic. Does comprehension of a stimulus involve cognitive processing or is emotional processing enough to meet the comprehension criterion?

 5.   *Allows for consideration of whether the advertising stimulus should be exposed more than once.* This principle reflects the industry controversy over whether it is preferable to expose consumers to the copy once or more than once. The principle is worded in such a way as to allow proponents of both positions to endorse it.

 6.   *Recognizes that the more finished a piece of copy is the more*

TABLE 11.1 Summary of Action Standards

Persuasion Comparison to Control		Recall Comparison to Brand or Category Norm		Recommended Decision
Purchase Intent	Key Strategic Benefit	Overall	Key Strategic Benefit	
Significant +	Significant +	Significant +	Significant +	Easy — Go! Run
Significant +	Significant +	Average	Significant +	Easy — Go! Run
Significant +	Significant +	Average	Average	Easy — Go! Run
No change	Significant +	Average	Average	Consider Changing
No change	No change	Average	Average	Do not change campaigns
No change	No change	Significant +	Average	Do not change campaigns
No change	No change	Significant+++	Significant+++	Change
No change	No change	Significant+++	Average	Consider changing
No change	No change	Significant+++	Significant +	Change
No change	Significant −	Significant+++	Significant +	Do not change
Significant −	Significant −	Significant+++	Significant+++	No not change

285

soundly it can be evaluated and requires, as a minimum that alternative ex-ecutions be tested in the same degree of finish. Obviously, other things being equal, everyone would prefer testing finished executions. However, every-thing is not equal. If it is assumed that the pool of funds available for copy testing is relatively fixed, testing finished executions means testing fewer al-ternatives than would be possible if executions were tested in rough form. (More about this later.)

7.   *Provides controls to avoid the biasing effects of the exposure context.* This recognizes the fact that there is interaction between the execution and the vehicle which acts as a carrier. The question of how best to take this into account remains an open one.

8.   *Is one that takes into account basic considerations of sample defini-tion.* One of the greatest potential weaknesses of copy testing is the methods by which samples of the population are obtained. National probability samples are rarely, if ever, employed. And there are serious questions as to what constitutes an "adequate" sample.

9.   *Is one that can demonstrate reliability and validity.* Although there are concerns about how reliability should be measured (e.g., split-half ver-sus test/retest), at least the necessary data are frequently available. Validity is another question. In 1979 the Copy Research Validation Council of the Advertising Research Foundation surveyed 125 of the leading advertisers of consumer goods as measured by Leading National Advertisers data to see whether validation information existed in corporate files. Very little was found; certainly not enough to support a claim that any method had been validated.

During the same survey corporations were queried about their use of syndicated services. The five most frequently mentioned services were asked to take part in a one-day workshop on Copy Research held in New York on November 3, 1981. After each of them had presented evidence of (or opinions as to) why the results produced by their services should be con-sidered valid, one of the CRVC committee members, Dr. Kevin Clancy of Boston University, spoke. His first sentence was "Well, obviously no one has final validation proof." The net result of the conference was that the CRVC agreed to proced with its plans for a carefully designed experiment aimed at providing the missing evidence.

Final agreement was obtained on the basic design in June of 1982. It called for testing six generic copy testing systems.[7] (A diagram of these is

---

[7] The alternative of testing specific systems was rejected because any ARF simulation of an existing service might be unable to fairly represent the administrative skills which each service has evolved over many tests with its own system. Also it was feared that, if each system was asked to run the test commercials through it, the tests might be run more care-fully than usual.

shown in Figure 11.7.) Plans call for comparing cell 3 with cell 4 to obtain insights into the kinds of differences that may occur between on-air and off-air tests. Similarly contrasting cell 6 with cell 4 allows comparison about how well a pre/post-design functions relative to a post-only design. And cell 1 versus cell 2 allows assessment of the choice between a self-selected audience and one that is prerecruited. Finally the differences between cells 4 and 5 allow evaluation of single exposure tests with tests involving an exposure and a reexposure.

These choices reflect the contrasts that were reported to be of greatest interest in a survey of members of the Advertising Research Foundation. But although quite a few firms indicated interest in each of these contrasts, one appeared to be of overriding importance—the choice between testing commercials in a natural on-air environment as opposed to testing them in a laboratory setting under tightly controlled conditions.

As a target it was decided that planning would be based on the assumption that 10 pairs of commercials would be cycled through each of the six cells. The 10 pairs would represent 10 brands drawn largely from the package goods industry.

Costs for conducting "forward" experiments are extremely high. Using the preferred services of Behaviorscan and Ad-Tel to obtain sales information, it was estimated that the project would cost $2 million or $3 million, and it was doubtful that the amount could be raised. For that reason, and to reduce the likelihood that no sales differences would be found for some pairs of commercials, it was decided to run a retrospective experiment. In a retrospective experiment the sales information is obtained first and the reasons for differences are sought afterward. Thus in this instance Behaviorscan and Ad-Tel were approached to see if it was possible to obtain pairs of commercials that appeared to be producing significant differences in sales performance. If so, these commercials would be cycled through the five generic copy testing systems as quickly as possible.

As of the publication date, funds are being raised to launch the tests. A modular approach has been decided upon to allow testing to begin when participants with qualifying pairs are located and the money to finance the testing of those pairs has been accumulated.

Present copy testing practices generally have their roots in beliefs about how advertising works. (See the models in Chapter 2.) Specific tests are tied to the copy platforms, examples of which were shown earlier in this chapter. However, there are also some basic differences in philosophies about how copy testing is best used. For example, few companies would agree on all of the answers to the following questions:

1. *How early in the process should testing be done?* As mentioned previously, the amount of research done early in the copy develop-

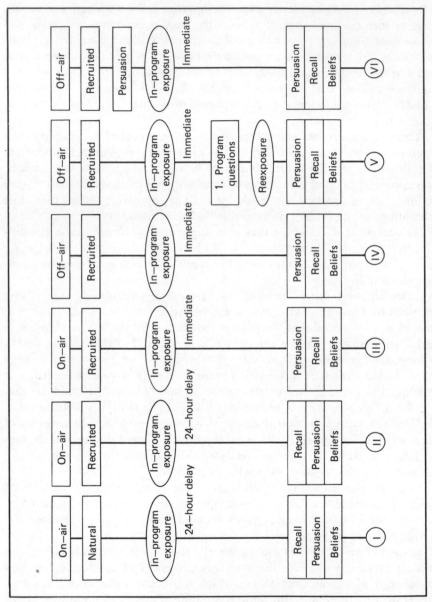

Figure 11.7. ARF copy research validity project

ment process has been growing steadily. However, some firms such as Coca-Cola prefer to test in finished form and that generally means late in the process.

2. *How many alternative executions should be developed and how many of these should be tested?* Obviously the more alternatives tested the greater the chance of locating effective executions. However, the cost of testing is almost directly proportional to the number of alternatives tested. So there are differences of opinion on this point.[8,9]

3. *How often should copy tests be conducted?* Should every execution be tested? Or should tests only be conducted when a fresh pool of executions is introduced? If the fresh pool is similar in nature to the last one (e.g., new poolouts), is testing required? Or should it be tested when the strategy remains the same but the executions are judged to be different than those that have been used in the past? Or should copy testing be reserved for those situations in which the communications strategy itself is changed?

4. *Should copy testing be used to measure wearout?* A related question is how large each pool of executions should be. It is reasonable to assume that large pools of executions built around a single theme will have more staying power than a single commercial used repeatedly.

5. *What copy testing measures are most appropriate for measuring wearout?* How do tracking study data relate to copy testing measures of potential wearout? At what level of wearout measures is it discrete to introduce fresh commercials into the market?

6. *What is the role of copy testing in strategy development?* Most researchers would probably agree that strategy work should be done before copy development begins, and that one important criterion for evaluating copy is whether or not it is on strategy. When impressive copy testing scores are obtained, however, it is tempting to rewrite the strategy enough to permit the copy to be used. At least one small agency advocates developing strategy directly from consumer reactions to a large number of executions rather than via the more traditional consumer survey route.

7. *Should copy research be primarily diagnostic or should it be evaluative as well?* One school holds that, because of the well-

[8] I. Gross, "How Many Ads Does It Pay to Pretest?" Operations Research Discussion Group, Report of the Tenth Meeting, ARF, March 10, 1964, pp. 1–24.
[9] K. A. Longman, "Remarks Concerning Gross Paper," 13th Annual Conference, ARF, November 1967.

known limitations of copy testing, it is best employed to help creative people build advertisements. On occasion the copy testing function has even been removed from the market research department and assigned to the creative department. Sometimes diagnostic research is done for the creative people and evaluative research for the client. In the latter instance it is usually used to help decide whether or not a particular copy execution should be used.

8. *How should the copy platform be expressed?*   This point has already been covered, at least indirectly, through examples of current practice.

9. *Should a syndicated copy testing system be employed or would a custom system be preferable?*   When syndicated systems are compatible with beliefs about how the advertising process works and what sorts of research biases are acceptable, they offer excellent value. On the other hand, custom systems are generally more flexible and can be tailored to reflect the consensus judgments of the organization.

10. *How can copy of differing sizes and lengths be compared?*   Does the copy work best in 30-second format or can it function equally well in 20 seconds? And a related question is whether the same copy will work better in print media or in broadcast media.

11. *Should copy testing for new and established brands be done in an identical manner?*   Some firms believe that developing effective copy for new products is a completely different problem than that of testing copy for an established brand and, therefore, that a completely different system should be used. Others believe that the same general model applies but that criteria should be weighted differently in the two situations (e.g., emphasis on brand awareness for new products and on persuasion for established products).

12. *Should competitive copy be tested?*   Some firms test new competitive copy as well as their own. The objective is to learn as soon as possible whether it poses a threat and, if so, to decide how best to respond to it.

In addition to differences in points of view concerning the best use of copy testing, there are differences in opinions of the types of measurements that should be taken, the degree of finish to be associated with the copy to be tested, the exposure conditions, the sampling system, the experimental design, and how action standards should be set.

THE GENERAL MEASUREMENT APPROACH

The general measurement approach in copy testing may involve sales measures, measures derived from observing respondents, measures obtained from physiological instruments (e.g., brain waves, voice patterns, pupil dilation), from projective tests, or from verbal responses. The latter can be obtained through direct questions from an interviewer, from a self-administered questionnaire filled out by a respondent with or without an interviewer present, or from a combination of approaches.

Although good advertising copy is expected to have a positive effect on sales at some point, sales are generally considered to be primarily criteria of the performance of the total marketing effort rather than specifically of copy content. Copy can make an important contribution but usually its effects are at least partially obscured by the influences of media weight, the media types chosen, media scheduling, pricing, sales promotion, distribution, display, packaging, and the combined efforts of competitors. Consequently although split-cable sales tests of copy are being done, and although supermarket scanners are being used increasingly in conjunction with copy tests, sales are not among the most frequently used copy test criteria.

Observational measures also are uncommon. They are used to measure attention, respondent purchase behavior, and respondent reactions. In the latter area some interesting work bordering on physiological measurement is being done with respect to coding of movements of the facial muscles signifying various emotions.

Physiological devices have received increased attention in recent years because of their objectivity, the fact that respondents have little control over them, and their promise of greater diagnostic power. They have been used to measure attention, interest, negative reactions, and brand attitudes. However, the research community remains cautious about their use. Because respondent measures usually must be obtained one person at a time, they are generally slow and expensive to use. Although they provide measurements not obtainable otherwise, at the present time they must be considered experimental.

Projective tests (e.g., figure drawing, sentence completion, thematic aperception tests, balloon tests, etc.) are particularly useful in situations in which nonverbal communications are dominant. However, their interpretation generally requires someone specially trained in their use. Additionally, the extent to which interpretations are reproducible from analyst to analyst has been questioned, but this is also an experimental area. Further validation of the implications seen by the analysts who use them will be required, as well as evidence of their reliability, before they are more broadly accepted as important copy testing tools. Until then their primary use remains intuitive and diagnostic, and their accepted function is to provide fresh insights into why respondents react to copy as they do.

Verbal responses are the most flexible of all measurement devices. Consequently, they are more frequently used in copy testing than any other type of measure. However, some important distinctions between open-end questions and structured questions, should be kept in mind when setting up a copy testing system based on verbal responses.

Open-end questions can be very helpful for measuring factors such as comprehension, recall, and information processing activities. They have shortcomings when attempts are made to use them in an evaluative fashion, however. As normally asked, they do not permit the reseacher to handle variations in articulateness of respondents. Some people may provide a single succinct answer to a direct question, whereas others may respond in great detail. If all responses are simply totaled, the more articulate respondents have more weight in the research findings. Moreover when an interviewer asks a respondent about things in which he or she has not been very deeply involved (such as viewing a commerical), she is bound to receive a large number of highly stereotyped answers.

Interviewer variability is also likely to be considerably greater when open-ended questions are used than when structured questions are used. In part this is due to the tendency of some interviewers to vary the phrasing of questions slightly in order to establish better rapport with respondents. In part it is due to variations in the abilities of interviewers to record the full answer as given by the respondent.

Open-end questions also raise coding problems. In translating responses into a form suitable for tabulation, coders must divine the underlying meaning of the phrases recorded by the interviewer. This process is often difficult in the absence of the facial expressions, voice qualities, and gestures of the respondent. At best it is highly subjective. At worst it can be imprecise or even erroneous. As a result inconsistencies in the ways in which individual coders respond to a specific response are quite commonplace.

For these reasons it is safest to restrict open-end questions as much as possible and to make relatively heavy use of structured approaches, such as rating scales. Rating scales are not only more reliable than standard open-end questions, they can engage the interest of respondents and increase their cooperation through the game-playing situation usually involved in obtaining scaled responses.

MEASUREMENTS TO BE TAKEN

Measurements fall into two categories—response measurements and respondent measurements. The former group concerns various communications, awareness, attitudinal, emotional, and perceptual effects of the copy. Some of the more frequently used measures of this type include:

Physical exposure—message delivery (e.g., commercial audience)

Attention—message receipt (both the verbal and the visual message)

Physiological reactions

Psychogalvanometer (blood pressure, heartbeat, respiration, perspiration)

Basal skin response

Eye camera (number of fixations, speed of eye movements)

Pupil dilation

Coding the facial muscles of the respondent, measuring changes

Eye blink rate

Twitchmeter (the extent to which respondents move around in their seats)

Voice pattern analysis (VOPAN)

Brain wave measurement (left brain/right brain)

Response latency

Involvement (continuous attention)

Comprehension (playback of intended message)

Believability (acceptance of the message)

Negatives (barriers to effectiveness)

Learning (factual and perceived informativeness)

Brand awareness, salience, registration, inclusion in evoked set

Advertising recall

Confusion (attributing message to the wrong brand)

Brand image, benefit delivery, delivery of key strategic benefit

Emotional response, mood

Reactions to the commercial/advertisement itself

Probability of decay in advertising effects

Brand preference, purchase intent, brand choice in lottery (often called persuasion)

Reinforcement

Curiosity

Intermediate actions (actions short of purchasing)

Sales, coupon redemption

Some comments on these measures are in order. Physical exposure refers to having the test advertisement pass before the eyes of the respondent. Frequently as pointed out in Chapter 2, the chapter on selective processes, respondents do not "see" the ad even though they are exposed physically. Attention refers to the conscious direction of a respondent's mind toward an ad or commerical. In other words, it involves the respondent "turning on" his or her mind. This is a difficult measure to obtain. One approach, employed by Benton & Bowles and a syndicated service called Copylab, is to have respondents placed in an anteroom, presumably waiting to be called into an interviewing room. In the anteroom are two television monitors placed in different corners of the room. Both run continuously; one shows a situation comedy, and at normal intervals television commericals appear on the screen. The other monitor shows traffic on the New Jersey Turnpike on a continuous loop. Observers are placed in the room to record the reactions of respondents when the test commercial appears. The attention measure is the percentage of those who continue to watch the commercial rather than turning their heads to check what is happening on the Jersey Turnpike. (There goes a truck! There goes a Volkswagen!) Attention measures are usually correlated with recall and recognition measures, shortly to be discussed. Thus recall and/or recognition are sometimes used as substitutes for attention measures.

Use of physiological measures fluctuates in popularity. They are attractive because they are more objective than questionnaire responses. However, they are normally gathered in one-on-one situations (an interviewer and one respondent) and, consequently, are relatively expensive to obtain. Also some investigators have encountered problems with their reliability[10] or have found that the same response can be attributed to more than one causal factor. At the moment the conventional wisdom is that such measures are of interest because they generally measure some form of arousal, but that they are best used in conjunction with more conventional measures rather than as substitutes for them.

Involvement with the commercial usually refers to continuous attention. One way in which this has been measured is via the CONPAAD machine.[11] This is a device that places one respondent at a time in front of a television set. The respondent is told that he can pump the two foot pedals as much or as little as he would like. One pedal controls the brightness of the screen and the other the loudness of the sound. A program is in progress as the respondent begins to pump. The measure of involvement is the rate at which he or she continues to pump when the commercial appears and throughout its length.

[10] Les Dorny, "Four Probes Into Space and Time," *Proceedings, 13th Annual Conference ARF,* November 14, 1967, pp. 3–10.

[11] R. C. Grass, L. C. Winters, and W. Wallace, "A Behavioral Pretest of Print Advertising," *Journal of Advertising Research,* Vol. 11, October 1971, p. 11ff.

Involvement can also refer to the amount and kinds of information processing activities that take place as respondents accept, distort, or reject the message of the advertisement. In this context it includes support arguments (sharpening), counterargumentation (leveling), connections,[12] and source derogation.

Comprehension is one measure that is obtained in almost every copy test conducted. It concerns the ability of the respondent to play back the sales message that the advertising was designed to communicate. It has been found to be a reasonably reliable measure, even when smaller than average samples are employed.

It is customarily measured by a question such as "Tell me everything that went through your mind as you read the ad." This phrasing permits involvement and information processing activities to be measured as well. "How would you describe the product to a friend who had never heard of it?" focuses more sharply on the central message as does "What did the advertiser intend to tell people?" "Tell me everything you remember about what the ad said or showed" gives more complete playback of the visual elements. Although actually a recall question, it allows inferences about comprehension as well.

Believability is a more controversial measure. It was originally designed to pick up out advertisements that were being rejected because the claims made were not accepted by the people exposed to the advertising. However, Maloney[13, 14] has suggested that lack of believability does not necessarily mean that the ad is weak. Instead, for example, if the ad is for a cosmetic and the implied claim is that it will make the user beautiful, the respondent may reject the claim but still be anxious to try the product—just in case.

Many companies have standards concerning the level of unsolicited negative comments that are acceptable. One popular standard is that no copy will be run if more than 10 percent of the comments generated by questions such as "What went through your mind as you looked at the commercial?" are considered to be negative in nature.

Learning is almost always one of the criteria by which advertising for new products is evaluated. It also comes into play when new facts are introduced into the copy for existing products and when corporate or brand slogans or taglines are changed. Broadly speaking it applies to the acquisi-

[12] A method suggested by Krugman wherein the number of times the respondent relates the message to his life are counted.

[13] J. C. Maloney, "Is Advertising Believability Really Important?" *Journal of Marketing*, Vol. 27, October 1963, pp. 1–8.

[14] ———, "Advertising Research and an Emerging Science of Mass Persuasion," *Journalism Quarterly*, Vol. 41, Autumn 1964, pp. 517–528.

tion of any new information about the brand, product, or corporation. A standard question is whether anything new, important, or interesting was learned from the advertisement.

Brand awareness, especially top-of-mind brand awareness,[15] is an important criterion, perhaps the single most important criterion, for marketers who believe in the ATR model of consumer behavior. The primary function of advertising in this school is to call attention to the brand, to place it in consumers' evoked sets, and thereby to increase its probability of purchase. For others awareness is used in much the same sense as negatives—to screen out questionable commericals. When the level of awareness is lower than some prespecified level, the commercial will not be run.

Advertising recall is probably the oldest standard of advertising effectiveness. Thirty years ago it was argued that people could not be affected by advertising that they did not remember; even today some marketing people believe this to be true. However, now there is substantial evidence that people's attitudes, and even their behavior, can be affected by advertising they do not remember.[16] Nevertheless, recall remains a frequently used criterion of copy effectiveness, although today largely in concert with other criteria. Recognition is another measure of retention. Some people believe that it is a more appropriate measure of the impact of ads featuring user imagery.[17] But Lucas and others have shown that people claim to recognize ads that they cannot possibly have seen—probably because they are similar to other ads that they have, in fact, seen.

Confusion is another negative criterion. Given the steady increases in advertising clutter, the erosion of product protection (rules about the permissible proximity of advertising for products of the same type), and the generally low levels of attention that consumers pay to advertising, the misattribution of commercial sponsorship has increased. Among creative people this is frequently called "vampire video." When only the execution is remembered and not the brand advertised, it "sucks the blood out of the message." Some confusion is, of course, inevitable; however, it is not unusual to set maximum acceptable levels.

Brand images are another criterion measure of long standing. Often one or two aspects of the brand image are singled out as being of special importance (key benefits) and their performance after exposure to the advertising is carefully watched. At least one major agency uses shifts in a key brand image item as their primary measure of the effectiveness of advertising copy.

[15] The percentage of the time the brand is mentioned first when consumers are asked "What brands of (category) can you think of?"
[16] D. A. Aaker and G. S. Day, "A Recursive Model of the Relationship of Attitude Change and Behavior Change," *Journal of Applied Psychology*, June 1974, Vol. 59, No. 3, pp. 281–286.
[17] "Foote Cone Study," *Marketing News*, Vol. 14, No. 25, June 12, 1981, p. 1.

Measures of emotional response or mood are a relatively recent addition to the copy researchers' tool kit. It is increasingly being recognized that advertising is a highly complex stimulus and that only part—perhaps a very small part—of its total effect is being measured by conventional copy testing measures. Currently the most popular means of approaching this problem is through adjective checklists,[18] but there is an active search for new and more effective measures. The traditional tools of clinical psychology, such as figure drawing, sentence completion, thematic apperception tests, and balloon tests, are being reexamined for their potential as are newer approaches such as perceptual mapping[19] and physiological response. Clinical approaches tend to be slow and expensive in copy testing applications, however, and the limitations of physiological measures have been discussed. Mapping, although potentially of interest, suffers from its statistical complexity and from the lack of accepted measures for applying statistical confidence intervals to the kinds of shifts that appear to take place on perceptual maps.

Some people believe that it is helpful to ask people direct questions about the advertising itself.[20] Sometimes people are simply asked if they enjoyed the commercial and if there is anything in it which they find annoying or objectionable. Other times the commercial is reexposed for the specific purpose of asking respondents to evaluate it. Adjective checklists are frequently used in this context.

Potential wearout is an important issue in the choice among alternative copy executions, but few attempts are made to measure it. Rather it is conveniently assumed that the copy which scores best on the first exposure or two is least likely to wear out. A few systems do attempt to deal with this problem. For example, in the Warner-Lambert system, respondents are asked after two exposures whether they would like to see the copy again. Responses are believed to be related to the probability of message decay.

Persuasion, as measured by brand choice, purchase intent, or constant sum measures, has replaced recall as the most popular single criterion measure. (Persuasion measures were covered in detail in Chapter 3.)

When brands have high market shares and a great many satisfied users, it may be difficult to obtain shifts on persuasion measures in copy tests. Obviously if all repondents gave a brand the highest possible score on a rating scale *before* exposure, it would be impossible to obtain a positive shift. In

[18] W. Wells, C. Leavitt, and M. McConville, "A Reaction Profile for TV Commercials," *Journal of Advertising Research*, Vol. 11, December 1971, p. 11ff.
[19] A. D. Beard, "Suggestions for Making Multidimensional Scaling More Useful in Exploring Styling and Other Aesthetical Dimensions," AMA National Educators Conference, August 10, 1981, Washington, DC.
[20] R. Bartos, "Ads That Irritate May Erode Trust in Advertised Brands," *Harvard Business Review*, July–August 1981, pp. 138–140.

such situations the function of the advertising is to hold them there, to reinforce attitudes so that they are more resistant to subsequent decay. This too is rarely measured, but it does have potential value. One comparatively straightforward way of measuring reinforcement is to apply a "sureness" scale after the basic persuasion measure has been taken. In such an approach people are asked how sure they are that the point of view just expressed is an accurate reflection of their feelings toward the brand. Thus it is possible for feelings of sureness to increase among top-box raters even though the level of their attitudes does not improve. In practical terms the "sureness" ratings can be used as a set of weights for the ratings on the persuasion scales.

Curiosity is another infrequently used criterion measure. It is, in effect, a scale designed to measure how likely the respondent is to take some followup action short of a purchase. In other words it is a measure of interest in following up something said in or implied by the advertisement.

Intermediate actions themselves can be measured, of course, and sometimes are. These are positive actions taken between the time at which a favorable predisposition toward the brand has been created and the actual sale. They include such things as coupon redemption, inquiries of friends or retailers, searchers for additional information, store visits, and trial by means other than a purchase. In some situations the function of the advertising is only to complete this step—to deliver prospects to the automobile salesperson for a trial ride or prospective army recruits to a recruiting office for more information on the alternatives open to them. The sales force is expected to make the final sale.

Sales, of course, are the ultimate criterion of copy effectiveness. As noted earlier, however, the effects of an individual piece of copy are hard to measure, and it is expensive to attempt to do so. In fact, the time period over which the effects of exposure to copy are likely to affect sales is not at all clear. For these reasons sales measures are a relatively infrequent criterion.

Given the wide variety of potentially useful measures, most copy researchers are in agreement these days (as evidenced by the PACT statement of principles) that no single measure is adequate for evaluating the effectiveness of an advertising execution. Advertising copy quite clearly operates on a variety of levels. Debate has continued for more than 20 years about whether recall type measures or persuasion type measures are better indicators of copy effectiveness. Quite a few studies have shown that recall and persuasion are virtually uncorrelated.[21] Thus different choices will be made depending upon which of these two criteria is given the greater weight. If a

[21] S. Young, "Copy Testing without Magic Numbers," *Journal of Advertising Research*, Vol. 12, February 1972, p. 3ff.

choice has to be made, the weight of evidence currently would seem to be on the side of those favoring persuasion measures. However, most copy researchers would also agree that a high persuasion score coupled with zero recall is suspect and, conversely, that so is a high recall level with no persuasion. However, there may well be no need for complete exclusion of either measure. It seems likely that in concert they may predict sales more effectively than either measure can be expected to do alone. The experiment being planned by the Copy Research Validation Council should shed considerable light on this possibility.

DIAGNOSTIC MEASURES

Thus far the measures discussed have been criterion measures—measures of whether or not the copy can be expected to achieve its goals. There is another type of measure concerned not so much with *whether* or not the copy is having a positive overall effect but with *why* it is having certain kinds of effects. As in the case of the criterion measures there are a number of different approaches to answering this question:

Analysis of verbal playback

Changes in image ratings

Adjective checklists

Physiological measures

Continuous measures of attention and interest

Nonverbal elements (presence of)

Each of these areas is analyzed in relationship to the performance of the criterion measure it is thought to influence. Sometimes this is done by cross-tabulation, occasionally through correlation or multivariate analyses. When relationships are discovered, they are tested in subsequent commercials. If, for example, symbols are found that heighten the impact of the advertising, they may be permanently incorporated into the advertising and even carried over to packaging or sales promotion.

For diagnostic analyses it is helpful to specify a model of the process that you believe to be taking place. One popular model is shown in Figure 11.8. In this model the "significant element" can be a piece of the open-ended playback or it may simply be the presence of a nonverbal stimulus, such as a visual element, symbol, or spokesperson used in the advertising. Anything that can be coded can be analyzed. Most frequently, however, analyses are confined to recall elements and to changes in brand images.

The brand image aspects in this sort of example are usually a dozen or so

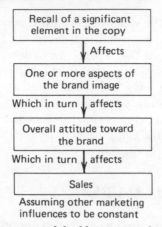

Figure 11.8. A diagnostic model of how copy elements can affect sales

carefully selected benefits and product characteristics, respondents having rated them on an "agree or disagree" scale for the brand of interest. The overall attitude measure (or so-called persuasion measure) is the purchase intent, brand choice, or constant sum measure that is favored. If, for example, the test involves a constant sum measure and a before/after design, it is desirable to have obtained a significant positive shift before deciding upon a diagnostic analysis. So let us assume that the test has produced a significant positive shift on the constant sum measure.

The analysis is usually worked backward from the changes in the overall measure to the changes in the individual brand image factors that may be causing it. A customary first step is to score each respondent plus one, zero, or minus one on each of the dozen or so image factors to indicate whether their ratings have shifted positively, negatively, or remained the same on each of those items. Respondents are scored similarly on changes in their constant sum allocations to the brand of interest. Then a simple table such as Table 11.2 can be generated.

Analysis of this table suggests that Image Item No. 1 is more strongly related to constant sum shifts than items No. 2 or No. 3. So scanning this type of table allows the items that are most strongly related to the positive constant sum shift to be identified. The hope is that some, if not all, of the changes in image items are related causally.

The next question to be investigated is why those image items have shifted. Again we can go to cross-tabs, this time, for example, cross-tabbing the changes in Image Item No. 1 by the various recall elements. The resultant table should look something like Table 11.3. Analysis of this table suggests that recall of Element No. 1 is positively associated with the observed

TABLE 11.2 Relationship of Changes in Image Perceptions to Direction of Attitude Shift

Average Shift in Image Item Number	People Whose Constant Sum Shifted Positively	People with No Change	People Whose Constant Sum Shifted Negatively
1	+0.3	-0-	−0.01
2	+0.1	+0.1	+0.1
3	+0.3	−0.1	+0.2
↓ 12	etc.	etc.	etc.

shifts in Image Item No. 1. From Table 11.2 we know that that image item is in turn associated with the constant sum shift. So from these two tables it can be hypothesized that recall of Element No. 1 affects attitudes toward the brand on Image Item No. 1, and that this affects the overall predisposition toward the product. Outside the scope of the copy test it is also presumed that the positive attitude shift will affect sales performance.

It is possible, of course, to assume a simpler model and, for example, to relate elements recalled directly to overall attitudes. This would require only one table with the three shift groups in the head and the recall elements in the stub.

A similar analysis can be made with "after only" design. In this case the first tale would contain *levels* of image ratings instead of the shifts shown in the illustration. Additionally, the header would consist of just two columns—one for exposed people and one for unexposed people, the control group. In this kind of analysis, however, it is very important that the exposed and unexposed groups be carefully matched on all relevant variables.

TABLE 11.3 Relationship of Recall of Copy Elements to Direction of Shift on Image Item

Recall of:	People Whose Rating of Image Item Number 1 Shifted Positively	People Showing No Change	People Whose Rating of Image Item Number 1 Shifted Negatively
Element 1	43%	27%	16%
2	12	15	11
3	50	47	50
etc.			

Nonverbal Communications

Unfortunately, the analytical model described in the previous section frequently does not provide the needed insights into why changes have occurred in the criterion measure. This is particularly true when the criterion measure is attitude shift.

Reasons are not hard to find. It is a well-known fact that recall scores and attitude shift scores are not well correlated with each other. Consequently, it is a rare phenomenon when the points recalled explain a large proportion of the variation in attitude shift scores.

Going one step further, it may even be unrealistic to expect respondents in a copy test situation to be able to recognize and play back to an interviewer all of the factors that are affecting him or her positively and negatively. A television commercial is a highly complex stimulus, packed with a variety of nonverbal forms of communication. Undoubtedly respondents are affected by factors such as music and the voice qualities of presenters, but they may not realize it at the time of exposure. And if they are asked to pay close attention to a factor such as music, their reactions may be different than when the music assumes its usual background role.

MEASURING NONVERBAL FACTORS

If respondents are not able to retrieve them, how then can nonverbal effects be measured? One strategy is to return to the stimulus and conduct a content analysis. If the center of interest is nonverbal communications, however, a special nontraditional form of content analysis may be required. Because nonverbal elements have not received much attention, the coding systems to be employed are not as evident as those that have been employed (e.g., in coding the content of newspapers). Television commercials consist of complex settings, people, cognitive messages, symbols, music, and a variety of sights, sounds, and motions, any of which may say more to the respondent than the cognitive message that the advertiser usually intends to deliver. Standard codes are not available for most of these areas. However, it seems that their development deserves to be assigned a high priority.

Research on nonverbal communications is widely scattered[22-24] and

[22] Thomas V. Bonoma and Leonard C. Felder, "Nonverbal Communication in Marketing: Toward a Commercial Analysis," *Journal of Marketing Research*, Vol. 14, May 1977, pp. 169-180.
[23] Daniel Druckman, Richard M. Rozelle, and James C. Baxter, "Nonverbal Communication: Survey, Theory, and Research," Sage Library of Social Research, Volume 139, 1982.
[24] John M. Wiemann and Randall P. Harrison, "Nonverbal Interaction," *Sage Annual Reviews of Communication Research*, Vol. 11, 1983.

little of it relates specifically to television commercials. Yet it seems certain that television commercials contain important nonverbal elements that are likely to be decoded affectively and, consequently to affect probability of purchase. In fact, work on interpersonal communication suggests that non-verbal factors are many times *more* important than cognitive, factual, literal communications. For example, Mehrabian[25] has concluded that only 7% of interpersonal communications is traceable to words, whereas 55% comes from facial expressions and 38% comes from paralanguage—the way in which people use their voices. Of course, it can be argued that communication via mass media is quite a different situation. In any case the possibility that nonverbals play a key role is clearly worth investigation.

The purpose of this section is to provide a "top line" report on some research that was begun at the University of New Hampshire in September 1982, the broad objective of which was to obtain insights into nonverbal communications in television advertising.

The planned research involves two stages. The first has been largely exploratory. Its purpose was to examine various types of nonverbal communication and to attempt to identify the most promising subcategories. The second stage is to be an in-depth investigation of several of the more promising types. As of the date of publication, the first stage has been completed and the second is well under way.

Stage I

Stage I was begun with a literature search. The complexity of the field of nonverbal communications quickly become apparent. A number of subdisciplines are involved and research in each has been developing in its own fashion. Investigations and areas of coverage overlap to a considerable extent. No overview that might be directly applicable to television was found. Consequently, for purposes of Stage I, 17 areas of nonverbal communication were arbitrarily defined. No attempt was made to prevent overlap among these areas. Rather the intent was to avoid overlooking areas of potential significance. The areas designated for study included:

1. *Paralanguage—the way in which voice(s) are used.* This includes factors such as the number of voices heard, whether they are male or female, whether a voiceover or an on-screen voice is used, pitch, tonal qualities, pace, use of silence, hesitations, and so on.

2. *Glance—the way in which eyes are used.* Amount of eye contact between cast, amount with audience, amount directed at the prod-

---

[25] Albert Mehrabian, *Nonverbal Communication*, Chicago: Aldine, 1972.

uct, winking, blinking, opening eyes in surprise, crying, redirecting of gaze, and so on.

3. *Proxemics—distances between cast members and between the cast and the audience.* This includes the amount of touching, who is touching whom, where, the manner of touching, relative postures, orientations, and kinesthetic factors (distances).

4. *Gestures—use of hands, arms, legs, fingers, heads, and other parts of the torso.* A wide variety of gestures was covered, including touching fingers to one's face, clapping, pounding, pushing, fumbling, pointing, waving, nodding, kicking, and so on.

5. *Body Language—this pertains to motion and stance.* It includes leaning, standing, sitting, rocking, running, dancing, and various modes of deploying arms and legs.

6. *Facial Cues—use of mouth, eyes, and forehead.* Covered here are smiling, frowning, squinting, starry-eyed expressions, raising eyebrows, wrinkling forehead, and a variety of expressions as shown by the principal character in the commercial (when there is one).

7. *Spokesperson Characteristics—how he or she is perceived.* Covered are level of familiarity, accent, type (human, animal, animated character, robot, etc.) and attributes ascribed to the spokesperson (authoritative, likeable, trustworthy, attractive, etc.).

8. *Music—characteristics of the music, if music is employed.* This includes the amount of time during which music is present, whether it is vocal or instrumental, familiarity, type, use technique, and a series of bipolar adjective scales.

9. *Dress—how people in the cast are attired.* Occupations suggested, status, fashion, use of jewelry, colors the same as the product, formality, and appropriateness to the situation.

10. *Semiotics—signs, symbols, and artifacts that provoke specified types of associations.* Under this heading fall the number of artifacts, their apparent purpose, and specific types of artifacts present in the commercial.

11. *Setting—the location of the commercial.* Is it indoor or outdoor, country or city, in a busy or distracting location? What sorts of colors, people, and products are involved?

12. *Tonality/Mood—the feelings projected by the commercial.* These are usually measured by a series of adjectives, and measurements used in this study were no exception. Among the dimensions scaled were different/ordinary, humorous/solemn, loud/quiet, sentimental/detached, and loud/soft.

13. *Commercial Format—the general plot of the commercial; its type.* This relates to the way in which the commercial is constructed. Among the types coded were comparative advertising, demonstration, news, emotional, problem/solution, slice of life, straight sell, animation, jingle, product as hero, and user as focal point.

14. *Sound Effects—types of sounds used and their intended effects.* Covered here are whether the sounds are machines, nature, animals, humans, mechanical, or musical; whether the intended effect is for attention, romantic, humorous, sexy, and so on; the number of effects detected, and the location of the loudest part of the commercial.

15. *Deception Cues—a category, crosscutting the others, which suggests to viewers that the commercial is not truthful.* Among the cues covered were fast, glib talk, overly used settings, coy or cute antics, false ethnic endorsements, paid sports personalities, and exaggerated demonstrations.

16. *Camera Use—the role that the camera plays in the execution.* This, strictly speaking, is not an area normally classified under the heading of nonverbal research. However, it seems relevant for television commercials. Codes relate to the number of camera shots, zooms, product closeups, supers, dissolves, how people are shot, and the amount of time spent on the different types of shots.

17. *Brand Identification—showing or saying the brand name.* Showing the brand name is also a form of nonverbal communication, although specific to television or print advertising. Among the factors measured were elapsed time until the brand name is seen, the number of times seen, the amount of time the name is visually exposed, type of exposure (name or package), and similar data on oral mentions.

Other factors could perhaps have been measured and, in fact, some were investigated after the original categorization (e.g., pitcher/catcher relationships—who is interacting with whom and their apparent relationships). However, the coverage appears reasonably comprehensive. In all some 510 individual codes were developed.

The Warner-Lambert Company provided 47 commercials for the Stage I analysis, together with several possible criterion measures obtained via the Richardson-Haley copy testing system. Some of the commercials were finished; some were photomatics, and some were animatics. Dummy variables were used in the analysis (described in the next section) to represent differences in degree of finish as well as product categories.

The Richardson-Haley system is used corporately at Warner-Lambert to select from several candidate executions the specific commercials that will be aired. It is a double exposure system, using a prerecruited audience and a cable on-air exposure method. Several alternative performance measures are available, depending upon the objectives of the advertising. The criterion measure selected for primary attention in this chapter is the pre/post persuasion measure, a constant sum measure that has been validated by tracking subsequent purchase behavior.

To launch the analysis, student teams developed extensive codes in each of the 17 areas to be investigated. These were based partly on the literature search, partly on interviews with other investigators at the University working in allied fields, and partly on intuition.

The preliminary list of codes was reviewed, reliability checks were made, items were added and deleted, and a more refined set was developed. The number of variables coded within each area varied substantially, ranging from about 15 in the smaller areas to around 50 in the larger ones. Over the next year and a half more than 175 students were trained in the use of these codes and, once trained, they reviewed and coded the 47 commercials.

ANALYSIS OF THE RESULTS

Data were keypunched and read into the UNH DEC-10 computer. As a first step, Pearson correlations were generated between each of the 510 variables coded and four possible criterion measures—constant sum attitude shift (persuasion), brand salience, proven recall, and perceptual shifts on a benefit designated as the "key benefit." The results are shown in Table 11.4. The number of nonverbal variables found to be related to the persuasion measure and to top-of-mind brand awareness is encouraging. However, the latter number is upwardly biased by the inclusion of the brand identification variables.

Returning to Table 11.4, it can be seen that 132 of the 510 nonverbal variables were significantly related to persuasion when evaluations were made at the .10 level of significance and 75 at the .05 level. Because it is hypothesized that nonverbal effects are especially important in persuasion, and because outside research suggests that the persuasion variables bear a more significant relationship to sales than does recall,[26] diagnostic efforts in this chapter are focused on the persuasion variable. Past diagnostic efforts

[26] L. D. Gibson, "Not Recall," *Journal of Advertising Research*, Vol. 23, No. 1, 1983, pp. 39–46.

TABLE 11.4   Correlations Between Nonverbal Variables[a] and Alternative Performance Criteria

	Performance Criteria			
	Persuasion	Related Recall	Top of Mind Brand Awareness	Key Benefit
Number found significant at 10% level	132 (25.9%)	90 (17.6%)	142 (27.8%)	62 (12.2%)
Number found significant at 5% level	75 (14.7%)	38 (7.5%)	89 (17.9%)	28 (9.9%)

[a] Total number of nonverbal variables = 510.

have generally attempted to explain the magnitude of attitude shifts by cross-tabulating points recalled by people with positive shifts against points recalled by those whose attitudes did not change or changed negatively (assuming use of a pre/post research design). In view of the typically low level of association between persuasion and recall (for these commercials $R^2 = +.047$) it is easy to understand why this procedure is often not helpful. The relatively high correlations for nonverbals suggest that they hold substantially more potential for explaining persuasion than do recall data.

A second finding of interest was that the preponderance of significant effects of nonverbals were negative in direction. Of the 132 significant variables, 90 of the effects were negative. Thus it can be hypothesized that nonverbal effects are more likely to work *against* a commercial than to enhance its effectiveness. This is not hard to explain. Studies on selective perception[27] suggest that people generally approach advertising in a casual, uninvolved, and more than slightly suspicious manner. They are aware that advertising messages are usually biased in favor of the advertiser. Thus they are reluctant to change their preconceptions on the basis of advertising and so they are alert to any cues which suggest that they can comfortably ignore the commercial. Nonverbals may be a crucial medium in supplying such cues. In other words, by guiding people into or away from the message they may play a critical role in the ultimate success of the advertising message.

Table 11.5 shows positive and negative effects by type of nonverbal com-

[27] Russell I. Haley, "Marketing Implications of Selective Perception," AAPOR Annual Conference, Lake George, N.Y., May 22, 1970. Note also that recall norms generally hover around 20 percent, suggesting that one day after exposure four out of five of the people who have been exposed to it cannot play back enough to prove that they have seen the commercial.

TABLE 11.5 Number of Simple Correlations Significant at the 99% Level

Nonverbal Area	Positive Relationship	Negative Relationship	Total Number Significant	Total Number of Variables Tested	% Significant
Paralanguage	2	3	5	16	31.3%
Glance	2	0	2	15	13.4%
Proxemics	1	0	1	44	2.3%
Gestures	0	0	0	29	0.0%
Body language	0	2	2	54	3.7%
Facial cues	2	0	2	25	8.0%
Casting	1	2	3	30	10.0%
Music	0	1	1	39	2.6%
Dress	0	0	0	31	0.0%
Semiotics	0	2	2	35	5.7%
Setting	0	2	2	16	12.5%
Tonality/mood	0	1	1	12	8.3%
Format	0	0	0	19	0.0%
Sound effects	0	0	0	16	0.0%
Deception	0	1	1	26	3.8%
Camera use	0	0	0	12	0.0%
Brand identification	0	0	0	10	0.0%
Pitcher/catcher/voiceover	0	0	0	81	0.0%
Totals	8	14	22	510	4.3%

munication. To provide greater discrimination between areas, only items that show significance at the 1% level are shown. It should be cautioned that comparisons among areas are affected not only by the importance of the area but also by the variability of the commercials available for analysis and by the appropriateness and sensitivity of the codes involved. Obviously if all of the commericals available for analysis use the same commercial formats (e.g., a problem/solution format), then that format will not appear as an important nonverbal consideration. Similarly, if important nonverbal variables have been missed or coded using an inferior measurement instrument, the potential influence of that variable will not be properly reflected in the results.

On the other hand, when large numbers of statistically significant effects do appear within a given nonverbal category, it suggests that that area warrants further investigation. Viewed in this way the areas of paralanguage, glance, setting, and spokesperson characteristics (casting) look particularly promising.

A similar method of screening categories is to select the single variable within each category that shows the highest simple correlation with the criterion measure—in this case attitude shift—and then to rank order those variables. This was done in Table 11.6. Viewed in this way, areas deserving special attention include Body Language, Facial Expression, Casting, and Tonality.

A more subjective, but perhaps equally valid method of screening cate-

TABLE 11.6 Nonverbal Variables Most Strongly Correlated with Persuasion

Variable	Simple Correlation	Area
Hands at side	−.5624	Body language
Principal character's expression is contentment	+.4789	Facial expression
Likable spokesperson	−.4662	Casting
Humorous mood	−.4510	Tonality/mood
Busy setting	−.4172	Setting
Wink	+.4150	Glance
Number of voices	−.4094	Paralanguage
Number of artifacts	−.4043	Artifacts
Music type is "other"	−.3527	Music
Exaggerated demonstration	−.3492	Deception
Relation of pitcher to others is unknown	−.3021	Pitcher/catcher/voiceover
Occupation suggested by dress is entertainment	−.2484	Dress

gories is to make an assessment as to categories in which substantial improvement in coding may be possible. Music is such a category. More discussion on categories with major potential for code improvement will follow shortly.

One obvious limitation in looking at a sample of commercials from differing product categories is that nonverbal measures may function quite differently from product category to product category. Indeed a wide variety of variables beyond those directly involved in the commerical has been posited to have potentially significant effects on persuasion. Among them are factors relating to the program and media context, factors relating to the consumer receiving the message, and factors relating to the product being advertised.

One way of reducing brand effects is to code brands as dummy variables and to enter them into the estimating equation. This was done and it was found that 53.4% of the variance in attitude shift scores could be explained by brand differences. Of course, it could be argued that brand effects should *not* be eliminated from diagnostic efforts. If Product A uses one spokesperson and gets large positive attitude changes, and Product B uses a different spokesperson and does not obtain large shifts, it does not necessarily follow that the observed differences are brand effects. The differences could well be attributable to differences in the effectiveness of the spokespersons involved. Brand and spokesperson effects are confounded, however, and we cannot be sure whether the brand, the spokesperson, or interaction between the brand and the spokesperson is causing the differences in attitude shift.

The use of dummy variables for brands allows an examination of the incremental effects that can be attributed to nonverbal influences alone. Table 11.7 summarizes the incremental effects attributable to each nonverbal category. Again in interpreting the results, the limitations associated with the range of codes included and the limited variability of the commercials available for analysis should be kept in mind. It is apparent, however,

TABLE 11.7   Incremental Effects on Persuasion Attributable to Each Nonverbal Category[a]

Area	Adjusted R^2
Facial cues	.300
Setting	.109
Format	.094
Pitcher/catcher/voiceover	.073
Gestures	.070
Others	.000

[a] Dependent variables are residual variances after product effects have been removed.

that viewed from this perspective the areas of Facial Expression, Setting, and Format perform well.

Individual Nonverbal Variables

As noted earlier, the primary purpose of Stage I was to screen nonverbal categories in order to identify a comparatively small number of categories in which future diagnostic efforts are most likely to be productive. However, the temptation to look at specific variables within categories is very strong. And although it is clearly impossible to generalize from a preliminary investigation of the sort presented here, it may be possible, at least, to generate some interesting hypotheses based on what has been found to date. For example:

> Humor generally correlates negatively with persuasion. Obviously humor itself is a complex topic and the range of humor available in this sample was limited. However, these data suggest that use of humor involves substantial risks.
>
> Presence of a celebrity spokesperson also correlated negatively with persuasion, implying that spokespersons, if used, should be selected with a great deal of care.
>
> The use of sex (sex appeal) shows no relationship—either positive or negative—with persuasion. It is hypothesized that the key is the extent to which sex can reasonably be associated with the product being advertised.
>
> Gender differences frequently show significant relationships with persuasion.
>
> Nonverbal variables that communicate simplicity or single-mindedness are positively associated with persuasion.
>
> Variables communicating complexity (several voices, distracting motion, multiple gestures, fast cuts, lots of characters) generally produce negative results.
>
> Music not used to emphasize the meaning of a message but added simply to provide a pleasant atmosphere is likely to operate negatively.
>
> Coy, cute antics are a definite turnoff.
>
> Exaggerated demonstration is also a turnoff.

STAGE I CONCLUSIONS AND STAGE 2 PLANS

It has become fashionable to think of advertising messages as either cognitive or emotional. In truth it is virtually impossible to deliver either a completely cognitive or a completely emotional message; to be delivered it must be executed. And to be executed it must be translated into visual and/or aural form. Cognitive messages require people, or voices, or graphics. Each of these has emotional overtones. If the presenter is changed, or the voice, or even the type font, the message itself is changed. Similarly even if an emotional message is intended, the respondent is likely to read logical behavioral consequences into it on the basis of the cues that are provided to him. So a more realistic way of viewing messages then a dichotomous classification is to array them on a continuum with polar positions labeled "rational" and "emotional." Some messages lean more one way than the other; some have pronounced leanings. And nonverbal forms of communications are closely related to how the message is positioned on that continuum.

Diagnosis of attitude shift ratings has been a chronic problem for copy researchers. Recall information has not been too useful in this regard, partly because of the generally low levels of correlation that have been found to exist between recall and persuasion measures. Theoretically shifts in perception might be helpful in explaining why shifts in persuasion measures are sometimes large and sometimes not. However, few companies have been able to develop reliable measures of the individual perceptions that, when combined in a Fishbein model, determine overall attitudes. This is true partly because consumer perceptions frequently are not firmly anchored. Consequently responses to copy research questions often contain a sizable random response element. To the extent that it is possible to develop reliable ways to code the stimulus, perhaps reasons for shifts in persuasion or for lack of shifts can be inferred. This chapter reports on some research that represents a first step in that direction. The generalization that nonverbals correlate more strongly with attitude shift than with recall offers hope that the direction will be productive.

The finding that nonverbal effects are more likely to be negative than positive is also interesting and has important implications for future work with nonverbals. Many (most?) commercials do not have the intended positive effects on consumers, and this finding hints at possible reasons.

Several areas have been designated for more intensive attention in Stage 2. They include Paralanguage, Facial Expression, and Music. The latter area is included as a result of a review of the somewhat naive coding employed in this category in Stage 1. Stage 1 codes included such considerations as whether the music was vocal or instrumental, the amount of music included, whether the music was in the foreground or background, and the type of music employed (classical, rock, country, jazz, etc.) The naïveté of these codes is illustrated by contrasting them with the ways in which music is analyzed in music appreciation courses at the University of New Hampshire. Students are taught to analyze music in terms of rhythms, melodies, textures, and harmonies. Terms such as *duple, triple,* and *complex* are applied to meter, for example. And terms such as *consonant, tertian, triadic* and *triad-plus* are applied to the character of the harmony. It is hypothesized that more sophisticated codes based on concepts such as these may do a better job of explaining changes in attitudes than the simplistic codes used in Stage 1. Work on developing such codes is now under way.

As a final step, recognizing the limitations of this process at this point in the investigation, a model was constructed to see how much of the total variance in persuasion scores could be explained by a combination of nonverbal factors. As mentioned earlier, brand differences accounted for 53.4% of the total variance. Nonverbals were found to account for 38.7% of the residual variance. If brand differences are ignored, nonverbal effects can explain 61.3% of the total directly.

Longer term it is hoped that, once the best possible codes have been developed for the more important nonverbal areas, it will be possible to model nonverbal elements so that an even larger proportion of total variance in attitude shift can be explained. Such a model would be useful in two respects.

It would allow screening of alternative executions at an earlier stage than has heretofore been possible. As pointed out by Gross in 1964, the more executions it is possible to consider the higher the effectiveness of the ultimately aired commercials is likely to be.[28]

As indicated by Stage 1 results, it should provide a substantial amount of diagnostic help for those interested in explaining attitude shift scores.

Finally, the learning that would result from a consistent and systematic application of this kind of diagnosis offers the possibility of substantially improved advertising effectiveness.

Measures for Matching Purposes

The issue of matching samples closely is the justification for including still another kind of variable in copy tests. These are variables which in the matched group design allow the analyst to be sure that observed differences are the result of commercial exposure and not simply a reflection of the fact that the two groups contain different types of people. They are useful in the

[28] Irwin Gross, "How Many Ads Does it Pay to Pre-test?" Operations Research Discussion Group Report of the Tenth Meeting, Advertising Research Foundation, March 10, 1964, pp. 1–24.

before/after design as well. Although in that design the "before" measure for each person serves as a control against which the "after" measure can be compared, it is frequently necessary to compare one commercial with others—either to decide which of several executions should be selected for airing or to see whether a new commercial has performed satisfactorily in relation to a "norm" based on performance of past commercials. In such cases it is crucial that the groups to be compared be matched on a "before" basis.

Among the kinds of variables most frequently included for matching purposes are the following:

Benefit importance/needs
Beliefs about the product category
Personality and lifestyle measures
Centrality of the product category
Centrality of the brand of interest
Involvement in the interview situation
Response stereotypes (the kinds of guesses people make about advertising when they remember seeing it but not what it said)

A popular program for sample balancing and one that has excellent documentation is commercially available from Marketmath.[29]

Timing of the Measurements

The timing decisions involve choices of the interval between exposure and the time at which measurements are taken. For designs that call for "pre" measures to be taken, there is a question as to how far in advance of exposure they should be taken. And for designs calling for multiple exposures there are questions both as to the length of time that should elapse between exposures and whether or not measures should be taken during that period (and, if so, what types of measures).

These choices revolve around the twin issues of decay and sensitization. Most advertising people believe that the effects of exposure to a commercial decrease as time passes and the exposure is not repeated. This deterioration is called decay. However, although the presence of decay is generally accepted, there is very little research on the results of measuring the effects of exposure to a commercial after the passage of varying amounts of time. In a different context, Luh[30] has shown that there is no such thing as a stan-

---

[29] Sample balancing program; Market Math, Inc., 1860 Broadway, New York City.
[30] C. W. Luh, "The Conditions of Retention," *Psychology Monograph*, Vol. 31, 1922, p. 142ff.

dard decay or forgetting curve. He measured decay five ways and obtained five different decay curves. Decay rates depend both upon the stimulus and upon the approach employed to measure decay. Moreover, it is virtually impossible to simulate real-world decay in a laboratory situation because it is vitally affected by the frequency, quantity, and content of competitive messages. And these are usually not known in advance.

The recall criterion has received more attention than any other, perhaps because decay in recall is relatively easy to measure. Procter & Gamble did a substantial amount of work on decay rates of their criterion measure, called related recall, in the 1950's. They systematically tested immediate recall in relation to recall obtained 24, 48, and 72 hours after exposure. They found that the list of points recalled immediately after exposure was slightly different and less discriminating than the points recalled after 24 hours had elapsed. The lists of points recalled after 48 hours and 72 hours had elapsed were similar to the 24-hour list but, of course, because of decay the levels were substantially lower. Thus the longer interviews were postponed beyond 24 hours the more expensive it was to obtain a fixed sized sample of people who were able to play back the contents of the commercial. So the decision was made to use a 24-hour delay. The 24-hour delay for on-air recall rapidly became standard practice and it remains so today.

Laboratory approaches such as ASI and ARS regularly obtained substantially higher recall levels for their tests because of the heightened attention levels inherent in captive audience situations. To make their recall data more comparable with the levels familiar to people accustomed to on-air recall tests, they experimented with delays of longer periods of time. They found that if the interval between exposure and the followup interview was extended to 72 hours (and if the highest and lowest scoring commercials were adjusted statistically), they not only could produce similar levels of recall but could do a reasonably good job of predicting on-air recall scores of individual commericals.

When attitude shift measures began to grow in popularity in the late 1950s, the 24-hour standard was frequently adopted, probably because it was a familiar delay period. Then as the years passed and commercial clutter increased, the proportion of commercials achieving significantly positive shifts was found to be approaching zero.[31] The most frequent response of copy testers wedded to attitude shift measures was either to move to some form of multiple exposure or to attempt to measure persuasion on an immediate basis.

Emotional response data are almost always gathered immediately after

[31] R. Haley, "The Marketing Implications of Selective Perception," AAPOR, Lake George, N.Y., May 22, 1970.

exposure when the commercial is still fresh in the minds of the respondents. Frequently the commercial is reexposed for this express purpose.

The sensitization issue concerns whether measures can be taken before exposure without affecting the responses that follow exposure. This will be discussed in detail in the following section.

Experimental Design and Action Standards

The term *experimental design* refers to the procedure used to net out the effects of exposure to the copy from the effects of other variables on the selected criterion measures. Three experimental designs are used much more frequently than any others. These are the "post-only" design; the "matched group" design; and the "pre/post design, also called the "before/after" design.

Post-only designs measure people after exposure to the copy and compare their reactions with those of other groups who have been similarly exposed in the past. Although this procedure begs the question of whether or not all of the commercials are effective or, in fact, none of them, it does allow comparison of responses to an individual commercial to be compared with some sort of an average or "norm" for similar commercials to see if it is about average, a little above average, substantially above average, or a little or a lot below average. Then, depending upon the creative judgments of the marketing people involved, and whether the copy test suggests acceptable ways of strengthening the commercial, an appropriate decision can be made as to whether the commercial should be run as is, changed and run, changed and retested, or scrapped.

Often several commercials are tested simultaneously and comparisons made among them, providing another sort of control. "Norms" are determined in various ways. Sometimes they are based on averages across a very broad class of products (e.g., all household products), sometimes across a more limited set of products (e.g., liquid laundry detergents), and sometimes they are made specific to the brand of interest (e.g., all past tests for that brand, on the last five tests for the brand). The more narrowly defined the norm the more pertinent it is but the smaller the number of cases on which it is likely to be based. So once again there is a tradeoff.

Some companies prefer to compare the performance of any new commercial for an established brand with the performance of the commercial it is scheduled to replace. This introduces additional complications, however. The commercial to be replaced is usually being aired currently and has been frequently aired in the past. Is it then fair to compare one or two exposures of a new commercial with what may be the twenty-fifth and twenty-sixth exposures of the old commercial? Some people claim that it is, arguing that this sort of test represents a real-world situation. If the new commercial replaces the old, its first few exposures will be obtained instead of those twenty-fifth, and so on exposures. However, that leaves unanswered the question of wearout. What if the new commercial, by virtue of being new, generates enough interest to outscore the old commercial on its first two exposures but wears out quickly, and by its fifth or sixth exposure is then scoring substantially lower than the old commercial would have scored had it continued its run?

One approach that purports to avoid this problem is to compare the performance of the new commercial not with incremental exposures of the old commercial but with the performance of that commercial when it was new. This reduces the problem of comparing two commercials that may be at quite different points in their life cycles, but it raises other concerns. How long ago was the old commercial introduced? If it was quite a while ago, are market conditions the same now as they were when it achieved its introductory score? Is the brand share similar? Are competitive shares similar? Have competitive themes and amounts of advertising remained relatively stable? Is the time of the current test seasonally similar to that of the earlier test? To the extent that conditions are the same, this practice is probably reasonably safe. But to the extent that they are different, caution is advisable.

One reasonably safe, but necessarily subjective, process is to use multiple norms. Then if they all provide the same evaluation of the new commercial, the analyst can feel secure in his or her recommendations. If they point in different directions, however, they will have to be studied, the reasons for the differences analyzed, and choices made.

The matched group design solves the problem of potentially inappropriate norms by building the controls directly into the test. For each test of a new commercial, reactions are obtained not only from a group of people who have been exposed to the commercial but from a parallel group that has not been exposed. Differences on the criterion measures are then ascribed to the effects of exposure. Problems of timing, city differences, and interviewer effects are largely neutralized by gathering responses from the exposed and unexposed groups under *exactly* the same conditions, the only difference therefore being the exposure itself.

The key to a successful matched group test is how the matching is done. One approach is to gather exposure on an "every second person" basis. For example, let us assume that a copy test is being done in four shopping centers. People are intercepted, asked if they would like to preview a new television program, then exposed to a program with a commercial in it and, as a reward for participating are given a handful of coupons, one of which is for the brand of interest. The criterion of commercial performance is the redemption rate of the coupon.

In the "every second person" approach every second person is shown the same program *without* the commercial in it. Everything else about the exposure situation is handled identically. Both the exposed people and the unexposed people receive the same sets of coupons. The only known difference between the two groups is that one has seen the commercial and the other has not. Therefore, if the redemption rate among the exposed group is significantly higher than among the control group, it can be presumed that the commercial is doing its job. Norms from past tests can also be used, of course, as a second level sort of control.

The every second person procedure, however, has faults. It is relatively easy to administer in a laboratory type of test, but it is not compatible with a natural exposure on-air test. In this approach people are called after they have been exposed, their brand preferences are obtained, and the facts of exposure are determined. Thus the program audience is self-selected. This has important advantages from the research standpoint because respondents do not know that they are involved in a test of any sort at the time of exposure. Thus they react to the commercial in a completely natural fashion. It also has some disadvantages, however, such as the difficulty of allowing for the effects of program environment. (These will be discussed later.) The point here is that it makes the matched group design more difficult to apply.

The sample balancing program mentioned on page 123 can be used to good advantage in natural exposure situations. To parallel the every second person procedure as closely as possible, a control group is drawn from people favorably inclined to the program on which the commercial is aired. This is done 24 hours in advance of the actual airing by asking people their viewing intentions, or it is done at the same time the regular postexposure interviews are conducted. In the latter case the control group is often constructed from people who view the test program from time to time but did not see the episode that was aired 24 hours previously.

Sample balancing still should be done between the exposed and unexposed groups to make sure that they are matched on important factors such as brand usage, volume of consumption, and key demographic characteristics for the product of interest.

Another wrinkle which is sometimes used to obtain a good control group and to preserve the spirit of the every second person procedure is prerecruitment. Again several variants of prerecruitment are in use. In one instance people are phoned a day before the program is aired and recruited either to watch that program or one that is being aired at the same time but on a different channel. In other words every second person is asked to watch a program opposite it. In another variant every second person who intends to watch the test program is paid *not* to do so. Each of these procedures results in reasonably well-matched test and control groups, and the statistical sample balancing program is left to take care of any important remaining differences.

Pre/post designs are also popular. Theoretically at least, they are most efficient from a cost standpoint because, however done, it is almost always less expensive to recontact people known to have been exposed to the commercial than to find fresh groups of similar people who have not been exposed. Also, because each person serves as his or her own control, the pre/post design is very efficient statistically. Because the variance between pre- and post-measures is normally smaller than the variance of the same measures taken from two different groups of people, the pre/post design can detect smaller differences. This is an important advantage because often, the attitude shifts caused by exposure to a commercial are small and transitory. Then too, with a pre/post design, and unlike the matched group design, it is possible for an analyst to identify the *individuals* whose attitudes have changed. This substantially increases the possibility of useful diagnostic analyses and of making useful inferences about the reasons for any observed attitude changes from them.

Despite its many impressive advantages, however, the pre/post design suffers from one important disadvantage. When this design is used it is always possible that the taking of the "before" measures has in some way affected the "after" results. Some years ago a group of British researchers conducted an interesting experiment.[32] They measured attitudes toward a number of brands and then, after a short interval, *and with no intervening stimulus,* repeated the measures. Statistically far more significant shifts were found than could be accounted for by chance.

When respondents were interviewed once more and asked why they had changed their minds, they said that the first response had been given with very little thought. In the period between the two interviews they had considered the answers they had given and decided that in some cases they were not accurate. Hence the changes. So based on this experience an argument could be made, and was made in the article summarizing the findings, that a single "pre" interview is at best an unreliable base from which to measure change and, at worse, potentially misleading.

Other evidence that sensitization is a potential problem comes from a series of experiments done by Cornelius DuBois[33] in the early 1960s. He reported that the pre/post and matched group designs frequently produced different results and concluded that the matched group design was superior.

[32] P. J. Macarte, "Multivariate Attitude Shift Analysis," *Admap*, October 1971, pp. 338–340.

[33] C. DuBois, Copy Research Discussion Group, New York Chapter of the AMA, October 15, 1960. See also, T. A. Nosanchuk and M. P. Marchak, "Pretest Sensitization and Attitude Change," *Public Opinion Quarterly*, Spring, 1969, pp. 107–111.

Of course, it could be argued by proponents of the pre/post design that its results, although different, are nevertheless superior. Matching is an approximate process and it is always possible that the samples, although matched on demographic and behavioral variables, are not matched on some important psychological or belief variable. Moreover in the matched group design it is impossible to know how the exposed group felt before exposure. Although their beliefs can be measured after exposure it is not possible to determine whether the beliefs held at that point are the same as they were before exposure or whether they were changed by the exposure.

Adding fuel to the controversy over which of these designs is the better choice is a series of unreported experiments. These experiments were conducted during the development of the Richardson-Haley procedure to determine on which of a series of demographic attitudinal and behavioral variables it was most important to match groups exposed to different commercials in order to maximize their comparability. The criterion measure, it will be recalled, was pre/post change in a constant sum attitude measure. It was found that belief measures were the best predictors of attitudinal shifts. In other words, the beliefs that a respondent brings to the exposure situation are the most important single determinant of whether he or she will be persuaded by the commercial. This, of course, is completely in line with the premises on which Benefit Segmentation is based. The conclusion drawn was that it was important for samples to be matched on their going-in attitudes if the performance of different executions was to be properly evaluated.

Various devices are used to reduce the risks of sensitizing the audience to the purposes of the research; some are more effective than others. Where consumers are recruited to watch a program containing the commercial of interest, they are usually told that the research firm is interested in their reactions to the program—to the plot, to the casting, and to other program elements. Then in the postinterview situation they are asked what they had thought the purpose of the research was before the current interview. Responses are used in three ways. One is to evaluate the level (in relation to historical norms) of people who say they knew the true purposes of the research. A second is a simple cross-tabulation to see whether the people who were aware of the masking attempt responded differently from those who were not. If they didn't, there is no problem. If they did, however, the decision must be made on whether or not to drop them from the sample. The third use is somewhat of a compromise. It simply accepts people's responses as input to the sample balancing program. In other words, no one is dropped from the sample. But samples are weighted so that each copy test, in effect, contains the same proportion of people who anticipated the nature of the test in which they were involved.

Where the interview focuses on a single brand, and this fact is readily apparent, respondents are sometimes told that different interviewers have been assigned to ask about different brands and that *this* interviewer's assignment is to talk about Brand X. How effective this is as a cover story is highly questionable, but perhaps it is better than no cover story at all.

Where respondents are to be interviewed about the brand of interest both before and after exposure to the copy, two systems are used. One method is to ask the minimum possible amount of information about the brand during the "pre" interview and to hide that in a battery of other questions. For example, brand choice can easily be obtained under the pretext of a prize drawing, the participation in which is a reward for taking part in the research project. However, the "pre" interview must avoid focusing too heavily on product information if respondents are not to be sensitized to the true purposes of the research. This can be accomplished by having most of the questions deal with such things as demographics, lifestyles, and reading and viewing preferences.

A second method is to cover the category of interest in some depth but to precede it with another category, also to be covered in some depth. Again questions that are not product oriented are included in the "pre" interview. Evidence suggests that each of these approaches can hold sensitization to tolerable levels.

Another simple device aimed at reducing sensitization is to conduct the "pre" interview somewhat farther in advance of the exposure (e.g., 48 hours instead of 24 hours). However, although this does help to reduce sensitization, the longer interval between the pre- and post-interviews allows more extraneous variables to intrude. Also if respondents have to be recontacted, respondent recovery rates may be slightly lower than with a shorter interval.

A more complex approach is to choose an experimental design which allows the effects of sensitization to be measured statistically and discounted in the evaluation of the effects of the copy. Such a design is the Solomon Four-Group design diagrammed in Figure 11.9.[34] In this design cell A is the traditional pre/post design and cell C is the post-only design. Cells B and D are control cells. The people in cell B are interviewed twice, at the same times that people in cell A are interviewed, but without an intervening copy exposure. The people in cell D are interviewed at the same time as the people in cell C, but they have not been exposed to the copy.

Results can be analyzed by traditional analysis of variance methods. Viewed more simplistically, the differences between the *column* totals

[34] See also D. A. Aaker and G. S. Day, *Marketing Research*, New York: 1980, pp. 275–276.

	Exposed to Copy	*Not Exposed to Copy*
Pre-Interview	A	B
No Pre-Interview	C	D

Figure 11.9. Solomon four-group design.

measure the effects of exposure to the commercial (A + C versus B + D), and the differences between the *row* totals provide a measure of the effects of the pre-interview (A + B versus C + D). It is hoped the latter difference will be small; however, that is what the test is designed to measure.

This attractive design is rarely used, perhaps because of perceived difficulties in administration.

Now let us turn to a problem that is related to the choice of the experimental design, namely that of setting action standards. The term *action standards* refers to advance decisions about the kinds of action that will be taken when different types of copy testing results are obtained. Sometimes these are simple and not formalized in written form. Sometimes they involve several different criteria, and a wide variety of permutations and combinations of results must be anticipated and incorporated into the standards. Sometimes they allow for a substantial amount of subjectivity. It is important that the action standards be agreed upon *before* the results of the copy test become available. Otherwise the final decision tends to rubber stamp the predispositions of the marketing team. If, in its initial screening in the agency or at the client's office, a commercial was enthusiastically received, the data have a way of being interpreted so as to endorse proceeding with the commercial. If, on the other hand, the commercial was viewed with a considerable number of reservations, only a blockbuster score is likely to remove them. The presence of action standards sharply reduces (but does not eliminate) these biases.

In actuality one of four decisions must be made: (1) run the commercial in its present form, (2) make minor revisions and run the commercial, (3) make significant revisions and retest, or (4) scrap the commercial.

One major agency kept records on the frequency with which each of these actions was recommended by the copy research people over the course of some 333 tests, and of whether their recommendations were followed. A percentage breakdown is shown in Table 11.8. In this table suggestions for minor revisions are combined with the "use as is" category. The influence of action standards is apparent. Recommendations were overturned in fewer than 10 percent of the tests.

TABLE 11.8   Actions Taken Based on Copy Testing Recommendations

Research recommendation was followed:	91.3%	
Recommendation was to use as is		26.1
Recommendation was to revise		21.7
Recommendation was to abandon		43.5
Research recommendation not followed:	8.7%	
Total commercials tested	100.0%	

One pragmatic method for setting action standards is to apply several acceptance levels to tests already completed to see what proportion of the commercials tested would have been rejected at each level. Obviously action standards cannot be set so high that all commercials will be rejected. Equally obviously, they should not be set so low that all commercials tested pass with flying colors. Thus the effects of choosing differing levels should be carefully examined before the level is locked in. Also there is the question of balancing the risks of losing good commercials against the risks of accepting inferior ones. So the final choice of level is important judgementally.

As for specific types of action standards, one popular one is simply beating the norm, however determined. If the commercial scores higher than the norm, it is run. If it comes close but falls short, it is revised and tested again. If it falls substantially short, it is scrapped.

In the matched group design the control group score is often handled as a norm. The data in Table 11.9 come from a major agency that uses the matched group design and top-box scoring of a hedonic overall attitude scale. It can be seen that, at the time these commercials were tested, the average attitude shift was +2 points. In fact this particular agency used the control group score as its norm. Thus in the chart the zero point is the norm. However, it would have been possible to set the action standard at +2, because that is the overall average, or to vary the action standard by product category or by brand.

Pre/post designs are handled in much the same way as matched groups. The pre measure is often considered the norm, but a tougher norm would be the average amount of change.

Double action standards are frequently used, most often considering both the persuasion score and the recall score in some fashion. The agency whose data are presented in Table 11.9 uses their persuasion score as their criterion measure and the recall score as the tiebreaker when several executions are tested at the same time. Thus if two commercials are tested and the first commercial scores a significant win over the second on persuasion,

TABLE 11.9 Extent of Top-Box Attitude Shifts

Magnitude of Shift (percentage points)	Number of Commercials
Below −9.5	1
−9.5 to −7.6	1
−7.5 to −5.6	4
−5.5 to −3.6	3
−3.5 to −1.6	7
−1.5 to +0.4	25
+.5 to +2.4	39
+2.5 to +4.4.	33
+4.5 to +6.4	20
+6.5 to +8.4	12
+8.5 to +10.4	7
+10.5 to +12.4	4
+12.5 to +14.4	1
+14.5 to +16.4	—
+16.5 to +18.4	—
+18.5 to +20.4	—
+20.5 to +22.4	—
+22.5 and above	1

it is run, assuming that it exceeds the norm as well. If both commercials exceed the norm but their persuasion scores are not significantly different from each other, the choice reverts to a comparison of recall scores. If one commercial has significantly better recall than the other, it is chosen.

The other approach to the double action standard is to use high and low brackets to spotlight what constitutes an unusually high or low score on the first criterion. Then if the score is not unusually high or low on the first criterion, the choice reverts to performance on the second criterion. Thus recall might dictate the choice if recall scores are unusually high (an automatic "run" decision) or unusually low (an automatic "scrap" decision), but the choice would be based on persuasion scores when recall scores were in the midrange as they most frequently would be.

Triple criteria are also used by a few firms. One has worked out all combinations for three criteria (persuasion, recall, and key benefit) (see Table 11.1). Another procedure is to include the same multiple criteria in each test and to allow each manager to specify the order in which they are to be applied in evaluating the results of the copy test. Thus a brand manager for an established brand in a category that usually involves a cognitive brand choice may choose the best commercial executions using a criterion sequence such as the following:

Constant sum scale (persuasion)

Overall hedonic scale (persuasion)

Fishbein measure (persuasion)[35]

Shift on key benefit

Related recall

Brand salience

However, a brand manager for a low involvement product may prefer a sequence such as brand salience/awareness, related recall, and constant sum scale. And a new product brand manager may select executions on a criterion sequence of brand salience/awareness and brand image profile (the characteristics that should stand out).

THE FORM OF THE ADVERTISING

The central question in this area is the appropriate level of finish for the copy to be tested. As PACT principles state, the closer the level of finish is to the final product the better the results of the test in terms of their projectability. It is also true, however, that the higher the level of finish the more expensive the test is likely to be. Few companies can afford to reject many finished commercials when the cost of those commercials is likely to be 10 times the cost of testing them. Consequently, most copy researchers hope to make some compromises concerning the levels of finish used. Opinions differ on just how much is tolerable. Table 11.10 shows a menu of selections.

The stimuli listed higher in the table are less expensive, but they also represent greater departures from the final product and hence greater risk. Before proceeding with a discussion of the kinds of compromises that are being made, some definitions are in order.

Concept cards represent the lowest levels of finish. They are plain white cards containing so-called core ideas around which advertising can be built. One major agency, Ogilvy & Mather, has developed an approach to building copy which they call *promise* testing. It begins by testing the appeal of a large number of ideas (or promises) expressed on white cards. These are screened down to a small number which appear to have potential, and copy with a higher level of finish is developed around the promises that are best received.

Although this is an efficient approach for deriving successful *cognitive*

[35] M. Fishbein and I. Ajzen, *Beliefs, Attitudes, Intentions and Behavior: An Introduction to Theory and Research,* Reading, MA: Addison-Wesley, 1975.

TABLE 11.10 Alternative Levels of Finish

Television Commercials	Print Advertisements
Concept cards	Concept cards
Print translations	Rough layouts with headlines
Storyboards	
Cartoons	
Cartoons with voiceover	Black-and-white photostats (scrap art)
Animatics	
Photomatics	C-print (color photostats)
Rough live	
Live-a-matic	
Finished (air quality)	Finished print advertising

selling messages, it runs the risk of screening out ideas where the finished execution rather than the underlying logical idea is the reason for the commercial's success. Many of today's most successful campaigns (e.g., the Charlie fragrance campaign) would never have evolved if the creative people were forced to start their planning with "winning" white cards. A substantial amount of evidence indicates that the way in which a commercial is executed is at least as important as its underlying idea.[36]

Print translations are print versions of a television campaign. They usually adhere to a standard executional format (e.g., an illustration, a one-line headline, 75 words of body copy, and the brand name in the lower right-hand corner). They are a sharp step up from concept cards and sometimes a reasonable choice in testing print advertising. They sacrifice sound and motion, however, and sometimes this is too great a sacrifice.

Storyboards started out as an internal tool used by creative departments in advertising agencies to help to plan commercials. A storyboard for a 30-second commercial usually has 12 "windows," each representing about 2½ seconds of the commercial. The windows show the sequences of visual action that will take place when the commercial is filmed. Under each window there is room for several lines of typing, which contain the words and sounds that will be heard as the commercial unfolds. Storyboards help creatives to plan a smooth, flowing commercial. They are easy to revise and inexpensive. And they allow artists, copywriters, and production people to communicate with each other (see Figure 11.10).

Early efforts using storyboards to allow consumers to envision the finished commercial had limited success. Many consumers found the gap be-

[36] R. I. Haley and R. Gatty, "The Trouble with Concept Testing," *Journal of Marketing Research*, Vol. VIII, May 1971, pp. 230–2.

Canon®

PRODUCT: CANON AE-1 PROGRAM   GREY ADVERTISING, INC.

1. PRO PHOTOG: (VO)
   Covering a champ like
   Jerry Pate

2. is a super opportunity for
   a photographer.

3. PATE: If I win this
   tournament, I'm gonna make
   you famous.

4. PRO PHOTOG: (VO)
   I counted on my Canon AE-1
   Program

5. with all the features a
   pro wants

6. to capture all the sides
   of Pate's game.

7. FANS: (VO) Go for it, Jerry.

8. PATE: Now it's your turn.
   I told you I was gonna
   make you famous.

9. PRO PHOTOG: (OC) Me?

10. The AE-1 Program

11. in any light makes the
    toughest shots simple.

12. The Canon AE-1 Program.
    So advanced – it's simple.

Figure 11.10. Normal storyboard layout (Used with permission of Canon U.S.A.,
Inc., and Grey Advertising)

tween a storyboard and a commercial too large to bridge.[37] One inventive firm turns storyboards into the kinds of color cartoons that we see in the Sunday comics, assuming that this will allow consumers to respond to a type of stimulus with which they are familiar. This process has been in use for a number of years and is reported to be working quite well.

Cartoons with voiceover are usually exposed one frame at a time via a slide projector with a recorded sound track synchronized with the slides. Animatics are a slightly more sophisticated form, in which the cartoons have limited motion. An arm moves and feeds a person; a mouth smiles, eyes register surprise, and so on. Photomatics use the camera to give the appearance of motion through zooms, fades, fast cuts, and so on.

Although terminology varies among different sections of the country, and even among agencies, this class of executions (voiceover, animatics, and photomatics) is often called *rough.* Roughs are comparatively inexpensive to use and over the past 10 years have probably experienced a greater increase in use than any degree of finish. In a speech that had a substantial impact on the copy testing community, Dr. Donald Kanter (now of Boston University) thoroughly recapped the evidence on the correspondence between copy testing scores of rough and finished commercials.[38] He concluded that "the professional research community appears to have reached a consensus on the subject of Roughs versus Finished commercials. The consensus is that rough treatments . . . do a more than adequate job of providing copy-testing materials."

Since that landmark summary a number of exceptions to that general conclusion have arisen. For example, ARS, based on an analysis of their own, has concluded that although roughs do an excellent job of predicting outstanding *failures* of finished commercials, they are of considerably less value in predicting outstanding *successes.*[39] That finding dovetails with the author's experience in trying to predict the sales of finished greeting cards from reactions to roughs.

In many respects the greeting card problem parallels the problem of trying to predict the relative success of print advertisements. The print ad has a headline; the greeting card has a caption. The print ad has an illustration; the greeting card has artwork. And the print ad has copy; the greeting card has a verse. In one important area, however, predicting which greeting cards are best is less of a problem. When people are favorably affected by a greeting card, they buy it right then. There are none of the many variables

[37] One commercial copy testing service Bruzzone, Research Company of Alameda, CA, uses storyboards for recognition tests.
[38] D. L. Kanter, "Finished or Unfinished Test Stimuli—The TV Testing Dilemma," *Proceedings of the ARF Conference,* 1976.
[39] Unpublished ARS paper.

TABLE 11.11 Relationships Between Panel Ratings and Sales Performance

		Consumer Panel Ratings[a]			
		High	Average	Low	Total
	High	28.0	10.8	0.4	39.3
Subsequent	Average	7.9	27.9	2.0	37.8
Sales	Low	3.9	3.9	15.0	22.9
	Total	39.8	42.7	17.5	100.0

[a] Columns do not add exactly because of rounding.

that can intrude between exposure to an effective print ad and the sales of the product it is attempting to promote.

Table 11.11 compares consumer ratings of greeting cards presented in rough form with the actual sales of those cards in finished form. Ratings and sales data have both been split into three categories because the evaluation of greeting cards involves a three-way decision.[40] If the card is highly promising, it is reprinted. If it is a slow seller, it is scrapped and removed from displays. If it appears to be about average, a normal production run (usually enough to last about six months) is made.

It is apparent that consumer panels do a much better job of anticipating slow sellers than they do of identifying "hot" items.

Other exceptions occur both when the finished ad focuses on mood or user imagery rather than upon a cognitive selling story and when a famous personality is used as a "presenter." In these situations the consumer is often unable to project his or her probable reactions to the finished ad from the rough.

Coca-Cola, for example, has developed a sophisticated model to predict their sales performance relative to Pepsi-Cola. It involves media weight and recall and persuasion scores from copy testing. They have found that accurate predictions are possible only when finished copy is used. Of course both Coke and Pepsi advertising rely heavily on music and other nonverbal communications.

So as a general rule, the choice of degree of finish depends upon a judgment call as to whether the verbal and nonverbal elements are adequately communicated by the rough.

Returning to the menu of alternatives, the term *rough live* refers to roughs made with live actors. For instance, it is possible to rent an entire recording studio and all of the equipment in it for an hour or two. The pro-

[40] This applies to "everyday" cards, such as birthday, sympathy, get well, cards, which may be applicable any day of the year. Holiday cards are a different matter.

duction team can then come in and shoot as many roughs as they can squeeze in, using as the cast people from the agency, people from the client, and anyone who happens to be around the studio and is willing to take part. So a number of roughs can be shot relatively inexpensively. To the consumer these are often a much better simulation of what the final commercial is likely to be like than, say, an animatic.

Live-a-matics are a special form of rough live where the actors and actresses are superimposed on realistic backgrounds. It is the closest simulation to a finished commercial available to date, and is frequently so well done as to be virtually indistinguishable from the final product.

On the print side of the ledger the best simulation of a finished ad in current use is the C-print or color photostat. Art departments generally have collections of finished artwork on a variety of topics, and these can be cut up and asssembled to give the appearance of a finished advertisement. This process is usually called a "scrap art" process.

To sum up, there is a tradeoff between the amount of testing that can be done and the degree of finish used. Most copy researchers like to do as much testing as they can before laying their reputations on the line. Consequently most testing tends to be done at whatever level is chosen as minimally acceptable. This choice in turn depends upon the combined judgments of the researchers, the creative people, the account executive, the brand manager, and senior people charged with advertising responsibility. It revolves around the relative importance of the informational and logical aspects of the advertising they are likely to run versus the nonverbal communications of the advertising. Nonverbals include the factors mentioned earlier—setting, casting, music, voice qualities, colors, pace, lettering styles, and so on. When these are critical parts of the advertising, it is discrete to test using higher levels of finish. When the central idea is logical and demonstrable, however, it should be possible to make compromises concerning the degree of finish used.

Exposure Considerations

Another important decision area relates to the choice of conditions under which the advertising will be exposed to consumers. This in turn involves choices with respect to:

Location of exposure
Message delivery method
Exposure environments
Message context

Clutter conditions
Exposure intensity

Exposure to copy test commercials occurs in a variety of settings. Among the more frequent are:

At home
    on regular channel on own TV sets
    on special channel on own TV sets
    on portable rear screen projectors
In theaters on large screens
In trailers on TV monitors
In rented storefronts in shopping centers
In focus group facilities
In anterooms
In stores

and print exposures can be delivered via:

Canadian magazines
Supplements
Dummy magazines
Tip-ins in old magazines
Tip-ins in advance copies of popular magazines
Portfolios
Flats

The issue of whether people react the same way toward commercials when they see them in stores, in an anteroom, or while on a shopping expedition as they do in their own homes has not yet been investigated.

A related issue is the message delivery method—the effect of screen size and type. Every known device is in use somewhere, whether it be large movie screens, home movie screens, TV monitors, portable projectors, or home TV sets.

The concern here is for the naturalness of the exposure. Questions have been raised, for example, about whether the impact of a commercial on a large movie screen may not be significantly different than the impact of the same commercial when it appears on a 20-inch screen. Opinions abound, but data are scarce.

Then there is the question of exposure environment. As that term is used here it refers to the numbers and types of people present at the time of exposure. The exposure environment ranges from individual exposure to exposure of groups of family members to exposure of groups of three or four, or 20 or 30, or several hundred strangers. In the natural exposure situation, people are usually exposed individually or with family or friends. Do they react the same toward commercials when they are among strangers? Certainly there are risks of contamination when group exposure situations are used. An audible and unsolicited comment, or even a laugh or a groan can affect the way in which the commercial is received. Of course, from a cost standpoint it is more efficient to expose people in groups. Where group exposure methods are employed, however, it is wise to have an observer present in each group. In that way situations in which something untoward happens can be spotted and discarded.

Another consideration is the context in which the commercial is embedded. As mentioned in Chapter 2, Yuspeh has shown that program context can affect copy test scores. What should be done about this? Should a standard program be chosen and all copy exposed in it? Or is it sufficient to have a variety of innocuous backgrounds such as situation comedies, travelogues, and so on? But what if the type of program on which the commercial is to be aired is known? Should an effort be made to test the commercial in a typical vehicle rather than a neutral vehicle? Or is it best to strip away the program context entirely and show the commercial in a "naked" situation?

Another environmental consideration is the amount and type of commercial clutter that should be present. If the commercial of interest is the *only* one present in the program presented during the copy test, the risk of "transparency bias" is a real one. As soon as questions are asked about the advertised brand, people will see through the purpose of the research, recognize which brand is sponsoring it, and this knowledge may bias their responses.

One simple way to eliminate that problem is to include a commercial for a competitive brand in the same program. However, although that largely solves the problem of transparency it creates another. Some consumers are bound to confuse the two brands and their messages, attributing the claims made by one brand to the other.

A compromise is to include what has become known as "noncompetitive clutter." These are commercials for other similarly priced products and ones with similar market targets. They avoid focusing respondents on the commercial of interest, provide a more realistic exposure situation in the sense that on-air programs always contain several commercials, and, although they do not eliminate the transparency bias, they help to reduce it.

Still another decision area relating to exposure is the number of exposures and their spacing. Copy testing had traditionally been done with a single exposure, but the trend has been toward incorporating multiple exposures. Sometimes a second exposure is made so that the commercial will be fresh in the minds of respondents when diagnostic questions such as adjective checklists are administered. Sometimes they are done to find elements of the message that were not played back on first exposure but that are picked up with additional exposures; some believe that this information will help to predict wear-in. But most often they are included because the commercials will be exposed many times in real life and because available evidence suggests that multiple exposures aid discrimination.[41]

As recently as 1972, when the Advertising Research Foundation issued a thorough bibliography covering copy testing and other research areas,[42] multiple exposure copy tests had not been done often enough to justify inclusion in the index. Since 1972 rising advertising costs have forced manufacturers to move from 60-second to 30-second commercials and there are predictions that 15 seconds will soon become the most frequent commercial length. The resultant clutter has driven down both recall and attitude shift scores based on single exposure testing, and has reduced ability to discriminate among alternative commercial executions. As a result of the increased difficulty in using copy research to help to make choices, the relationships between creative departments and research departments in agencies understandably became more strained and the credibility of copy testing, always open to some question, was further reduced. Agencies and their clients reacted in varying ways. Some dropped "on air" tests entirely and conducted laboratory and forced exposure tests to obtain heightened responses and thus better discrimination. Some classified copy research as primarily diagnostic and set up copy research activities within creative departments rather than independent of them, for the exclusive use of creative people in developing advertising. And finally, some used multiple exposure testing.

Researchers began to call increasingly for multiple exposure tests. For example, Joel Axelrod wrote a pamphlet for the Association of National Advertisers[43] on copy testing. In it he concluded that multiple exposure systems were more sensitive and recommended their use. Greenhalgh and Smith,[44] writing in the *Journal of the Market Research Society*, pointed out

---

[41] M. J. Naples, *Effective Frequency: The Relationship Between Frequency and Advertising Effectiveness*, New York: Association of National Advertisers, Inc., 1979.

[42] *An Annotated Bibliography of Copy Testing, 1960–70*, New York: ARF, 1972.

[43] J. Axelrod, "Choosing the Best Advertising Alternative," *ANA*, 1971.

[44] "Pre-testing Press Advertisement Campaigns," *Journal of the Market Research Society*, April 1972, pp. 88–110.

that single exposure testing may penalize mood ads and give an undue advantage to ads that are word oriented and educational. They hypothesized that the latter type ad might win after the first exposure but that by the third exposure the mood ad might prove superior. Parallels were drawn between copy testing and the well-known taste-testing situation, in which the product that wins after the first trial is not necessarily the product that wins after an extended use test.

Agencies too began to develop copy testing systems of their own involving multiple exposures (e.g., the METS system of Ogilvy & Mather. METS is an acronym for Multiple Exposure Testing System).

The single exposure systems were developed largely as a matter of economics. Also it was not clear what sorts of time intervals between exposures would provide a sufficiently accurate simulation of the kinds of effects that were likely to be generated by the media schedules. It was apparent that different people would receive differing numbers of exposures. Moreover, because of varying media habits they would receive them with different time intervals between exposures. Simulating this sort of environment appeared to be virtually impossible.

Reinforcement for avoiding the problem came from copy testing organizations, such as Schwerin Research, who presented data in one of their well-read newsletters. These data suggested that, in comparative testing, the commercial with the best score after the first exposure usually was the best commercial in a multiple exposure situation as well. The readily accepted implication was that the added expense of using a multiple exposure situation was not warranted.

Now, however, substantial evidence has appeared on the other side of the issue. For example, Naples presented the data shown in Table 11.12 in support of the thesis that multiple exposures on-air are more sensitive than a single exposure in a laboratory situation.[45] All data are indexed to Commercial A. It had been shown previously that single exposure laboratory situations are more discriminating than single exposure on-air tests.[46]

Tables 11.13 through 11.17 are taken from a sizable on-air test of a single exposure to three different commercials versus up to 10 exposures of the same three commercials. A recruited audience approach was used. People were telephoned the day before the first show on which commercials were to be aired, were offered a choice of several substantial incentives to watch the programs, and were given a cover story to the effect that the firm sponsoring the study wanted their opinions of the programs in which the com-

[45] M. J. Naples, "Facing Up to Evaluative Copy Research," New England Advertising Research Conference, ARF, New England Advertising Day, 1976.

[46] R. Haley and R. Gatty, "Measuring Effectiveness of TV Exposure by Computer," *Journal of Advertising Research,* Vol. 9, No. 3, September, 1969, pp. 9–12.

TABLE 11.12 Comparison of Single and Multiple Exposure Copy Tests

Commercial	Single Exposure Laboratory Situation	Multiple Exposures On-air Split Cable
A	100	100
B	84	42
C	81	71

mercials were imbedded. The research design controlled for the effects of time, city, program, and respondent characteristics such as brand usage. Approximately half of those recruited were interviewed an hour after the first exposure. The remainder was interviewed an hour after the tenth exposure.

The recruitment questionnaire obtained demographic and behavioral information. The latter was obtained for several product categories to disguise the area of interest. The postexposure questionnaire covered opinions about the show and copy test measures of awareness, persuasion, brand image, and commercial recall. Results are shown in Tables 11.13 through 11.17. They clearly support the position that multiple exposure tests are more sensitive than single exposure tests.

Additionally the laboratory work of Mike Ray at Stanford University suggests that the commercial which starts off best is by no means a certain

TABLE 11.13 Awareness (% of respondents)

	Single Exposure Commercial			Multiple Exposure (9–10) Commercial			Control Commercial
	A	B	C	A	B	C	None
Top of Mind	20	26	22	42	39	28	4
Unaided	59	57	60	77	63	55	25

TABLE 11.14 Purchase Intent (% of respondents)

	Single Exposure Commercial			Multiple Exposure (9–10) Commercial			
	A	B	C	A	B	C	Control
First Choice	12	13	14	32	31	24	6
Other Choices	27	35	28	34	20	18	19
In Evoked Set	39	48	42	66	51	42	25

TABLE 11.15   Constant Sum Attitude Score (% of respondents)

	Single Exposure Commercial			Multiple Exposure (9–10) Commercial			
	A	B	C	A	B	C	Control
Client Brand	4.61	4.62	4.41	5.18	4.86	4.46	3.45

TABLE 11.16   Recall (% of respondents)

	Single Exposure Commercial			Multiple Exposure (9–10) Commercial			
	A	B	C	A	B	C	Control
Unaided	49	50	44	60	53	33	1
Produce cue	6	9	6	13	16	16	1
Brand cue	6	7	7	14	13	21	0
Total	61	66	57	87	82	70	2

TABLE 11.17   Brand Image (% of respondents)

	Single Exposure Commercial			Multiple Exposure (9–10) Commercial			
	A	B	C	A	B	C	Control
Image characteristic 1	17	14	23	30	25	23	11
2	43	42	45	57	52	48	31
3	23	24	24	38	34	29	14
4	28	39	39	51	52	48	25
5	33	37	33	53	53	41	25
6	7	8	9	12	17	14	2
$\bar{x}$	25.2	27.3	28.8	40.2	38.8	33.8	18.0

winner. In tests with 18 ads with six exposures of each ad and samples of 168 respondents for each exposure level, he found significant interaction between individual ads and repetition levels both for recall and for persuasion measures.[47] In one instance, for example, he found that repetition had a strong effect on recall of an ad for one brand of hand soap (Phase III) but not for another (Ivory). However, the situation was reversed on the persua-

[47] M. L. Ray and A. G. Sawyer, "Repetition in Media Models: A Laboratory Technique," *Journal of Marketing Research*, Vol. 8, February 1971, p. 27.

sion measure. Ivory benefited from repetition, but Phase III did not. And this pattern of results was replicated in a second study. In general, Ray found recall leveling at the fourth exposure and purchase intent starting upward at the third exposure and peaking at the fourth or fifth exposure. Again there were frequent exceptions to this pattern.

Summing up, multiple exposure tests are more discriminating than single exposure tests, although they are often more expensive as well. Furthermore multiple exposure tests sometimes produce results that differ from those produced by parallel single exposure tests. The issue of validity remains open, however. Not everyone is convinced that multiple exposure designs are preferable to single exposure designs.[48] And certainly many people continue to use single exposure tests. The choice depends on how you believe advertising works and, in particular, how you think the copy to be tested will achieve its results in the marketplace.

SAMPLING

Sampling considerations include:

The definition of the universe from which the sample will be drawn
The method of selection
The size
Dispersion (number of locations)
Location selection criteria

The definition of the universe from which copy test respondents should be drawn is often a controversial issue. The controversy revolves around whether people in the market target can be expected to respond in a similar fashion to those who are not in the target—especially insofar as rank order responses to alternative executions is concerned.

Whether or not they do appears to depend upon two considerations— how the target is defined and which criteria have been selected as measures of copy performance. If the target is defined very loosely and in demographic terms (e.g., all male adults between 18 and 65 years of age) and if recall is the primary criterion of performance, there is a substantial body of information[49] indicating that rank order results are likely to be quite stable

[48] R. Chay, "The Myths and Realities of Single Exposure and Double Exposure Copy Tests," Annual Mid-year Conference of the Advertising Research Foundation, Chicago, 1981.
[49] *The Effect of Environmental and Executional Variables on Overall Memorability*, Cincinnati: Burke Marketing Research, n.d.

(e.g., if females are included in the sample, the rank order performance of the commercial executions will be unchanged.) However, the more narrowly the target is defined, the more it is defined in benefit terms, and the more emphasis placed on persuasion criteria, the less likely is the target to respond similarly to the balance of the population. In fact a major part of the rationale of target definition is that the people in the target will respond differently. When they do not, it suggests either that the appeal being used is so universal that everyone responds to it or that the target has been poorly defined. The balance of opinion in the research community seems to have swung fairly sharply behind the position that testing should be done among people in the market target.

Despite this opinion there are some definite advantages in including nontarget persons in the sample provided that the number of target persons is large enough to permit their responses to be analyzed separately. Obviously some nontarget people would not be included under any circumstances (e.g., nondog owners for a dogfood commercial or nondenture wearers for a denture cleanser commercial). However, all category users are worthwhile respondents. Not only can they often be included at very little additional cost, but they allow assessment of the extent to which the effects of the central buying incentive carry over to the balance of category purchasers. Certainly it is desirable to persuade as many category users as possible, if the market target has been effective. And experience suggests that the spillover can vary substantially from commercial to commercial.

Inclusion of nontarget category users has other diagnostic value. If a mild increase in persuasion is observed across the board, it may suggest that the commercial execution causing it has not been attuned precisely enough to the perceptions, beliefs, needs, and desires of the market target. If general effects are observed for several successive executions, it suggests that the method of defining the target should be reviewed. Or, alternatively, perhaps the creative people do not understand and empathize with the target as fully as they might.

Respondent selection methods depend upon the research design and exposure system being used. As the PACT document specifies, however, basic principles of good sampling practice should be observed wherever it is possible and economically feasible to do so. In other words, the sample should be selected so that its results are projectable back to the universe from which it is drawn. Where telephone interviewing is done some variation of random digit dialing *with callbacks* is advisable. Where recruiting is done in shopping centers, respondents should not all be recruited at the same time of day or on the same day of the week.

Sample sizes in copy testing have been under cost pressure, especially because doubts have been expressed about the relationships between copy testing scores and sales performance. If the emphasis of the copy tests is on diagnostic use, small samples can be very helpful. Some agencies routinely use samples of 30 to 50 respondents for all of their copy testing.

Sample sizes tend to be larger for captive audience situations involving group exposure, ranging from 300 upward. The historical standard for on-air tests was 200. In general, however, the trend seems to be toward smaller sample sizes. Ten years ago the most frequent sample size for copy tests was probably about 200. Today it is more likely in the vicinity of 150. Minimum acceptable sample sizes for subgroup analysis vary from company to company, but 100, 120, and 75 are popular choices.

The decision about the number of testing locations to be used is another tradeoff situation. The more locations used the more projectable the results are likely to be; however, the more cities the higher the cost is likely to be. Testing in a single location is dangerous because in the absence of contradictory data there is a tendency to assume that results from other cities would be the same if they were available. Where more than one location is employed, it is not unusual to observe sizable differences from city to city. For this reason testing should always be done in at least two locations, with four cities being a popular industry choice. When several cities from diverse locations are used, the city-to-city variation can provide a good intuitive measure of sample reliability. If results are stable from city to city, we can assume that city differences are not a serious concern in interpreting the results of the test. On the other hand, sharply differing results should be taken as a warning that they may not be reliable and that, if the decision is an important one, it will be wise to replicate the test in additional cities.

If a limited number of markets is to be employed and if there is some degree of flexibility in their choice, the final sampling question is how they should be chosen. With only two to four selections to be made, purposive samples make a great deal more sense than random sampling. What then are helpful selection criteria? Certainly the pragmatic factor of available facilities and availability of a high-quality interviewing service are primary considerations. Also if a syndicated service is being used, choices may be limited. Where choices exist, however, they should be evaluated, as a minimum, in terms of city size, brand development, and category development. City size is especially important when on-air tests are planned because this usually bears a direct relationship to media costs. The larger the market the higher the media cost. Of course, it can logically be argued that media dollars invested in a copy test are no more wasted than media dollars invested in regular advertising. However, this argument seems to carry little weight with budget-conscious marketing executives.

Brand development refers to the per capita sales rate of the brand being advertised. This is available on a market-by-market basis in most package goods companies. Similarly category development refers to the per capita sales rates of the combined brands within the product category. Again this is customarily available.

Where the test is to be conducted in just two markets, preferred practice is to choose markets that are about average in terms of both brand development and category development. Where more markets are covered, more diversified development situations can be represented. For example, if history has shown that sales of the brand of interest are more responsive to differences in brand development than to differences in category development, and if four markets are to be used, it would be customary to choose two markets with average levels of brand development, one with high brand development and one with low brand development. In other words, selection criteria can involve any factors that experience has shown to be related to responsiveness. The factors already cited are frequently believed to be in that category. Others sometimes considered include brand development of the leading competitior, distribution levels, price levels, advertising weight for the brand at issue, competitive advertising weight, media costs, and media coverage. One final factor that is almost always considered is geographical dispersion. To the extent that it is possible to do so efforts are made to draw the markets from different sections of the country.

SYNDICATED SERVICES

In reviewing the choices which have to be made if a copy testing system is to be built from scratch, we have set up a framework that allows a succinct review to be made of any existing copy testing system. Additionally it permits alternative systems to be compared in such a way that differences among them become apparent and their relative strengths and weaknesses can be evaluated in terms of the personal preferences of the reviewer. All that is necessary is a recap of seven factors—their measurement method, the specific measures taken, timing of the measurements, experimental design, forms of advertising tested, exposure mechanics, and sampling procedure.

To illustrate this let us compare five services which an Advertising Research Foundation survey in 1981 had shown to be among the most widely used (see Table 11.18). Action standards are not included in this table because different clients using the same syndicated service would, in all likelihood, have different action standards. Had the table compared the practices of major manufacturers, it would have been desirable to include an additional row specifying the action standards being used. Such a table is not included here for two reasons—companies consider this information to be semiconfidential and are reluctant to release it, and the systems in use tend to be modified in some respect every year or two.

TABLE 11.18 Summary of Methods of Leading Copy Testing Services

Burke*	ASI	AC-T	ARS	Mapes & Ross
		Measurement Approach		
Verbal Response	Verbal Response (Self-Administered Physiological Measures)	Verbal Response (Self-Administered)	Verbal Response (Self-Administered with phone followup)	Verbal Response
		Measurement Taken		
Related Recall	Recall (50 minutes after exposure)	Clutter Awareness	Recall (72 hrs. later by phone)	Proven and related recall
Communications (copy and visual recall)	Communication	Communication	Communication	Communication
Verbatims	Adjective checklist	Persuasion (brand choice—market basket or purchase intention)	Persuasion (first and second choice, shopping bag lottery)	Persuasion (brand choice scale)
	Persuasion (brand choice—door prizes and purchase intent)	Diagnostics (custom)	Diagnostics (custom)	Brand image
				Custom Diagnostics

341

TABLE 11.18 (*Continued*)

	Burke*	ASI	AC-T	ARS	Mapes & Ross
		Profile curve		Verbatims	Verbatims
		Interest curve (dial)			
		Diagnostics (focus group of 12)			
		At extra cost —refocus—open end, 6 people —Delayed recall (24 hours)			

Timing of the Measurements

	Burke*	ASI	AC-T	ARS	Mapes & Ross
	24 hours after exposure	Immediate	Immediate	Immediate except recall delayed 72 hours	24 hours after exposure

Experimental Design

	Burke*	ASI	AC-T	ARS	Mapes & Ross
	Post only	Pre/post	Pre/post	Pre/post	Pre/post

Form of the Advertising

	Burke*	ASI	AC-T	ARS	Mapes & Ross
	Finished	Rough or finished	Rough or finished	Rough or finished	Rough or finished

Exposure

Service	Location	Message Delivery Environment	Method	Message Content	Clutter Conditions
Burke*	Flexible (25–30 cities)	Home	Own TV set	Original TV programs	Natural
ASI	One 300 seat theater, others at additional cost, primarily Chicago	Large groups	Theatre Screen	Ads exposed naked *after* half hour pilot program	Non-competitive (five commercials, one control)
AC-T	Hotel or other large public meeting room	Small groups (N=25)	23″ TV monitors (closed circuit TV)	In between performer auditions	Non-competitive for first exposure, alone in program for the second
ARS	Hotel meeting rooms	Small groups (N = 30–40)	23″ TV monitors (closed circuit TV)	In program for first, naked for second	Non-competitive
Mapes & Ross	Three markets	Home	UHF over own TV set	Prime-time movies and lower interest reruns	Position and product protection controlled

TABLE 11.18 (*Continued*)

Service	Number of Exposures	Universe	Sampling Method of Selections	Size	Dispersion
Burke[*]	One	People willing to be program viewers	Pre-recruited by random dialings from phonebooks	200 programs, 150 commercial	Three or four markets
ASI	One	Not well-defined	Recruited in shopping centers, business districts and by phone	N = 200–300	Los Angeles
AC-T	Two	Phone households	Recruit by phone	N = 250–300	Six + mkts
ARS	One, extra exposure of 100–200 respondents for diagnostics	Listed phone households	By mail from random phone book selection	n = 400–600 for persuasion, 150–200 subsample for recall	Two standard & custom markets
Mapes & Ross	One	People willing to watch movie	Prerecruited by phone	N = 200	Three markets, others at added cost

Comments

	Burke*	ASI	AC-T	ARS	Mapes & Ross
	Central location interviewing	Brand preferences for 4 categories	Recall is obtained between prepost persuasion measures	Recall gathered individually to avoid contamination	Central interviewing
	Establishes commercial audience	Ads are exposed singly with intervening questions	Questions asked by prerecorded interviewer	Clean prepost measure Brand preference for 10 categories	Percent mentioning animatics is used as a control for tests in that form
	Client and agency are responsible for airing commercial	Adjective checklist and purchase intent obtained between prepost persuasion measures	Locations changed from time to time	Preference questions are accompanied by pack shots	Commercial audience not established

* Since the 1981 conference Burke has introduced an on-air testing system called SELECTOR that combines recall and persuasion measurements.

For a review of syndicated print copy testing services and syndicated television copytesting services not included in Table 11.18, see Stewart, Furse and Kozak.[50]

COPY TESTING IN A SEGMENTED MARKET

Given the fact that a Benefit Segmentation study has been conducted and that a communications strategy has been developed, there are a number of implications for copy testing. The starting point is to prepare a copy strategy statement that summarizes what the copy is intended to do. As indicated previously these vary to some extent from company to company. Some are not more than a few key sentences, whereas others may involve a half-dozen pages of discursive text. Sometimes they are prepared by the creative people and sometimes by brand managers or account executives. However, in one way or another they define:

> The market target (the segment chosen for primary attention) and sometimes secondary targets
>
> The central buying incentive (and sometimes desirable secondary buying incentives; alternatively the personality they hope to create for the brand)
>
> The user image (how the person who uses this product is differentiated from the world at large)
>
> Copy tonality (forceful, friendly, reassuring, informal, etc.; a related area is the mood to be projected by the advertising—sometimes called the emotional response)
>
> Executional direction (setting, casting, pace, etc.)

Because these are prepared before the copy is tested, they serve the very useful function of providing guidelines for evaluating consumer reactions to the advertising. In other words, they can be used to measure how well the copy is accomplishing what was intended. They permit key questions such as the following to be answered:

> Is the profile of message playback in line with the communications strategy? This is the most basic communications problem.
>
> Is the central buying incentive playing through more clearly than alternative benefits? In theory this seems as though it should be easy to do. In practice it is not always accomplished.

[50] "A Consumer's Guide to Commercial Copy Testing Services," Working Paper No. 81–118, Vanderbilt University, August 1981.

Is the user characterized in the intended manner and is the projected image judged to be attractive by people in the market target? This is particularly difficult to guarantee in advance because of the potent and unpredictable effects of casting, setting, music, dress, grooming, and other nonverbal factors.

Is the mood created by the advertising the intended one and an appropriate one?

To this sort of information can be added the ability of the commercial to meet whatever action standards have been established with respect to persuasion, salience, recall, attitude shifts on key benefits, and so on.

Next there is the question of how best to gather information designed to classify copy test respondents back into the benefit segments discovered in the course of the original Benefit Segmentation study. There are two major alternatives for doing so: The original ratings can be gathered in total and respondents can be classified into segments at the tabulation stage, or a "doorstep screen" can be developed. With the latter approach the interviewer asks a few short classification questions and, based on the pattern of responses, decides on the spot whether the respondent qualifies as a member of the segment or segments of interest.

Usually it is not practical (and unnecessary) in the context of a copy test to repeat the extensive list of benefits used to derive segments in the original study. So the "doorstep screen" is to be preferred. A stepwise discriminant function analysis will identify a subset of items, usually no more than 8 or 10, which will allow new respondents to be classified into the original segments with perhaps an 80% accuracy. (More will be said about that shortly.)

Probably the most popular procedure is to run a normal copy test, adding to the questionnaire the 8 or 10 benefit items required to code people into the appropriate segments. Then when the completed questionnaires are available, it is a simple matter to determine the proper codes for each respondent by cycling each individual's pattern of responses through the equations produced by the discriminant function analysis.

This approach has the advantage of allowing comparison of reactions in the target segment with those of each of the other segments. And because each of those segments is understood in depth, the way in which they react to the copy can provide diagnostic insights into how it is working and why it is operating as it is. These insights provide the means of strengthening the specific copy and point the way to producing still stronger copy in the future. Also if the copy is accomplishing its goals, the persuasion, recall, salience, and other action standard measures should perform more favorably for the target segment than for other segments.

The disadvantage of this approach is that segment sizes are determined by the luck of the draw. Thus researchers cannot know in advance how many people in the target segment will be obtained. Where fixed sample sizes are desired, this is a definite drawback. To be sure that enough people in the target segment will be reached it is necessary to oversample and that, in the long run, is a wasteful practice.

Another form of waste occurs when the target segment is relatively small. If, for example, the target segment amounts to only 20 percent of the population, then the huge preponderence of those interviewed will not be people in whom interest is greatest. So although there is definite value in including nontarget people in the sample, the inclusion of too many is certainly an inefficient use of copy research dollars.

As mentioned previously, the alternative procedure attempts to utilize a "doorstep screening" procedure to identify target prospects immediately. Then it is possible to use either of two frequent variations in the procedure in interviewing practices. The first variation involves screening out all nontarget people and interviewing only those estimated to be members of the target benefit segment. This has the advantage of concentrating the copy research investment on the people who have to be influenced if the campaign is to succeed; however, it gives no measure of their relative responsiveness.

The second variation is to split the sample on a fifty/fifty basis so that approximately half of the people interviewed will be members of the target segment and the remainder will be members of the other segments.[51] This gives a standard of comparison but, of course, at the cost of reducing the number of target people interviewed.

There are several ways in which doorstep screens can be conducted. In some situations the method used can be exceedingly simple. For example, if the target consists of health-conscious persons, the screen might involve interviewing those who express strong agreement with two or three belief statements centering on health. However, that ignores the problem of response styles and the fact that those same people might have agreed with quite a few statements, many of which would not be endorsed by those who were members of the segment of interest.

A second method is self-classification. Under this system respondents are given descriptions of the various benefit segments and asked which one they believe they most closely resemble. Attempts to validate this approach have been discouraging. Some segments appear to be more socially desirable than others and consequently are chosen more frequently than they would be with a more objective classification system. Table 11.19 shows the results of two experiments with self-identification. The columns are original segment memberships as determined by multivariate analysis. The rows show

[51] Some analysts use the sample balancing program to bring segment sizes into line.

TABLE 11.19 Two Experiments in Respondent Self-classification

| | Experiment No. 1 Actual Segments | | | | | Experiment No. 2 Actual Segments | | | | |
	I	II	III	IV	Σ	I	II	III	IV	Σ
Respondent self-classification										
I	42	22	20	63		66	6	11	22	
II	9	46	9	31		10	109	15	16	
III	7	36	11	41		12	32	31	25	
IV	11	26	13	68		36	15	10	69	
sample size	69	130	53	203	455	124	162	67	132	485
% correct	61%	35%	21%	33%	37%	53%	67%	46%	52%	57%

349

respondents' attempts to classify themselves in a repeat interview situation.

In general people did choose the proper segment for themselves more frequently than any other single segment, the exception being the third segment in the first experiment—the smallest segment there and not a very appealing one from the standpoint of social status. Note that Segment III people see themselves as similar to Segment I people when faced with descriptions of all four segments. However, Segment I people rarely confuse themselves with Segment III people—again a matter of status.

The second experiment was much more successful than the first because segment descriptions were rewritten several times and pretested to be sure that they were considered accurate descriptions by the people belonging to each segment. That particular experiment yielded the highest level of predictive accuracy of a half-dozen experiments of this general type. And even in this instance misclassifications were almost as frequent as correct classifications. Moreover it was found that the screening process was now taking an inordinate amount of time. To do the job right segment descriptions had to be fleshed out rather fully and time requirements for respondents to read all of the descriptions, consider which was most like themselves, and make a choice were rendering the self-identification approach impractical.

Currently doorstep screens are the most frequently used method. And they are normally based on responses to a small number of items. As Table 11.20 illustrates, if items are chosen through stepwise discriminant function analysis, losses in predictive accuracy due to reduction in the number of predictors can be minimal. Tables such as these can be used diagnostically as well as for choosing a specific number of predictors. Segments that show joint misclassification patterns (e.g., Segment I is confused with Segment II and vice versa) can sometimes be approached by similar copy. At the very least the patterns of confusion can indicate the likely directions of spillover for copy targeted at one particular segment.

Five items is perhaps a smaller number than economic conditions usually dictate. However it is not unusual to find that the 80% level can be reached with about that number of items. (See Table 11.21 for results and Figure 11.11 for the format in use with the doorstep screener.)

One frequent question in this area is how high a level of predictive accuracy should be sought. The more items included the higher the predictive accuracy; however, the more items included the larger the amounts of interviewing time. Also as accuracy levels increase, incremental gains become harder and harder to achieve and larger numbers of additional items are required to get each additional point of accuracy. As might be expected the answer to the above question depends to some extent upon the number of segments obtained and how well differentiated they are from each other. The fewer the segments and the more distinct they are the smaller will be the number of items required.

TABLE 11.20 Clasification Accuracy and Number of Benefits Employed

Predicted segments	Predictions Based on Responses to 106 Items					Predictions Based on Responses to 25 Items					Predictions Based on Responses to 5 Items				
	Actual Segments					Actual Segments					Actual Segments				
	I	II	III	IV	V	I	II	III	IV	V	I	II	III	IV	V
I	44	4	3	1	—	37	4	1	3	1	35	7	3	3	—
II	2	29	—	—	2	4	31	1	1	2	7	28	2	—	3
III	—	2	35	2	1	3	1	35	—	—	—	1	32	1	2
IV	1	2	—	16	—	1	1	3	16	—	—	2	2	13	—
V	1	3	3	1	7	2	4	1	—	7	5	2	2	3	5
Total	47	40	41	20	10	47	40	41	20	10	47	40	41	20	10
% Correct	94	73	85	80	70 (83)	79	78	85	80	70 (80)	74	70	78	65	50 (72)

Interviewer: Using the "Opinion Rater," ask respondent to sort the five benefit cards. As she does, place an "x" on the corresponding box on the rating scales below and post the number below in "x" in the box to the right of the scale (in the column labeled "Point Total")

	Extremely	Very	Quite	Rather	Slightly	Not at all	Point Total
1. Mild tasting	0	3	5	8	10	13	
2. Makes you look younger	19	15	12	8	4	0	
3. Comes in size I like	0	5	10	15	20	25	
4. Makes you feel you belong	20	16	12	8	4	0	
5. Breath stays fresh longer	20	16	12	8	4	0	

Interviewer: Total the numbers in the five boxes in the column labeled "Point Total." If the total is 52 or more, continue the interview.

Figure 11.11. Format for doorstep screener to identify target segment

TABLE 11.21 Sometimes Accuracy Can Be Obtained with Very Few Items

	Example A—Based on 6 Items Actual Segments				Example B—Based on 5 Items Actual Segments				
	I	I	III	Σ	I	II	III	IV	
Predicted segments									
I	48	4	11		27	0	7	10	
II	1	51	4		2	47	1	3	
III	2	3	26		1	2	23	0	
IV					2	4	1	20	
Total	51	58	41	150	32	53	32	33	150
% correct	94	88	63	83	84	89	72	61	78

As a rule of thumb, derived from tests in perhaps 50 product categories, 80% is a realistic target level. It can generally be reached with between five and 12 items. However, the best procedure is to develop an accuracy curve at varying levels and to make the choice as to the number of items after examining that curve. It can always be argued that some misclassification is acceptable. If, for example, people are misclassified as target people and mistakenly interviewed, it is likely that the reason for the mistake is that they are similar to target people. If they are similar in terms of the benefits they seek, they should respond similarly to advertising stimuli as well as to (although perhaps at less intense levels than target people) to communications that are exactly on target.

One final observation on this topic may be helpful. The decision about how many items to include in the screener should not be based on the overall level of predictive accuracy. Some segments, quite naturally, are much more interesting to a given marketer than others. And it is not unusual for the addition of an item to improve overall accuracy by *lowering* the accuracy of predictions for one segment while increasing it for two or three others. Thus the pattern of predictive accuracy by an individual segment must be considered as well as the overall level of predictive accuracy.

TWELVE

Media Planning and Other Forms of Follow-Through

MEDIA PLANNING IN A SEGMENTED MARKET

Package goods marketers find that, next to geographical coverage, advertising copy normally bears the primary burden in a communications strategy based on a Benefit Segmentation study, operating through the selective processes that people use subconsciously in deciding when to turn on their minds and to process the message. As has been pointed out, they do this when an ad appears likely to contain information of interest to them, to entertain them, or to reinforce their behavior, opinions, or perceptions. The power of the benefit approach, supported by the kinds of executional formats and ingredients that allow a respondent to project him- or herself into the ad, is that it is very effective in capturing the attention of those interested in a particular benefit or set of benefits. Thus ads involving health maintenance will almost automatically pull out of the physically exposed audience the people (segment) more interested in that area.

The role of media is to put the copy before as many primary target people as possible and, as might be expected, some media have considerably more prospects in their audiences than others. Moreover the general media environment and specific vehicle environment can play an important role in helping to capture the attention of the prospect. The same prospect may be considerably more attentive to a particular type of message in some media environments than he or she is in others. If the ad is custom tailored

355

to the interests of the prospect, however, it is likely to capture this person's attention in any of a fairly broad range of vehicles.

Because quite a wide variety of vehicles is potentially suitable, cost per thousand considerations, combined with the judgment of the media professional concerning the appropriateness of a given campaign for a particular medium and the vehicles in it, become paramount. However, we are not concerned so much with cost per thousand in the sense that the term is customarily used by media people; rather we are interested in cost per thousand turned on minds.

Thus the first job of a media planner in attempting to implement the results of a segmentation study is to try to understand the primary market target, and the secondary target (if there is one) in as much depth as possible. Once the planner feels he or she understands the market target (and the project team should be prepared to work with the media planner in developing this understanding), he or she should attempt to build an ideal media plan for reaching the intended target. In doing so the same standard media sources should be used that are customarily used in developing media plans.

Some analysts prefer to try to use the data gathered in the media section of the segmentation study. However, there are a number of good reasons for not attempting to do so.

It is impractical to attempt to include all vehicles that might conceivably be of interest. Consequently media schedules that come out of segmentation studies tend to be strongly biased in the direction of the vehicles fortunate enough to have been included in the questionnaire—a sort of circular logic.

Samples used by standard media sources such as Simmons/TGI are much larger than those employed in the typical attitude segmentation study. These permit substantially greater accuracy on a market-by-market or region-by-region basis.

Sample dispersion in media surveys generally provides much better coverage of C&D counties. For reasons of maximizing the amount of information per research dollar invested, these are often undersampled in segmentation studies.

Media services frequently gather information at several points throughout the year. In doing so they sample time as well as geography. They are able to do this because their clients customarily buy a series of reports. So they are surveying more or less continuously. Those who use segmentation studies, on the other hand, usually cannot afford to devote a full year to their fieldwork. Consequently their samples are more susceptible to seasonal biases.

Media planners are intimately familiar with their resources and are highly skilled in their use. The media data from segmentation studies are less familiar and therefore more likely to be misused.

When media vehicles are included in segmentation studies, they should be as diverse as possible so as to cover the full gamut of types of viewing, reading, and listening preferences. Additionally, the set chosen should include specific vehicles used by the brand of interest and its competitors. To the extent that time and space permit, the more popular media vehicles should be included also. These vehicles have two functions:

One is to show individual media vehicles and/or media types which have above-average ability to reach the segments of greatest interest. The second function is to aid in clarifying the nature of the segments for media planners. The profile of interest and lack of interest in specific media vehicles can be as revealing to professional media planners who understand the precise nature and content of those vehicles as personality inventory responses are to a trained psychologist. Once the planner sees that a specific segment reads some magazines regularly and avoids others, he or she can speculate with surprising accuracy on other vehicles likely to have above and below average exposure in that segment. Doubters can put their own media experts to the test when the media data from the segmentation study become available by choosing a segment and telling the media planners about one or two vehicles with above and below average penetration in the given segment, and then asking them to guess about other vehicles for which information is available. Needless to say, to protect reputations this is best done informally and in private. In the experience of the author, however, the successful guesses far outnumber incorrect guesses.

Once the media planner has constructed his ideal plan using his understanding of the nature of the market target, his intuition, and his standard media sources, he can, as a last step, review the media data produced by the segmentation study to be sure that it is generally in line with his recommendations and that he has not overlooked any opportunities.

In this process the key factor continues to be the judgment of the media professional. Although this fact is not widely appreciated, building media plans is a creative act rather than a statistical procedure. Although more data are available for the media selection process than perhaps any other advertising decision, and although a number of sophisticated media models are available to aid in the selection process,[1] the development of a truly effective media plan is primarily a creative effort. An experiment from the world of media planning may serve to illustrate this point. But first some background on media models may be helpful.

[1] J. Z. Sissors and E. R. Petray, *Advertising Media Planning*, Chicago: Crain Books, 1976.

Almost every media selection model involves a variety of input data. Typically they require:

A list of media vehicles to be considered

Data on their audience sizes, characteristics, and geographic dispersion

The cost of each media unit in each vehicle

Special restrictions such as the maximum frequency permitted or the maximum proportion of budget to be put in any one media type

Weights indicating the relative importance of various respondent types

Weights indicating the relative impact of each media unit and each vehicle

Weights reflecting the cumulative impact of multiple exposures

The first four of these are relatively easy to obtain. Even the fifth can be supplied if problems of persuasibility are overlooked and volume of consumption is accepted as a measure of importance. However, the media impact weights and cumulative impact weights are much harder to obtain. As of now they rest heavily on judgment. Nevertheless in sensitivity tests these weights can be shown to have a large influence on the ultimate results, probably more than any other single factor.

Of course, the importance of media impact weights raises no special problems provided there is a reasonable consensus among media professionals as to how they should be assigned to individual media vehicles. The experiment about to be reviewed casts strong doubts on this premise.

Participants were 60 media professionals, six each from 10 major advertising agencies. They were first briefed thoroughly on the product for which media was to be bought—on its marketing strategy and the best prospects for the product. As part of the briefing they were shown samples of how the creative people intended to communicate the central buying incentive.

Uniform instruction on rating procedures was given to all participants. They were asked to rate a series of vehicles on a zero to 100-point rating scale with five-point intervals. Before doing so, however, they were given a personal briefing on how to use the scale and were issued a set of written instructions, recapping the briefing. All raters were media professionals, none with less than five years experience in media planning, and they were each trying to implement an identical strategy.

Under such conditions it might be expected that the range of variations for a standard unit such as a 30-second network TV commercial or a 30-second prime spot might be about 20% to 30%. In point of fact the range turned out to be 250 percent. In other words, the highest rater assigned an impact weight that was 2½ times the impact weight assigned by the lowest rater.

Of course, there weve 60 raters and perhaps expectations of a 30% range were too conservative. However, even when the *average* within-agency range is computed—with only six people involved—the highest rater assigned double the impact of the lowest to a 30-second network TV commercial. And the variability increases sharply when less frequently used media units are examined. For example, the highest rater in a six-person set in the same agency assigns, on average, a weight that is almost four times that of the lowest rater to quarter-page black-and-white newspaper ads.

As a final step in the analysis, the variation among raters *within* agencies was compared with the variation *among* agencies to test the hypothesis that there are definite points of view within agencies and that they differ from agency to agency. This hypothesis was rejected.

What are the implications of these findings? Perhaps the most important one is that, although the process of media selection involves mathematical models and appears to be highly scientific, it is, in fact, quite subjective. If a company does not like a media plan its agency has recommended, it need not consider a change in agencies. All it needs to do is request that a new plan be developed by a different planner in the same agency. Results are likely to be quite different.

A good case can be made for the idea that good media planning requires just as much creativity as developing good advertising copy. Obviously it is difficult to tell when a truly outstanding media schedule has been put together. As indicated in Chapter 11, however, it is not easy to judge when outstanding copy has been produced either.

Returning to the value of segmentation study data for media planning purposes, at the very least, if a strict statistical approach to media planning is favored, the media portion of the segmentation study can be helpful in choosing both prospect weights and weights for individual media vehicles. At the most, media planners will obtain insights into the media habits of the kinds of people who represent the best prospects and will be able to use these as guidelines for their creativity.

PACKAGING, SALES PROMOTION, PRICING, AND PRODUCT PLANNING

Segmentation studies are helpful in other areas involving communications. For example, segmentation research provides guidelines for evaluating alternative forms and designs of packaging, labels, and logos. Are they helping to reinforce the desired personality of the brand? For example, does the shift in images from when they are measured with just the name on a plain white card to when they are measured with a package or logo present move the image in the desired direction? As noted in the discussion of perceptual mappings, image shifts, because they deal with perceptions rather than evaluations, tend to be homogeneous across all segments. It is especially important, however, that changes occur in the anticipated directions among people in the target segment.

Sales promotion is also generally considered to be an element of communications. It too can be tailored to the needs and interests of the target segment, and it can involve promotions that strongly reinforce the central buying incentive. For example, if premiums are to be employed, they can be tested in much the same way as copy. Those that are most attractive to people in the target group can be selected. Similarly, coupons can be sent to people whose names are drawn from telephone directories or mailing lists. Afterward these people can be contacted, classified into segments via the doorstop screening approach, and redemption rates determined, Thus the relative appeal of the promotion to those in the target segment can be estimated.

Market tests, consumer panels, or controlled store tests can be used in a similar fashion to evaluate the success of promotional alternatives. Frequently, however, it is not necessary to resort to special research to determine the kinds of promotions that are likely to be most appropriate for the target segment. Knowledge of the nature of the segment and its interests will permit the marketer to make accurate guesses as to the kinds of promotions that will and will not find the target group receptive.

Even in the area of pricing segmentation, studies have utility. Price elasticity can be estimated separately for the target segment and for the remaining segments. These allow the marketer to anticipate the extent to which price increases are likely to cut into the volumes of the individual segments and thus to decide on the desirability of pricing changes. Again the responses to questionnaires allow reasonably accurate predictions of *relative* impact. Where more precise estimates are needed, market experiments can be run either with a pre/post design involving people coded into segments before being exposed to the test stimulus, or they can utilize a post-only design with people coded into segments after the fact.

Next to communications the most frequent area of application for segmentation studies has probably been product planning. Most product markets are segmented in one way or another—sometimes by price, sometimes by product form, and sometimes by variations in the sorts of benefits that different brands are perceived to deliver. As Purnell H. Benson has demonstrated it is not impossible for the brands with the highest overall appeal to have lower shares than brands with less appeal to the total market.[2]

This happens in the manner illustrated by the Corning Dinnerware ex-

[2] P. H. Benson, "Consumer Preference Distributions in the Analysis of Market Segmentation," *Proceedings of the Winter Conference of the AMA*, December 1962, pp. 320–335.

ample summarized in Chapter 5. Let us assume that there are five products in the chocolate cake mix market. A paired preference taste test is administered for each pair of cake mixes with the results shown in Table 12.1.

TABLE 12.1 Pained Preference Taste Test

		% Preferring				
		A	B	C	D	E
	A	—	50	50	30	30
	B	50	—	50	30	30
To:	C	50	50	—	30	30
	D	70	70	70	—	50
	E	70	70	70	50	—
	$\bar{X}$	60	60	60	35	35

The first three brands appear to be the stronger brands. However, now let us assume that the market is segmented by the darkness of the chocolate. Some people prefer a dark, bittersweet recipe, some prefer a very light milk chocolate, and most people prefer an average chocolate—neither dark nor light. Let us further assume that Brand D is a dark, bittersweet cake, Brand E is a very light milk chocolate and Brands A, B, and C are at the center of the market—average chocolate cakes.

If demand in the underlying segments of the market for chocolate cake is distributed as shown in Table 12.2, the two brands with lower preference will, other things being equal, actually have larger market shares than the three more popular brands. Although the segment interested in an average chocolate cake is the largest of the three segments (50%), there are three brands fighting for it. Thus other things being equal, each could be expected to have a little less than 17% of the market. However, Brand D will capture the full 25% of the market looking for dark chocolate (25%) and Brand E will capture the segment preferring a very mild milk chocolate, again 25%. These are the facts of life in segmented markets. And many more markets are segmented than is generally believed to be the case. So the implication is that segmentation must be understood and that, in order not to be misleading, product tests should be conducted in the target segment.

TABLE 12.2 Preference by Strength of Chocolate Flavor

	% of Total
Dark bittersweet chocolate	25
Average chocolate	50
Light milk chocolate	25
	100%

As in the case of copy testing in a segmented market, nontarget people can be included in the test for control or for diagnostic purposes. However, they should generally be undersampled when this is done.

Segmentation research is sometimes used for product lining purposes. Where there are several market segments in a given market, the manufacturer of the dominant brand in one of the segments often finds it advantageous to offer line extensions with appeals tailored to segments other than the one he or she dominates. Such product lining strategies are often assumed for defensive purposes.

Product modification is an occasional outcome of a segmentation study. In a benefit segmentation study done for a dental product it was found, for example, that either, by luck or by plan, marketing efforts were targeted on the proper segment. Because of a lack of full understanding of the nature of that segment, however, marketing efforts were slightly out of focus. But often with a little fine tuning, in this case a slight product modification in the flavor of the product, the product can be moved closer to the preferences of the center of its target segment.

Last there is guidance in new product work. R&D efforts can be directed toward expanding segments. Concept and concept/product tests can be conducted among those who will be responsible for their success or failure. And profiles of the satisfaction sought by the various segments can point to specific new product opportunities. This subject has already been covered in detail in Chapter 9, so it will not be discussed fully here. As mentioned earlier, although segmentation studies have value in this area, their value should be considered supplementary. Their primary advantage is still in improved communications strategies and executions.

Summing up, Benefit Segmentation research can be of some help in almost every area of marketing. It is particularly helpful in the task of coordinating all of the elements in the marketing mix so that they work in concert and reinforce each other. Segmentation research provides explicit goals for marketing actions and standards of evaluation for almost every research project that follows the segmentation study. It also provides a common frame of reference for the marketing team, encouraging its members to look at the market in a similar fashion and helping to focus their activities on significant problems and significant opportunities.

One final phase is required—the feedback loop.

FOLLOW-UP TRACKING SYSTEMS

Although a Benefit Segmentation study represents a substantial investment in both time and dollars, a major part of the potential value is lost if it is not followed up. The careful review of the market that is implicit in a Benefit Segmentation study inevitably suggests a number of promising marketing experiments or supplementary research projects with attractive payoff prospects. Additionally, although the typical study is exceedingly thorough and produces large quantities of detailed data, it is conducted at a single point in time. Important changes are taking place in American society today. Working women are becoming more and more prevalent, family sizes are shrinking, population is shifting in the direction of the Sun Belt, and lifestyles have become more informal and more individualized. These and other important changes will probably continue and they will be reflected in consumption patterns for consumer products and services. Consequently a consumer tracking system, a series of repetitive consumer surveys at fixed points in time, is necessary to make sure that any important changes that begin to occur in the sizes and/or characteristics of market segments are detected at the earliest possible moment. Also systematic checks at regular intervals can answer such questions as:

Are the members of one segment gravitating to another segment or segments as they age?

Into which segments are younger people being classified as they enter the market?

In which segments is growth greatest for corporate brands? Which are increasingly competitive strongholds and why?

To what extent are beliefs, perceptions, and benefits sought changing over time?

Are significant new segments emerging?

Do segment trends suggest new product opportunities?

Tracking studies can be conducted via telephone, mail, or personal interviews (including dropoff questionnaires) or through combinations of these methods. For example, some companies conduct detailed personal interviews on an annual basis and shorter telephone interviews at intervening periods (e.g., quarterly).

Sampling is sometimes done monadically with fresh samples drawn for each wave of interviewing. For example, if unaided brand awareness is considered an important criterion measure, a monadic sampling plan is generally preferred.

Other companies favor the "bathtub" sample, named for the procedure often used to keep the water warm in a bathtub. As the water cools, perhaps half of it is drained off and replaced with an equal amount of hot water. In the sampling application approximately half of the respondents are dropped at each wave of interviewing and the remaining half is recontacted. The people who are dropped are replaced with an equal number of fresh respondents.

Interviewing the same people twice has distinct advantages in situations in which brand switching is of central interest. The behavior of a fixed sample of individuals can be compared at two points without having to worry about sampling variations. If the entire sample were recontacted, however, there would be concerns about the extent to which reported behavior in the second time period was influenced by the first interview—the sensitization issue again. When the sample consists half of a fresh group and half of people who are being recontacted, the fresh group can be accorded the greatest attention for measures such as unaided awareness, whereas the recontacted people can be analyzed not only for directions and magnitudes of change but also in terms of the characteristics of the individuals who changed.

Some analysts prefer a third type of design—continuous sampling. In this approach interviews are conducted every week of the year, although they may be cumulated and summarized less frequently, say quarterly. Annual sample sizes are no different with this approach than with designs involving, say, quarterly interviews. Spreading out the interviews over time has several advantages. First, it provides a better sample of time, involving, as it does, a large number of points in time. Also once the research system is operating, it allows excellent before/after measures of competitive marketing actions. If a competitior lowers his price on a given date, or introduces a new advertising campaign, or changes his product formulation, the analyst can simply cumulate interviews before and after the action was taken and assess its success.

The design, however, has corresponding disadvantages. It adds slightly to the cost of the fieldwork, although the increase in cost is generally tolerable. It also makes the geographical sampling plan substantially more complex. Ideally, each week's sample should be separately projectable to the universe to which the total sample is to be projected. Finally if consumption varies substantially by season of the year, there will be seasons during which a large portion of the interviews will be more or less wasted.

Tracking studies have four major purposes:

Monitoring
Prediction
Measuring the effects of market experiments
Diagnosis and hypothesis development

In the monitoring application the tracking study acts as an early warning system.[3] As long as results are in line with expectation, no special action is taken. However, should any unusual trends develop—a brand that is steadily increasing its market share or a growing number of people agreeing with a particular belief—the reasons for the changes are investigated, often through a separate research project custom tailored to the trends of interest. When the reasons are understood, appropriate marketing actions can be taken. Sometimes where costs of such actions are high or when they involve a sizable risk, they are tested in a limited number of markets before being taken on a broader scale.

The prediction function involves projecting the trends that appear to be developing by means of a mathematical model such as the Markov model[4] or the Box-Jenkins model[5] and evaluating their implications. In other words, this is an anticipatory function rather than a corrective function as is primarily the case with systems designed to monitor the market. One important use of this function is to anticipate competitive actions and reactions on the basis of the past history of the companies involved.

Market experiments can also be designed within the context of a tracking system. Experiments may concern advertising weight, media types, campaign evaluation, advertising weight allocation, new product introductions, pricing, promotion, or other marketing actions. For example, the highly successful "Soup Is Good Food" campaign for Campbell Soup was first tested on the West Coast and, when it was seen to have a positive effect there, was extended to the rest of the country. Monitoring was continued for several years and copy was revised as evidence was received on the kinds of image changes that were occurring.

Diagnosis and hypothesis generation is a continuing activity with most tracking systems. Not only the facts of change but the *reasons* for changes need to be established. The tools of diagnostic analysis include standard cross-tabulation, brand-switching analyses, leverage analyses, analysis of changes in evoked sets, quadrant analyses, perceptual mapping, clustering, and various forms of multivariate analysis. When a new advertising campaign is introduced, the key question is whether it is working as anticipated. If the campaign is designed to increase brand awareness and then to change the brand image in directions believed to be favorable, is that what is hap-

[3] "Monitor Your Markets Continuously," Harvard Business Review, Vol. 46, No. 3, May–June 1968, pp. 65–69.

[4] J. G. Kemeny and J. L. Snell, *Finite Markov Chains*, New York: Van Nostrand, 1960.

[5] A. J. Adams and M. M. Moriarty, "The Advertising-Sales Relationships: Insights from Transfer-Function Modeling," *Journal of Advertising Research*, Vol. 21, No. 3, June 1981, p. 41–48.

pening? Are the people in the market target responding more favorably than those who are not in it? Are the intended points in the advertising copy being recalled? Are those who recall them more favorably inclined toward the brand than those who do not? Are there signs that the campaign is influencing trial rates and/or repurchase rates? It is rare to have a campaign work in exactly the fashion anticipated. Consequently tracking studies, when properly designed and conducted, almost always result in a significant amount of learning about the process being monitored. And this knowledge, once tested and verified, can be put to good use in future marketing activities of a similar nature. Obviously a tracking study need not be restricted to a single function. It is usually intended to serve several purposes simultaneously.

Tracking surveys are often accompanied by parallel sales data. Although survey information is useful in spotting trends and, particularly in diagnosis, it is less well suited to volumetric estimates. All marketers maintain shipments records, but shipment data have important drawbacks in tracking applications. There is sometimes a sizable delay before the effects of changes in consumer usage are felt in shipments. Products such as soup, gelatine, and cranberrry sauce are on the shelves of most consumers. Consequently the first effects of increased consumption are often a reduction in consumer inventories. But at a certain point inventories must be replenished and effects begin to appear in retail sales. Again there is likely to be a period in which retail sales growth is accomplished at the expense of reduced retail inventories. But sooner or later reordering will be stepped up and wholesale sales will register gains. And then there is a final lag between the period in which wholesale inventories are drawn down and effects are passed along to factory shipments.

There can be even more confusion when sales slow down. Inventories can pile up in homes and at the retail and wholesale levels while shipments continue at their normal rate. In such cases the day of reckoning (which is bound to come) can be traumatic to everyone concerned. This is especially true of new products. There is always a substantial amount of pipeline filling when a new product is introduced, and this may seem very encouraging at the shipments level. If the product is not being consumed, however, sooner or later everything will come to a screeching halt, and there will be a great deal of distress merchandise on the market.

To guard against the problems caused by lack of knowledge of merchandise flow throughout the channels of distribution, most package goods marketers subscribe to syndicated audit services such as Nielsen or SAMI or both. A few have established custom panels of their own at the wholesale and retail levels. Whatever the source, audit information represents an invaluable supplement to a consumer tracking study.

Other useful supplementary information includes the spending level of the brand of interest and of major competitive brands (if possible, broken down by medium and by market), data on promotional expenditures (or, as a minimum, the presence of promotional activity by brand), and pricing information.

Returning to the consumer survey, most tracking surveys involve short questionnaires and large sample sizes. The following question areas are normally covered:

Awareness.   Top-of-mind and/or unaided awareness

Purchase/use.   Brand bought last or most often, brand bought the time before last (for switching analyses), frequency or volume of consumption, and, for new products, the number of times bought (sometimes called "depth of purchase")

Advertising recall.   Claimed and proven

Overall attitudes.   Purchase intent, constant sum, and/or hedonic ratings plus measures of evoked set and brand loyalty

Demographics

Depending upon budgetary constraints and the depth of analysis desired, other questions are often added to this basic set. They are likely to include things like:

Brand image items, especially those related to the primary and secondary benefits of the communications strategy

Occasions of use

User characteristics, including lifestyle items

Category beliefs

Media habits

Analysis of results depends upon the objectives of the tracking study. It is made difficult by random changes from period to period. These can be held to a minimum by repetitively sampling the same markets, using an identical questionnaire from wave to wave,[6] and, to the extent that it is practical to do so, using exactly the same interviewers. Moving averages can also be used to advantage in smoothing out period to period fluctuations, and sample balancing should be used from wave to wave to be sure that the sample composition of the people contacted is as stable as possible.

---

[6] Some tracking studies involve a set of standard questions plus a set of custom questions that vary from wave to wave, depending upon issues of interest at the time. The custom questions are placed at the end of the interview so that they do not affect the standard questions.

A number of tracking study ratios are helpful in flagging possible marketing problems. Such ratios are no more than rules of thumb, and they suffer to some extent from sampling errors. Thus they should be examined carefully to be sure that observed differences are statistically significant. Also they are frequently open to alternative interpretations, but they have the advantage of permitting comparisons across brands. And when they show sharp changes from one period to the next, the investigation of causes often leads to a better understanding of the influences underlying the dynamics of the marketplace. If for no other reason, they are worth checking for the hypotheses they suggest.

Before considering the ratios themselves six key measures need to be defined operationally:

1. *Preference.* When an individual assigns a brand 6 or more points on a 10-point constant sum scale. Or when monadic evaluative scales are used, when a respondent rates a given brand higher than other brands.[7]

2. *Satisfaction.* A top-box rating. Alternatively the percentage of those who use the brand most often and indicate preference for it.

3. *Acceptance.* Assigning any points on a constant sum scale. Or ratings in the top two boxes of a monadic evaluative scale.

4. *Supportability.* An image rating among the "most often users" of a given brand that is as high or higher than the ratings given to other brands by the "most often users" of those brands.

5. *Trial ratio.* People who have "ever tried" a brand expressed as a percentage of those who are aware of it.

6. *Conversion ratio.* People who have brought the brand recently (e.g., within the past two purchase cycles) expressed as a percentage of those who have "ever tried" it.

Table 12.3 summarizes some of the more frequently used ratios and some of the hypotheses they are believed to suggest. When tracking studies are used for purposes of market experimentation, it is important that test markets and control markets be closely matched. Key matching criteria include brand share, trend in brand share, per capita consumption of the product category, trend in per capita consumption, benefit segment sizes, demographics related to consumption, distribution levels, advertising and promotional spending levels, media considerations, and competitive considerations.

Because matching markets is a complex and imprecise area, modeling

---

[7] Some analysts simply use any top-box rating as a rough measure of preference.

TABLE 12.3   Key Ratios for Tracking Studies

Situation	Hypothesis
Low awareness plus high preference	More advertising weight is called for
High awareness plus low preference	Product problem
Drop in ratio of satisfaction to "bought last"	Product problem
Drop in ratio of bought last to acceptance	Distribution problem
High awareness, low acceptance, high satisfaction	Copy problem
Low ratio of preference to acceptance	Fuzzy image
High awareness, high acceptance, drop in bought last	Point of purchase problem
Percent newly aware of brand and giving it midscale ratings	Copy problem
Movement down rating scale by triers	Product problem or ad overclaim
Ratio of preference to advertising exposure	One measure of advertising effectiveness
Ratio of share of market to share of advertising dollars	A measure of advertising efficiency
Ratio of advertising exposure to advertising dollars	Reflects media choices and/or scheduling
High trial, low conversion	Product or price/value problem
High satisfaction scores	Reinforcement advertisements are called for
Low recent use plus high acceptance	Reminder ads (e.g., occasions of use) called for
Low recent use plus low acceptance	Try product sampling then withdraw brand

the history of a test market and extrapolating it often provides a superior form of control. Some analysts prefer to hedge their bets by using both types of control. Both the test markets and control markets are modeled and projected. Test results are evaluated by subtracting the differences between actual sales in control markets and their projections from the differences between the actual sales of the test markets and their projections, a process known as *double difference analysis.*

When all possible care has been taken in the planning and execution of a tracking study, inexplicable differences tend to disappear. But, it is not unusual to encounter the opposite problem—to find that total market statistics indicate that most marketing actions are having a relatively minor impact on sales, at least in the short term. In part this is due to a misconception— the expectation that a readily visible response will occur in the total market. A major thesis of this book is that any such responses are likely to be selective, occurring only in one or two segments. So an important key to understanding what is going on is to know among whom it *should* be going on. It is extremely difficult to move the entire market and, in most cases, unrealistic to attempt to do so, especially on a short term basis.

Most major consumer products marketers make regular use of market tracking studies. For example, General Electric has conducted what they term the Quarterly Index of Corporate Relations for almost 20 years. This involves 3000 telephone interviews each quarter. Questions include attitudes on public issues that directly or indirectly affect GE, ratings of large companies including GE, and media exposure patterns. Among the analyses regularly performed are comparisions among readers of a given magazine for quarters in which General Electric ads appeared in the magazine and for those in which no GE ads appeared in the magazine. Similarly, comparisons are made for television with respect to viewers of differing numbers of shows—shows on which GE advertising had appeared.

Individual GE divisions also maintain tracking systems of their own. For example, the Lamp Division, under the direction of James A.Rafert, established a tracking system in the early 1960s for use and purchase of flashbulbs, and successfully integrated the consumer survey information with retail audits and factory shipment data. And at about the same time Dr. Robert Pratt and David Case instituted a large omnibus tracking survey covering major appliances. Although the latter survey is no longer being conducted, it was done for more than 15 successive years before being discontinued.

Coca-Cola accumulates approximately 16,000 consumer tracking interviews a year and has been using its tracking systems since 1953. They measure brand and advertising awareness, attitudes, user characteristics (including heaviness of use), occasions of use, volume per occasion, package size mix, brands purchased, and brand switching. Also they have developed suggested remedies for changes considered to be undesirable. For example, a drop in frequency of use may suggest an increase in couponing, whereas a drop in volume per purchase may suggest promotions on the order of "buy two, get one free."

A particularly thorough review of the tracking systems of a major corporation was given by James F. Donius, Manager of Survey Research for the General Foods Corporation, at the December 1981 Advertising Research

Workshop of the Association of National Advertisers.[8] At General Foods, Market Tracking Studies are distinguished by two key characteristics—data integration and total market perspective. Quoting from Mr. Donius,

> The studies combine conventional survey data with related spending, audit and panel information to examine the relative position in the mind of the consumer of *all* the brands in a market at regularly occurring points in time. In this way, these unique market overviews provide the reoccurring report card function necessary to marketing decision making.

General Foods uses such studies for monitoring and for reassessment. Most of their studies involve advertising copy and advertising media decisions. However, they also occasionally influence promotion, product, and pricing decisions as well.

In the advertising area tracking studies influence decisions to continue or to abandon advertising, provide guidance for modification of campaigns, and signal the need for strategy changes. With respect to media they bear on target definitions, scheduling, spending levels, allocation of funds between advertising and promotion, media mix, and the selection of specific media vehicles. Survey results have frequently been validated by changes in the marketplace. For example, price increases have led to declines in incidences of usage, and brand substitutability questions correlate with panel switching data.

These studies typically measure advertising awareness, brand awareness, copy point playback, brand attribute ratings, brand substitutability, category usage, brand usage, and demographics. Their analyses involve standard cross-tabulations, monitoring key performance ratios, and a close examination of what they call the "consideration frame," a concept borrowed from the evoked set.

In summary, tracking studies are a vital follow-through activity, one that is favored by a large number of the nation's most progressive consumer product marketers. The requirements of an effective tracking study include:

Realistic objectives.   The magnitudes of responses expected from marketing actions must be reasonable in relation to those that have been obtained from similar actions in the past.

Samples of an appropriate size.   Samples must be large enough to permit the effects of interest to be separated from the random variations inherent in any sample.

---

[8] "A Perspective on Market Tracking of Established Brands," Association of National Advertisers, Advertising Research Workshop, Plaza Hotel, New York City, December 1981.

Well-defined targets.   Tracking surveys should allow the examination of attitudinally defined subgroups. Total market responses are rare.

Proper statistical matching.   Between waves of the tracking study and between test and control groups in experimental situations.

Adequate controls of experiments or quasi-experiments.   Often this means modeling and projecting historical patterns of change.

Sensitive measures.   Recognition that responses to changes in marketing strategies and tactics may take a variety of forms, allowing for that variety by covering the hierarchy of possible effects.

THIRTEEN

Successful Benefit Segmentation Case Histories

A relatively small number of Benefit Segmentation case histories has found its way into the marketing literature. There are two primary reasons for this. First, the corporations for whom these studies have been done consider them confidential and see no advantage in informing their competitors about their communications strategies and the information upon which they are based. Often the strategies developed from communications studies are adhered to for a substantial number of years. Thus the research is slow to become outdated and to be declassified, and by the time that has occurred interest levels in reports of past marketing actions are likely to be modest at best.

The second reason concerns the nature of the professional literature, which is largely written by and refereed by academic researchers. However, it is unusual to find academics who have participated in both a number of segmentation studies and in the follow-through activities involved in the implementation of their findings. The most experienced people tend to be professional consultants, advertising agency researchers and, in some cases, client researchers. These people have considerably less incentive to publish and, not infrequently, are prevented from doing so by company policy.

There are some notable exceptions, however. One of the most detailed summaries available of a full-scale Benefit Segmentation study, the Ocean Spray study, has also been one of the best-selling Harvard Cases.[1] Unfortu-

[1] Ocean Spray Cranberries, Inc., Parts A and B, Cambridge, MA: Intercollegiate Clearing House, 1975. (See Appendix D.)

373

nately, however, budgetary limitations sharply restricted follow-through activities relating to that study, so the full marketing value of the study was never tested. It remains a stimulating example of the kinds of marketing actions that might (or might not) have been successful at that particular time. Without trying them, obtaining feedback, recalibrating efforts and trying again, one can only speculate on the potential value of the study.

One of the earliest recognized successes was the previously noted Benefit Segmentation study conducted for Old Gold Spin filters in 1964. Four segments were uncovered, one of which appeared to be an ideal communications target for Old Gold. The single characteristic that best identified this segment was high scores on a series of beliefs reflecting an independent personality. Because Old Gold Spin Filters had a fractional share of market, smokers who chose it *had* to be independent. They received very little reinforcement from other smokers showing similar preferences.

At first this seemed to pose a difficult problem. How was it possible to develop a campaign that would select and involve, from those physically exposed to it, persons who were independent? The very fact of their independence suggested that they would be unlikely to respond uniformly to any specific stimulus.

The answer was to appeal to them directly in terms of their independence. A series of commercials was developed, each featuring the satisfactions associated with independence.[2] For example, one commercial showed a man caught in bumper-to-bumper thruway traffic. He turned off the thruway and drove down a beautiful country road, all by himself. Another showed a herd of cattle and admonished smokers not to be one of the herd. The theme line was "Get away from the crowd; get the flavor you want." During the year following the launching of this campaign, Old Gold Spin Filters was the only brand in the entire Lorillard stable to post an increase in sales. As a reward for this success the much larger brand, Kent, was assigned to the agency that produced the Old Gold campaign, Grey Advertising. The campaign was run consistently, with minor modifications, from 1963 to 1973.

Other early successes at Grey included a study for Jif Peanut Butter, a study that marked the beginning of a steady 10-year growth in share, and a Tidewater study which focused attention on a segment that wanted their service station to take over their car care worries. The latter campaign featured a basset hound and a tagline of "Oh, do we worry!" Sales showed a substantial jump following the introduction of this campaign. Its success was even reported in England, where it was called "a dramatically suc-

[2] Previous campaigns had dealt mainly with the filter and the strength of the product, and sales had been experiencing a slow decline.

cessful campaign."[3] But the initial gains were overshadowed by the even more successful introduction of the first gas station game promotion, "Win-a-chek," shortly thereafter.

Other agencies were also reporting on Benefit Segmentation success. In a speech to the New York Chapter of the American Marketing Association on November 19, 1970, Ronald deLuca, then Associate Creative Director at Kenyon & Eckhardt Advertising, summarized several cases in which he had personally been involved. One was a study for Milk Bone dog biscuits. A segment was discovered that was entitled "Reciprocators." They were most positively disposed to their dogs and to the client's brand, and were sufficiently numerous to represent a satisfactory marketing opportunity. A commercial called "Cleaner Whiter Teeth" was developed to focus on the benefits they considered important and was executed "with a feeling tone responsive to what they were like." Sales of the product jumped 14 percent in the first Nielsen period following its introduction and "continued to climb thereafter." The campaign ran for more than five years.

DeLuca also reported successful campaigns for Kotex (sales up 25 percent) and for Lysol spray deodorant, and closed by characterizing Benefit Segmentation as "the most meaningful contribution research has made to help the creative man. I haven't seen anything like it in my twenty years in the business—on behalf of the guys on the creative floor, thank you."

Leo Burnett, although placing primary emphasis on lifestyle segmentation, was also finding that attitude segmentation pays off. In one instance the creative department had developed a "space-age" campaign for a floor wax. On finding that their most logical target group consisted of home-oriented compulsive cleaners, they voluntarily scrapped their campaign—a huge concession given the amount of time and effort that had gone into its development.

The famous "Have it your way" campaign for Burger King was a product of Benefit Segmentation research, as was the "Feeling Free" campaign by BBDO for Pepsi-Cola during a period in which Pepsi was gradually closing the gap between its share of market and that of Coca-Cola.

CPC International was one of the earlier major corporations to make full use of Benefit Segmentation studies. Their first study was of the market for spoonable salad dressings and was done on behalf of Hellman's Mayonnaise.[4] The market was defined as "spoonables" to include both Hellman's and what they perceived as their principal competitor—Miracle Whip salad dressing. At the same time they wished to exclude "pourable" salad dressings under the assumption that, although they represented a form of

[3] *ESOMAR Marketing Research Review*, Vol. 7, No. 1, Summer 1972, p. 3.
[4] The same product carries the label "Best Foods" on the West Coast.

competition, that form was less direct than that represented by Miracle Whip and Kraft Mayonnaise.

Hellman's was a healthy brand with an annual growth rate of about 5 percent at the time of the study. But senior management at CPC reasoned that the brand represented such an important factor in corporate profits that its market should be understood in as much depth as possible, especially from the standpoint of any vulnerabilities it might have. So the study was undertaken for what were essentially defensive purposes.

The study exceeded expectations, however, producing both a sharply defined Benefit Segment target and ways of significantly strengthening copy. During the periods following the introduction of new copy, based on the research, the rate of year-to-year growth in Nielsen sales rose to 17%.

Stimulated by this success the corporation undertook another Benefit Segmentation study, this one for their Mazola brand of cooking oil. At the time of the study the cooking oil market was dominated by three brands—Crisco, Wesson, and Mazola. Mazola was a distant third, however, and it was feared that it might be vulnerable to the higher rates of advertising spending for the two leading brands.

The Benefit Segmentation research showed that the market was clearly segmented into a number of benefit segments, some of which were primarily concerned with taste and others of which were more concerned with health. Not surprisingly it showed that Mazola, a 100% corn oil product, had its largest share among health-conscious people. It also showed that users of Crisco and Wesson, vegetable oil brands containing no corn oil, believed that their brands contained corn oil as well. .

From these findings came a hard-hitting comparative advertising campaign stating that, "of the three leading brands of cooking oil only one is 100% corn oil."[5] Although this campaign was helpful to the Mazola brand, it had the side effect of calling the attention of Procter & Gamble (the makers of Crisco) and Hunt-Wesson (the makers of Wesson) to what appeared to be a significant marketing opportunity. Within a short time both had introduced new brands aimed at what they saw as the health market—Puritan from Procter & Gamble and Sunlite from Hunt-Wesson. Moreover, both new brands appeared to have significant health assets in relation to Mazola. (Both were lower in cholesterol.) But things are rarely as simple as they may seem. With the knowledge afforded it by its Benefit Segmentation research and followup studies, CPC has been successful in fighting the efforts of its large competitors. As recently as the end of 1981 it was able to defend successfully a challenge by Hunt-Wesson through the National Ad-

---

[5] This campaign was cited by the Federal Trade Commission as an example of the best type of comparative advertising—advertising that provides the consumer with useful information.

vertising Division of the Council of Better Business Bureaus, Inc. to its important claim of parity on lightness.

Another notable success was the Benefit Segmentation study conducted for the Corning Glass Works during the introductory period for its Corelle line of dinnerware. This identified a functionally oriented segment that was the ideal target for the Corelle line. It also showed the limitations on the extent to which the line could be expected to penetrate the dinnerware market. It brought into clear relief a segment of style-conscious dinnerware buyers who had lukewarm reactions to the Corelle line. These people wanted more attractive patterns, which in their eyes were of a completely different type from the rim designs being offered by the Corelle line. Moreover, they had the financial resources and the willingness to pay more for them. Based upon this information the Expressions line was developed and successfully introduced.

This is the study that produced a supplementary bit of information to the effect that dinnerware purchasers would like to have a mug available for purchase. As the marketing director liked to point out, profits from the sale of the mug during its first year more than paid for the cost of the entire Benefit Segmentation study.

Shirley Young, Executive Vice President and Director of Research Services and Marketing at Grey Advertising, Inc., presented three successful case histories at the 19th Annual Conference of the Advertising Research Foundation.[6] The first study resulted in repositioning Canada Dry Ginger Ale as a soft drink (rather than as a mixer) for modern sociable people. The campaign was followed by share increases in 24 of the 26 months following its airing.

The second study concerned the Ford subcompact, the Pinto. The research identified a segment that was more practical than other car prospects and was oriented to functional basic transportation. The benefits they sought were dependability, durability, and economy.

Accordingly, a campaign was developed that positioned Pinto as exemplifying basic economical transportation and which traded on Ford's heritage with the Model A.[7] The campaign theme was "When you get back to basics you get back to Ford."

The campaign ran consistently for three years, and by the third year Pinto was the largest selling subcompact, outselling its formidable Volkswagen competitor by a sizable margin.

The third case concerned the radial tires of B. F. Goodrich. Strategic research on communications showed that their then current strategy of em-

---

[6] "Which Role for the Professional Researcher-Problem Solver or Data Producer?," 19th Annual Conference of the Advertising Research Foundation, New York Hilton, November 1973.

[7] Previous advertising had positioned the car as a carefree, small, romantic car.

phasizing safety, durability, and equality was on target. However, there was confusion between Goodrich and Goodyear and, as is normal, it operated in favor of the market leader. In effect a large portion of Goodrich advertising was being attributed to Goodyear.

The problem was attacked directly and with humor. It enabled Goodrich, which ranked fourth in advertising dollars, to jump into the lead in the tire category in brand awareness and to improve its brand preference with respect to radial tires. Both of these conclusions came from the results of a tracking study. Presumably sales were favorably affected as well, but Ms. Young did not present data in this area.

Another well-publicized success was a Benefit Segmentation study described by Elizabeth Richards at a 1977 New York Chapter/AMA conference on Fashion Management.[8] It was conducted under her supervision as Director of Marketing Information and Analysis at Warnaco and was done for one of their divisions, White Stag Women's Sportswear.[9] The research uncovered five segments among consumers of women's sportswear, one of which stimulated a change in White Stag marketing strategy and a new line of clothing. The study also provided White Stag with valuable insights into the people to whom its "Miss" fashions had their primary appeal. And, as a final payoff, the results of the research were converted into a valuable merchandising device. A brochure summarizing the main findings was developed and sent to retailers to demonstrate the need for younger, more spirited sportswear, which would revitalize somewhat drab Missy departments. A 15-minute film summarizing the findings and their practical implications was also prepared and shown to buyers and at trade and professional meetings. Response was reported to be enthusiastic and stores exposed to it, especially the larger stores, did in fact change their buying patterns.

The study was prompted by a problem, as often is the case. In this instance the stimulus was a drastic slowdown in the sale of polyester pull-on pants and coordinates, until then the backbone of women's sportswear sales. Reasons for this development were not at all clear, and White Stag decided that large-scale consumer research was called for.

To quote Ms. DeKupsa,

What emerged from the information obtained was a measurable complex human being—our customer—whose fashion preferences we could define

[8] "Fashion Management and Consumer Life Styles," New York Chapter/AMA, Biltmore Hotel, January 1977.
[9] The study was also reported on by Steve Sturman of Wells Rich Green, the White Stag advertising agency and by Claire DeKupsa, Vice President, White Stag sportswear. See E. A. Richards and S. S. Sturman, "Lifestyle Segmentation in Apparel Marketing," *Journal of Marketing*, Vol. 41, October 1977, pp. 89–91.

and were able to act upon. The study showed all of us in detail that the so-called "Missy Customer," that person we all professed to know was not the person we thought she was. It turned out she was five different women with varied lifestyles whose common denominator is that they shop in upstairs missy sportswear departments and in specialty shops that carry related merchandise.

The five segments were described as follows:

Segment A (22% of the market), named the "Jet setter"

Psychographics: Fashion conscious, interested in being well dressed, willing to try new styles and new bras.

Behavior: Wears Missy sizes 12 and 14, tends toward pantsuits and conservative, traditional clothing, shops in better priced sections of larger stores.

Demographics: Age 30–39, household income over $20,000, suburban.

Segment B (15% of the market), named the "Homebody"

Psychographics: Value conscious, conservative, willing to trade off softness for durability.

Demographics: Age 30–39, household income $10,000–$20,000.

Segment C (21% of the market), named the "contemporary"

Psychographics: Likes the stretch bra and the contemporary look. Prefers soft and sheer bras.

Behavior: Wears sizes 8–10, shops in better-priced sections of department stores, specialty shops, and boutiques.

Demographics: Age 18–29, household income $10,000–$20,000.

Segment D (24% of the market), named the "Functionnaire"

Psychographics: Desires full comfort. Tends to be full-figured.

Demographics: Age 50–59, household income $10,000–$15,000

Segment E (18% of the market), named the "No-nonsense Woman"

Psychographics: Prefers prepackaged bras.

Demographics: Age 40–49, household income $15,000–$20,000

In interpreting the results of the survey the first important findings were the new insights that were provided into the nature of the primary White Stag customer. They were found to be much more fashion conscious and more interested in being well dressed than had been anticipated, and they were well represented in the first segment. Accordingly, that segment was designated the primary market target. An updated line, involving more colorful and more fashionable clothes, was designed for them and presented to retailers with excellent results. It was found that retailers had tended to confuse Segment A and Segment B people, considering them both to be conservative and price conscious.

Segment C was considered to be a major new product opportunity. To exploit it White Stag designed younger, more spirited sportswear than their traditional lines. A young guest designer was also invited to contribute a group design for Segment C. Presentations of the research results and the new lines of merchandise were first made to the White Stag sales force to acquaint them with the nature of the White Stag market targets and to emphasize the sales potential of younger, more fashionable clothes. Subsequently presentations were made to retailers in White Stag showrooms and sales offices to convince them that they could attract additional customers by investing in the new lines. Followup brochures were distributed both personally and by mail. The results, according to Ms. DeKupsa, were "millions of additional dollars in Spring volume."

Benefit Segmentation has also been applied successfully in the tourism industry.[10] A study of the U.S. market for travel to Canada produced six benefit segments.

Segment I (29% of the potential market) named the "non-active Visitor."

Key Characteristics: Visiting friends and relatives, familiar surroundings, low participation in vacation activities.

Segment II (12% of the potential market) named the "Active City Visitor."

Key Characteristics: Visiting friends and relatives, familiar surroundings, participation in activities such as city sightseeing, shopping, cultural, and other entertainment.

Segment III (6% of the potential market) named the "Family Sightseers."

Key Characteristics: New vacation location, a treat for the children, enriching experience.

Segment IV (19% of the potential market) named the "Outdoor Vacationer."

Key Characteristics: Clean air, rest and quiet, beautiful scenery, camping, availability of recreational facilities, children are an important factor.

Segment V (8% of the potential market) named the "Resort Vacationer."

Key Characteristics: Water sports such as swimming, good weather, popular place, big city atmosphere.

---

[10] "Marketing Canada as a Vacation Nation," in B. M. Rusk, Y. Wind and M. G. Greenberg (Eds.), *Moving A Head with Attitude Research*, AMA: Chicago, 1977.

Segment VI (26% of the potential market) named the "Foreign Travel Vacationer."

Key Characteristics: A place not visited previously, foreign atmosphere, beautiful scenery, good accommodations, good service, not price conscious. Looking for an exciting enriching experience.

The last three segments were designated as the primary market targets for Canada's tourist industry. Creative and media strategies were refocused on the basis of the data generated by the research, and guidelines were obtained for direct mail and for publicity.

The new creative executions centered on the specific benefits of interest to each segment (separately). At the same time they attempted to reinforce positive aspects of the Canadian image and to correct any negative misconceptions that might have existed. Focus group sessions were used extensively to evaluate and fine tune the creative efforts. This, incidentally, is an exceedingly appropriate use for focus groups. Often they are stereotyped as valuable only in the exploratory stage of marketing surveys, but they also have great value in putting the flesh back on the statistical bones that too often are the final result of a segmentation study. Holding focus group sessions among people in the target segment can be extremely helpful in developing appropriate communications.

Media planning was a more difficult problem because the research did not measure media exposure directly and, as so often happens, the six benefit segments were not well differentiated by demographic data. Consequently, emphasis was placed on matching the editorial environments of eligible magazines with the benefits offered in individual advertisements. The expectations with which readers approach various magazines were also taken into account.

Magazine inserts of eight and 16 pages were prepared for target segments for appropriate regions of Canada. For example, the Quebec and Ontario inserts were designed with the Foreign Travel Adventurer in mind, whereas those for Manitoba and Saskatchewan were aimed at the Outdoor Vacationer. Again focus group sessions were used to evaluate and revise the inserts.

Results of the Canadian program have, in the words of Myron Rusk of the Canadian Government Office of Tourism," been so successful that we have continued and broadened this program." Applications of this study were also reported to have been made by the two major Canadian air carriers and by provincial government tourist offices. The vacation products they offered were tailored to the trip benefits sought by U.S. vacationers.

The Benefit Segmentation approach has been found to be applicable to other nonpackage goods areas. Ardyce Haring successfully applied it to claims for unemployment compensation in New York City. Sawyer and Arbeit compared Benefit Segmentation with other segmentation strategies and found it more effective in determining the market segments appropriate to the banking industry[11] and Lewis found it an insightful tool in the restaurant industry.[12] Quoting from Lewis,

> Restaurant positioning and Benefit Segmentation are powerful tools on which to base advertising strategy and to determine marketing direction. In short, this study provides the means to find new approaches to restaurant advertising both for the industry and for a particular restaurant type. Further similar research can provide individual tools for leading restaurant advertising out of clichés and demographics, and for understanding that the joint-interaction effects of attribute beliefs represent a whole larger than the sum of its parts.[13]

[11] A. Haring, "Work or Welfare: An Attitude Segmentation of ADC Clients," Human Resources Administration, New York City, July 1973.

[12] A. G. Sawyer and S. Arbeit, "Benefit Segmentation in a Retail Banking Market," in *1973 Combined Proceedings*, T. V. Greer (Ed.), Series No. 35, Chicago: American Marketing Association, 1974.

[13] R. C. Lewis, "Restaurant Advertising: Appeals and Consumers' Intentions," *Journal of Advertising Research*, Vol. 21, No. 5, October 1981, pp. 69–74.

FOURTEEN

An Overview of Attitude Segmentation Research

Most major package goods marketers have conducted one or more attitude segmentation studies in the past 10 years, with Benefit Segmentation the most popular type. In recent years attitude segmentation has been attempted in an increasingly diverse range of markets. But as noted, most attitude segmentation studies have been conducted in highly competitive industries, and there are relatively few instances in which the results of these studies have been published. In the few cases in which studies have been reported, the reports rarely contain details of the findings, how they have been used to guide marketing decisions, and the results of such applications. Most summaries, including even some of those cited in the preceding chapter, are generalized and glossy; often they are very outdated.

Although Benefit Segmentation studies are likely to continue to be popular in applied research circles, a number of misconceptions about them,[1] largely based on limited experience with them, have slowed their more general acceptance. Therefore, in concluding this book it may be productive to summarize some of the primary complaints that have been voiced about them and to respond to those complaints as someone thoroughly experienced with Benefit Segmentation research might respond.

Criticisms have come from three general sources—from marketing people, from methodologically oriented market researchers, and from academic researchers. Among them have been the following:

---

[1] See E. M. Tauber, "Editorial: Stamp Out the Generic Segmentation Study," *Journal of Advertising Research,* Vol. 23, No. 2, April/May 1983, p. 7.

383

From marketing people:

We did a segmentation study and it didn't work. This could mean almost anything. The most frequent reasons for this particular comment relate to:

Unrealistic expectations such as expecting that a series of complex multivariate analyses will somehow automatically indicate the kinds of marketing actions that should be taken.[2]

Not understanding that the primary payoffs of a Benefit Segmentation study are in the area of communications.

Not taking time to organize properly for the study. Also not forming a project team and staffing it with the right people in the organization and its agency or agencies.

Not undertaking a series of follow-through actions once the study is complete. Assuming that the study will provide "answers" and that all that is required is to put them into effect.

Segmentation studies are not action oriented. This comment suggests that the person offering it did not specify the objectives of the study in advance. This usually means that the most productive ways of analyzing the data have not been decided upon before the data become available. In such cases it is not unusual for the research team to virtually drown in the data—to generate such a huge volume of tabulations from so many different perspectives that it is almost impossible to extract a coherent analysis from them.

The segments we came up with didn't make sense. This could be a technical problem (see Chapter 8). It can also stem from strong preconceptions about the market, however, and a lack of willingness to change those preconceptions. Although it may seem ludicrous it is nonetheless true that in one instance a major corporation decided that a pro forma segmentation grid, used at the study proposal stage to illustrate the sorts of data that *might* be provided by the research, was preferable to the actual data produced by the research—and based their marketing planning upon it!

The segments we found were not clear-cut. This could be a technical problem relating to the choice of attitude items included in the research or to their reliability. In the experience of the author it is *always* reasonable to expect significant differences in brand shares when the segmentation work is done thoroughly, but it could also signify unrealistic

---

[2] This is what Tauber calls the Generic Segmentation study. He points out, that, properly understood, "segmentation research does work and can be immensely valuable."

expectations about the kinds of differences likely to occur. Although most segmentation studies produce sizable differences among segments, a few markets do not appear to have sharply defined segments. Operating in a radarlike fashion, however, Benefit Segmentation can provide a general outline of the nature of the segments that exist, even in these markets. Moreover small statistical differences often mean large differences in responses to alternative marketing actions. Finally if no one has recognized the existence of a given segment and concentrated their marketing activities on it, the boundaries of the segment may remain somewhat vague. This situation can change quickly, however, when the segment is addressed in a custom-tailored fashion.

Segmentation research is not an effective way to find new product opportunities.   This is probably an accurate comment. If the primary objective of the research is the development of new products, there are more efficient ways to proceed. This does not mean, however, that segmentation studies do not turn up new products—they do. But their primary value is in market target identification, repositioning existing products, and defining competitive environments.

"Even if segmentation research were successful, implementation would be difficult because media, which provide the information, do not have data relevant for segmentation purposes"[3] Because this was written, media planning databanks have added the information needed for lifestyle segmentation (PRIZM, Acorn, and VALS). Although lifestyle information is less useful than benefit information (see Chapter 1), this is a step in the right direction. In focusing on media and ignoring the function of copy, however, this statement misses the point. Copy is a much more potent tool than media in segmenting audiences. Through the mechanisms of selective processes (see Chapter 2) it can pull in substantially different market segments through variations in its content. Benefit Segmentation studies provide a great deal of assistance in the area of copy. They also can be helpful in media selections, as has been pointed out elsewhere in this book. But contributions with respect to copy development are undoubtedly larger than to media selection and scheduling.

No matter which segment we choose as our target more of our purchases come from outside the target than within it. So targeting through Benefit Segments is a waste of time.   Of course, this is not always the case. When it is, however, it is invariably true that the *per capita* rate of purchase *in* the target segment is *higher* than *outside* it. Also as experiments will verify, it is always easier to obtain incremental volume from the tar-

---

[3] "Book Based on FTC Study Skeptical of Brand Managers, Market Research," *Advertising Age*, March 19, 1973, p. 88.

get segment than elsewhere provided the segment has been properly identified. Thus the return per unit of effort invested is higher when attention is concentrated on the target segment.

If you're considering attitude segmentation research, lifestyles offer a much larger payoff than benefits.   This is rarely true. In the great majority of product categories the product benefits sought by individuals are much better predictors of their brand choice behavior than their lifestyles.[4] Specific actions such as brand choice are rarely predicted accurately by generalized statements about how people are living their lives. Thus although increasing numbers of consumers were agreeing with the statement "It's important to be attractive to the opposite sex," use of hair colorings was declining. And although more people were agreeing with the idea that "meal preparation should take as little time as possible," use of frozen vegetables and frozen dinners was declining.[5] It is certainly true, however, that services such as VALS and the Yankelovich Monitor are very popular, and that major agencies such as Leo Burnett and Young & Rubicam have publicized their regular use of lifestyle information in copy development. Fortunately it is not necessary to choose either benefits or lifestyles to the exclusion of the other universe of content. Intelligent marketers will include both benefit ratings and lifestyle ratings in their segmentaiton research studies, and they will use them in concert in their final market segment interpretations.

We can't afford the time and energy that a segmentation study requires.   The payoffs for an effective communications strategy are huge in relation to the costs involved. Most companies can't afford to bypass a tool that holds so much potential.

People play games in interview situations. They do not answer questionnaires accurately enough to predict their behavior.   The evidence suggests otherwise. The more favorable a consumer's attitude toward a brand the more likely he or she is to use it. When a person's attitude toward a brand improves, the probability that he or she will switch to it increases. And when a consumer's attitude toward a brand in use deteriorates, the likelihood that he or she will try another brand increases. Similarly, if a person places a high value on convenience and a low value on price, he or she is likely to choose brands perceived as more convenient even if they cost a little more.[6]

---

[4] W. Willkie, "An Empirical Analysis of Alternative Bases for Market Segmentation," Unpublished doctoral dissertation, Stanford University, 1970.

[5] W. Wells, "Do Trends in Attitudes Predict Trends in Behavior?," ANA Advertising Research Workshop, New York, December 9, 1981.

[6] A. A. Achenbaum, "How Advertising Works: A study of the relationship between Advertising, Consumer Attitudes, and Purchase Behavior," New York: Grey Advertising, 1968.

From market researchers:

Emotional and sensory benefits are short-suited in the typcial Benefit Segmentation study.   This is an unfortunate limitation of Benefit Segmentation research as it is normally conducted. It is also a limitation of every form of questionnaire research in which the stimuli are provided to respondents in the form of words and phrases on white cards or in the form of a self-administered questionnaire. Theoretically it should be possible to overcome this shortcoming by presenting respondents with more complex stimuli (e.g., ads or commercials) which focus on the kinds of emotional benefit that are not well communicated by white cards. Unfortunately we do not, at the present state of the art, know enough about nonverbal and emotional communications to be sure that we can accomplish this in a single-minded fashion. As messages take a more complex form they run a high risk of departing from the "single-minded" standard. Experimentation is badly needed in this area,[7] perhaps more so than in any area of communications research. Some efforts are already under way and there is good reason to hope for significant progress in our understanding of these areas over the next five to 10 years.[8]

Segmentation research almost never shows the package to be an important factor in purchase. Yet we know it often is very important in actual purchase situations.   Again we are dealing with a nonverbal stimulus and consumers' cognitive responses to questionnaires. In an interview situation it is unlikely that consumers will attach sufficient weight to the influence of in-store factors such as package and display, and perhaps even price, on their brand choices. Experience has shown, however, that when ratings for these factors are comparatively high for a given respondent (in relation to the average level of his or her ratings and relative levels for other respondents),[9] he or she is likely to be more responsive than the average consumer to marketing actions focused on that item.

Another approach to dealing with the specific problem of packaging is to use the physical package or color photographs of it during the exposure situation.[10] Previous research on the role of the package should be helpful in deciding how far to go in this respect.

---

[7] R. Haley, "Advertising Research: We've Come a Long Way Baby," Keynote address, 8th Annual Midyear Conference of the ARF, Chicago, September 15–17, 1982.

[8] R. I. Haley, J. F. Richardson, and B. M. Baldwin, "The Effects of Non-verbal Communications in Television Advertising," *Journal of Advertising Research,* August/September 1984, Vol. 24, No. 4, pp. 11–18.

[9] This point holds for emotional items as well.

[10] In the Corning dinnerware example a detailed study was done to determine whether respondent preferences from color photographs would parallel those based on exposure to the actual dinnerware. They did.

We couldn't interpret one (or more than one) segment in our last segmentation study. This suggests that either not enough time was allocated to the analysis of results, that there are important technical shortcomings in the statistical methods employed, or both. Although some sequences of statistical analysis seem to be more effective than others, and although each analyst has his or her favorite procedures, no one set of methods is "best" for all configurations of the data. To determine whether the methods used are at fault it is advisable to test the effect of using alternative approaches. For example, there are several methods of factor extraction in factor analyses and a large number of alternative rotation schemes. Similarily a wide assortment of clustering algorithms is available for use.

If time and money are available, it is a good idea to test alternative methods on each study, but that is frequently not the case. As long as the approach used (presumably one that has worked well on other studies) produces segments that meet the test of face validity and that are discriminated on key variables, it is reasonably safe to proceed. Where results are puzzling, however, it is best to backtrack and see if the methods are at fault.

To a large degree the selection of a system of segmentation is arbitrary. To some extent this is true. There is no way to assure that you have developed *the* best segmentation of a given market, but there are some objective criteria for assessing the quality of alternative segmentations. For example, they can be compared in terms of how well they discriminate on key measures. Also they can be compared in terms of their split-half reliability. In the last analysis, however, the test of a segmentation system is how well it leads to productive marketing actions. And the appropriate standard of comparison is the analytic framework being used to understand the market before the new segmentation perspective became available.

The importance of benefits depends upon occasions of consumption. Therefore, occasions are a more meaningful way of segmenting markets than benefits. In some markets segmentation by occasions turns out to be a highly effective mode of segmentation. But even in those markets there is no reason to exclude benefits from the analysis. Occasions and benefits are often inseparably intertwined. Moreover, when segmenting by benefits is compared with segmenting by occasions, the strategy of forcusing on a selected benefit or benefit set across occasions often turns out to be more effective than focusing on a single occasion or set of occasions.

Benefit segmentation doesn't carry you far enough. For example, it's not enough to know that people would like a pleasant flavor. You need to know whether it is peppermint, spearmint, wintergreen, or some other flavor.   Benefit segmentation is strategic research. Followup tactical research, including product tests, is always needed. However, it is helpful to know about those who are particularly sensitive to the flavor issue. In that way custom communications can be designed to reach them. Also the ability to identify the flavor-oriented segment should help in the development of sampling specifications for product testing.

The phraseology of individual benefits is important. That is why so much up-front work is recommended in selecting the precise items to be used in the final phase (Phase III) of interviewing. Usually no one item stands alone. If flavor is represented in a questionnaire, it is represented by several items. And when a respondent, through his or her ratings, signals interest in all or most of them, this respondent can accurately be labeled as flavor conscious.

We didn't find a segment we know is there.   Again this suggests insufficient up-front work. In Phase I and Phase II research hypotheses about the market should be developed, together with ways of measuring key factors in a sensitive, reliable, unambiguous, and valid way. If the proper items are included in the measuring instrument, the segmentation procedures should uncover all major segments. If you have confidence in your measuring instrument, perhaps it is time to reexamine the evidence that led you to believe in the existence of the missing segment.

Segmentation procedures don't predict an individual's membership in a segment accurately. When test-retest reliability studies are done, it is found that many individuals are classified in different segments the second time.   In part this is due to the popular practice of forcing *all* individuals into a relatively small number of segments, usually between three and six. Some individuals have low levels of association with *any* of the segments, and thus their classifications are not reliable.

Another contributing factor is the practice of classifying each respondent into one and only one segment. Some respondents have similar probabilities of membership in two, and even three, segments. When they are forced into one segment on the first occasion, a slight shift in their probabilities on the second occasion can cause a change in their classification. This does not mean that the classification method is unstable.

On the contrary, there is a substantial amount of evidence[11, 12] that the

[11] R. J. Calantone and A. G. Sawyer, "The Stability of Benefit Segments," *Journal of Marketing Research,* Vol. 17, No. 1, February 1977, pp. 60–68.
[12] I. Fenwick, D. A. Schellinck, and K. W. Kendall, "Assessing the Stability of Psychographic Analysis," Working Paper No. 9, School of Business Administration, Dalhousie U., Halifax, Canada, August 1981.

nature of major market segments remains very stable over time. The author was involved in one large tracking study, for example, where segments were reliably reproduced each quarter for three and one-half years. Groups are always easier to predict then individuals[13] and the facts indicate that despite the greater variability and greater difficulty in predicting *individuals* when groups are predicted (e.g., Benefit Segments) their sizes and compositions generally show little change from one year to the next. Over longer periods of time, of course, they do change, but only as a reflection of actual changes occurring in the marketplace.

A classic case of the problems that can beset a two phase segmentation study was reported by Yuspeh and Fein.[14] A Benefit Segmentation study was done among a sample of 1200 people using a 72-item battery of benefits, and a combination of personal and self-administered interviews was conducted. Q factor analysis was applied to the responses, and five intuitively pleasing segments were revealed. A split-half reliability test of the five-group structure was conducted, and it was found that 74% of all core members (defined as people having factor loadings of at least .30 on their Q group and requiring that that loading be at least .10 higher than their loading on any other Q group) could be correctly classified into the equivalent segment in the opposite half.

Using predictive equations developed with a reduced set of 12 items, samples drawn in subsequent copy tests and a telephone tracking study were classified back into the five original segments. In comparing behavioral and demographic information from the tracking study with parallel information from the original segmentation study, it was found that major discrepancies existed from segment to segment. Respondents from the original study were then recontacted by telephone,[15] and it was found that the prediction equations were unable to classify them properly back into their original segments. The situation was remedied when new predictive equations, utilizing demograhic and behavioral information, as well as benefit ratings, were developed and were found to do a satisfactory job of classification.

A postmortem on this case provides several useful guidelines for researchers who wish to avoid similar problems.

1.   *Benefit items should be tested for reliability.*   Unreliable items can substantially reduce predictive power.[16] In the study under review the 72

---

[13] F. M. Bass, D. J. Tigert, and R. F. Lonsdale, "Marketing Segmentation: Group versus Individual Behavior," *Journal of Marketing Research*, Vol. 5, August 1968, pp. 264–270.

[14] S. Yuspeh and G. Fein, "Can Segments Be Born Again?" *Journal of Advertising Research*, Vol. 22, No. 3, June/July 1982, pp. 13–22.

[15] The original segments had been developed on the basis of responses gathered via in-home personal interviews.

[16] J. C. Nunnally, *Psychometric Theory*, New York: McGraw-Hill, 1967.

items were presumably selected intuitively. Although split-half reliability tests were conducted to check the stability of the five segments they produced, it is not clear how the reliability of individual items was determined.

2. *Relationships among items should be tested for reliability.* Fenwick, Schellinck, and Kendall[17] have suggested that this can be accomplished by first factor analyzing the benefits using the full sample of respondents, and then using the Jacknife technique,[18] which splits the sample into a number of equal-sized subgroups and repeats the analysis, dropping a different subgroup each time. Because rotation affects factor loadings, it is also necessary to rotate each of the solutions obtained to the solution obtained from the total sample. One procedure for accomplishing this is the CLIFFMATCH program.[19]

3. *Using a combination of R factor analysis and cluster analysis is preferable to using Q analysis.* A number of investigators have pointed out the shortcomings of Q analysis and have suggested that cluster analysis is a more effective procedure for segmentation problems.[20]

4. *In deciding when predictive equations are sufficiently accurate for regular use, it is important to look at accuracy by individual segment as well as overall accuracy.* Although the equations in the study in question were able to achieve a 74% accuracy rate overall (only slightly below the 80% norm cited earlier in this book), this was largely because of the 84% accuracy rate obtained in one of the segments. Three of the remaining four segments showed only two-thirds of their members being accurately classified, substantially below the desirable 80% rate.

5. *Core group membership should be defined conservatively.* In this instance it was possible to be assigned to a segment with a loading of only 0.3. A more conservative level, depending on opinions as to the desirability of assigning *all* respondents to segments, might have been 0.5.

6. *Equations developed from one mode of interviewing cannot be applied, without modification, to other modes of interviewing.* In the study under review the original segmentation was based on scaled responses obtained from *personal* interviews and self-administered questionnaires. Responses were obtained by *telephone* in the tracking study and recontact

[17] I. Fenwick, D. A. Schellinck and K. W. Kendall, "Assessing the Stability of Psychographic Analysis," Working Paper No. 9, School of Business Administration, Dalhousie University, Halifax, Canada, August 1981.

[18] J. W. Tukey, "Bias and Confidence in Not-Quite Large Samples," *Annals of Mathematical Statistics,* Vol. 29, June 1958, pp. 614ff.

[19] N. Cliff, "Orthogonal Rotation to Congruence," *Psychometrika,* Vol. 31, March 1966, pp. 33–42.

[20] *American Marketing Association Combined Proceedings,* 1975, p. 211. Also, D. W. Stewart, "The Application and Misapplication of Factor Analysis in Marketing Research," *Journal of Marketing Research,* February 1981, pp. 51–62.

surveys. Because scaled response patterns in personal interviews are different than responses to the same items over the telephone, the lack of predictive power found in the original equations is not surprising. If tracking studies are to be used to follow up the segmentation study (as they should be), it is important that the interviewing methods in both studies be identical. Thus if telephone interviews are to be used to obtain scaled ratings in the tracking study, they should also be used in the original Benefit Segmentation study. Alternatively if personal interviews are required for some reason in the benchmark study (e.g., so that pictorial material can be exposed to respondents), ratings should be obtained orally, in the same manner that they will be obtained in followup research on the telephone.

Aside from the problem of using different modes of interviewing, however, the Yuspeh/Fein study was conducted in accordance with procedures in common use and was probably above average in terms of the quality of effort involved. Extensive reliability checking, although important, is expensive, thus this step is often omitted. The risks of doing so are clarified by the results obtained in this instance.

The clustering procedures themselves are unreliable. An article by Funkhouser questions the reliability of some clustering algorithms.[21] His illustration involves seven clusters. It is certainly true that the larger the number of clusters produced the greater the risk that unreliability will become a problem. The problem is less severe at the most frequent four- and five-cluster solution level, however, particularly if item reliability and correlation structure reliability can be assured before the clustering begins (93% of the respondents were in similar clusters at the four-group level). Funkhouser also suggests that, to minimize reliability problems, unstandardized input be used and that cluster membership not be decided at levels of precision that are higher than those justified by the precision of the input data.

People don't have to be divided into groups. The segmentation job can be done more thoroughly via perceptual mapping.[22] The approach suggested has a number of technical advantages; however, it suffers from communications problems when attempts are made to give all members of the project team a strong intuitive grasp of the findings. Maps, especially if they involve more than two or three dimensions, are often hard for marketing people to translate into suggested marketing actions.

On the other hand, marketing and creative people are accustomed to

[21] G. R. Funkhouser, "A Note on the Reliability of Certain Clustering Algorithms," *Journal of Marketing Research*, Vol. 20, February 1983, pp. 99–102.

[22] R. M. Johnson, "Market Segmentation: A Strategic Management Tool," *Journal of Marketing Research*, Vol. 8, February 1971, pp. 13–18.

thinking in terms of target groups and in attempting to personify them. Also they are familiar with and have been exposed to a great many cross-tabulations. The process of contrasting target people with other people in great detail so as to understand them is almost inevitably well received. Thus the project team is able to proceed to the implications of the research findings as they should, without becoming involved in the technical methods employed in the research. Mapping is a useful adjunct to segmentation studies and is especially helpful in defining competitive environments. However, the process of dividing people into segments and examining each segment individually is invaluable.

From academic researchers:

People are members of overlapping segments in actuality. Segmentation studies generally ignore this factor and they should not.[23]   Segmentation studies do ignore overlapping segments, but whether they should continue to do so is debatable. The virtues of the simplicity of the conceptual frame and the accompanying ease of communicating research results have already been discussed. Actually there is nothing in present Benefit Segmentation procedures to prevent overlapping segments from being used. A score reflecting the association between the desired benefit profile of each individual and the desired benefit profile for each segment is developed in the course of the research. All that is required is deciding what level of this score is required for membership in a given segment. With a very small change in the programming, overlapping segments can be produced. How well they will be understood by marketing people is an open question. It seems doubtful, however, that any reformulation which introduces overlapping segments would significantly alter the implications of a Benefit Segmentation study.

The fact that academics have not given more emphasis to Benefit Segmentation in their textbooks indicates that the method is not worth extended study.   Only occasionally do academics get involved in Benefit Segmentation research. And even more infrequently do they get involved in the numerous follow-through activities that occur once the initial three-phase project has been completed. Thus it is difficult for them to accumulate enough experience to generalize about the utility of the method. So although it is referenced, it is rarely covered in depth.

Contributing to the lack of academic coverage are the numerous approaches that have been suggested as potential solutions to the attitude

[23] P. Arabie, J. D. Carroll, W. DeSarbo, and J. Wind, "Overlapping Clustering: A New Method for Product Positioning," *Journal of Marketing Research*, Vol. 18, August 1981, pp. 310–317.

segmentation problem. In attempting to give some coverage to all of these (most have been suggested by academicians rather than by applied practitioners), it may be inevitable that less coverage has been given to the methods favored by practitioners than they deserve.

Benefit Segmentation involves outmoded techniques. There are better methods of segmenting markets. This comment mistakes the main thrust of Benefit Segmentation. The main thrust is philosophical rather than technical. This book presents the case for Benefit Segmentation. In doing so it lays out procedures that, if followed, will virtually guarantee useful results. The statistical methods are a relatively small part of those procedures, however. The main point is that if the objective of the marketer is to develop an effective communications strategy, it is useful to consider the market as being composed of several market segments, each comprised of people seeking different combinations of benefits. Moreover in most situations the benefit orientation is likely to be the best of several alternative orientations, all of which are worth testing.

An overview of alternative methods of market segmentation was provided by Frank et al.[24] a decade ago. Since then alternative procedures have been suggested at the rate of two or three every year.[25] And there are advocates for conjoint analysis, tradeoff analysis, canonical analysis, componential segmentation, Benemax, Q analysis, cluster analysis, discriminant mapping, and other approaches. These should not obscure the fact that Benefit Segmentation has withstood the test of time. It is still being used successfully more than 20 years after its initial development. No other market segmentation research approach has produced more successes, and no research directions suggested thus far appear likely to make it obsolete. But that is because its success is not based on statistical methods. Rather the keys to success are realistic objectives, careful organization, adequate time for analysis, and coordinated follow-through activities. Finally it has one saving grace. Although it by no means represents the ultimate in statistical sophistication, and although it inevitably involves some subjective elements, in a world of confusing, complex, highly mathematical, and frequently disappointing approaches, this one works!

[24] R. E. Frank, W. F. Massy and Y. Wind, *Market Segmentation*, Englewood Cliffs, NJ, Prentice-Hall, 1972.

[25] R. C. Blattberg and S. K. Sen, "Market Segmentation Using Models of Multidimensional Purchasing Behavior," *Journal of Marketing*, Vol. 38, October 1974, pp. 17–28. P. P. Dickson, "Person-Situation: Segmentation's Missing Link," *Journal of Marketing*, Fall 1982, Vol. 46, No. 4, pp. 56–64.

Copy Executions from Experiment on Predicting Attention

See pages 144 to 159 for a detailed description of the experiment.

There's one place we'll never fly to.
DULLSVILLE

An airline is an airline is an airline.
Or is it?

The difference is in the service. Courteous. Friendly. Genuine. When our stewardesses greet you with a cheery "Good morning", they *mean* have a **good** morning.

There's more fun in flying for *us* when it's more fun for you. That's why we place a little more stress on our friendly service. It makes your flight a fun flight.

A smile goes a long, long way. Even on a short hop.

United Air Lines

396

Name your travel dream...we'll put it all together

Here's the way to have a vacation you and your family will remember for years to come. Just tell us your dream and we'll do all the planning, make all the reservations, get you things you couldn't have gotten yourself—*and bring it in within your budget.*

Our name? Eastern Airlines. Our business? Making vacations really fun. Relaxing. Smooth. Unforgettable. Sensibly budgeted. Do as thousands of others have done—name your travel dream and let Eastern Airlines put it together.

 EASTERN

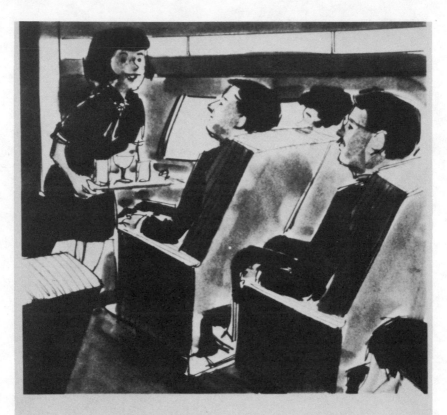

It's fun and friendly on American Airlines

They say that getting there is half the fun and American Airlines makes sure its true. From the sidewalk check-in to the baggage claim area, friendly American Airlines personnel are there to serve *you*.

There's complimentary coffee 'n cake in the boarding lounge. And on board, you'll be served h'ors d'oevres when you purchase a cocktail. Playing cards, puzzles and a wide assortment of reading materials are available to help you wile away the hours. And, on flights taking four or more hours, you'll see an Academy Award movie. So make sure getting there really is fun. Fly American Airlines.

American Airlines

"Now that you have arrived..."

...it's time for that Chevrolet. Remember, when you put your foot on the first rung of the ladder, the promise you made yourself? That when you reached the top, you would buy nothing but the finest. Well, now you have arrived, and it is time to keep your promise. The world's finest motor car is waiting for you.

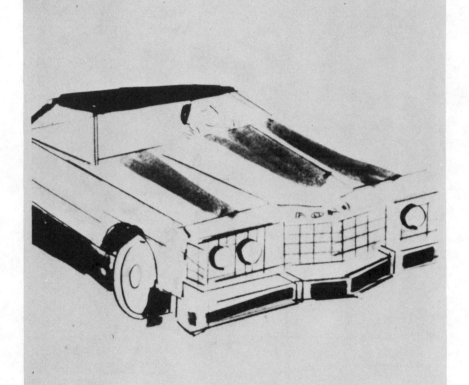

"Meet your 1978 Ford"

Funny thing . . . looks just like the '73, doesn't it. Well, it is. But if you're like most Ford owners, there's a good chance that the Ford you buy today will be giving you the same reliable service five years from now. Toughness . . . durability . . . reliability . . . they're built into every model we make, and every part of every car. The result is a machine that will keep you rolling, year after marching year.

How to become the envy of your neighborhood in one easy lesson

Simple. Drive home in a brand new Saab. See the eyes of your own kids light up. Catch the envy in the faces of your neighbors as they touch the chrome, open and slam the doors, listen to the 8 track hi-fi system and touch the deep lustre, vinyl upholstery.

Now . . . in one easy lesson . . . you'll suddenly comprehend the prestige of owning and driving a brand new Saab. See your own pride of ownership reflected by your wife as she slides in beside you for her first drive.
Be the "King of the Road." See your Saab dealer today.

Saab

401

THE SLUM SCHOOL
THAT WORKS

LEAPschool opened four years
ago in a storefront New York's
lower east side. It was started by a
young educator, Michelle Cole, and
grew out of her work with her
Psychologist husband, Larry.

They wanted to give street kids
a better chance. A place where they
could live and grow up and survive
the usual pitfalls of street life.

These are kids who failed in the
public schools, or maybe the public schools failed them either way.
LEAPschool gives them a last chance.

It's not like any school you remember, but then the world isn't
the way you remember either.
LEAPschool has no deans, no
hall guards, no enforcers, no drug
problem.

Nobody says you kids better
come to school, and nobody goes
out looking for them if they don't.

Each kid has basic courses that
he has to take, but kids and adults
decide together what other courses
should be taught and which ones
each kid should attend.

Adults and kids also make the

rules, and if they're broken they
deal with each other. These kids
grow up hating authority suddenly
they are authority.

It's a school that has 'houses'
and 'segments' and 'group trips'.
And the teachers talk to the kids
eyeball to eyeball, on an equal basis.

because it makes them better
teachers.

When a kid graduates and decides on college, that's great. Or
when he decides to work in his
community equipped with the necessary skills to succeed at whatever,
that's great too. But what's greatest
is kids able to make decisions.

Last year the Cole's took over an
old A&P and built a permanent
school. The student 'hustle committee' got corporations to donate
tile and bricks and pipe but one job
that's never finished is finding the
cash to keep going.

The Cole's have turned down
government money, because that
means doing things the government way and that would kill the
spirit of the school. Right now

LEAPschool works. Losing that
would be a shame.

Maybe you can help out, or maybe you work for a company that
sees the value in educating kids
who want an education, but who
have left the system. If so, please
write:

LEAPschool
540 East 13th Street
New York, N.Y. 10009

We guarantee that one hundred
cents of every dollar you give goes
directly to LEAPschool. And if
you'd like to visit the school, the
results will be there for you to see,
in black and white and brown, or
whatever color a kid may be.

LEAPschool

402

This Sunday, don't let the light go out on the children of Biafra.

This Sunday, keep a light burning in your window through the night. A light that says you believe in a lifeline for Biafra, not a deadline.

This Sunday, an Interfaith Service will be held at St. Thomas Church, 53rd Street and Fifth Ave., New York City at 2:00 P.M.

This Sunday, "a little child shall lead them." The service will be followed by a children's march to the United Nations.

This Sunday night, keep the light burning for the children dying in Biafra.

The American Committee to Keep Biafra Alive, 2440 Broadway, New York, N.Y. 10024

Only God can make a tree

But happily, we can plant them. Each year, thousands of trees must be sacrificed in order to provide us with essential needs. Paper, furniture—the very houses in which we live. St. Regis recognized the need for conservation of our forests a long time ago. And we're doing something constructive about it by re-seeding the millions of acres in our care. St. Regis has a future, and so do their forests.

ST REGIS

Why HAMMERMILL is a good neighbor

Hammermill operates plants in 29 American cities, distribution centers in 68 and sales offices in 142 more. In total, the Hammermill family numbers more than 158,000 Americans.

We are proud of our associates and the contributions they make to their home communities. Hammermill supports and encourages local bowling leagues, softball teams and Little League Baseball. We provide professional leadership to local charity drives, and urge our associates to participate in an active way.

Hammermill is an Equal Opportunity Employer. We operate a wide variety of innovative apprentice and job training programs designed to open up additional employment opportunities for people from all walks of life. If you seek a better future, come see us at the Hammermill installation nearest your home community.

HAMMERMILL

- A good place to work
- A good company for growth
- A good neighbor

HAMMERMILL

Save for retirement the easy way

Planning for your retirement is sound and sensible, but it shouldn't put you in the poorhouse.

Home Insurance is just as concerned about your financial well-being today as it is about your retirement well-being. And so Home Insurance developed an insurance plan that makes paying premiums almost easy.

We arrange for your employer to deduct just pennies a day from your salary and send these deductions directly to Home Insurance each month. All you do is watch your retirement income grow as you receive your quarterly statements.

So call your Home Insurance representative today. He can develop a plan for *you* that will make paying premiums almost easy.

Save $20 a week now...retire on $400 a month!

Imagine the security and peace of mind that can be yours to retire on $400 a month *plus* social security *plus* your organization's retirement benefits. And that $400 a month is *interest* not principal.

How do you do it? Easy. If you're 35 years old or younger, come in and join our Golden Years Club. Deposit $20 a week. Let the Golden Years Club high interest rate compound, and at retirement, you'll have a *minimum* of $400 interest a month for the rest of your life.

Come in today and join the Golden Years Club.

Allstate
You're in good hands

A vacation requires two very precious commodities: Time and money. We specialize in making the most of both

It's your time and money. Would you entrust them to just anybody?

At TWA we have specialists to serve you in your travel and vacation planning. They've personally checked out whatever place you want to visit. That's part of their job.

Just let us know where you want to go (or merely the *type* of place you're looking for), when you want to go, and whatever likes and dislikes you'd care to list. We'll plan your vacation around them. At TWA we don't think of our customers as fussy. We think of them as fastidious.

408

*Economy car? After 50,000 miles
only the tires had to be changed*

Meet the Prescott's of Old Westbury, N.Y.

For the first 50,000 miles, following their dealer's routine maintenance schedule, they spent less than $65 for repairs. That doesn't, of course, include the cost of the new steel belted radials which had to be replaced at 48,000. The Prescotts report that after all those miles, many of them grueling, the car still glides smoothly along the road, just as it did the first day they owned it.

We have always made the Volvo to be durable, lasting and to hold its value for many years. That is what makes it such a worthwhile investment.

Perhaps the nicest thing you can say about a Volvo is that it's worth every penny.

A job is a job is a job...

410

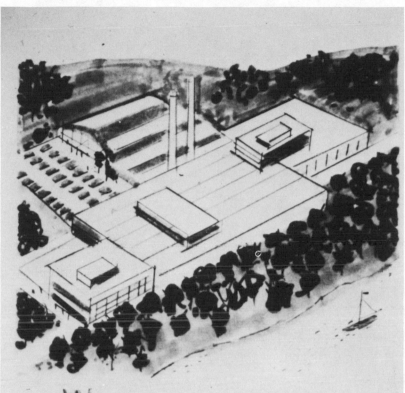

Waste not...want not

Manufacturing paper involves more than you might think. Chemicals, solvents and other materials necessary in production eventually become waste matter. And this is what pollutes the air and fouls the water.

But once we set our minds to it, the problem was solvable. We hired a team of chemists who were able to develop safer, purer means of disposal. Our smokestacks have cooled down since the installation of sophisticated blowers designed to disperse waste matter more evenly, so that the air remains clean. And we'll continue our responsibility by keeping up with new developments designed to save our environment.

At IBM - we care!

Benefit Segmentation Exercise

1. GENERAL DIRECTIONS

Select a product category of interest to you, then conduct exploratory research within it. For example, you may wish to visit outlets where the product or service is sold and talk to the people who sell it. Or you may want to observe people buying it. Or you may simply want to talk with people who can be considered a part of the market for it. Or you may want to look through magazines to see what sort of advertising is being done and to draw inferences about how the advertisers and copywriters view their customers and their interests. Because this phase is largely qualitative, almost any line of inquiry that you feel might be productive is worth pursuing. The objective is merely to obtain insights into the kinds of things that people consider when they make a purchase decision and the ways in which they decide that some alternatives are attractive and others are not. (If you would prefer a more structured approach, one is outlined in the following section.) Once you have a fairly good idea about the kinds of benefits being sought, speculate as to the kinds of segments that exist. Which are seen as attractive targets by the major competitors in the category? Which marketers are competing for the same segments? Which for different ones? Are any segments being missed entirely? To aid in your analysis of the market fill out the Segmentation Grid on page 415. It provides space for up to seven segments. Use only as many as you feel are appropriate to the market being analyzed. Similarly fill in only the rows that are relevant for your product or service.

413

2. SOME SUGGESTED PROCEDURES

From current or prospective customers, and using your own judgment, compile a list of the more important benefits sought. Make sure that the items you list do not overlap each other any more than is necessary. Present this composite list of the benfits for your product/services to respondents on a sheet of paper. Ask the respondents to place 10 points (pennies, poker chips, etc.) in the boxes next to the benefits that are most important to them in selecting the product for their use. If you have more than four benefits, 20 points may be a better number of points. Allow the respondents to re-arrange the points, pennies, and so on, as often as they wish in order for them to weigh the tradeoffs of the benefits you have presented them. First make sure those questioned are users of your generic product; that is, does the respondent use razor blades, drink coffee, and so on?

Generic Product Class—Bread

☐ Freshness

☐ Nutrition/nourishing

☐ Economy

☐ Taste

☐ Good sandwich bread

☐ Good smell

After you have collected data from 15–20 respondents, you should construct a matrix of the data. Make sure every column adds to 10.

RESPONDENTS (20 respondents identified 1–20)

		1	2	3	4	5	6	7	8	.	.	.	.	20
B	Freshness	3	5	2										
E	Nutrition	2	1	1										
N	Economy	0	2	5										
E	Taste	3	0	2										
F	Good sandwich bread	1	2	0										
I														
T	Good smell	1	0	0										
S	Other benefits	0	0	0										
		0	0	0										

Figure B.1. Sample instrument for consumer tradeoff analysis.

Segmentation Grid

	Segment 1	Segment 2	Segment 3	Segment 4	Segment 5	Segment 6	Segment 7
Name of the segment							
Benefits sought							
Category beliefs							
Brands/products favored							
Volume of consumption							
Occasions of use							
Media habits							
Personality/lifestyle							
Demographics							

415

From a visual inspection of the data you should be able to see groups of consumers who have similar configurations of benefits sought. Persons who are generally high on similar benefits and, at the same time, low on similar benefits are considered to be those with similar configurations. Circle all values of 3 or higher to help you spot the patterns of response. If you find you have too many circles, use 4 as your cutoff level instead of 3.

When you find a similar group of people, you can begin to fill out your segmentation grid. Start by entering the benefits of interest to them in the row labeled "Benefits Sought." Then go down the column, fleshing out the nature of the segment by filling in as many of the elements in that column as possible. It is perfectly all right to make reasonable guesses wherever you feel able to do so. When the column is filled out as completely as possible, go back to the top row and give the segment a name. Ideally the name should capture the essence of the segment. Then continue the process with the next segment, and the next, until you feel there are no further segments worth the attention of marketers. Your segmentation grid now gives you an overview of the market of interest.

3. DEVELOPING MARKETING IMPLICATIONS

One of the major uses for this sort of grid is the development of communications strategy. Assume that you are in charge of a hypothetical major brand in this market. Assume further that your brand is a "me too" brand. In other words, it is similar to other brands on the market. Make whatever additional assumptions you feel are needed. For example, you may wish to make additional assumptions about your product, its price, its packaging, its distribution, its market share, its sales trend, and so on. You may also wish to specify the size of the budget available for advertising and promotion.

Consider and specify the following:

1. *Objectives:* your promotional objectives for the year.
2. *Market Target:* your primary market target, and secondary targets to which you would like your appeal to extend.
3. *Buying Incentive:* your central theme, including suggested copy visuals, symbols, and tonality.
4. *Competitive Positioning:* how you intend to favorably differentiate your product or service from competitors.
5. *Media:* the media types and vehicles you would recommend, together with comments on timing, reach, and frequency, where appropriate.

Another use for the segmentation grid is to speculate about new product opportunities. Look at the benefits that people are seeking and the extent to which they are being delivered by products currently on the market. Is there an opportunity for a new product? Describe the type of product that you believe might be successfully introduced and specify its introductory communications strategy (steps 2, 3, and 4 in the preceding list). Assume that the new product is to be marketed by the same company you worked with in the earlier part of this exercise. In other words, be sure that you take into consideration *total company* penetration of the market as well as the penetration of the new product under consideration.

Wine
Segmentation Grid

Name of Segment	Aristocrats	Taste	Price	Entertainers	Boy/Girl
Benefits sought	Taste-dryness, vintage bouquet	Taste-sweetness, fruitiness, effervescence	Inexpensive	Special occasions	Romance
Category beliefs	Imports are superior to domestic products				
Brands/products favored	Mouton Cadet Chateau de Pope	Reunite Yago	Gallo Paul Masson	Mateus	Asti, Spumanti Harvey's Bristol Cream
Volume of consumption	Above average	Average	Average	Below average	Below average
Occasions of use	Daily—luncheons, dinner	Dinner, evenings, socializing	Parties, social gatherings	Social gatherings, dinner parties	Dinners for two, afternoon picnics for two
Media habits	*Wall Street Journal*, PBS, *The New Yorker*	*Time/Newsweek*, *Woman's Day*	Radio, local papers, Evening News, Good Housekeeping	*Boston Globe* "20/20" "60 Minutes"	Old movies, radio, *Playboy/Playgirl*
Personality/Lifestyle	Cultured, refined, well-traveled	Gregarious, family oriented, provincial	Frugal, family oriented, conservative	Outgoing, sophisticated, traveled	Upscale, idealistic, ambitious
Demographics	Lower-upper, upper-middle	Lower-lower, upper-lower	Lower-middle	Upper-middle	Lower-middle, upper-middle

Sports Market
Segmentation Grid

	Segment 1	Segment 2	Segment 3	Segment 4	Segment 5	Segment 6
Name of segment	Socialite	Purist	Relaxer	Relative	Sports fan	Winner
Benefits sought	Social interaction and companionship	Top quality action	Tension release, emotional outlet, and fun	Family pride, love, and cohesiveness	Vicarious involvement and entertainment	Association and indirect involvement
Category beliefs	Look at sporting events as "something to do"	His/her grasp or knowledge of the sport is very good	Sporting events are a good time to "let yourself go"	Important to provide emotional support to loved ones	Sports and athletic events are a positive force in our society	If I support a winner, I'll be perceived as a winner
Brands/products favored	Any level sport with familiar faces in the crowd	Sport with high caliber of play. Pro or large college	A sport with lots of action and excitement	Event or sport with a relative involved	A wide variety of sports and levels of performance	Follows a winner, whether they are consistent or flash in the pan
Volume of consumption	On occasion; could be often or seldom	Weekly	Weekly during season	Depends on number of family members involved and when they play	Weekly or daily	Weekly or daily during season
Occasions of use	Gathering of friends or family; homecoming	Game Day	As a reward for a long week on the job; weekends	Whenever a relative is playing	Game day	Every Game Day

Sports Market
Segmentation Grid (Continued)

	Segment 1	Segment 2	Segment 3	Segment 4	Segment 5	Segment 6
Media habits	Heavy user of TV and radio	Reads special topic and general interest magazines, some TV, radio, and newspaper	Heavy TV watcher	Younger relatives all heavy TV and radio. Older relatives heavier on magazines and newspapers.	Moderate TV and heavy on sports magazines, and newspapers	Average use of TV, radio, and newspaper
Personality life-style	Socially conscious, outgoing, semiliberal	Informed, intelligent, conservative, professional	Blue collar, easy-going, "one of the boys"	Conservative, family oriented	Active, extroverted, involved, interested	Fanatical at times, gregarious, excitable
Demographics	18–35 yrs, female, upper-middle college-educated, white	25–45 yrs, male, lower-upper, white, college educated father	20–45 yrs, male, lower-middle, high school education	20–50 yrs, male or female, middle-class, large family	15–40 yrs upper-middle male, college bound or graduate	20–50 yrs, male, middle-class, high school

Car Repair
Segmentation Grid

	Segment I	Segment II	Segment III	Segment IV
	Price Conscious	Convenience Seekers	Quality Conscious	Worriers
Benefits sought	Price	Convenience	Competence	Peace of mind
Category beliefs	Auto repair is expensive	Auto repair is for crises	Auto care is important	Auto care is necessary
Brands/products favored	Service stations	Service stations	Expert repair services	Both
Volume of consumption	Low	Low-moderate	Moderate	Moderate-high
Occasions of use	Something wrong with car	Emergency/crisis	Regularly scheduled	At least when regularly scheduled
Media habits	Local paper Network TV WERZ Radio	Local paper Less TV WOKQ, WMYF	Local paper Little TV WHEB, Boston Radio	Local paper Network TV WMYF, Boston Radio
Personality/lifestyle	Conscientious, hard-working, struggling to make ends meet	Seek to avoid hassles	More sophisticated, informed, discriminating	Local homeowner native
Demographics	Lower-income working families	Lower-income, older	Upscale, professional	Middle-income, working, older

**Cereal
Segmentation Grid**

Segment Name	Nutrition seekers	Sensory	Traditionalists	Weight watchers
Principal Benefit sought	Healthy food balanced diet	Unusual color, size, shape, texture	Familiar taste Proven product	Fills you up Low calorie
Personality/lifestyle	Introverted Worries	Venturesome Hedonistic	Conservative Traditional Values	Active Independent
Behavioral characteristics	Heavy users	Heavy users, Premium oriented	Light users	Average users
Brands favored	Prefer cereals that emphasize nutritional aspects, hot cereals, bran	Presweetened cereals	Well-known company	Extruded cereals
Media favored	Print	Saturday AM tv	Television	Print, FM radio
Demography	Larger families Upscale	Larger families Young children	Older downscale Smaller families	Middle-aged Upscale

Tire
Segmentation Grid

Segment name	Long mileage	Maximum Performance	Sports-minded	Low Price
Principal benefits sought	Long-run value	Top quality regardless of price	Appearance, modernity	Price
Brand perceptions	See some brand differences	See major brand differences	See major brand and type differences	See no meaningful brand difference
Behavioral characteristics	Average loyalty Own low-priced standard cars Buy radials	Highly loyal Own higher-priced luxury cars Luxury cars Buy premium-priced tires	Highly loyal Own sportscars Highly knowledgeable Buy wider tires, white-walls	Low loyalty Own compacts, used cars Buy price line
Personality/lifestyle	High autonomy	Conservative	Venturesome, sociable	Active
Demography	Not discriminated	Upscale	Younger	Larger families

Hosiery
Segmentation Grid

Segment name	Fashion Oriented	Practical	Aloof	Passive
Buying incentive	Attractiveness, shades	Fit durability	Attractive package/display	Attractive package/display
Personality	Self-preoccupation, exhibitionism	Efficient, conservative, puritans	Flexibility	Rigid shy
General attitudes	High fashion and brand consciousness	Brand consciousness	All brands equal, not interested in stockings	Low fashion consciousness
Behavior	Buy in department stores, interested in new products	Brand and price conscious, stick to old reliables	Average	Buy in variety stores, poor new product prospects
Demographics	Younger upscale, high percentage of working women	Lower income lower education older blue collar	Upper income	Lower income, lower education older blue collar

Airlines
Segmentation Grid

Segment name	Independent	Worrier	Pleasure Seeker	Family Man	Striver
Buying incentive	Trouble-free trip, to be left alone	Personal attention	New, unusual experiences	Ease of family travel	Frequent on-time trips
Business or pleasure travel	Business	High percentage of pleasure	Pleasure Takes more and shorter vacations	Pleasure, usually drives on vacations	Business
Traveling circumstances	Alone	With others	With other pleasure seekers	With wife, children	Alone
Use of travel agent	Relatively low	Average	High	Low	High
Choose own airlines	Sometimes	Usually	Usually	Usually	Rarely
Airline choice	Varies	Large, well-established airlines	High percentage of smaller airlines	Varies	No strong preference
Personality and life-style	No close relationships with family/friends	Insecure	Carefree, venturesome	Average guy, main interests are family/friends	Ambitious Extrovert Enjoys work
Predominant demographic characteristics	Businessman, upper income	High percentage Women, black	High percentage college	Large family size	Businessmen, upper income

Snack
Segmentation Grid

Segment name	Children-concerned	The Entertainers	The Worriers	The Utilitarians
Principal benefit sought	Good for children	Good taste	Lightneess and digestibility	Price
Personality	High family involvement	High sociability	High hypochondriasis	High self-involvement
Lifestyle	Conservative	Active	Liberal	Value-oriented
Behavioral characteristics	Heavy users	Medium users	Light users	Heavy users
Brands/products favored	Name brands	Premium special products	Health products	Store brands
Demography	Children	No children	Few children	Teen-agers

Automobile
Segmentation Grid

	Segment 1	Segment 2	Segment 3	Segment 4	Segment 5	Segment 6
Segment Name	Status seekers	Best buy seekers	Longevity seekers	Basic transportation seekers	Foreign car fanciers	Extras first/cars later
Benefits sought	Style	Price/durability	Durability Ease of finding repairs and maintenance parts	Durability Gas mileage Ease of finding repairs and maintenance parts; style, performance	Performance	Front-wheel drive Comfort Price
Category beliefs	"Once your car breaks down, it's no good. When mine breaks down, I buy a new one."	"You need to shop around for the best buy."	"Cars should last a long time."	"All you need is basic transportation. You've got to look out that you don't get a raw deal."	"Foreign cars are better built and run better than American cars."	"It's such a big investment. I like to be comfortable."
Brands/products favored	Volvo Chevrolet Camaro Toyota	Chevrolet Camaro Datsun Dodge Colt	Buick Chevrolet Malibu Plymouth Horizon Olds Starfire	Honda Accord Olds Starfire Renault LeCar Toyota Corolla	Volkswagen Toyota Cellica BMW	Tornado
Purchase frequency	Average	High	Low	Average	Average	Average
Occasions of use	Primarily work	Primarily work, some pleasure	Equally for work and pleasure	Pleasure Work, travel vacation	Pleasure Work	Pleasure Work
Media habits	TV and newspapers	Magazines and newspapers	TV only	Radio Newspapers TV	Magazines	TV and newspapers

Automobile
Segmentation Grid (Continued)

	Segment 1	Segment 2	Segment 3	Segment 4	Segment 5	Segment 6
Personality/life-style	High in needs for achievement, cars are reflections of lifestyles, upward mobility; perhaps reflect more affluence than achieved	Homebodies who value family and domestic activities, go out when nec. such as shopping	Easygoing, set in their ways, followers vs. leaders	Politically conscious, self-conscious about being conspicuous, try to appear worse off then they really are	High achiever, politically liberal, otherwise highly conservative	Brought up in affluent environment, self-important socially sophisticated
Demographics	Male, age 30–45, managers/administrators Income: $30–35,000	Age: 25–35 Income: 15–20,000 service workers	Age: 30–40 blue-collar Income: 15–20,000	Age 20–30 Mixed occupations Income: 20–30,000	Age 25–35 Professionals, owners, managers Income: $30–40,000	Age 40–50 Female, married Income: $25–35,000

Cocktail Mixes
Segmentation Grid

	Convenience Oriented	Insecure Mixer	Economy Oriented	Swinger
Benefits sought	No fuss	Comes out right every time	Can buy just what you need	Up-to-date conversation piece
Volume of consumption	Above average	Average	Below average	Above average
Personality/lifestyle	Venturesome	Introverted	Cerebral Cognitive	Extroverted
Media habits	Sports action/adventure	Soap operas Game shows	News Print	*Playboy, Cosmopolitan* Radio *New York Magazine*
Demographics	Upscale	Housewives	Urban apartment dweller	Young

Welfare Clients
Segmentation Grid

	Worker	Mother	Hostile	Timid
Attitudes toward work	"I want to better myself. I'd like a job that pays well. It's important to have a job."	"A mother belongs at home taking care of her kids. I'd like to be a nurse or a teacher."	"I'd like a job that pays well. I want to better myself. Most jobs poor people get just help the rich."	"I like to work. I'd like a job that pays well. A job means security."
Attitudes toward welfare	"I'm not as well off on welfare as with most jobs I've found."	"Caseworkers really care about you. Welfare means security."	"You have to fight to get anything from welfare. Welfare doesn't keep you from worrying. Welfare is a step down. Welfare changes your ideas about honesty."	"Welfare is security for me. This policy of taking people off welfare really make me mad."
Attitude differentiators	"Welfare's a plot against poor people. I'd feel like a different person if I had a job. I want a regular job. It's embarrassing to use food stamps. I feel good when I have a job."	"I'm getting off welfare as soon as I can get trained."	"I like to do my best at whatever I do. On welfare you learn to make up a story. I'd cheat if I weren't afraid of being caught. You have to teach your kids to hustle in this world."	"I don't have a lot of confidence when it comes to getting a job. I don't know where to look for a job." Doesn't like to be the boss.
Behavior	Has held more clerical/sales jobs than other segments. Higher skills level. More likely to be working currently. Made above average wages on last job. Has been on welfare a shorter time but has been on before.	High on "never worked." More likely to have done bench work. Lower skills level. Made below average hourly rate. Left last job for child care or pregnancy. On welfare for the first time now.	Has held more clerical/sales jobs. Higher skills level. Worked a shorter period at last job. Made above average wages. On welfare for the first time now.	Has held more service and bench work jobs. Average skills level. Has not had job training. Less likely to be working currently. Held last job longer than average. Made below average wages. Less likely to be on welfare for first time.

	Older	Older	Younger	A little younger.
Demographics	More likely to have completed high school. Has lived longer in the city. Reads and writes English very well. More likely to be black. More likely to have a larger family.	Less likely to have completed high school. Likely to have been born out of the city. Reads and writes English less well. More likely to be Hispanic. Larger family.	More likely to have completed high school. More likely to have been born in the city. Reads and writes English very well. More likely to be black. More likely to be single.	Average education. More likely to be single.
Personality/lifestyle	High on honesty, achievement, independence, helping, and leadership.	High on honesty and resignation. A traditionalist.	High on sociability, achievement, independence, and leadership.	High on self-blame, resignation, need. Low on confidence.

Fast Food
Segmentation Grid

	Reward Oriented	*Work Oriented*	*Socially Oriented*
Benefits sought	Treat Wholesome, nutritious food A respectable restaurant Pleasant atmosphere Not a teen hangout Not a place catering to truck drivers	Fast, efficient service Food specialists Being able to see food prepared High-quality food	A place to relax A place to have a good time Where you can socialize with friends Inexpensive meals
Occasion	After a hard day's work When I don't feel like cooking With family	Occasions relating to work or school Lunch After work Alone	After movies After sporting events Celebrating special occasions While visiting friends When you feel like a snack When you have nothing else to do
Volume of consumption	Below average	Heavier users	Heavy users
Behavior	Likely to bring food home Likely to eat with their families	Sandwiches and coffee Eat by themselves	Spend longer per visit in restaurant Eat with friends
Demographics	Above average on female Middle-aged Middle to upper social status	Middle-aged Employed Buinessmen More males	Younger Heavy on teens
Personality	Homebodies Enjoy cooking Enjoy preparing meals Enjoy tending to their families	Aggressive	Self-indulgent Active Outgoing
Media patterns	Daytime television Women's magazines	Above average radio	Rock radio stations

Banks
Segmentation Grid

Segment Name	Convenience Seekers	Financials	Service Oriented	Switches	Venturesome
Key Benefit	Convenience (hours & location)	High interest loans at lower rate	Friendly service, good management	Gifts Easy to get loans	New/progressive Best management
Financial behavior	Primarily savings and checking	Uses bank services selectively	Many instruments Many financial services	Savings and checking only	Savings clubs
Loyalty	Average switching	Low switching	Low switching	Frequent switching	Moderate frequent switching
Reasons for switching when it occurs	Change residence or job hours	Better deal elsewhere	Mishandling of errors, slow service	Incentives from other banks	Change residence or job
Primary savings reasons	General security	Retirement illness/disability	Children's education General security	Vacation Christmas/Chanukah	General security Car
Media habits	Television	Heavy newsp.	Magazines	Magazines	Radio, newspapers
Median income	Average	Above average	Above average	Below average	Average
Age	Average	Older	Slightly older	Younger	Younger
Occupation	Services/sales	Professionals	Mixed profile	Clerical/sales	Services
Marital status	Average	Married	Average	Single	Average
Education	Average	Average	Above average	Slightly below average	Above average

433

Soft Drinks
Segmentation Grid

Segment Name	Actives	Taste	Meal Accompaniers	Price
Key benefits	Satisfy thirst After strenuous activity Refreshing	Strong Goes well with food Good taste	Goes well with food High-quality ingredients	Inexpensive, lots for the money
Brand decider	Female H H	Teenager	Male H H	Mixed
Brands used	Nonmajors	Major brands	Majors	Nonmajors
Volume of consumption	High	High	Below average	Average
Occasion of consumption	Sports	Work/school	Relaxing at home	With friends
Frequent activities	Exercise Evening snacks Eating out	Often bored	Eating out Relaxing at home	Meeting with friends
Age	20–35	20–35	45+	30-45
Education	Above average	Below average	Above average	Average
Marital	Single, widowed, divorced	Average	Single, widowed, divorced	Married
Income	Above average	Below average	Average	Average
Family size	Large	Average	Smaller	Average
Age of children in households with children	Younger	Few children	Older	
Lifestyles	Independence	Doing things with friends	Parties and social get-togethers Traditional	Community minded
Media	Heavy TV, soap operas	Heavy TV movies	Lighter TV news	Average TV variety shows

Liquor Segmentation Grid

Segment Name	Light Drinkers	Traditionalists	Price Buyer	Blue-Collar Drinker	Progressives
Attitudes					
Key benefits:	"Light taste." "Good for special occasions."	Hearty; can be enjoyed straight.	"Less expensive than other brands." "A good buy"	"Keeps taste when diluted. Won't cause hangovers." "Easy going down." "Drinking is a masculine activity."	"Consistent quality." "More expensive than other liquor but worth it."
Key belief:	"Heavy drinking ruins a party."	"Being offered a drink makes me feel welcome."	"On a limited budget if I had to choose between quality and quantity, I'd choose quality."		
Behavior					
Overall consumption: Above average on:	Below average / Gin Rum Wine Cordials	Average / Bourbon Beer	Average / Vodka	Above average / Bourbon	Slightly above average / Scotch Rum Wines Cordials
Occasions:	With spouse / Before dinner / At home	With spouse / Before dinner / At home	Average	Alone or with friends / Straight / At home	With friends / Late evenings / In bars, restaurants
Characteristics Distinctive demographics:	Married / Female	Male, older / Some college / Upper-income	Nothing special	Older, male / less educated / Blue-collar	Younger, male single, more educated / Upper-income
Lifestyles:	Cultural / Eats out for fun / Enjoys cooking	Active / Energetic / Traditionalist	Inactive / Enjoys movies / Insecure	Hunter/fisherman / Heavy smoker / Believes drugs to be extremely dangerous	Sociable / Likes foreign products

Dinnerware
Segmentation Grid

Segment Name	Modernists	Traditionalists	Price	Functional
Pattern preference Material preference	*Impressionistic* Stoneware	*White and Central Floral* China	*Geometric* Plastic	*Rim-design* Laminated glass, melmac
Beliefs	"The way the table looks before the food is served is very important."	"I believe in the same kinds of things my parents did."	"Dinnerware need not fit in with room decor."	"One set of dinnerware is enough for a household."
Location of use	Dining room	Dining room	Kitchen	Kitchen
Media influence	Magazines	In-store and word of mouth	In-store	Television
Personality/lifestyle	Independent sociable	Formal traditionalists	Enjoys the simple things of life Informal	Conservative Family oriented Enjoys cooking
Demographics	Younger More educated Higher-income	Older Lower-income	More children Age 25–45 Middle-income	Age 25–34 Average education Homeowners Average income

Recorded Music[a] Market Segmentation Grid

Segment Name	Sophisticated Classicists	Casual Listener	Sound Specialists
Key Benefit	Emotional satisfaction Outstanding artist High-quality sound	Price Socially acceptable Nostalgia Convenience	Clear sound Reproduces original sound accurately
Listening occasion	Solitary	Background, escape	With guests
Playing style	Medium	Soft	Loud
Role of the package	Protection, durability Provide information	Decorative	Functional
Volume of purchase	Heavy	Light	Average
Frequency of playing	High	Lower	High
Demographics	Over 40 Above average income Equally male and female	Under 30 Female	Middle-aged Average income

[a] Classical music only.

Gasoline
Segmentation Grid

	Clean Modern Facilities	Gasoline Performance	Convenient Location	Personal Service	Brand Reputation	Price
Key benefit	Clean station appearance	Gas performance, car repair	Conveniently located	Personal reassurance	Well-known brand	Low price
Believe brands differ in quality	Average	High	Low	Low	High	Average
Volume of consumption	Low	High	Average	Average	Low	High
Number of cars owned	Average	Average	Low	Above average	Below average	High
Late model owned	Average	High	Average	Low	High	Low
Amount of driving	Average	Average	Low	High	Low	High
Credit card ownership	High	Average	Low	Average	Average	Low
Demographics	Income slightly above average. Average otherwise	Younger Upper-income	Female Younger Blue-collar Less educated Below-average income	Male Older White-collar More education	Female More education Below-average income	Male Older Less education Above-average income

Cruise Market
Segmentation Grid

	Informal Vacations	Nightlifers	Personnel Oriented	Ship Oriented	Price/Value
Attitudes Key benefits	Informal atmosphere Informal parties/dress. Lots of activities Meeting people	Gay, exciting nightlife Formal dress	Clean, well cared for ship Efficient personable service Good food	Comfortable, spacious cabins Large ship Well cared for ship Relaxing, comfortable atmosphere	Interesting ports of call
Behavior	Longer vacations Winter vacations	Recent cruiser Frequent cruiser	Longer vacations Frequent cruiser	Summer vacations With friends	Vacations with children by auto Inexpensive
Characteristics	Sociable Male Younger Below-average education and income	Sociable Leadership Female Younger Less-education Higher-income	Venturesome Less sociable Female Middle-aged Well-educated Higher-income	Family oriented Strongly attached to friends Male Older Less well educated Average income	More children Younger Well-educated Average income

439

Soluble Coffee Segmentation Grid

	Mild Coffee Seekers	Coffee Tolerators	Strong Coffee Preferers	Coffee Lovers
Attitudes				
Beliefs	Caffeine-free coffee is flavorful	"All coffees bother me."	"I prefer strong coffee."	"I prefer strong coffee."
	Caffeine-free coffee is healthful	"I prefer mild coffee."	"Coffee is a good morning catalyst."	"Coffee is a leisure-time drink."
	Coffee is a leisure-time drink	"My coffee making could be improved."		"I'm particular about how coffee is made."
	Ground coffee bothersome			"Caffeine-free coffee is not flavorful."
Benefits	Mild coffee	Good value for the money	Physical stimulation	Tastes good black
	Low in caffeine	Mild taste	Strong taste	Rich taste
	Doesn't keep you awake	Goof-proof	Real coffee aroma	A refreshing pick-me up
	Proud to serve to guests		Made from good beans	Tastes like ground
			Fresh taste	
			Well-known brand	
Type preference	Regular instant	None	Regular instant	Ground
	Freeze-dried instant		Freeze-dried instant	
Behavior				
Volume	Above average	Below average	Average	Far above average
Regular brand	Sanka	Nescafe	Instant Maxwell House	Taster's Choice
Coffee habits	Less coffee per cup	Less coffee per cup	More coffee per cup	More coffee per cup
	Buy at regular price	More likely to reheat	Adds both milk and sweetner	Drink coffee black
		Low brand loyalty	Above average on serving coffee at breakfast	Coffee is the dominant beverage in the household
			Children more likely to drink coffee	Deal prone for accepted brands
Characteristics				
Demographics	Older	Younger	Less educated	Upper-income
	Married	Professional	Middle-income	
		Above-average income	Not geographically mobile	
Lifestyle	Culinary interests	Consider themselves a little "unwell"	Organized homemaker	Enjoys reading, lone activities, smoking, drinking, and being sociable
	Traditional	Low on organized home-making	Patriotic	

Flow Chart for Prototypical Benefit Segmentation Study

See pages 171 to 276.

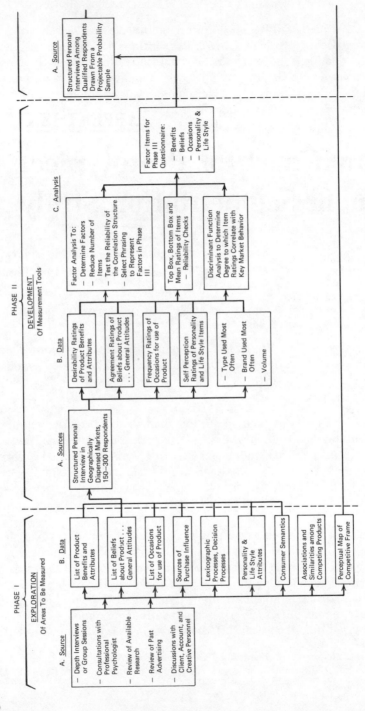

442

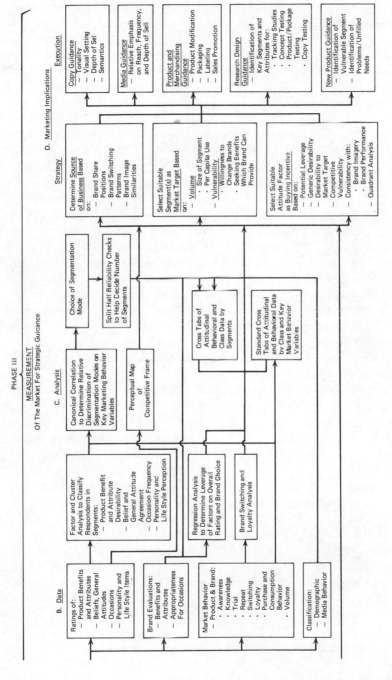

PHASE III

MEASUREMENT
Of The Market For Strategic Guidance

Benefit Segmentation Study

OCEAN SPRAY CRANBERRIES, INC. (A)

"THE FRUIT POSITIONING STUDY"

In December, 1971, the research team from Appel, Haley, and Fouriezos, Inc., under the direction of Mr. Russell Haley, presented the results of a survey among 200 cranberry sauce users to Mr. Jerry Melvin, Brand Manager of Ocean Spray's cranberry sauce products, and Mr. Ken Witham, Manager of Marketing Research at Ocean Spray. Brand management had requested the study to find ways of repositioning its cranberry sauce, which had experienced no sales growth in the latter 1960's and had actually registered a six-percent decline in fiscal year 1970. The research team had completed a pilot study which was to be the basis for an expanded survey of consumers' product attitudes, personality patterns and life style characteristics relevant to canned cranberry sauce and cranberry jelly. The management group had requested the presentation as an interim review of the project, which had resulted in expenditures of about one third of its allotted budget.

445

The Company and the Cranberry Industry

Practically all processing and marketing of cranberries[1] have in recent years been made by various cooperatives. The sales of fresh cranberries were lower than in the 1950's and early 1960's, while the processed products had almost doubled their sales. However, the yield per acre increased faster than the amount which could profitably be marketed, so the industry became confronted with a significant surplus problem. The surplus was by 1968 serious enough to cause growers to resort to the Agriculture Marketing Agreement Act of 1937.[2] The Cranberry Marketing Act of 1968 stipulated that no new acreage was to be developed over the next six years. Eighty-seven percent of all growers voted in favor of the order making it binding on all cranberry growers.

In the early 1970's 99 per cent of the industry's sales of cranberries had been made by various cooperatives. In 1970 production was slightly above two million barrels. Around 370,000 barrels went to fresh sales and 1,400,-000 barrels to processing. The difference between production and utilization represents economic abandonment. The "set aside" amounted in 1970 to more than 40 million pounds. Between 1965 and 1971, the production and utilization (i.e., fresh sales and processed) of cranberries developed as follows:

U.S. Industry	1965	1966	1967	1968	1969	1970
Production, 1000 barrels*	1,437	1,599	1,404	1,468	1,823	2,037
Utilized, 1000 barrels	1,423	1,578	1,313	1,413	1,760	1,845
Average price received by growers, $/barrel**	$15.60	$15.60	$15.50	$16.50	$16.30	$12.90

* 1 barrel = 100 lb.
** Price per barrel is based on utilized cranberries.
Source: Annual reports of Crop Reporting Board, Statistical Reporting Service, USDA.

The cooperatively owned Ocean Spray Cranberries, Inc. of South Hanson, Massachuetts (OSC), dominated the cranberry growing, processing, and distribution in the United States. Its sales volume had developed as follows:

[1] Cranberry is according to *Webster's New World Dictionary* "a firm, sour, edible red berry, the fruit of any of several trailing evergreen shrubs of the heath family."
[2] Under this act growers can regulate and control the size of an agricultural crop if the Federal Government and more than two-thirds of the growers by number and tonnage agree to a plan for restriction.

	Fiscal years ending in August:					
	1965	1966	1967	1968	1969	1970
OSC sales, 1000 barrels	967	1,036	1,054	1,145	1,265	1,197
OSC sales, $ millions	$44.4	$50.9	$55.4	$62.5	$70.8	$71.4

Source: Company annual reports.

As a growers' cooperative, OSC was tax exempted as long as 95% or more of its business was cranberry-based. Year-end operating profits were determined by deducting from sales all manufacturing, marketing, administrative and other expenses, advances on berries delivered by the growers, and any retained earnings. Total net proceeds (equivalent to operating profits before taxes) were then divided by the number of barrels of cranberries received by OSC, and the resulting average pool price was used to pay each member-grower on the basis of cranberries delivered to OSC. Operating figures from 1963 through 1970 are listed in Exhibit 1.

OSC was the largest cooperative and had operations in all the principal growing areas of North America: Massachusetts, New Jersey, Wisconsin, Washington, Orgon, British Columbia, and Nova Scotia. Over 800 growers were members of the OSC cooperative in 1971, and there was very little year-to-year change in that number.

The "Ocean Spray" brand name had been in use since the 1920's for canned cranberry products. Product development activities over the years expanded the retail line of Ocean Spray cranberry products to include the following as of late 1970:

Fresh cranberries	Cranapple drink
Jellied cranberry sauce	Cranprune juice drink
Whole berry cranberry sauce	Grape–berry juice drink
Deluxe cranberry–raspberry sauce	Low calorie cranberry products
Cranberry juice cocktail	Institutional cranberry products
Cranberry–orange relish	Industrial cranberry products

Operations were divided among four divisions: Food Service, Government and Industrial, International, and Retail. The retail operations accounted for the major part of OSC's total sales. Brand managers were responsible for retail marketing. Exhibit 2 shows the marketing organization.

Many of the OSC products enjoyed good retail distribution. The company used 85 food brokers to contact the retailers. These brokers were assigned all OSC retail products in their areas, which could be quite large.

EXHIBIT 1. Ocean Spray Cranberries, Inc. (A)
Financial Review 1963–1970 (thousands)

Fiscal Year Ended August 31	1963	1964	1965	1966	1967	1968	1969	1970
Net sales ($000)	32,294	37,430	44,401	50,909	55,429	62,513	70,815	71,365
Barrels sold (000)	938	978	967	1,036	1,054	1,145	1,265	1,197
Per 1,000 barrels ($)	34.4	38.3	45.9	49.1	52.6	54.6	56.0	59.6
Selling, marketing and administrative expenses ($000)	6,314	7,441	9,264	10,590	11,774	11,512	12,983	12,896
Per 1,000 barrels ($)	6.73	7.61	9.58	10.2	11.2	10.1	10.3	10.8
Net proceeds ($000)	11,369	13,607	15,788	17,584	17,534	18,652	20,298	20,536
Net proceeds as per cent of net sales (%)	35.2	36.4	35.6	34.5	31.6	29.8	28.7	28.8
Total capital employed ($000)	7,190	7,198	6,597	6,858	7,201	9,781	11,628	13,699

Source: Annual reports.

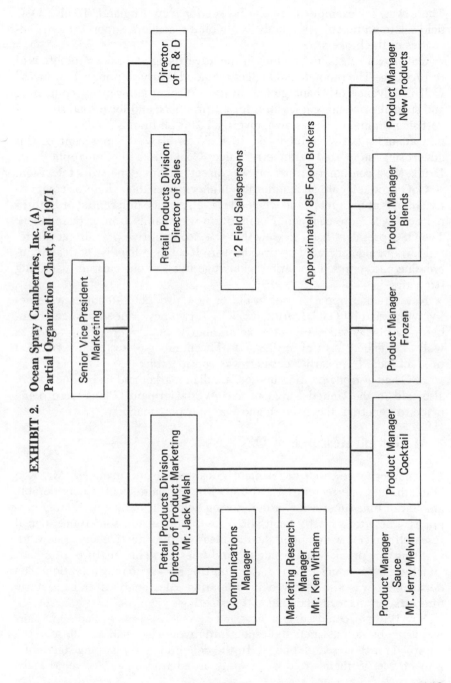

EXHIBIT 2. Ocean Spray Cranberries, Inc. (A)
Partial Organization Chart, Fall 1971

449

There was, for example, only one broker for New England. Twelve OSC field salesmen functioned mainly as regional managers, supervising the activities of the brokers.

OSC spent substantial monies in the advertising and sales promotion of its products. The promotional budget included "early shipping allowances" well in advance of Thanksgiving, in-store display allowances, couponing and special price-margin features for all products, and local food store advertising programs. OSC's own advertising for all brands exceeded $5 million annually between 1968 and 1970. Well above 75 per cent of this advertising supported Cranberry Juice Cocktail, and Cranapple Juice Drink. Most consumer advertising was directed through network television.

OSC products sold at significantly higher prices than those of competitive brands at both retail and wholesale level. A price differential of 10 to 15 per cent was quite common. Competition was mainly from private labels. The OSC president had the view that the "competitive pressure at the retail level being generated by private store-label merchandise is steadily increasing and represents a serious challenge in all of our current marketing strategies."

New product opportunities in old or new product categories were actively pursued by OSC. During fiscal 1970 two new sauce products (cranberry–raspberry sauce and a deluxe cranberry sauce) were being tested as well as a jellied form of applesauce. The number of tested but rejected product ideas from earlier decades was considerable.

OSC had a strong position in the Canadian market and its products were also sold in the United Kingdom and West Germany. Plans were being made to penetrate the Swedish and Dutch export markets.

Marketing Research at OSC

The marketing research department consisted of one manager, Mr. Ken Witham, and one secretarial assistant. Mr. Witham spent a considerable amount of time supervising or monitoring field tests of new marketing programs. These tests mostly dealt with new products, but sometimes special research projects were undertaken to measure the effectiveness of new advertising or promotional vehicles and messages for mature products. Usually, new product tests required most of Mr. Witham's attention. The department was also involved in preparing sales analyses and quarterly forecasts for financial planning and budgeting.

Mr. Witham could suggest new marketing research projects but normally the brand managers took such initiatives. They had also to seek the approval for the research budget. In the definition and planning stages of a project, Mr. Witham's role was mainly an advisory one. He would make comments on how the new project related to previous research, and the costs and benefits of different research approaches and techniques. He would also be in charge of establishing and maintaining contacts with outside suppliers of marketing research. Outside firms were used in the data collection and analytical phases of special projects, and Mr. Witham participated in the interpretation phases of each study with the brand managers and representatives of the research supplier.

In a typical year there were 5 to 10 projects with a total budget of around $150,000. This sum did not include salaries, which amounted to around $30,000. The advertising agencies responsible for various product groups would occasionally undertake marketing research in connection with their handling of OSC accounts.

Apart from these research efforts OSC also bought syndicated marketing information. OSC management received Nielsen Index reports bimonthly on all retailed cranberry products. These reports contained information gathered by retail store audits about price, shelf position, in-store promotion, and estimated sales volume of OSC and competing brands. Monthly SAMI reports on warehouse withdrawals were purchased for the sauce products during the main selling season. For beverage products only, a third syndicated data base was purchased from the operators of the MRCA National Consumer Panel, a diary-based service reporting within household purchasing activities over continuous time periods for a variety of consumer products. Occasionally, OSC would buy other syndicated information, like the MRCA National Household Menu Census. In a typical year, OSC spent approximately $200,000 for syndicated marketing information.

Marketing of OSC Cranberry Sauce

Industry sales of cranberry sauce totaled about 6 million cases (1 case = 24 lb) annually. It had been learned from previous research that more than 90 percent of all U.S. households consumed some cranberry sauce during a year. A large consumer segment with very high usage consisted of relatively old people. For most consumers cranberry sauce was purchased and used a couple of times a year. The four months from October to January accounted for 60 per cent of retail sales.

OSC's sauce was sold in two forms—whole berry and jellied. A cranberry–raspberry sauce and a deluxe sauce were in test markets during the fall of 1970. Retail sales and marketing expenditures for the OSC jelly and whole-berry sauce were as follows (year ending August 31) [see page 451]. The overall marketing strategy for sauce during the latter half of the 1960's was characterized as a milking strategy. Marketing support was sharply

curtailed in 1964 for two reasons. First, the brand had not responded to previous advertising, and second, cutbacks were necessary in order to fund introduction of the juice product and still maintain grower returns. The only
noticeable advertising efforts for sauce during this period were an outdoor
campaign in 1965–1967 and newspaper supplement ads at Easter in 1970.

	1965	1966	1967	1968	1969	1970
Million cases						
Retail sales (sauce)*	4.25	4.53	4.54	4.64	4.55	4.25
($1,000)						
Advertising (sauce)**	$240	$226	$214	$—	$—	$72
Promotion (sauce)	446	473	312	182	344	605
	$686	$699	$526	$182	$344	$677

* A. C. Nielsen.
** Company records.

OSC retailed 8-ounce and 1-pound packages at a higher price than competitors. A retail price of around 27 cents was common for the 1-pound can.
Other brands, if any, were usually sold at 3 to 7 cents less per can. It was
difficult to estimate the retail mark-up on sauce, because retailers set price
drastically different dependent on whether or not it was in-season or off-
season. During off-season, a common retail mark-up was 18 per cent. However, many retailers used sauce as a "loss leader" during the peak season.
One New York retailer had sold the OSC sauce for one cent to those customers who made more than $5 worth of other purchases.

The brand manager for sauce worked with the sales division in planning
in-store promotion activities. Broker commissions varied between 3 per
cent and 5 per cent based on OSC factory prices, depending on volume
generated in the broker's market. Management was satisfied with the results
obtained by the brokers during the major season, but less so regarding off-
season activities.

Limited couponing was used before or after the main fall season, but
brand management could not find economic justification for using coupons
in connection with peak selling seasons. However, some food retailers included coupons for OSC sauce in their newspaper ads during the major
selling season.

Despite some losses to private labels, OSC still had a dominant position
in cranberry sauce. Its brand name was truly a household name. No other
manufacturer of sauce had a national market. The competitors relied almost
entirely on selling their cranberry sauce under private labels. Many fruit or

vegetable cooperatives as well as other manufacturers having a canning operation were active during the main season. On an annual basis, the private labels accounted for around 26 per cent of the sauce volume in 1970–1971 and this share had been increasing very slowly.

OSC did participate in cranberry private-label business to a very limited extent in the 1960's. No concerted effort was made to gain such business. In fiscal year 1970, OSC sold around 100,000 cases of sauce under private labels, which represented an addition to regular sauce sales of around 2 per cent. OSC usually received 2–4 cents less for the one-pound can of sauce when sold as private label. This was offset by savings in distribution and production costs (another sauce formula was used). The private-label business was not the responsibility of the OSC sauce brand manager although he was kept informed about it.

OSC sold three times more jelly than whole-berry sauce. This ratio had been very stable during the 1960's. However, the ratio was about 4 to 1 in New England and 2 to 1 in California. The brand manager had so far not found any good explanation for the regional differences. He knew, however, that the whole berry sauce was relatively more often used as an ingredient in preparing a meal. The two products were always jointly advertised and promoted. It was felt that management did not have a clear indication as to how the marketing of the two variants could be beneficially differentiated.

Previous Market Research for Sauce

While handling the OSC sauce and drink accounts the McCann-Erickson advertising agency undertook in 1962 an "Exploratory Motivation Survey of Consumer Attitudes Toward Cranberries." This study followed a general format which McCann-Erickson called "MARPLAN '62." The study had a great impact on OSC management and it was often referred to or reviewed in the following years.

The MARPLAN study found that cranberry sauce was tradition-bound, almost synonymous with Thanksgiving and turkey. It indicated that this aspect of the image was not likely to change. The rejection of cranberry sauce by nonusers who have tried it seemed to be a fairly permanent factor. Close analysis of the verbatims and ratings suggested that rejection was primarily based on taste.

It seemed unlikely that nonusers could be taught to like cranberries by advertising. The study concluded that if advertising were to be used, the effort would have to be substantial. Advertising should be aimed at overcoming the force of habits and traditional views among year-round users and in-season-only users rather than persuading rejecters to become triers again.

However, OSC management opted for the implicit alternative of minimal advertising and promotional expenditures.

In 1967 OSC had purchased information from the MRCA National Household Menu Census. The survey gave demographic data on sauce users and nonusers. When the results of the 1967 study were compared with those of MARPLAN '62, a shift in the age distribution of the sauce franchise to a reduction in the annual usage in younger age groups was apparent.

**Incidence of Cranberry Sauce Usage
in Preceding 12 Month Period**

Age of Female Head of Household	1962 MARPLAN* $N = 2027$	1967 MRCA** $N = 4000$
Under 25	68%	59%
25–34	85	75
35–44	91	99
45–54	88	95
55+	83	81
Average	85	85

* Based on claimed usage.
** Special survey conducted among members of the MRCA National Consumer Panel.

MARPLAN '62 and the Menu Census also revealed that even though many households used sauce with chicken servings, sauce was only used in connection with 6 per cent of all chicken servings. In the brand manager's eyes this was an opportunity for growth. Another possibility for growth read from these reports was the fact that if the "seasonal" users could be stimulated to buy one additional can, this would represent around 25 per cent increase in total volume.

Apart from reports from the sales organization, the brand manager received Nielsen retail audit reports and SAMI warehouse shipment figures during the peak sales season. These standardized reports were helpful for short-term marketing planning and control. However, it was equally clear that they were not particularly designed to be used in analyzing and developing long-term strategy for OSC's cranberry sauce.

Developments During 1969–1971

Before joining OSC as a brand manager in 1969, Mr. Jack Walsh worked with the General Foods Company. He had there been witness to many attempts to increase sales and/or market share of commodity-like food products. These attempts centered primarily around advertising, positioning and occasionally around product quality since changing other marketing variables like price or distribution was deemed unprofitable. According to Mr. Walsh, the management and marketing process dealt with trying to identify large consumer groups which seemed to be similar to medium or heavy user groups. If one group of consumers only differed markedly as to the amount consumed of a certain product when compared with another group, then it ought to be possible to "convert" this group of lighter users to a group of heavier users.

A central question in these studies was choosing which specific consumer characteristics to measure. In addition to traditional measures of product usage, demographic and socioeconomic characteristics, some market segmentation studies had begun experimentation with newer measures of consumers' life styles, their attitudes toward a product class, and their beliefs about the kinds of benefits a product should provide. Though studies of consumers' attitudes and product usage patterns were not new, it became fashionable to refer to the more recent research efforts as psychographic studies. Whereas demographics referred to the characteristics of an individual or a population in terms of its age, sex, and location, psychographics included any of a range of more-or-less systematic measures of a consumer's (or a group's) personality as it related to the scenarios of purchase and consumption of a given product category.

Mr. Walsh's first task was brand management of the cranberry cocktail and sauce businesses. He saw three ways to increase sauce sales and profits: (1) gain in market share by selling part of production under private label; (2) by more aggressive pricing and merchandising of the OSC sauce; or (3) expansion of sauce demand by stimulating heavier usage among various consumer segments. Various opinions were held by the members of the OSC management as to which was the best way to go and, above all, whether or not any offensive marketing action was likely to help OSC's position in the market for cranberry sauce. Mr. Walsh himself argued that there were opportunities to expand the sauce market. "We have a premium brand of an inexpensive food product which two out of every three U.S. households buy once or twice a year. The marketing challenge is to raise this to twice or three times a year."

Possible reasons for infrequent usage of sauce came easily to mind, and the following explanations were popular among OSC managers: "Many consumers consider cranberry sauce as a tradition strictly connected with the Thanksgiving and Christmas holidays and the turkey meal"; "many find it inconvenient to serve"; and "many housewives don't buy it more often because some family members don't like the taste."

Management's thinking about the role of consumer advertising was affected by the experiences from the substantial effort made in the early 1960's. The objective at that time had been to promote sauce consumption year-round. Cranberry sauce as an accompaniment to a variety of meals was featured in the advertising copy. The advertising program was stopped because little consumer reaction was observed. Measurements of advertising results showed the early 1960's program had failed to make consumers more aware of sauce advertising in out-of-season periods.

Mr. Walsh thought the sauce market was ripe for an application of psychographic research along the lines he had experienced while at General Foods. The sauce business was very important for OSC, because it accounted for around 40 per cent of growers' returns. Top management, on the other hand, was not convinced that advertising would be a sound investment for these reasons:

The "milking" strategy seemed to be successful.

Past advertising efforts had not succeeded in generating sufficient sales growth to "pay-out."

Marketing funds would have to be diverted from OSC drinks which were growing rapidly.

Lack of any OSC exclusivity in previous creative submissions made it likely that growth resulting from successful advertising would be disproportionately shared with price brands, whose cranberries were supplied by growers who were not members of the Ocean Spray cooperative.

For these reasons it had been reluctant to spend money on the advertising of OSC sauce, or for that matter, invest substantial sums in sauce marketing research.

When the sales of OSC sauce products decreased by nearly 7 per cent in fiscal year 1970, management became more willing to take action. The decline was due to a combination of a 3 per cent drop in total sauce sales and the inroads of low-priced private-label products in selected major markets.

Management abandoned the milking strategy of 1965–1969 and implemented a merchandising and promotion program in 1970 that was credited with stabilizing a declining situation. While advertising spending in fiscal 1970 was limited to a $72,000 Easter campaign, $605,000 was spent on promotion and merchandising activities. Brand management's plan for the 1971 fiscal year, approved late in the summer of 1970, called for an increase of over $500,000 in spending for sauce to be divided approximately equally between advertising and promotion, and some of those funds could be diverted for research studies if properly justified with top management.

In this situation, just after the selling season of fall 1970, Mr. Walsh outlined a marketing research project which could give management information about how the apparent market expansion opportunity should best be seized. His memorandum to key personnel at OSC and the advertising agency, Young & Rubicam (who had obtained the sauce account late in the 1960's), stated that the project would:

(a) observe the psychodemographic characteristics of heavy sauce users; (b) generate hypotheses for their high service frequency; and (c) develop selling propositions which, delivered against similarly profiled light/nonusers, will position regular sauce service as complementary to their life style.

The ultimate objective was to "turn on" some segment of light and/or nonusers of sauce.

As Mr. Walsh saw it, the direction for development of communication approaches would come from observation and analysis of heavy user subgroups. He gave the following simplified example of how this would be done:

One segment of heavy users may be characterized by a "Family Centered" orientation, where meals are a medium for expressing affection for family and where it can be concluded that the role of sauce is to communicate affection at common, easily-prepared, or otherwise "unspecial" meals.

Next, this segment would be viewed against normative data to determine potential (that is, incidence in the total consumer universe) and reachability (in terms of media habits).

Were the above completed and were "Family Centered" concluded to be the optimal target, the Agency would go to work. Advertising would be produced which communicated the life style of the target audience and positioned cranberry sauce service as complementary to or supportive of that style. The desired end result would be target prospects "self-selecting" ("Hey, that's me"), perceiving sauce service out-of-season as desirable and commencing to buy the product. For the heavy users necessarily reached, the advertising would reinforce and, hopefully, stimulate their already profitable behavior pattern.

Mr. Walsh foresaw the need to work with "an agency trained in psychodemographics who would provide the formal game plan." In the meantime, he indicated that the following research activities would take place:

Screen for a statistically reliable sample of heavy users.

Segment sample through psychological testing and analysis by a research firm (include demographic and media habit data by segment).

Generate hypotheses for the sauce usage of each segment in context of their now available psychographic profiles or life styles.

Select the most promising segment.

Develop and test the selling platform for that segment.

Late in December of 1970, Walsh's superiors agreed to a marketing research project for sauce, mainly to help management better evaluate and plan the increased marketing spending on sauce.

Having set out research objectives, guidelines for the methods to be used, and organization of the project, Mr. Walsh initiated and participated in a series of meetings with agency and OSC marketing managers and research specialists. Late in the spring of 1971, OSC invited the agency and two other marketing research firms to submit proposals and bid for the project. These two firms were Daniel Yankelovich, Incorporated, and Appel, Haley, Fouriezos, Incorporated. The latter came out as the winner. An important factor was that Mr. Russell Haley of AHF had successfully completed similar consulting assignments for General Foods. Mr. Walsh was familiar with this work.

In the spring of 1971, Mr. Walsh was promoted to Group Product Manager and Mr. Jerry Melvin became Brand Product Manager for sauce. Mr. Melvin was earlier an assistant to Mr. Walsh.

The Fruit Positioning Study

By the end of the summer 1971, the research project was a major concern of Messrs. Walsh, Melvin and Witham. Mr. Haley's proposal had called for "a benchmark study of the market for cranberry sauce." The overall proposed study was to be the development of an understanding of cranberry sauce users—their behavior, attitudes, opinions, and beliefs. Mr. Walsh decided the study would focus only on the sauce product category and would not investigate other OSC products in any depth.

The research objectives were formulated as follows:

To identify and describe the kinds of women who use cranberry sauce;

To provide an understanding of what consumers are seeking in choosing between complementary products for use—in salads, and with main food courses;

To look into the consumption of various food types as sources and potential sources of cranberry sauce usage;

To describe consumer usage patterns with regard to cranberry sauce;

To identify broad media types of OSC sauce in getting across its message to consumers; and

To investigate new product or line extension possibilities.

It was argued that guidance for formulation of three basic components of the marketing strategy would result from a fulfillment of the above research objectives. The three components were in the words of the AHF proposal as follows:

1. *Positioning.* Where are additional sales most likely to originate? Should the product or its image be modified, to maximize its long-term sales appeal, and if so, how?
2. *Market Target.* Who are the best prospects for cranberry sauce?
3. *Buying Incentives.* What should be said about OSC's cranberry sauce to make it most attractive to its market target?

At the meeting between the brand group, OSC research and Mr. Haley, it was agreed that the project should have three phases with a final report in early spring 1972. The cost of the three phases would be about $45,000 with a plus or minus 10% contingency for unforeseen costs or savings. The three phases were to cover (1) exploration of areas to be covered, (2) development of measurement tools, and (3) measurement of the market on a national basis.

Phase One—Exploration of Areas to be Covered

The immediate purpose of the first phase was to define the competitive environment and to compile lists of product attributes, consumer beliefs, and personality and life style characteristics of special relevance for cranberry sauce consumption. Past research on the cranberry sauce market consisted mainly, as has been mentioned above, of the MRCA study from 1967 and the so-called MARPLAN study from 1962. These studies were reviewed in research of areas to be measured. Mr. Witham put down a one-page list of hypotheses concerning the activities, opinions, life styles and demographics of heavy users of cranberry sauce.

Heavy Sauce Users
1. Use cranberry sauce with a variety of meats and numerous preparations—i.e., fried, broiled, cold meats, as well as baked;
2. perceive sauce as a part of the meal rather than a garnish or a symbol of tradition;
3. have sauce in their kitchen as a staple year-round;
4. often make their own sauce or relish when fresh cranberries are available;

5. feel sauce has a food value as well as an attractive appearance and good taste;
6. often use sauce as an ingredient in cooking;
7. consider sauce a convenient, inexpensive food item;
8. have (demographics)

    larger families

    several children living at home

    better education

    a 30–45 year old female head-of-house

    a higher family income

    up-scale socio-economic characteristics; and
9. have a life style which includes

    a wife/mother who enjoys cooking

    active participation in community affairs

    being concerned with nutrition of the family, quality of environment

    preference for natural foods versus synthetics

    a planned food budget and shopping from a shopping list

    strong family ties.

Mr. Melvin, the sauce brand manager, gave the AHF team a list of 41 cranberry sauce usage hypotheses, for example, "since sauce is perceived as appropriate for formal meals, the difference between heavy and light users has to do with the number of formal meals served," and "new products like Shake 'n' Bake are cutting into the sauce business."

To supplement management's judgment, two focused group sessions were conducted among women who used cranberry sauce. The first group session was conducted in Boston among ten heavy users. The light user group was gathered in Kansas City. A light user had to have used only one can of cranberry sauce within the past year, and not served any within the past month.

One finding was that several of the women were concerned about serving a colorful meal. A difference between the two groups was the food items chosen to make a meal more colorful. The heavy users primarily chose cranberries while the light users specified a combination of green and yellow vegetables, salads and beets. Cranberry sauce was not mentioned by this group particularly because they considered it to be strictly a traditional food.

Twenty women were also the subjects for a perceptual mapping exercise. Each respondent was asked to make judgments about which two out of a set of three food items were most alike in terms of use. Twenty-four food ac-

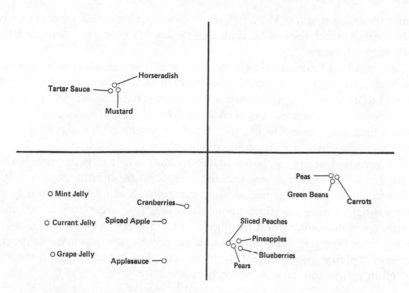

Figure 1. Perceptual map of various food accompaniments.

companiments, including cranberries, were considered in this way. Figure 1 was developed using the perceived similarities data, and suggests how the 20 respondents positioned cranberries relative to other foods. In discussing this map with OSC managers, Mr. Haley suggested that the two dimensions could be interpreted as "spicy–nonspicy" and "condiment–side dish." Cranberries were perceived as average on the first scale and more of a side dish or fruit than a condiment on the second scale.

Phase Two—Development of Measurement Tools

The qualitative results from Phase 1 were used to design a questionnaire. Marketing management made several extensions and modifications of the questions which the research team first suggested, and the list of questions became quite lengthy. Management and the AHF staff came up with 75 questions dealing with attributes of ideal canned fruit products, 103 questions on overall opinions and feelings about cranberry sauce, and 55 on personality and life style. The 75 questions on attributes were to be replicated for jellied and for whole berry cranberry sauce, respectively. Traditional questions on product usage and on various demographical variables were also to be included.

A pilot test was conducted in fall 1971 to try to determine which of the many items best reflected strong, underlying consumer dimensions in the cranberry sauce market. That such dimensions of attitudinal or other character existed was believed by both OSC marketing management and the AHF research team.

Two hundred females living in ten different market areas were personally interviewed in their homes. The procedure to select the sample was thought to acceptably approximate a national probability sample. Potential respondents were personally screened to determine if they had purchased canned cranberry sauce in the past year. Around 220 females had to be contacted to yield a sample of 200 qualified respondents.

The personal interview lasted about 30 minutes. It covered purchasing and usage of cranberry sauce, brands, frequency of serving various foods, and demographical and socioeconomic variables. A self-administered questionnaire containing questions about the subjective areas mentioned previously (overall opinions and feelings about cranberry sauce) was given to the respondent at the end of the personal interview. The interviewer picked up the completed questionnaire later the same day. A promised gift was delivered in return for the completed questionnaire.

Analysis of Pilot Test Data

A major objective of the pilot test was to investigate the extent to which consumers in fact exhibited the characteristics that management had hypothesized. The self-administered portion of the pilot survey questionnaire contained 383 separate items covering five separate areas of inquiry:

Set	Type of Data	No. of Items
1	Attributes of an Ideal Canned Fruit	75
2	Perceived Attributes of Jellied Cranberry Sauce	75
3	Perceived Attributes of Whole Berry Cranberry Sauce	75
4	Overall Attitudes and Feelings About Cranberry Sauce	103
5	Self-Description of Personality and Life Style	55
	Total Number of Self-administered Items	383

The pilot questionnaire had been constructed to cover as many different characteristics of consumers and the product category as could conceivably be relevant to the purchase and use decision process of important market segments. The research strategy involved letting the data and subsequent analysis determine which subsets of all the original items were of more or less analytical and managerial interest, rather than strictly relying on "expert judgment" as a basis for building a more succinct list of final items. Whatever redundancy might be present in the original items would thus be identified and could be eliminated, and furthermore, if certain items seemed to be tapping a fundamental consumer or product characteristic not explicitly measured, that characteristic could be inductively identified. The pilot questionnaire, then, was thought of as a preliminary and exploratory vehicle that would shape the form and content of a smaller, final set of questions to be employed in Phase 3 of the project.

The five data sets were analyzed one at a time—however, always in combination with a sixth group of variables. This sixth group consisted of the following variables:

1. cranberry sauce usage—heavy or light;
2. age—young or old;
3. meat consumption—heavy or light;
4. fruit (and vegetable) consumption—heavy or light; and
5. education—high school or further.

Respondents were given the values "1" or "0" in the coding of these variables. It was hoped that by including these basic marketing variables, the analyses would give results which were easier to understand.

The computerized data analysis was done in five steps and repeated for each of the five sets of data. Appendix 1 illustrates the analytical procedure as it applied to the fifth data set—"Description of personalities and life styles." The steps were as follows:

Step	Analysis
1.	Calculation of means and standard deviations of the responses to each item (Exhibit 3).
2.	Preparation of a matrix of the pairwise correlations between these items (Exhibits 4 and 5).
3.	The use of a computerized data analysis technique called principal components analysis to identify which sets of variables tended to be scored by respondents according to a consistent pattern. The output of the principal components analysis was a series of factors.
4.	Each factor consisted of a set of weights (called loadings) which showed the degree of association between each variable and an underlying theoretical pattern of responses. Loadings could range between -1.0 and 1.0, and loadings that were near zero indicated

EXHIBIT 3. Analysis of "Descriptions of Personalities and Lifestyles" Data
Table A-1. Means and Standard Deviations of "Descriptions of Personalities and Lifestyles"

Variable		
No. Label	Mean	Standard Deviation
1. I like to have friends over for dinner	2.04	1.02
2. I prefer fresh vegetables to canned or frozen products	2.23	1.15
3. I watch my calories carefully	3.17	1.31
4. I like to rough it and live simply	3.22	1.17
5. I'm not a good cook	3.60	1.29
6. I believe in things my parents believed in	2.68	.91
7. I'm a nervous sort of person	3.09	1.28
8. I usually get together with the family for holiday meals	1.73	1.04
9. When I see something I like, I buy it	2.65	1.02
10. I prefer natural foods to ones with artificial ingredients	1.95	1.06
11. I really enjoy eating	1.63	.88
12. I don't feel well, but don't know what is wrong	4.30	1.03
13. I enjoy having lots of people around	2.43	1.07
14. I tend to be good to myself	2.44	.97
15. I like to cook new dishes	2.08	1.05
16. I usually serve several relishes and other extras at holiday meals	1.70	.87
17. I try to serve my children the things they like to eat	2.01	1.00
18. I like to have my meals planned and organized in advance	2.16	1.10
19. I often buy store brands instead of national brands	2.91	1.17
20. I like to look for sales in the grocery store	1.92	1.10
21. I am frequently on a diet	3.25	1.35
22. I think Sunday is a traditional day	2.38	1.24
23. I have few pains	3.20	1.40
24. I enjoy cookouts	2.19	1.16
25. My family appreciates the work I put into a meal	2.05	.97
26. I like to prepare fancy dishes even if they take a long time	2.70	1.30
27. I am in better health than most of my friends	2.67	1.15
28. The foods I serve reflect my moods	2.86	1.14
29. I like to keep busy in leisure time	2.03	1.06
30. I usually get to cook things for my husband	1.88	1.19
31. I plan my life carefully	2.79	1.10
32. I enjoy cooking more for guests than for the family	3.47	1.25

EXHIBIT 3. (Continued)

Variable		Mean	Standard Deviation
No. Label			
33. I like to balance my meals carefully to make sure they're nutritious		1.84	.87
34. I like to prepare colorful salads		2.15	1.04
35. In running my home—I think how mother would do things		3.50	1.19
36. I enjoy entertaining at home		2.10	1.04
37. I wish I were not so shy		3.57	1.33
38. I try to get color and taste contrast in my main meals		2.00	.97
39. I rarely serve leftover foods		3.32	1.25
40. Food advertising interests me		2.56	1.22
41. In enjoy taking time to prepare meals		2.28	1.03
42. I serve quite a few casseroles		2.90	1.05
43. I always keep some fruit around for the family		1.51	.75
44. We prefer plain and simple foods		2.19	.90
45. I believe we are on earth to enjoy ourselves		2.23	.95
46. I like to cook		1.84	1.01
47. I think the meat is the most important part of the meal		1.78	.85
48. I enjoy being active		1.63	.73
49. I enjoy serving spicy dishes		2.89	1.11
50. Meals are a way to express affection for the family		2.11	1.05
51. I feel guilty about wasting food		1.84	1.12
52. Sauce: heavy/light user		.52	.50
53. Age: younger/older		.39	.49
54. Meat: heavy/light user		.43	.50
55. Fruit: heavy/light user		.51	.50
56. Education: high school/+		.65	.48

Keys to variable number:

1-51. Respondents answered along a five-point scale—ranging from "describes me completely" (1) to "describes me not at all" (5);

52. Respondents who stated that they had purchased ≥ 7 cans of cranberry sauce in the past year were considered to be heavy users. Heavy users were given the value "1" and light users "0" on this variable;

53. Respondents in the age $\angle 34$ years were given the value "1";

54. Heavy users were those who reported a total score ≥ 31 on questions regarding the frequency of eating meats during an average month. Nine different meats were mentioned and a seven-point scale was used. Heavy users were given the value "1";

55. Heavy users ("1") were those who reported a total score ≥ 56 on sixteen fruits and vegetables;

56. Respondents with high school as highest grade were given the value "1."

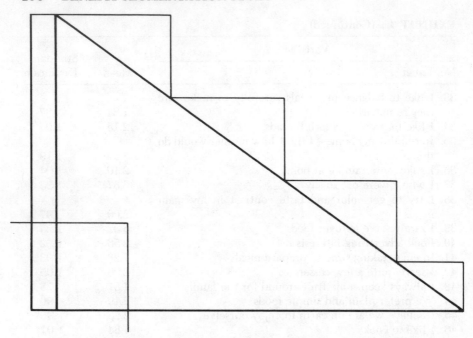

EXHIBIT 4.   Correlation Matrix: Description of Personalities and Lifestyles Data

there was no association between a variable and a particular fctor. Exhibit 6 lists the loadings of the 56 Personality and Life Style variables on the first of the 13 factors.

5.   The theoretical response pattern represented by a given factor was then identified using the following procedure: a list of highly loaded variables was compiled for each of the 13 factors. Exhibit 7 is such a list as prepared by the Factor Analysis program for Factor One. The list was then inspected and the research team made a judgment regarding what underlying phenomena seemed to best explain the factor. Factor One was judged to be a measure of cooking enthusiasm and was so labeled. This process was repeated for the remaining 12 personality and life style factors, resulting in the labels listed in Exhibit 8.

The use of the principal components analysis had suggested the possible underlying dimensions of consumers' attitudes toward the product category, and had identified a relatively small subset of important variables in each of the five types of measurements. The research team then began construction of a revised questionnaire—with no redundant or irrelevant items—to be used in a full-scale survey.

The revision of the pilot questionnaire resulted in changes so that instead of the 75 original questions on attributes of ideal canned fruit products, jellied and whole berry cranberry sauce, the research team now wanted to use 33 questions; 43 of the original 75 had been dropped and one added. Furthermore, of the 103 questions on overall attitudes and feelings about cranberry sauce, only two were retained. An additional set of 20 question items would be included. Finally, of the 51 statements regarding personality and life style, 17 were dropped. This part would consist of the remaining 34 plus one additional item.

Preparations for a Full-Scale Survey

A meeting was held between the research team and the marketing research and brand managers from OSC to report on the results of the pilot test. In discussing the planned full-scale consumer survey, the research team reiterated the earlier objectives for Phase 3 of the project. A larger sample would result in more reliable estimates of the attitudes and behaviors of cranberry sauce users. Furthermore, the pilot test had enabled the research team to develop a better version of the questionnaire.

Mr. Haley's brief to the OSC managers contained the following question areas suggested for Phase 3:

In the personal interview:

Usage of main dishes with which cranberry sauce may be eaten
Usage of and overall attitudes toward competitive complementary products
Occasions of use
Brand awareness and trial
Brand loyalty
Demographic characteristics

In the self-administered questionnaire:

Attitude ratings of whole berry and jellied cranberry sauce
Desirability of product attributes and benefits
Images of branded and private label cranberry sauce
Perceived compatibility with various main dishes

EXHIBIT 5. Sample from Matrix of Pairwise Correlations of "Descriptions of Personalities and Lifestyles"

	1 I like to have friends over for dinner	2 I prefer fresh vegetables to canned or frozen products	3 I watch my calories carefully	4 I like to rough it and live simply	5 I'm not a good cook	6 I believe in things my parents believed in	7 I'm a nervous sort of person	8 I usually get together with the family for holiday meals	9 When I see something I like, I buy it	10 I prefer natural foods to ones with artificial ingredients
40 Food advertising interests me	.197	−.002	.172	.166	.108	.230	.144	.122	.081	.106
41 I enjoy taking time to prepare meals	.362	.145	.179	.193	−.234	.205	.005	.080	.090	.216
42 I serve quite a few casseroles	−.083	.172	.105	−.023	.027	.056	−.054	−.067	−.053	.102
43 I always keep some fruit around for the family	.184	.123	.132	.077	−.076	.056	.143	.111	.127	.162
44 We prefer plain and simple foods	−.046	.070	.060	.086	.126	.180	.078	.027	−.009	.136
45 I believe we are on earth to enjoy ourselves	.213	.166	.166	.171	.070	.091	.078	−.010	.184	.354
46 I like to cook	.328	.084	.182	.137	−.248	.149	.011	.018	.068	.147

I think meat is the most important part of the meal	47	.191	.052	.087	−.039	−.056	.163	.004	.111	.131	−.004
I enjoy being active	48	.225	.153	.108	.041	−.021	.179	−.111	.016	.080	.172
I enjoy serving spicy dishes	49	.161	.082	.120	.072	−.106	−.063	−.043	−.024	.142	.104
Meals are a way to express affection for the family	50	.207	.161	.085	.166	−.095	.218	.081	.031	.008	.248
I feel guilty about wasting food	51	−.026	.072	.074	.189	.031	.229	.145	−.076	−.259	.266
Sauce: heavy/light user	52	−.065	−.005	.024	.086	.102	−.047	.160	−.203	−.031	.054
Age: younger/older	53	−.038	.045	.143	−.025	.019	.046	−.013	−.042	−.066	.162
Meat: heavy/light user	54	−.020	−.101	−.054	−.001	.109	−.011	.031	.033	.005	−.157
Fruit: heavy/light user	55	−.015	−.091	−.052	−.033	.114	.028	−.005	.028	−.123	−.109
Education: high school/+	56	.129	.002	.037	−.198	−.132	−.076	−.091	−.180	.004	−.052

EXHIBIT 6. Detailed Listing of Factor No. 1[1]

Variable No.	Loading	Variable No.	Loading
1	.3181	29	.0059
2	−.0005	30	.1188
3	.0222	31	.0052
4	.1522	32	−.0747
5	−.4790	33	.0713
6	.0026	34	.1572
7	−.0962	35	.0830
8	−.0224	36	.2865
9	.0163	37	−.0482
10	−.0274	38	.1051
11	.3798	39	.0970
12	.0591	40	−.0651
13	.0576	41	.6165
14	−.0359	42	.0987
15	.5778	43	.0274
16	.2069	44	−.3540
17	.0666	45	−.0569
18	.1351	46	.7470
19	−.0125	47	.1416
20	−.0444	48	.0265
21	.0629	49	.4987
22	−.0020	50	.4555
23	.0866	51	.1326
24	.2609	52	−.1613
25	.3921	53	−.0679
26	.5584	54	−.0393
27	.0945	55	−.0539
28	.1781	56	.0460

[1] Loadings determined by Equimax rotation of the 13 factor principal components solution.

Beliefs

Personality and life style characteristics

Exposure patterns to different types of media

It was suggested that personal interviews should be conducted regarding consumer usage of cranberry sauce and the demographic profile of the respondent. Live questions would ask about the frequency of serving various meats and complementary products (like cranberry sauce) with these meats, cranberry sauce purchases, etc.

EXHIBIT 7. Factor Analysis of "Descriptions of Personalities and Lifestyles": Managerial Summary
Factor One (5.9 per cent variance explained)

Assigned[1] Variable No.	Loading	Label
46	.7470	I like to cook
41	.6165	I enjoy taking time to prepare meals
15	.5778	I like to cook new dishes
26	.5584	I like to prepare fancy dishes even if they take a long time
49	.4987	I enjoy serving spicy dishes
5	−.4790	I'm not a good cook
50*	.4555	Meals are a way to express affection for the family
25*	.3921	My family appreciates the work I put into a meal
11*	.3798	I really enjoy eating
44*	−.3540	We prefer plain and simple foods
24*	.2609	I enjoy cookouts
16*	.2069	I usually serve several relishes and other extras at holiday meals

Interpretive label: "Cooking enthusiast"

[1] A variable was assigned to Factor No. 1 if the absolute value of the largest loading of that variable on any of the 13 factors was equal to or greater than .30 and the absolute value of the loading of the variable on Factor 1 was within .15 of the absolute value of the maximum loading. An * indicated that the variable had been assigned to more than one factor.

EXHIBIT 8. Summary of Interpreted Factors for the "Descriptions of Personalities and Lifestyles"

Factor Number	Interpretive Label	Percentage of Total Variance	Cumulative Percentage
1	Cooking enthusiast	5.9	5.9
2	Sociable	5.8	11.7
3	Conscious meal planner	4.9	16.6
4	Traditional values	4.4	21.0
5	Active	4.2	25.2
6	Husband/family oriented	4.1	29.3
7	Dreamer	3.9	33.2
8	Weight watcher	3.9	37.1
9	Self-indulgent	3.7	40.8
10	Economically minded	3.7	44.5
11	Youth orientation	3.7	48.2
12	Light users	3.4	51.6
13	Healthy	3.1	54.7

EXHIBIT 9. Ocean Spray Cranberries, Inc. (A)
Labels Given to Factors Extracted from Five Types of Data

First Ten Factors in Order of Extraction	Attributes of Ideal Canned Fruit Products	Attributes of Jellied Cranberry Sauce	Attributes of Whole Berry Cranberry Sauce	Overall Attitudes and Feelings about Cranberry Sauce	Self-Description of Personality and Life Style
1	Convenience orientation	Appropriate for all meats	Appropriate for trad./formal meals	Rejection of frequent use	Cooking enthusiast
2	Attractive appearance	Attractive color	Easy accessibility	Family usage and interest	Sociable
3	Used with a variety of meats	Nourishing	Brings out variety of meat flavors	Perfect for special occasion meals	Conscious meal planner
4	Nutritive value	Traditional yet formal	Consistency	Appropriate for all meats	Traditional values
5	Fancy/special meals	Easy accessibility	Appetizer/snack	Elegant/fancy food	Active
6	Unique taste	Snack food	Wholesome	Tastes good/good for you	Husband/family oriented
7	Less frequent uses	Sharp taste	Sharp taste	Jellied form preferred	Dreamer
8	Adaptable	Everyday food	Heavy users of meat/fruit	Unique taste	Weight watcher
9	Relish association	Sweet/unusual taste		Negative taste aspects	Self-indulgent
10	Heavy users of meat/fruit	Smooth		Because of mom	Economically minded

The other items discussed above would be measured by a self-administered questionnaire. The questionnaire would include some questions on television, radio and newspaper exposure patterns as well as questions regarding readership of 24 general or female audience magazines. This magazine list was, according to the account manager at Young & Rubicam, "totally representative of the books which would be considered for a magazine effort for sauce." In the communication to the AHF team he had, however, added that it was "highly improbable that all of the magazines would ever be used."

In order to obtain around 1000 qualified respondents (purchased one or more cans in the last year), it seemed likely that around 1200 women would have to be contacted in their homes. If standard estimates for the costs of this kind of field work were used, the OSC managers figured that the additional expenditure for Phase 3 would amount to around $30,000. About $12,000 had been spent through the completion of Phase 2. Phase 3 costs would include the data collection, analysis and reporting to OSC management. The research team promised delivery of a report in March 1972. The field interviews would be made in late January and early February. Mr. Melvin was concerned about the timing because he had to prepare the marketing plan well before the new fiscal year started in September 1972!

Preliminary reports for the 1971 fall selling season indicated that OSC cranberry sauce sales were up by around 5 per cent compared to the previous year. Mr. Melvin attributed the increase to the fact he had mustered an almost 80 per cent higher marketing expenditure budget in fiscal 1971 than in fiscal 1970. He certainly hoped that the AHF study would give indications about how the marketing effort should be directed to give even better results in 1972. Since Phases 1 and 2 largely confirmed the brand manager's assumptions about cranberry consumers, it was not clear to him whether the final phase would produce the desired direction for future marketing.

OCEAN SPRAY CRANBERRIES, INC. (B)

FINDINGS OF THE FRUIT POSITIONING STUDY

Mr. Russell Haley of Appel, Haley, Fouriezos, Incorporated, presented in March 1972 the conclusions of the Fruit Positioning Study to the managers of marketing and marketing research at Ocean Spray Cranberries, Inc. (OSC) and the advertising agency personnel involved with OSC sauce products.[1] A 305-page report and additional computer printouts were also handed over by Mr. Haley. The study was generally given a favorable reception by the OSC managers. They noted that some findings confirmed those of a study undertaken in 1961–1962 by McCann-Erickson.

According to Mr. Haley, the central marketing problems for cranberry sauce were (1) relatively low per capita use and (2) an aging franchise. He suggested the following as five promising ways of increasing consumption:

1. Promoting cranberry sauce as a versatile poultry and meat accompaniment;
2. Changing people's perceptions of cranberry sauce;
3. Reminding people to use it;
4. Focusing communications efforts more sharply on potentially productive market segments; and
5. New product introductions.

The AHF research team stated in its 305-page report that "four clearcut attitudinal segments were found in the cranberry sauce market." These were labeled as follows:

Segment 1: Convenience oriented

Segment 2: Enthusiastic cooks

Segment 3: Disinterested

Segment 4: Decorators

Each consumer segment was described in a variety of ways. For instance, when compared with all consumers, the convenience-oriented segment was said to have "a higher preference for jellied form of cranberry sauce relative to whole berry," and "a higher share of people 45 years or older."

Background

At the invitation of OSC management, the marketing research firm Appel, Haley, Fouriezos, Inc. had conducted the final phase of a three-phased consumer research study about cranberry sauce. The overall purpose of the study was to develop a better understanding of cranberry sauce users—their

---

[1] For details of the exploration and pilot test phases of this research and for additional industry and company background, see Ocean Spray Cranberries, Incorporated (A).

behavior, attitudes, opinions, and beliefs. This would be accomplished by achieving the following research objectives:

1. Identify and describe the kinds of persons who use cranberry sauce
2. Provide an understanding of what consumers are seeking in choosing between complementary products for use such as in salads or with the main course
3. Look into the consumption of various food types as sources and potential sources of cranberry sauce usage
4. Describe consumer usage patterns with regard to cranberry sauce
5. Identify broad media types for OSC sauce for getting across its message to consumers
6. Investigate new product or line extension possibilities.

The cost of the whole project would be $44,500 ± 10 percent contingency for unforeseen costs or savings. The project was proposed in three phases which covered (1) exploration of areas to be covered, (2) development of measurement tools, and (3) measurement of the market on a national basis.

The purpose of the first phase was to define the competitive environment and to compile lists of product attributes, consumer beliefs, and personality and lifestyle characteristics of special relevance for cranberry sauce consumption. To this end, two focused group sessions were conducted among 20 women who were either heavy or light users of sauce in the past year. The results from Phase 1 were used in designing a questionnaire. The tentative list of questions was quite lengthy. The purpose of Phase 2 was to determine which of the many questions best reflected underlying consumer dimensions in the cranberry sauce market. Data for Phase 2 was collected by a pilot survey undertaken in the fall of 1971, in which a sample of 200 females living in ten market areas was personally interviewed.

Analysis of the pilot test data resulted in substantial revisions of the questionnaire. Between 30 to 98 percent of the items were dropped or exchanged within parts of the questionnaire. The structure of the questionnaire was, however, basically retained for later use in a national survey. Thus, most of the questions dealt with the following five areas:

1. Opinions about attributes of ideal canned fruit products;
2. Opinions about attributes of jellied cranberry sauce;
3. Opinions about attributes of whole berry cranberry sauce;
4. Overall attitudes and feelings about cranberry sauce; and
5. Descriptions of personalities and lifestyles.

The new questionnaire also included some questions on exposure patterns to broadcast and newspaper media as well as questions regarding readership of 24 national magazines for general or female audiences. At a meeting with Mr. Haley late in 1971, OSC management agreed to proceed with Phase 3.

Phase 3

The purpose of the third phase—a national survey—was to provide a better understanding of the attitudes and behavior of cranberry sauce users and to suggest potentially innovative ways of segmenting the existing demand for sauce. The respondents were sampled from 47 areas, 37 of which were Standard Metropolitan Statistical Areas, and the remaining 10 were nonmetropolitan counties. Quotas of persons to be interviewed were then established for each area, for example, 12 for Larimer County (Ft. Collins), Colorado and 100 for New York. Blocks or roads were randomly selected from maps of the sampling areas. A list with names of blocks or roads was given to each interviewer, who was directed to personally contact and screen a given number of females according to a specific procedure for choosing households within a block or road. The interviewers made daily reports through their supervisors to AHF of the number of completed interviews with eligible respondents. As in the pilot survey, potential respondents were personally screened to determine if they had purchased canned cranberry sauce in the past year. Around 1,300 women were contacted and 1,004 of them qualified as respondents and participated in the interviews.

Analysis of the Sample in the Aggregate

Before seeking the identity of potentially interesting homogeneous subgroups within the sample, the AHF research team examined the characteristics of the entire sample of 1,004 respondents. Frequency counts of the total sample on various demographic and socioeconomic characteristics, compared to available national distribution were as follows:

	AHF Sample, $N = 1004$	1970 U.S. Population Census
Age		
18–39	42%	44%
40–64	47	40
65 +	11	16
	100%	100%

Education
  High school or less   66%   79%
  Some college or more   34   21
                                                        100%   100%
Employment
  Full- or part-time employed   22%   42%
Children
  Have children 18 years or under living at
  home   63%   55%

The most commonly accepted opinions or beliefs about cranberry sauce reflected its traditional nature, food value, and integration as part of a meal rather than a garnish. The percentage of all respondents strongly agreeing or disagreeing with different belief statements is shown in Exhibit 1.

When consumers were asked about their inventory of cranberry sauce, 48% of them said they had at least one can at home. Of the 48%, 85% reported they had OSC cans. Since more than half of the respondents strongly agreed with the statement that "I probably would serve more cranberry sauce if I thought of it, but I don't," Mr. Haley suggested that promotions be directed toward building increased in-home inventories and stimulation of product usage.

It was found that "nutritious" and "has vitamins" were said to be "extremely important" characteristics of an ideal canned food product by 46% and 37%, respectively, of all interviewed cranberry sauce users. However, only 22% and 19%, respectively, "agreed completely" that jellied cranberry sauce had these characteristics. The research team concluded that a fortified product would help to provide reassurance in these areas.

The researchers thought that a secondary new cranberry sauce product might be one with "a consistency more similar to that of applesauce." They argued that "one principal reason for the popularity of cranberry sauce is its convenience in use. If it were made even more convenient (so that it could be easily spooned out of the can or stored in refrigerator dishes) it might provide a worthwhile stimulus to sales."

The research team found grounds for the statement that cranberry sauce is sold "in a somewhat ambiguous competitive environment, being perceived as something of a cross between a fruit and a garnish." A perceptual map developed as part of the Phase 1 research was put forward in support of this statement. Of the various food accompaniments, cranberry sauce products were perceived to be "closer" to applesauce than to catsup. This map was based on data collected from twenty women who had participated in the Phase 1 focused group interviews.

EXHIBIT 1. Ocean Spray Cranberries, Inc. (B)
Consumer Opinions or Beliefs (Overall Attitudes and Feelings) Regarding Cranberry Sauce

Variable Number	Belief Statement	Agree Completely/ Strongly	Disagree Completely/ Strongly	Difference
1	Cranberry Sauce Is a Traditional Food	92%	3%	89%
2	Cranberry Sauce Has Food Value as Well as an Attractive Appearance and Good Taste	87	4	83
3	Cranberry Sauce Is Part of the Meal Rather than a Garnish	72	17	55
4	I Usually Keep a Can of Cranberry Sauce in the Cupboard Year Round	65	26	39
5	I Probably Would Serve More Cranberry Sauce if I Thought of It, but I Don't	57	31	26
6	I Serve Cranberry Sauce with Turkey to Add Moistness	43	39	4
7	A Firmer Jellied Sauce Is a Higher Quality Cranberry Sauce	29	34	−5
8	Cranberry Sauce Is Served with Pork because It Cuts the Grease	26	37	−11
9	Cranberry Sauce Is Too Tart to Serve with Spicy Foreign Foods	16	56	−40
10	I Often Make My Own Cranberry Sauce when Fresh Cranberries Are Available	26	68	−42
11	I Use Whole Cranberry Sauce as a Cooking or Baking Ingredient	20	69	−49
12	Cranberry Sauce Is Appropriate for Roast Whole Chicken but not for Broiled or Fried Chicken	16	67	−51

478

EXHIBIT 1. (Continued)

Variable Number	Belief Statement	Agree Completely/ Strongly	Disagree Completely/ Strongly	Difference
13	I Often Use Jellied Cranberry Sauce as an Ingredient in Cooking and Baking	16	74	−58
14	I Feel Almost Patriotic When I Serve Cranberry Sauce	10	71	−61
15	I Don't Like to Serve Cranberry Sauce Too Often Because It Loses Its Significance	9	77	−68
16	I'll Eat Cranberry Sauce in a Restaurant, But I Don't Serve It Very Often at Home	12	80	−68
17	Cranberry Sauces Dries Up in the Can Before It Is Used Up	8	79	−71
18	All Brands of Cranberry Sauce Are Made by Ocean Spray	5	80	−75
19	Eating Cranberries Can Cause Health Problems	3	78	−75
20	I Serve Cranberry Sauce to Cool Hot Food	6	81	−75
21	Cranberry Sauce Should Be Served Only on Thanksgiving and Christmas	5	87	−82

Sample Size = 1,004

When the research team examined the ways in which cranberry sauce and jelly were served, they discovered the following reported usage patterns:

Application	Percent of Cranberry Serving Occasions
Accompaniment to meats	84%
As a vegetable substitute	3
In plain or molded salads	9
In cooking (glaze or topping)	1
In baking	1
In desserts or dessert toppings	1
	100%

By combining information on consumers' frequency of use of the sauce with various meats and the frequency of eating these meats, it was found that chicken, roast beef and pork were worth special considerations for future advertising copy and package label. The method and data which led the research team to this conclusion were the following:

Each respondent was given a score based on her frequency of use of cranberry sauce with an individual meat—5 for "always," 4 for "frequently," 3 for "sometimes," 2 for "seldom," and 1 for "never." The average score for light users was subtracted from the average score for heavy users. (25% of all users were classified as heavy users, and 28% as light users.) The results were multiplied by the frequency of eating an individual meat and this figure in turn was multiplied by 100. In other words, the numbers in the following table are indicative of the relative amounts of volume which would result if light users were to behave like heavy users.

Jellied	Index	Whole Berry	Index
Fried Chicken	187	Baked or Roast Chicken	180
Baked or Roast Chicken	180	Fried Chicken	119
Leftover Chicken	130	Pork/Pork Chops/Pork Roast	105
Roast Beef	125	Leftover Chicken	104
Broiled Chicken	120	Baked or Roast Turkey	102
Pork/Pork Chops/Pork Roast	105	Broiled Chicken	96
Hamburger	86	Hamburger	86
Ham	80	Roast Beef	75
Leftover Beef	76	Leftover Turkey	72
Leftover Turkey	60	Steak	68

Management observed that the aggregated sample analyses were not inconsistent with the findings of the MARPLAN '62 study which they had received in 1962. One of the major differences between the 1962 study and the AHF study, however, was AHF's determination to identify subsets of the entire sauce market in psychographic terms and to suggest variations in OSC's strategy based on the resulting market segments.

Determining Psychographic Market Segments

The method used by AHF to determine a segmentation strategy and structure for the cranberry sauce and jelly market was described to the casewriter by Mr. Tibor Weiss, Senior Vice President of AHF. The data collection phase of Phase 3 had produced three separate categories of information dealing respectively with lifestyles, personality, and product attribute judgments.

These data were eventually input to a cluster analysis program, but first the original data sets were reduced to a smaller number of important variables. Instead of using individual items of the questionnaire as possible bases for clustering, a small number of summed scales were constructed. For example, four scales of various belief items were constructed as follows. Using judgment supported by factor analysis, a few items were selected and their responses were added together to form a new scale, thus creating a new variable or item.[1] The four resulting belief scales and the tentative labels attached by the AHF research team were:

Scale 1 "Traditional"	6 — ("I usually keep a can of cranberry sauce in the cupboard year round") + "I don't like to serve cranberry sauce too often because it loses its significance." [Note $(6 - x)$ reverses the polarity of item x, thus $S_1 = (6 - x_4) + x_{15}$]
Scale 2 "Cook and Bake"	"I often use jellied cranberry sauce as an ingredient in cooking and baking" + "I use whole cranberry sauce as a cooking or baking ingredient." [$S_2 = x_{13} + x_{11}$]
Scale 3 "Serving Interest"	"Cranberry sauce is served with pork because it cuts the grease" + "Cranberry sauce should be served only on Thanksgiving and Christmas" + "I serve cranberry sauce to cool hot food" + "A firmer jellied sauce is a higher quality cranberry sauce." [$S_3 = x_8 + x_{21} + x_{20} + x_7$]

[1] This new scale is sometimes called a cumulative or Guttman scale.

Scale 4
"Food Value"

"Cranberry sauce is part of the meal rather than a garnish" + "Cranberry sauce has food value as well as an attractive appearance and good taste." [$S_4 = x_3 + x_2$

Similarly, six summed scales of personality items, and six summed scales of benefit items were also constructed. The full list of belief variables is included in Exhibit 1.

The belief scales, personality scales and benefit scales then were compared for their potential as bases for defining market segments. Each set of scales was used in the cluster analysis program separately producing three possible interpretations of market structure.

The cluster analysis program assigned individual members of the sample into groups such that all members of a given group were relatively similar in terms of the belief, personality or benefit characteristics input to the program, and such that each successive group would be relatively dissimilar when compared to all other groups. A more explicit description of the cluster analysis is included as Appendix A. The research team at AHF decided that the beliefs data provided the best of the three bases or clustering, and that there were four clusters that were of managerial consequence. Those clusters were named "Convenience Oriented," "Enthusiastic Cook," "Disinterested," and "Decorator." When the four segments were compared on some standard marketing variables, the results were as shown [see page 483].

To enrich the understanding of the four clusters, a variety of psychographic and traditional marketing variables were cross-tabulated against cluster membership patterns. The resulting tabulations were presented by Mr. Haley as a means of making the clusters more lifelike, more humanistic and more realistic potential targets for the OSC marketing strategy. In turn, the clusters were described according to their central tendencies as indicated by the following types of measurements:

1. Key benefits of ideal fruit products
2. Key beliefs about cranberry sauce products
3. Key food related lifestyle characteristics
4. Key attitudes toward cranberry sauce products
5. Product usage behavioral tendencies
6. Demographics
7. Media exposure patterns

Exhibit 2 lists the between cluster comparisons for each of the above characteristics, and also compares the individual clusters to the population means on many individual items.

Segment Size	Convenience Oriented 299	Enthusiastic Cook 257	Disinterested 270	Decorator 178	Total 1,004
Percent of all respondents	30	25	27	18	100
Percent of total volume purchased	34	32	16	18	100
Percent of jellied	35	29	17	19	100
Percent of whole berry	30	40	14	16	100
Percent heavy users (19 or more cans per year)	27	38	13	25	25
Percent medium users (7 to 18 cans per year)	48	45	40	54	46
Percent light users (6 or less cans per year)	25	18	47	21	28
Total	100	100	100	100	100
Percent who noticed price difference between OSC and other brands	34	37	30	36	34
Percent who purchased 10 OSC cans of last 10	75	74	76	76	74
Age distribution					
18–39	36	35	58	37	42
40–64	53	56	35	44	47
65 +	11	9	6	17	10
	100	100	100	100	100

EXHIBIT 2. Ocean Spray Cranberries, Inc. (B)
Characterization of Four Consumer Segments

Type of Measurement	Segment 1: "Convenience Oriented" N₁ = 299		Segment 2: "Enthusiastic Cook" N₂ = 257		Segment 3: "Disinterested" N₃ = 270		Segment 4: "Decorator" N₄ = 178	
	Benefit	%	Benefit	%	Benefit	%	Benefit	%
Key Benefits of Ideal Food Products Rated "Very Important"	Quick		Appropriate for holidays	4	Different taste	−1	Easy availability	12
	Goes well with turkey			4	Festive	−1	Appropriate for formal meals	11
	Easy to serve		Goes well in salads	3			Acceptable to everyone	10
	Smooth consistency		Colorful	3			Appropriate for holidays	9
							Variety of uses	9
							Available year round	9
							Festive	8
							Quick	8
							Has vitamins	8
							Sweet taste	8
	Belief	%	Belief	%	Belief	%	Belief	%
Key Beliefs, Rated "Agree Very Much"	Part of meal rather than garnish		Use whole cranberry sauce as a baking ingredient		Would serve more cranberry sauce if I thought of it, but I don't		Firmer jellied sauce is higher quality	23
	Has food value as	20	Usually keep can	21			Cranberry sauce	1

Characteristic	%
well as attractive appearance	
Usually keep can year round	15
Traditional food	13
	5

Characteristic	%
year round	
Often makes own cranberry sauce when fresh berries are available	14
Often use jellied cranberry sauce as a cooking/baking ingredient	10
Cranberry sauce is one of favorite foods	9
	7

Characteristic	%
is served with pork because it cuts the grease	17
Usually keep can year round	17
I serve cranberry sauce with turkey to add moistness	15
Cranberry sauce is one of favorite foods	8
Should be served only on Thanksgiving and Christmas	5

Characteristic	%
Prefer natural foods to ones with artificial ingredients	1

Characteristic	%
Enjoy being active	9
Like to cook	8
Like to cook new dishes	7
Enjoy taking time to prepare meals	7
Like to prepare fandy dishes	6
Like to prepare colorful salads	6
Sociable	6

Characteristic	%
Prefer fresh vegetables to canned or frozen products	0

Key Life Styles Rated "Describes Me Completely"

Characteristic	%
I believe we are on earth to enjoy ourselves	14
Nutrition conscious	11
Believe in things parents believed in	10
Interested in food advertising	10
Gets together with family for	10

EXHIBIT 2. (Continued)

Type of Measurement	Segment 1: "Convenience Oriented" $N_1 = 299$	Segment 2: "Enthusiastic Cook" $N_2 = 257$	Segment 3: "Disinterested" $N_3 = 270$	Segment 4: "Decorator" $N_4 = 178$
		Like beef on the rare side		holidays 8 Prefer natural foods to ones with artificial in-gredients 8 Serve children the things they like to eat 7 Like to look for sales in the gro-cery store 7 Enjoy taking time to prepare meals 7
		6		
Attitudes				
Main Attitude	See cranberry sauce as a conve-nient staple. High preference of jellied form relative to whole berry	High in seeing cranberry sauce as a cooking/bak-ing ingredient	See cranberry sauce as a change of pace	See cranberry sauce as a means of sprucing up meals

	Attitude	%	Attitude	%	Attitude	%	Attitude	%
Supporting Attitudes Rated "Agree Very Much"	High rejection of whole berry	6	Low on rejection of whole berry	−16	High rejection of whole berry by adults and children	9	Low on rejection of whole berry	−3
	High brand awareness	4	Low on rejection of jellied	−4	High rejection of jellied by adults and children	7	Low on rejection of jellied	−3
	High regular brand OSC	2	Low on preference of jellied over whole berry		High on preference of jellied relative to whole berry	−3	High on preference of jellied form relative to whole berry	9
	High future OSC purchase intention	2	High in seeing OSC as costing more	−3	Low on brand awareness	−3	Low on future OSC purchase intentions	7
	High in seeing OSC as costing more	2			Low on regular brand OSC	−2		−3

	Behavior	%	Behavior	%	Behavior	%	Behavior	%
Behavior Rated "Tend to do Frequently"	High on eating baked/roast chicken	9	High use of whole berry with turkey	13	High consumption of pork and fried chicken	5	Favors jellied and applesauce as accompaniments	
	High on eating leftover chickens	3	High on consumption of all meat, poultry, and fish		Low on accompaniments, including cranberries		Low on jellied with chicken	−7
	High on eating applesauce as accompaniment	2+4	High on use of 16 oz. cans	−1+6	Low on use of 16 oz. cans	−7	High on consumption of leftover chicken, leftover chicken, and broiled chicken	4−7
	High on use of cranberry sauce as meat accompa-		High on serving cranberry sauce	8	High on use of cranberry sauce as a meat accom-	8		

EXHIBIT 2. (Continued)

Type of Measurement	Segment 1: "Convenience Oriented" $N_1 = 299$		Segment 2: "Enthusiastic Cook" $N_2 = 257$		Segment 3: "Disinterested" $N_3 = 270$		Segment 4: "Decorator" $N_4 = 178$	
	Characteristic	**%**	**Characteristic**	**%**	**Characteristic**	**%**	**Characteristic**	**%**
(continued)	…piment High on serving cranberry sauce on all occasions, esp. informal meals	−5 +2 / 3 −6	on all occasions	10	paniment only; Low on serving cranberry sauce on all occasions; Serve cranberry sauce at Thanksgiving and Christmas	−11	Low on use of 16 oz. cans; Low on using cranberry sauce on all occasions	−3 / −4
Key Demographics	45 and older; Low on college; High on U.S. as parents' country	5 / −3	40 to 64; High on college or more; High on U.K. as parents' country of origin; High on upscale occupation of household head	6 / 2 / 7 / 3	18 to 39; High on some college; High on children living at home; High on U.S. as parents' country of origin; High on middle occupation of household head	10 / 3 / 11 / 5 / 3	65 and older; High on some high school or less; Low on children living at home; High on Germany/Austria, Italy, and Russia as parents' country of origin	7 / 8 / 8 / 3

Media	%	Media	%	Media	%	Media	%
Buy newspapers Above average readership of:	2	Buy newspaper Above average readership of:	3	Buy newspaper Low on magazines	−5	Buy newspaper Above average readership of:	−1
Ladies Home Journal	3	*Family Circle*	8			*True Story*	4
Reader's Digest	2	*Woman's Day*	8			*True Romance*	2
TV Guide	2	*Better Homes & Gardens*	6			*Reader's Digest*	2
Good House-keeping	2	*Good House-keeping*	5				
		McCall's	5				
		Ladies' Home Journal	5				

Note: The % number to the right of each item shows the difference between the frequency count (%) for the segment and the frequency count for the total sample on the item.

Presentation to Management

In his presentation to OSC management, Mr. Haley said the four clusters were "four clearcut attitudinal segments." He went on to say that "three of the four segments just described are attractive targets and, based on the information now available to us, tailormade campaigns can be designed for each segment." He described these campaigns in terms of buying incentives, copy visuals, copy tonality, promotions, and media, as follows:

	Target Clusters		
	"Convenience Oriented"	"Enthusiastic Cook"	"Decorator"
Buying Incentives	Position as a convenient, versatile meat accompaniment rather than as a special-purpose product. A natural food.	Both jellied and whole berry can be promoted for this segment. Color, versatility, and usefulness as a cooking/baking ingredient are desirable claims.	A good way of dressing up your meats and leftovers. A way of interjecting a festive note at mealtimes.
Copy Visuals	Informal settings, family meals, baked/roast chicken particularly good.	Larger family scenes or scenes with guests. Big eaters.	Mature models, slight accent permissible, leftovers particularly good.
Copy Tonality	Brisk, matter of fact. These women are not involved in cooking.	Friendly, sociable, reflecting interest in people and in cooking.	Reassuring, reinforcing. Emphasis on color. These people already love cranberry sauce.
Promotions	Tie-ins with chickens and meats.	Recipes, cookbooks, salads, not price conscious.	Price promotions are apt to be especially effective.

| Media | Small-space re-
minders in
newspapers.
*Ladies' Home
Journal,
Reader's Digest,
TV Guide,
Good House-
keeping.* | *Family Circle,
Woman's Day,
Better Homes &
Gardens, Good
Housekeeping,
McCall's,
Ladies' Home
Journal.* | *True Story,
True Romance,
Reader's Digest.* |

Comparisons of the clusters which differed in volume consumed and in types of cranberry products used led the research team to talk about "a cycle running through the market." The lightest sauce users seemed to strongly favor the jellied form. At the next heavier usage level people became somewhat more frequent users of the jellied form. At a still higher level were heavier users who used both whole berry and jellied sauce, favoring whole berry because of its usefulness in cooking and baking. Finally, there was the real cranberry enthusiast who employed fresh berries in making her own sauce.

The researchers did not think that efforts to attract nonusers held large promise. This had also been the conclusion of a similar though nonsegmented study undertaken in 1962 by McCann-Erickson. Moreover, only 23% of the households originally contacted were nonusing households. Some researchers thought that light users might be difficult to motivate because of their relatively low interest in cooking. Their general advice was that the best point of emphasis seemed to be somewhere in the middle of the usage cycle. "People at this point have shown their acceptance of cranberries. However, by the standard of heavy cranberry users or average applesauce users, their volume of consumption is still low. Thus we believe that a huge potential lies in this intermediate group. Moreover, we believe that a marketing strategy aimed at increasing the consumption of this group will, at the same time, draw new users into the market."

Mr. Haley also offered suggestions regarding pricing of jellied and whole berry sauce. "Since the jellied form has the greatest expansion potential, its price should be kept as low as is economically feasible. However, people who consume whole berry are less price conscious. Therefore, it should be possible to allow the price to float a little upward without damage to unit sales volume. Thus it appears that whole berry can safely be established as a higher profit margin item."

Shortly after OSC management had received the study, Mr. Melvin, brand manager for sauce, requested his advertising agency to develop advertising campaign proposals in light of the findings regarding market segmentation. Mr. Melvin's first reactions were that the study certainly was a needed updated version of the old 1962 study, a furthermore, that it would give him information to propose a more efficient advertising and promotion program. The right segmentation of the franchise should produce a much higher efficiency. There were, however, different opinions as to which of the four segments ought to be the prime target. Mr. Melvin felt the "convenience-oriented" group would be best, but Mr. Walsh, director of product marketing, argued for the "enthusiastic (or creative) cooks." The discussion about selecting a segment dealt also with the practical problems of identifying and reaching a particular consumer segment.

Mr. Melvin thought also that the broad approaches to advertising used in the previous two seasons had not worked too well and should be reevaluated in light of some of the new findings. He noticed that the respondents generally overstated their volume of sauce consumption. It seemed that OSC had a huge potential in just bringing actual volume up to claimed volume of consumption.

APPENDIX A.
OCEAN SPRAY CRANBERRIES, INC. (B)

CONSTRUCTION AND INTERPRETATION OF BELIEF CLUSTERS

The Appel, Haley and Fourezios, Inc. research team used two complementary data analysis techniques to form the four belief clusters presented to the Ocean Spray Company brand management team. The two techniques require the use of large digital computers and have many specific forms depending upon how they are programmed, but generically they are known as cluster analysis and multiple discriminant analysis. While both methods have been applied to impersonal objects and to variables observed over classes of objects, it is most illustrative to think of the two methods as they are routinely applied to samples of individual consumers. Cluster analysis is a procedure for forming an arbitrary number of relatively homogeneous subgroups of individuals within a larger, heterogeneous sample of respondents. Multiple discriminant analysis is a procedure for interpreting the differences between a number of existing groups of respondents.

Cluster Analysis

Cluster analysis can be performed in a variety of ways and many statistical algorithms have been written that have essentially the same objective: to form homogeneous groups of respondents drawn from a heterogeneous population. Procedures are either aggregative (proceeding by combining individuals into groups, and smaller groups with individuals or other smaller groups to form larger groups) or disaggregative (proceeding by taking the entire sample—the largest possible group—and breaking it into successively smaller groups of increasing homogeneity). Both aggregative and disaggregative procedures have been written that allow for an individual respondent to be reassigned from an existing subgroup to a newer subgroup that better matches the characteristics of that respondent.

Users of cluster analysis are not required to know in advance how many, or what kind of clusters they eventually will choose. The purpose of the analysis is to suggest several alternative clustering arrangements from which analysts must select one that best meets their particular information needs. The analyst, perhaps in consultation with management, must decide how many clusters will make up the "solution" to the grouping problem being addressed. The analyst has the additional burden of interpreting the solution, first in terms of descriptions of the central tendencies of the resulting clusters, and eventually in terms of what the clusters imply for purposes of marketing decision making.

Multiple Discriminant Analysis

Cluster analysis is used to form groups, and multiple discriminant analysis is used to interpret the statistical differences between a given number of existing groups. Given a set of existing groups, multiple discriminant analysis can also be used to predict into which existing group a new individual, not presently a member of any of the existing groups, is more likely to be classified. Thus multiple discriminant analysis, working with an existing set of groups, is used to perform tasks of interpretation and classification. Because it works with grouped data, it is a good counterpart technique to cluster analysis. Together, the two methods give the analyst a series of procedures that can be used to form groups from survey observations, interpret some of the underlying differences between those groups, and develop a classification scheme for predicting the group membership of individuals not represented in the original sample.

The AHF Segment Building Process—Cluster Analysis

The sample was split in two halves of 502 respondents each and separate cluster analysis solutions were determined for each sample. This split-half technique was used to give the researchers an opportunity to judge the stability of the cluster solutions. The two subsamples consisted of individuals with even and odd identification numbers; thus there would be reason to expect strong similarities between the two cluster solutions except in the event that the relationships between the beliefs variables and homogeneous population subsets were spurious. A series of cluster analyses were performed using a top-down, hierarchical, disaggregative algorithm. Briefly, this computer program worked in the following way:

1. All respondents were first assigned to a single group.
2. The respondent farthest from the cluster mean or centroid was then selected as the centroid for a second cluster.
3. All respondents were sequentially tested to determine if a reassignment to the second cluster would reduce the within group sum-squared error, a statistical measure of within group homogeneity.
4. When it was no longer possible to reduce the within group sub-squared error by reassigning any single respondent to the second cluster, then that individual farthest from either of the two centroids became the centroid for a third cluster and the reassignment process was repeated.
5. The number of clusters was allowed to increase to some maximum number of clusters, set by the researcher. This number was set at six.
6. When this limit was reached, the program automatically terminated.

After constructing 4 product belief scales, 6 personality scales and 6 product use benefit scales, each set of scales was used as the basis for two cluster analyses—one for the 502 respondents with even numbers and the second for the 502 with odd numbers. The clustering solution derived from the 4 belief scales led to the highest ratio of between group variation to within group average variation as calculated for all solutions.

The belief clusters were therefore selected as the basis for deriving the market segments eventually presented to OSC management. Mr. Haley considered the belief items to have the most direct implications for marketing.

Looking at the cluster solutions for the belief items, it seemed clear that the samples should be divided in no less than 4 clusters. With only 2 or 3 clusters, the third belief scale, Serving Interest, appeared not to be a basis for between-cluster differentiation as indicated in the table of F ratios shown below. On the other hand, it seemed that little was gained by using more than 4 clusters.

The similarities between the "even" and "odd" halves of the sample were judged quite acceptable and gave the research team confidence that there were systematic relationships between the belief measurements and stable consumer subgroups. One of the two 4-cluster solutions was chosen as the basis for a complete classification of the 1004 respondents. The "odd" solution was chosen because of apparently cleaner delineations, as measured by generally larger F ratios, of the 4 clusters on the 4 scales.

Classifying the Remaining Respondents—Multiple Discriminant Analysis

Having accepted a cluster solution, the AHF team used the structure of the "odd" groups to define a strategy for classifying the entire sample. The classification strategy employed multiple discriminant analysis (MDA).

The computer program used was a stepwise discriminant analysis program called BMDO7M selected from the Biomedical Computer Programs library written at the Health Science Computing Facility of the University of California, Los Angeles. The program calculated a discriminant function for each cluster with coefficients similar to those in regression analysis. The classification rule based on this set of discriminant functions was that a respondent should be assigned to cluster 1 if the value of L_1 was higher than the values of L_2, L_3 and L_4, which were obtained by plugging the respondent's values on each of the four X's into the functions.

As shown below, this classification of the "odd" sample using that rule led to a near perfect (92 percent correct) classification of the 502 respondents. The same set of discriminant functions was then used to classify the remaining 502 respondents from the "even" sample into one of the four clusters. A probabilistic estimate that the respondent belonged to a certain cluster was computed. The discriminant function coefficients were used to compute the four L-values for each respondent. The resulting L-values were then considered to be normally distributed around the L-values of the four cluster means and using the assumptions of the normal distribution, probabilities of group membership were computed. Respondent 256, for example, was found to have a .94 probability of being a member of cluster 2. The group membership probabilities for a few members of the odd sample are shown [on page 499].

Number of Clusters:	2		3		4		5		6	
Sample Halves:	Even	Odd	Even	Odd	Even	Odd	Even	Odd	Even	Odd
Items										
Beliefs	238	231	175	194	159	153	123	124	79	85
Personality	143	146	82	81	66	71	50	46	44	44
Benefits	112	119	101	101	59	66	57	51	36	51

Number of Clusters:	2		3		4		5		6	
Sample Half:	Even	Odd	Even	Odd	Even	Odd	Even	Odd	Even	Odd
Univaritte F ratios										
Scale 1, "Traditional"	1214	1117	337	413	340	377	392	347	358	289
Scale 2, "Cook and Bake"	101	53	452	600	275	307	380	283	330	294
Scale 3, "Serving Interest"	5	4	19	20	198	186	169	194	193	247
Scale 4, "Food Value"	228	318	407	320	273	255	248	345	268	295
Average within group sums of squares (W)	2.02	2.05	1.51	1.48	1.14	1.13	.92	.91	.78	.79
Between group sums of squares (B)	484	474	263	287	182	174	114	112	66	62
B/W ratio	238	231	175	194	159	153	124	123	85	79

Group	Size	"Traditional" X_1	"Cook and Bake" X_2	"Serving Interest" X_3	"Food Value" X_4
Cluster 1	134	3.15 (1.30)	2.51 (0.80)	7.60 (1.83)	9.40 (0.81)
Cluster 2	123	3.24 (1.38)	6.55 (1.82)	7.64 (2.04)	8.27 (1.45)
Cluster 3	148	6.51 (1.56)	2.90 (1.36)	8.33 (2.20)	6.99 (1.80)
Cluster 4	97	3.32 (1.48)	3.18 (1.71)	11.61 (2.44)	7.97 (1.65)
Total "Odd Half"	502	4.19	3.74	8.60	8.13

	Constant	"Traditional"	"Cook and Bake"	"Serving Interest"	"Food Value"
$L_1 =$	-24.66	$+0.2505X_1$	$-0.0915X_2$	$+1.128X_3$	$+3.984X_4$
$L_2 =$	-24.87	$+0.3488X_1$	$+2.123X_2$	$+0.8438X_3$	$+3.082X_4$
$L_3 =$	-21.73	$+2.187X_1$	$+0.2419X_2$	$+0.9776X_3$	$+2.521X_4$
$L_4 =$	-26.29	$-0.0481X_1$	$+0.0572X_2$	$+2.182X_3$	$+3.067X_4$

Classified by Cluster Analysis	Number of Respondents Classified by MDA				
	Cluster 1	Cluster 2	Cluster 3	Cluster 4	Total
Cluster 1	127	0	1	6	134
Cluster 2	11	111	1	0	123
Cluster 3	2	4	141	1	148
Cluster 4	8	4	1	84	97
Total	148	119	144	91	502

Respondent No.	Probabilities of Group Membership				Group Assignment
	Group 1	Group 2	Group 3	Group	
255	.52440	.31081	.00028	.16449	1
256	.04790	.93954	.00127	.01127	2
257	.00280	.99135	.00100	.00484	2
258	.00021	.78391	.21548	.00037	2
259	.49128	.13987	.32159	.04724	1
260	.24562	.00029	.00109	.75299	4

The respondent was allocated to the cluster he or she was most likely to belong to. The AHF analysts had by these procedures obtained the following four clusters:

Cluster	Number of Respondents
1	299
2	257
3	270
4	178
Total	1004

The discriminant functions were also useful in interpreting the obtained clusters; for example, since cluster 2 was strongly associated with high scores on scales 2 and 4, the interpretive label "enthusiastic cook" seemed appropriate. Additional interpretations of the clusters were made using cross-tabulations such as those presented in Exhibit 2.

Author Index

Aaker, D. A., 21, 296, 321
Achenbaum, A., 16, 90, 172, 386
Ackerman, S. J., 90
Acito, F., 89
Adams, A. J., 12, 173, 365
Adler, L., 60
Ajzen, I., 88, 325
Akerlof, G. A., 48
Alpert, L., 16, 215
Anderson, B., 89
Andrews, J. R., 279
Andrews, R. B., 148
Arabie, P., 393
Arbeit, S. P., 2, 382
Arndt, J., 215
Arnold, S. J., 219
Assael, H., 110, 191, 216
Athaide, K., 16
Atkin, C., 32
Axelrod, J. N., 46, 90, 156, 333
Ayres, R. V., 98

Baldwin, B. M., 387
Barach, J. A., 182
Bartos, R., 297
Bass, F. M., 49, 100, 102, 219, 390
Bauer, R. A., 23, 43
Baumwoll, J., 16
Baxter, J. C., 302
Beard, A. D., 297
Beckwith, N. E., 89, 129
Benson, P. H., 360
Berkowitz, L., 149
Bettman, J. R., 148, 178, 180
Blattberg, R. C., 394
Block, M., 32

Bogart, L., 37, 44, 47
Bonoma, T. V., 302
Boote, A. S., 3
Britney, K. E. A., 190
Britt, S. H., 37
Brunner, J. S., 33

Calantone, R. J., 389
Caples, J., 159
Carmone, F. J., 105, 108, 217, 218
Carroll, D. G., 217
Carroll, J. D., 104, 105, 393
Carterette, E. C., 104
Case, D., 370
Case, P. B., 64, 65, 85
Chang, J. J., 105
Chaplin, J. P., 33
Chave, E. J., 58
Chay, R., 337
Chestnut, R. W., 89
Chittenden, D., 127
Chotin, M., 16
Clancy, K. J., 16, 32, 45, 137, 218, 286
Clarke, Peter, 21
Cliff, N., 391
Cohen, J. B., 13, 250
Cook, F. L., 50
Coombs, C. H., 105
Cooper, A. S., 119
Courtney, Alice E., 19
Cox, D. F., 128
Crawford, Bruce, 1
Crespi, I., 60
Cutler, F., 61

Dalkey, N. C., 184

Day, G. S., 21, 97, 296, 321
DeKupsa, C., 378
DeLuca, R., 133, 375
Demby, E., 6, 7, 16
Deming, W. E., 135, 222
DeSarbo, W., 393
DeVita, S., 88
Dhalla, N. K., 22, 143
Dickens, W. T., 48
Dickson, P. P., 394
Donius, J. F., 100, 370
Dorny, L., 294
Douglas-Tate, Melody, 23
Druckman, D., 302
DuBois, C., 90, 319
Dunn, T., 16, 280
Dutka, S., 199

Eastlack, J. O., Jr., 135
Edwards, A. L., 12, 60
Ehrenberg, A. S. C., 143
Einhorn, H. J., 193

Fergin, B., 110
Fein, G., 390
Felder, L. C., 302
Fennell, G., 32
Fenwick, I., 389, 391
Festinger, L., 90
Fishbein, M., 88, 178, 325
Fisher, W., 89
Fishman, E., 16
Frank, R. E., 3, 13, 16, 216, 394
Frankel, J., 54
Friedman, H., 32
Friedman, M. P., 104
Funkhauser, G. R., 392
Furse, D. H., 346

Gage, C. W., 277
Galloway, J., 50
Gardner, Burleigh B., 35
Garreau, J., 2
Gatty, R., 16, 47, 86, 147, 155, 163, 215, 326, 334, 365
Gerhold, P., 279
Gibson, L. D., 306
Ginter, J. L., 90
Gold, B., 36
Goldberg, A., 16

Goldberg, L. R., 116
Goldstocker, J. L., 13
Grass, R. C., 46, 294
Green, P. E., 88, 105, 108, 209, 210, 217, 218
Greenberg, M., 16, 217
Greenberg, M. G., 380
Greenhalgh, C., 333
Greer, T. V., 382
Greyser, S. A., 43
Gross, I., 289, 313
Guilford, J. P., 58
Gutman, J., 110
Guttman, L., 59

Haber, R. N., 40
Haley, R. I., 14, 33, 36, 47, 64, 65, 78, 85, 86, 102, 111, 131, 138, 144, 147, 155, 161, 163, 211, 215, 226, 239, 241, 250, 307, 315, 326, 334, 365, 387
Hardin, D. K., 94
Hare, I., 34
Haring, A., 382
Harman, H. H., 87
Harper, M., 49
Harris, B., 192
Harrison, R. P., 302
Hartigan, J. A., 109
Haskins, J. B., 51
Heller, H., 16
Helmer, O., 184
Hendon, D. W., 41
Hershenson, M., 40
Holbrook, M. B., 36
Holman, R., 111
Hornik, J., 172
Howard, John, L., 22
Howard, N., 192
Hughes, G. D., 20, 61, 156, 228
Hyman, H. H., 37

Jacobs, B., 62
Jacoby, J., 5, 88, 89
Jain, A. K., 89
James, William, 31
Johnson, R. M., 13, 16, 88, 193, 213, 392
Johnson, S. C., 105, 191
Jones, R. R., 116
Juster, F. T., 62

Kalwani, M. V., 5

Kane, C., 237
Kanter, D. L., 328
Kapohen, Arthur, 7
Kassarjian, H., 89, 129
Kelly, G. A., 176
Kemeny, J. G., 365
Kendall, K. W., 389, 391
King, C. W., 100, 102
Klapper, J. T., 37
Klein, B., 48
Knapp, M., 165
Kominik, N., 21, 112
Kover, A. J., 17, 139
Kozak, R. P., 346
Kraw, T. S., 33
Kriewall, M. A., 89
Krishnamurthi, L., 89, 210
Krugman, H. E., 22, 32, 33, 46, 143, 154, 164, 295
Kurnit, S., 133, 279
Kweskin, D. M., 32, 45
Kyner, D. B., 5

Lambek, E., 16
Lamparter, A., 16
Lazarsfeld, P. F., 159
Leavitt, C., 112, 297
Leffier, K. G., 48
Lehman, C., 47
Lehmann, D. R., 36, 89, 129, 172, 190
Lemert, J. B., 59
Lessler, R. S., 269
Levine, J. M., 33
Levitt, T., 95
Lewis, R. C., 382
Light, L., 270
Likert, R., 59
Lipstein, B., 280
Longman, K. A., 289
Lonsdale, R. F., 390
Lucas, D. B., 37, 296
Luh, C. W., 314
Lutterman, K., 149
Lynch, J. G., Jr., 109

Macarte, P. J., 319
McConville, M., 112, 297
MacDonald, C., 46
McGinness, E., 33
McGuire, W. J., 39, 140

MacKuen, M., 34
MacLachlan, J., 62
McMennamin, J., 5
Maloney, J. C., 51, 295
Manning, B., 279
Marchak, M. P., 319
Marquis, K., 54
Massey, W. F., 13, 394
Mehrabian, A., 111, 303
Melvin, S., 16
Merton, R. K., 159
Meyer, E., 47
Miaoulis, G., 241
Miller, A. H., 34
Miller, W. B., 279, 328
Mitchell, A. A., 31
Moran, W. T., 5, 129
Moriarty, M. M., 365
Moriarty, R. T., 247
Morrison, D. C., 5, 185, 219
Moskowitz, H., 62
Mowen, J. C., 32
Murphy, G., 33
Myers, J. H., 102, 110

Naples, M. J., 46, 280, 333, 334
Neelankavil, J., 280
Nelson, P. J., 48
Nelson, R., 16
Neswald, D., 16
Norris, E. E., 111
Nosanchuk, T. A., 319
Nunnally, J. C., 390
Nutter, S. B., 89, 210

Ogilvy, D., 42
Olson, J. C., 31
Osgood, C., 60, 63
Ott, L. E., 16, 137
Overholser, C., 16

Palda, Kristian S., 21
Perrault, W. D., Jr., 31
Pessemier, E. A., 12, 100, 102
Petray, E. R., 357
Plummer, J. T., 12, 111, 280
Posner, F., 16
Postman, L., 33
Pratt, R., 370
Punj, G., 109

Rafert, J. A., 370
Rao, V. R., 209
Raphaelson, J., 42
Ray, M. L., 20, 21, 22, 31, 58, 143, 336
Reibstein, D. J., 214, 247
Reis, A., 232
Reisner, R. J., 16, 90
Richards, E. A., 378
Richardson, J. F., 23, 387
Robbin, J., 16
Roberts, M. L., 218
Robertson, T. S., 22, 143
Rokeach, M., 148, 165
Rosenberg, M. J., 88, 172
Rozelle, R. M., 302
Rusk, B. M., 380
Russo, J. E., 155

Salkind, W., 36
Sampson, P., 176
Sawyer, A. G., 336, 382, 389
Schellinck, D. A., 389, 391
Schoenwald, M., 16
Scotton, D. W., 218
Sen, S. K., 394
Shapanko, A., 98
Sharp, L. M., 54
Sheatsley, P. B., 37
Sheth, J. N., 22, 51, 87
Shiller, S. B., 16, 129
Shocker, A. D., 97, 110
Sims, J. T., 241
Sissors, J. Z., 357
Smith, G., 61
Smith, H. A., 334
Smith, R. E., 20
Smith, W. R., 2
Sneath, P. H. A., 109
Snell, J. L., 365
Sokal, R. R., 109
Solov, B., 16
Spielman, H., 38
Srinivasan, V., 88
Srull, T. K., 109
St. James, M., 88
Stapel, J., 60
Steffire, V. T., 100, 102
Stern, M. O., 98
Stewart, D. W., 109, 221, 346, 391
Strain, C., 216
Sturman, S. S., 378

Suci, G., 60, 63
Sutherland, M., 50
Swartz, J., 16
Swinyard, W. R., 20

Talarzyk, W. W., 87
Tannenbaum, P., 60, 63
Tauber, E. M., 17, 102, 137, 383, 384
Termini, S., 32
Thurstone, L. L., 58, 59
Tigert, D. J., 12, 390
Torgerson, W. S., 4
Tortoloni, R., 46
Trout, J., 232
Tuchman, B. W., 36
Tukey, J. W., 391
Twedt, D. W., 3

Valiente, R., 32, 144

Waddell, C., 112
Wallace, W. H., 46, 294
Ward, S., 22
Warwick, K., 16
Washington, R., 32
Wasson, C. R., 39
Watts, M., 16
Webster, F. E., Jr., 12, 37, 78
Wright, P., 89
Weigl, K. C., 89
Wells, W. D., 6, 12, 61, 112, 172, 215, 297, 386
Wiemann, J. M., 302
Wilkie, W. L., 13, 250, 386
Wilson, C. L., 12, 13
Wilson, W. J., 33, 35
Wind, Y., 13, 17, 217, 380, 393, 394
Winer, B. J., 187
Winters, L. C., 294
Wish, M., 104
Wittink, D. R., 89, 210
Woo, C. Y., 119
Wood, S., 143
Wright, J. S., 13
Wright, P. L., 39

Yankelovich, Daniel, 7, 16
Yoell, W., 180
Young, S., 16, 110, 298, 377
Yuspeh, S., 16, 45, 280, 390

Zallocco, R. L., 218
Ziff, R., 16, 226

Subject Index

ABC summary chart, 266–267
Action standards, 322
Advertising:
  basic principles reinforced by benefit segmentation research, 167–168
  how it works, 143
  importance of favorable attitudes, 165
  triggering effect, 165
Advertising copy, Gestalt effect, 164
Advertising planning process:
  developing advertising stimulus, 28
  development of communications strategy, 26
  exposure to consumers, 28
Answer booklet, 196–197
Arrowhead #9 study, 64
Attended self administered questionnaire, 198
Attention:
  copy testing measures, 293
  other factors affecting, 36
  two-step process, 164
Attitude change, 51–52
Attitude measurement, 53–92
  advantages of rating scales, 57–58
  limitations of physiological measurement, 57
  limitations of question-and-answer methods, 54–56
  obstacles to be overcome, 53–54
Attitudes, components of:
  affective, 51
  cognitive, 51
  conative, 51
Attitude scales:
  descriptive, 51
  hedonic, 52

purchase intent, 51–52
Attitude scaling alternatives:
  combination scales, 62
  constant sum, 61
  criteria for evaluation, 58–59
  Guttman Scales, 59–60
  Likert Scales, 59
  non-verbal, 61–62
  numerical scales, 60
  paired comparisons, 60
  semantic differential, 60
  Thurstone scales, 59
  verbal, 61
Attitude segmentation, importance of small differences, 174
Attitude segmentation research, 131–141
  defining objectives, 136–139
  forming research task force, 134
  organizing for study, 132
  what segmentation study can and can't do, 139
Attitude segmentation research overview, 383
  past criticisms:
    from academic researchers, 393–394
    from marketers, 384–386
    from market researchers, 387–393
Audience factors, 35

Backward segmentation, 215
Behavior prediction, 386
Beliefs, 28
Believability, 295
Benefits:
  ability to predict recall, 156–159
  as causal variables, 172
  importance of matching samples by interest

Benefits (*Continued*)
in, 122–123
relationship to attention, 144
types, 26, 110
what product is, 110
what product does, 110–111
how product makes you feel, 111
Benefit segmentation:
backwards method, 253
communications and other marketing implications, 239–243
direct derivation of generalized benefit segments, 251–261
early experimenters, 16
experiments demonstrating power of benefits, 160–163
fields to which it has been applied, 249
generalizations about segment types, 250–251
methodology, 171
origin of, 14
successful case histories, 373
BF Goodrich, 377–378
Burger King, 375
Canada Dry Ginger Ale, 377
Canadian Tourism, 380–381
Corning Glass, 377
CPC International, 375–377
Floor wax, 375
Ford Pinto, 377
Jif Peanut Butter, 374
Kotex, 375
Lysol Spray Deodorant, 375
Milk Bone, 375
New York unemployment, 381–382
Ocean Spray Cranberries, 373
Old Gold Spin Filters, 374
Pepsi-Cola, 375
Tidewater, 374
White Stag Women's Sportswear, 378–380
types of information gathered, 171
Benefit segmentation premises, 143–151
Benefit segmentation principles, 231–239
Benefit segmentation research:
ABC summary charts, 266
areas of coverage, 197
communicating with creative people, 271–278
communicating with task force, 267

conclusions and practical implications, 267
helpful tactics, 268–271
overall study design, 174
phase I (exploratory research), 175
phase II (questionnaire content), 185
phase II (refining measuring instruments and hypotheses), 182
phase III (analyzing results), 202
phase III (measuring market in detail), 195
phase IV (content), 200
presentation formats, 264
presenting results, 263
Benefit segmentation studies, primary advantage, 173
Benefit segmentation study followthrough, 277
copy research, 279
copy testing in segmented market, 346
with creative people, 277
packaging, sales promotion, pricing, product planning, 359
media planning in segmented market, 355
tracking systems, 363
Benemax method, 217
Binocular rivalry, 37
Brand choice:
prediction of, 172
relation to benefits, beliefs, and lifestyles, 172–173
Brand image, copy testing, 296
Brand ratings, methods of obtaining, 199–200
Brand switching behavior, 99
limitations of use, 100
British Market Research Bureau, 43–44
Bump-and-Push clustering, 192–193
Buying incentive:
being single minded, 109
choice criteria, 112–113
believability, 113
importance, 112
leverage, 114–118
supportability, 112–113
uniqueness, 113–114
vulnerability, 113
choosing, 109
Buying styles, 181

Cake mix market, 361
Camera eye method, 180
Cannibalization, 236

Canonical correlation, 216
    use of, in choosing between universes of
        content, 218–219
Channel characteristics, 31
Charting results, 263–264
Cluster analysis, 190–193, 221, 392
Clutter, 47
    simulation of, 332
Coca-Cola tracking system, 370
Coffee market, 237–238
    segmentation of, 121
Communications:
    effects, measurement, 151–155
    rules of thumb for communicators, 166
    strategies, 93
Communications process:
    general conclusions about, 164
    models of, 19
    two-way model, 164
Componential segmentation, 217
Comprehension, 295
Concept tests, 201–202, 230, 362
    light whiskey concept test, 230–231
Confusion, copy testing, 296
Conjoint measurement, 209
    appropriate uses, 212
    problems with, 210–212
CONPAAD, 294
Constant sum scale, 74
Constructing image measurement tool, 81
    areas of coverage, 82–83
    assigning importance weights, 87–90
    factor analysis, 86–87
    interviews, 83–85
    scale scoring, 85–86
    selecting stimuli, 81
Consumer panels, 329
Copylab, 294
Copy platform, 282–285
Copy research:
    knowledge gaps, 279–280
    limitations, 281
Copy Research Validation Council, 286
    validation project, 286–288
Copy testing:
    experimental design, action standards,
        316–325
    exposure considerations, 330–337
    form of advertising, 325–330
    general measurement approach, 291

identifying segment members for testing
        purposes, 347–353
    key questions regarding use, 287–290
    matching samples, 313–314
    measurements taken, 292
    sampling considerations, 337–340
    syndicated services, 340–346
    timing of measurements, 314–316
Copy testing measures, interrelationships,
        298–299
Core idea, 28
Creative department, working with, 168
Creative implications, 242
Cross relating attitudinal and behavioral
        segments, 258
Cross-tabulation, 203
Cruise market, 271–276
Curiosity, copy testing, 298

Decay, 29
Decision process:
    models, 177–178
    participation of family members, 178–179
Defense mechanisms, source derogation,
        discrediting spokespersons, distortion,
        counter argumentation, mental re-
        hearsal, 38–39
Depth interviews, use of, 179
Descriptive attitude scales, choosing aspects
        to be measured, 78
Diagnostic measures, in copy testing, 299
Diet, health, nutrition market, 252
Dinnerware market segmentation, 123–125
    pattern preferences, 123–124
Discriminant function analysis, 185–187
Doorstep screen, 350
Doorstep screening experiments, 350–353
Double blind procedure, 201

Emotional benefits, 85, 387
    affiliative, 112
    of buying, owning, using, 111–112
    sensory, 111
    user imagery, 112
Emotional response, copy testing, 297
Evaluative attitude scales:
    Arrowhead #9 study, 65–77
    extent to which scales measure same thing,
        72
    extent to which scales discriminate, 73

Execution, variation within themes, 155
Exposure to advertising, amount of, 43
Eye camera, 150–155

Factor analysis, 86–87, 185
  "Q" method, 216
    problems of using, 219, 221
  "R" method, 219
Factor analytic experiments with descriptive
  scales, 78–80
Focus groups, use of, 175–179
Functions performed by advertising:
  emotional reinforcement, 24
  entertainment, 24
  information function, 24

Gasoline market segmentation, 119–121
General Electric tracking system, 370
General Foods tracking systems, 370–371
Gifts as aids to cooperation, 200–201
Greeting card industry, 328–329
Grey Matter, 7

Heavy half theory, 3, 14
Hendry Corporation, 5
High involvement/low involvement, 22–23
How advertising works, 20, 143
  AIDA model, 21
  ATR model, 22
  Hierarchy of Effects, 21
  Howard/Sheth model, 22
  Staircase of Influence, 21
  see also Selective processes

Ideal brand profile, 230
Ideal points, use of, 13
Ideal product inventory method, 179–180
Importance scores, 207
Information processing, memory, 40
Information processing style, 28
Intermediate actions, copy testing, 298
Involvement, 35, 294–295
Item analysis, 190
Item selection grid, summarizing benefit
  choice criteria, 194

Learning, 29, 295
Leverage analysis:
  association with importance ratings,
    117–118

limitations of, 116
Lifestyle measures, limitations of, 12
Lifestyles, 386
Live-a-matic, 330

Market definition:
  Fleer *vs.* Topps (bubble gum), 94–95
  identification of primary competitors, 97
  method of concentric rings, 95–99
  through perceptions, 102
Marketing judgment, role of, 234
Market segmentation:
  behavioral, 3
  by brand loyalty patterns, 4–5
  constant sum scales, 4–5
  demographic, 2–3
  determining best method, 215
  forces behind, 1–2
  geographic, 2
  history of, 2–6
  by lifestyles, 7–13
  misleading nature of total market profile,
    119–125
  by occasion, 6
  primary objective, 25
  value of understanding segments, 119
  volumetric, 3–6
Market target selection, 118
  directed targeting, 129
Masking purposes of research, 320
Matched group design, 316
Mayonnaise market, 238
Media, 385
  implications, 242–243
    from benefit segmentation research, 168
Media selection, 13–14
  models, 357–359
Media weights, experiment with media
  experts, 358–359
Message(s):
  choice of, and audience selection, 158
  content of, 26
  elements of:
    context, 34
    novelty, incongruity, surprise, 32
    valued, pleasant stimuli, 33
  execution of, importance, 147
Miller Brewing Company, 232–234
Models of communication process, 19
Modified Delphi technique, 183–184

Multiple exposure copy tests, 333–337
  single *vs.* multiple exposure tests, 334–337

Narrowcasting, 2
Necessary number of exposures, 46
New products, 362, 385
Non-verbal communications, 302–313
Non-verbal effects, 165
Non-verbal factors, 28
  music, 312
  negative effects on persuasion, 307
Norms, 316
NPD Research, Inc., 251
Numerical scales, 69

Observational method, 180
Occasions, 388
  as use, 177

Packaging, 387
PACT document, 280–286
Paired comparison scale, 70, 73
Perceptual mapping, 102–110, 392–393
  discriminant function maps, uses of,
    228–229
  generalizations, 103–104
  interpretation of, 105
  suggested approach, 104
Perceptual maps, 176
  use of cluster analysis, 108–109
Persuasion:
  through brand salience, 48
  conditions under which it can occur, 166
  copy testing, 297
  by presence, 48
  relationship to non-verbal variables,
    306–311
  when most effective, 159
Physiological measures, copy testing, 294
Post-only design, 316
Preference maps, 106
Pre/post design, 319
"Problem" information, 230
Product implications, 243
Promise testing, 325
Psychographics:
  lifestyle measures, 7
  origin of, 6
Public service messages, 151–152
Purchase influence study, 35

Purchase intent scale, 69, 74

Quadrant analysis, 206, 231

Recall:
  copy testing, 296
  factors relating to, 41–42
  as measurement criterion, 151
Recognition, factors relating to, 41
Regression analysis, 187–190
Repetition, 34
Respondent fatigue, 198–199
Response style, 155–156
Retail market, 244–247
Richardson-Haley, 305
Richardson-Haley model, 23, 26, 27

Sales as copy testing measure, 298
Sample balancing, 318
Scale choice decisions:
  anchoring, 63
  balance, 63
  handling "no answers," 63–64
  length, 63
  odd/even numbers of points, 63
  single *vs.* multiple response, 64–65
Scree diagram, 221
Segmentation grids, use of, 241–243
Segmentation research, confidential nature of,
    14
Segmentation studies:
  failures, 17
  interpreting results, 225–239
  number of segments obtained, 224
Segment reliability, stability, 389–392
Segment selection, 125–130
  criteria, 125
  probability of generating sales, 127
    attending messages, 127–128
    changing buying behavior, 128–130
  size considerations, 126
  use of overlap, 127
Selective processes, 25
  effects of, on advertising, 42
  message avoidance and pursuit, 29–30
  selective attention, 30
    determinants of, 31
  selective perception, 36
  selective retention, 39
Semantics, consumer, 177

Singleton-Kautz clustering method, 192–193
Situational and environmental influences, 31
Social responsibility, 149
Source influences, 31
Sources of market growth, 95
Split-half reliability tests, 221
Spine charts, 207–208
Substitutability Index, W.T. Moran, 5

Targeting, 167, 260, 385–386
Task Force Survey, 182–183
Toothpaste market, 239–243
Top-of-mind brand awareness, 296
Tracking systems:
  areas of coverage, 367
  examples, 370–371
  key measures, 368
  key ratios, 369
  objectives, 364

requirements of effective system, 371–372
Tradeoff analysis, 212–215
TV-matic copy test, 44–45
Two-way communications, 23–25

UNH Non-verbal Research Program, 303–313
  stage I conclusions and stage II plans,
  311–313
Universes of content, choice between, 218
Unsolicited negative comments, copy testing,
  295

Validation evidence, Grey validation study,
  90–92
Values, 148–149
Verbal protocols, 180

Wear in, 335–337
Wear out, 297

You're in charge of marketing a product. It's a good one, too, certain to find a large and receptive audience—somewhere. But how do you determine who that audience is, and what kind of advertising they'll respond to? How do you decide on the right product image and the most powerful buying incentives? Most important, how do you carve out and defend that all-important niche? This book shows you how.

Developing Effective Communications Strategy familiarizes you with benefit segmentation, the classic market segmentation approach developed by the author and used with great effectiveness at America's most successful companies. Following benefit segmentation techniques, you'll learn how to isolate your most profitable audience and create advertising that pushes all their "hot buttons." Real-life examples of winning ad plans that have been built on benefit segmentation are included throughout the book.

Once you've pinpointed your target group, you'll learn how to develop a powerful, enduring communications strategy —encompassing copy, design, media planning, sales promotion, and tracking—tailored for your niche alone. You'll even learn how to judge if your strategy has been properly executed, using state-of-the-art copy testing techniques; if it's achieving the desired results, through sampling and scientific follow-up; and how to set a strategy back on course when it has strayed from the original plan.

Developing Effective Communications Strategy is backed by the results of over 120 benefit segmentation studies conducted by the author. From identifying consumer attitudes to selecting a market target, measuring communications effects, interpreting segmentation study results, communicating with creative people, analyzing creative output, packaging, pricing, and product planning, this book accomplishes a consultant's task in half the time and for a fraction of the price.